Privatizing China

Privatizing China

Socialism from Afar

EDITED BY

Li Zhang and Aihwa Ong

Cornell University Press
Ithaca and London

First published 2008 by Cornell University Press
First printing, Cornell Paperbacks, 2008

Printed in the United States of America

Library of Congress Cataloging-in-Publication Data
Privatizing China : socialism from afar / edited by Li Zhang and Aihwa Ong.
        p.   cm.
    Papers originally presented at a conference held in Shanghai, China, June 27–29, 2004.
    Includes bibliographical references and index.
    ISBN 978-0-8014-4596-5 (cloth : alk. paper)—ISBN 978-0-8014-7378-4 (pbk. : alk. paper)
    1. Privatization—Social aspects—China—Congresses.   2. Communism and individualism—China—Congresses.   3. Socialism—China—Congresses.   4. Social ethics—China—Congresses.
5. China—Social conditions—1976–2000—Congresses.
6. China—Social conditions—2000—Congresses.   7. China—Social policy—Congresses.   8. China—Economic conditions—1976–2000—Congresses.   9. China—Economic conditions—2000—Congresses.   10. China—Economic policy—1976–2000—Congresses.   11. China—Economic policy—2000—Congresses.   I. Zhang, Li.   II. Ong, Aihwa.   III. Title.

    HD4318.P755 2008
    338.951'05—dc22

Cornell University Press strives to use environmentally responsible suppliers and materials to the fullest extent possible in the publishing of its books. Such materials include vegetable-based, low-VOC inks and acid-free papers that are recycled, totally chlorine-free, or partly composed of nonwood fibers. For further information, visit our website at www.cornellpress.cornell.edu.

Cloth printing   10 9 8 7 6 5 4 3 2 1
Paperback printing   10 9 8 7 6 5 4 3 2 1

Contents

Acknowledgments

This collection draws on presentations at a workshop, "Privatizing China," which we organized in Shanghai, June 27–29, 2004. We are grateful for funding by the University of California Pacific Rim Research Program. In addition, we received support from the Institute of Governmental Affairs and the Center for State and Local Taxation at the University of California, Davis. We thank Professor Lu Hanlong of the Institute of Sociology (Shanghai) for his gracious hospitality, Jean Stratford (UC Davis) for handling the logistics of the meeting, and Shannon May (UC Berkeley) for keeping notes on the workshop discussion.

We received generous and insightful comments from Ralph Litzinger and Lisa Hoffman on a draft of our introduction to this book. We must stress, however, that the views articulated there are our own and by no means express a collective position. We are pleased to note, nevertheless, that the contributors to this volume constitute a kind of community mobilized by the shared goal of understanding China in today's world—with all its complexity, variability, and dynamism. Finally, many thanks to Peter Wissoker for his vigorous support and his confidence in the book project, and to Candace Akins for guiding us through the production process.

Earlier versions of the following chapters were published in journals:

Chapter 3, by You Tien Hsing, as "Land and Territorial Politics in Urban China," *China Quarterly* 187 (September 2006): 1–18.

Chapter 5, by Pun Ngai, as "Global Production, Company Codes of Conduct, and Labor Conditions in China: A Case Study of Two Factories," *China Journal* 54 (July 2005): 101–113.

Chapter 8, by Matthew Korhman, as "Should I Quit? Tobacco, Fraught Identity, and the Risks of Governmentality in Urban China," *Urban Anthropology* 33 (2004): 211–45.

Chapter 10, by Lisa Hoffman, as "Autonomous Choices and Patriotic Professionalism: On Governmentality in Late-Socialist China," *Economy and Society* 35, no. 4 (2006): 550–70.

To all our China students

Privatizing China

Introduction: Privatizing China

Powers of the Self, Socialism from Afar

Aihwa Ong and Li Zhang

"If you want to talk about modern China it's not only about money. During the Cultural Revolution there was no stage for the individual, just the government. Now there is a stage for everyone. And you can see a show every day."[1] This observation by Yu Hua, one of China's leading novelists, identifies the rise of a self-animating, self-staging subject in the post-Tiananmen era. In China the pursuit of personal glory has replaced selflessness, and the individual grasps his life with both hands. But Yu Hua is taking poetic license here, for the political unleashing of self-interest also constrains the fullest expression of private thought and behavior. Powers of the self, we mean to argue, are regulated and framed within the sovereign power of the nation. The emergence of China on the global stage is balanced against the struggles of the Chinese to stage their arrival as post-socialist subjects.

The breathless pace of market reforms has created a paradox in which the pursuit of private initiatives, private gains, and private lives coexists with political limits on individual expression. The neoliberal principles of private accumulation and self-interest—expressed in profit making, entrepreneurialism, and self-promotion—are not allowed to touch key areas that remain firmly under state control. For instance, despite ongoing land grabs by corrupt officials, thousands of peasant protests each year serve to remind the government that market forces must be reined in by socialist precepts. In March 2006, Premier Wen Jiabao warned that the major historical task facing the Chinese Communist Party is to "build a socialist countryside," and that the socialist project of eradicating poverty remains crucial to the party's survival. Clearly the market gains and the self-interested behavior permitted by privatization coexist with socialist state controls. This tense articulation between neoliberal logic and socialist sovereignty is reconfiguring contemporary China.

Despite two decades of spectacular capitalist growth, ambivalence over the hegemony of privatization persists. As an idea, privatization remains political dynamite in a socialist country undergoing wrenching transformation. This fact was brought home to us in 2004, when we convened a workshop at which the original drafts of several chapters of this book were first presented. A prestigious Chinese academy that had been extremely eager to host the event with University of California professors abruptly withdrew its co-sponsorship at the last minute because we decided to call the workshop "*Privatizing* China." Apparently the academy had been warned by the authorities that China has not officially recognized privatization (*siyouhua*) as a national policy. The withdrawal of official sponsorship, however, did not include canceling the academy's role in making business arrangements for our workshop.

This event revealed to us that there are multiple meanings, localizations, and entanglements of privatization in contemporary China. Privatization in the form of profit-making business is roaring along in some areas, but privatization as official policy is strictly denied. Going beyond official definitions, we view privatization as an ensemble of techniques that free up not only entrepreneurialism but also powers of the self. As we shall see, the government recognizes that, left unchecked, the individual freedom to pursue private objectives can spill beyond the business realm to include critiques of state power.

China is an emerging milieu that challenges Friedrich A. von Hayek's claim that collectivist planning can lead only to totalitarianism and modern-day serfdom, not free markets and entrepreneurial subjects.[2] Privatization was a deliberate shift in China's governing strategy to set citizens free to be entrepreneurs of the self. But these conditions of possibility came about not by dismantling the socialist apparatus but rather by creating a space for people to exercise a multitude of private choices, but always within the political limits set by the socialist state. In contemporary China, regimes of living are shaped by the intersection of powers of the self with socialism from afar.

As the editors of this volume we make a number of claims in this introduction, though not all of the contributors share our views. We challenge conventional notions of privatization in China by identifying the spread of a multitude of practices of self-interest and self-animation associated with neoliberal logic. At the same time, we maintain that the cross between privatization and socialist rule is not a "deviant" form but a particular articulation of neoliberalism, which we call "socialism from afar." We call it this because state controls continue to regulate from a distance the fullest expression of self-interest. The interplay between the power of the state and powers of the self is crystallizing a national environment of great diversity and contingency. Thus our analysis cannot be framed only at the scale of the nation-state but must capture the situated interplay of sovereign politics and self-governing practices that configure new milieus at multiple scales.

First, we challenge the Chinese discourse on privatization as limited to market activities. Instead we view privatization as a set of techniques that optimize economic gains by priming the powers of the private self. Since calculative activities deployed in the marketplace cannot be easily compartmentalized, they therefore come to shape private thinking and activities in other spheres of social action. In broad terms, we view privatization as a process that both produces free-floating values of self-interest and allows them to proliferate in daily life.

This subjectivizing aspect of privatization as a mode of thinking, managing, and actualizing of the self is a central element of the neoliberal doctrine espoused by Hayek and his disciple Milton Friedman.[3] Their proposal is that individuals should be free to become entrepreneurs of the self in confronting the uncertainties of the market. In a fundamental sense, the self-enterprising subject begins by developing basic individual capacities to make autonomous decisions, to take initiative and risk, and otherwise to act on his or her own behalf to achieve optimal outcomes. The point was never to limit such personally responsible and self-propelling behavior to the market environment but rather to embrace such a calculative logic as the ethic of subject formation.

The adoption of such neoliberal imperatives thus penetrates to the core of what it means to be (and to behave) Chinese today. The question for observers of China is: How can free markets, private property, and private pursuits normally associated with advanced liberal economies flourish in a socialist configuration?

Second, we respond to this question by considering privatization as a set of mechanisms associated with neoliberalism as a technology for governing and for achieving optimal growth. Privatization mechanisms include the corporatization of state industries, the adoption of profit-making policies, and the expansion of private property, as well as budgetary reforms, tax breaks, and entrepreneurial incentives. At a broader level, Nikolas Rose conceptualizes neoliberalism as a technology of rule that capitalizes on the "powers of freedom" to induce citizens to be self-responsible, self-enterprising, and self-governing subjects of advanced liberal nations.[4] Neoliberal reason informs a mode of governing subjects that mobilizes their individual capacities for self-government. This neoliberal strategy is called "governing at a distance" because subjects are left free to govern on their own behalf. At a basic level, privatization techniques entail self-governing practices, the "despotism of the self" that Rose argues "lies at the heart of liberalism."[5]

The central problem addressed in this volume is to determine how such calculations of the enterprising self can burrow into the heart of Chinese socialism
without entirely remaking the body politic. We do not want to give readers the
impression that there was a conscious choice in favor of neoliberalism by the
party-state; the Chinese authorities have clearly and firmly rejected the adoption
of neoliberal thinking and strategies. Nevertheless, many of the new policies and
practices introduced under the rubric of privatization have been deeply influenced by what we would consider a neoliberal line of reasoning. Privatization informed by neoliberal thinking helps the Chinese state break with failed practices
and resolve issues of growth and participation in globalization. Under slogans
such as "market reforms" (*shichang gaige*) and "opening up" (*kaifang*), the neoliberal logic associated with entrepreneurialism and self-enterprise have filtered
into an economy that is still to some extent controlled by the state.

At the same time, socialist rule is not disabled but reanimated by the infusion
of neoliberal values and an increasing mass of freewheeling citizens. Free-floating
neoliberal values can orient a largely urban population toward taking control of
their individual fates. The action of privatization logic in fostering private ownership, entrepreneurialism, and self-enterprise does not supplant state controls
elsewhere, however. Instead, state permission to pursue self-interest freely is
aligned with socialist controls over designated areas of collective or state interest.
For instance, while state-run enterprises have been converted to private ownership, state controls continue to limit foreign investment. Neoliberalism as a
technology of both governing and self-governing is usually introduced as an exception to political business as usual in emerging economies.[6]

We thus challenge claims that socialist rule is dead in China, or that China is
becoming a variant of Western models of neoliberalism. Rather the adoption of
neoliberal reasoning has made possible a kind of socialism at a distance, in which
privatizing norms and practices proliferate in symbiosis with the maintenance of
authoritarian rule. We argue that postsocialism in China denotes a reanimation
of state socialism realized through a strategy of ruling from afar. Citizens gain increased latitude to pursue self-interests that are at the same time variously regulated or controlled by the party-state.

Third, the mix of self-governing and socialist governing at a distance is con-
figuring a space we call "the new social." We thus differ from the approaches of
others who frame contemporary social change in terms of a split between an
emerging civil society and the authoritarian state. Rather, we maintain that in the
post-Tiananmen era, the new social space is produced through the interplay of
state authorities in combination with a multitude of self-interested actions that
give form and meaning to the popular experience of socialism from afar.

Fourth, such complex intersections of global and locally situated factors pose
a challenge to anthropologists and other scholars as they seek to define a space
appropriate to their inquiry. Some choose to study the spread of neoliberalism as

a total social force operating at the scale of the nation-state or even the global level. In contrast, we suggest that analyses based on large-scale categories such as "the state," "the market," and "society" miss the dynamism, multiplicity, cross-currents, and multiple scales of transformation that are unfolding unevenly throughout China. In order to identify and observe particular intersections of neoliberalism, situated politics, and cultural norms, anthropologists must stay close to the everyday practices and relationships that configure emerging situations.[7] This oblique angle of investigation captures the situated constellations of socialist rule, neoliberal logic, and self-governing practices that shape varied situations emerging across the nation. We suggest that these emerging milieus in contemporary China can be accessed through an analytics of assemblage, a concept that identifies the space of ethnographic inquiry at the complex intersection of global flows and particular situations.

The chapters that follow chronicle in vivid ethnographic detail the crystallization of neoliberal logic in a range of privatizing practices, from owning property, accumulating wealth, prestige, and rights, and operating a business to the realization of individual health, talent, and ethical well-being in a range of Chinese contexts. We distinguish between privatization powers connected with the ownership of property and privatization powers associated with the ownership of the self. Powers of property are explored through the relationships between private ownership, wealth accumulation, labor controls, and entrepreneurialism that are forming novel class configurations. Investigations of powers of the self focus more directly on the ethics of managing the self—one's health, career, and spiritual needs. Collectively the authors present a new ethnography of the multitude of micro-"revolutions within"[8] which are animating China's emerging neoliberal configuration.

Privatization: Socialism from Afar

In contrast to conventional approaches, we treat privatization as a range of activities that help realize the optimizing goals of (neoliberal) governing. Practices associated with neoliberalism include not just market-driven action but a wide array of techniques such as budgetary austerity, transparency, accountability, and self-enterprising behavior.[9] Privatization is a subset of a broad range of neoliberal techniques dispersed throughout different countries, where selective adoption has engendered different combinations of neoliberal and preexisting elements. Like other socialist countries, China has embraced aspects of market calculation and self-optimization, but not (yet), say, transparency in trade policies. While the Chinese government highlights privatization in market activities, we emphasize the fundamental effect of privatization in animating a new kind of self-consciousness and self-governing among Chinese subjects.

Before going further, we need to review briefly various models of privatization in Chinese history. The Chinese have long understood private interests underpinned by property ownership. For centuries, barely literate peasants engaged in bookkeeping, accumulated savings, used credit, and bought and sold land.[10] Chinese merchant capitalists were kept on a tight leash by emperors worried about the capacity of commercial power to undermine imperial rule.[11] The arrival of modern Western capitalism wreaked extensive havoc on early modern China, adding to the poverty, displacement, and misery of the masses already suffering from political misrule and natural disasters. The new Republic of China was greatly undermined by a chaotic warlord-driven—and gangster-driven—mode of rural appropriation. The communists were determined to destroy private property ownership and end the class oppression that they viewed as a major source of China's problems. In the 1950s the Chinese Communist Party (CCP) banned private property. Under the dictatorship of the proletariat, a multitiered system of collectivization—the collective, the commune, the household registration system, the family planning program, the Women's Federation, and the work unit (*danwei*)—shaped a resolutely public way of life that outlawed all forms of privatization, including private initiative and even the pursuit of private dreams.[12] The only forms of ownership permitted involved items of personal use, such as clothing, which were mostly rationed by the state. Thus, while private property has returned with market reforms, it is an explosive issue creating tensions and disputes across the social landscape.

By 1978 the economic impasse in China had caused Premier Deng Xiaoping to make a dramatic call for "market reforms" (*shichang gaige*), thus introducing a new mandate for privatization. The goal was to "open up" (*kaifang*) China to the forces of commodification and global markets. The Communist Party was careful to define "privatization" (*siyouhua*) as "systemic reforms" (*tizhi gaige*) limited to a market sector within the preexisting socialist system. The private sphere being opened up is officially associated with a well-defined space of market activities tightly contained within the Chinese state.[13] The major blow struck for privatization in the official sense was the dismantling of state-owned enterprises (SOEs) through acquisition by managers at low prices, along with the reorganization for efficiency which frequently involved laying off workers. Right-wing radicals influenced by Hayek promoted the view that privatized industries led by entrepreneurial managers were necessary for driving China's export-oriented growth to serve global markets. Nevertheless, despite more than two decades of China's rapid rise as the world's factory, protests against privatization continue to roil the Chinese peasantry, who are under assault from the ongoing appropriation of land which Marx called "primitive accumulation."[14]

Beneath the official view of privatization as entrepreneurial activities in economic zones, there is also a bottom-up view of "spontaneous privatization." This refers to the rise of private enterprise among ordinary people, especially the proliferation of entrepreneurs (*getihu*). In Chinese cities, private entrepreneurs have struggled to gain the attention of the state, which continues to focus more on pleasing foreign investors than in helping Chinese businessmen. Domestic companies claim, "We can only be the concubines of the state-owned enterprises or the mistresses of the multinationals."[15] Ever since the institution of market reforms, the state's ambivalence over privatization can be traced to the CCP's perception of its role in supporting state enterprises and increasing employment for millions of workers hired by big industries. More recently steps have been taken to increase official protections, such as the inclusion of entrepreneurs in the Chinese Communist Party and the passage of a law to protect private property.

Despite these shifts in regulation, privatization encompasses more than the dismantling of state enterprises, the spread of private property, and the spontaneous growth of entrepreneurialism. Indeed the most significant aspects of privatizing reforms may be in other realms of the private space opened up by the proliferation of neoliberal values in China. As we have noted, our concept of the private goes beyond the officially recognized economic forms to include a range of privatizing ideas and practices that are fundamental to neoliberal governmentality. Foucault defines governmentality—or the "conduct of conduct"—as a modern technique that governs not through discipline or oppression but by regulating the behavior of newly freed subjects.[16] In China, privatizing processes are accompanied by values of self-optimization that liberate subjects and induce them to pursue a range of self-managing goals in daily life. This proliferation of self-governing practices is widening the space between the socialist state and everyday activities that are now under individual control: the distancing of state regulation that we call socialism from afar.

We also challenge approaches that locate privatizing practices only within the "market sector," or a burgeoning "civil society," or a future market economy emerging out of socialism. Rather we find that neoliberal forms of self-management are not only flourishing within the mutating socialist landscape but also actually helping to sustain socialist rule. Privatization must be reconceptualized to take into account a diversity of market-driven strategies and calculative practices that crisscross and interweave between state and society, public and private, other and self. The private/interior and the public/exterior are becoming more and more enmeshed, with public interventions promoting private choices and self-interest directing public discourses. Despite the growth of powers of the self and powers of protest, there have been few demands for the limits of government, that is an absence of a liberal technology of government that is correlative of the notion of "civil society."

Indeed, Chinese idioms of neoliberalism specify micro-freedoms for citizens to experiment with—taking care of the self in the domains of livelihood, commerce, consumption, and lifestyles. In the 1990s citizens were urged to "free up" (*jiefang*) their individual capacities to confront dynamic conditions in all areas of life without seeking guidance from the state, society, or family. There were calls for people to shift from "relying on the state" (*kao guojia*) to "relying on yourself" (*kao ziji*). The privatization discourse was and continues to be a tool for people to engage in self-authorizing activities in uncertain times.

Increasingly individuals are obliged to exercise diligence, cunning, talents, and social skills to navigate ever-shifting networks of goods, relationships, knowledge, and institutions in the competition for wealth and personal advantage. At the same time, the promotion of self-care has also induced an enforced sense of autonomy in the midst of bewildering changes, conditions that spurred many to turn to varied sources of guidance, whether from the marketplace, religion, or the Internet. Neoliberal biopolitics have thus engendered new ethics of self-management and self-orientation.

Indeed the widespread adoption of self-animating practices is central to the new relationship between socialist rule and the citizenry. Increasingly, self-governing activities, through the promotion of responsibility for oneself, are recast as nonpolitical and nonideological matters in need of technical solutions from individuals in the course of their everyday life. The resultant gap between state action and self-interested endeavors permits the socialist state to govern at a distance. The space for self-managing subjects opened up by neoliberal tools of privatization is the space we call "the new social." It is emerging from the multitude of autonomous decisions, practices, and goals now freed from direct state control. One might say that neoliberal technology has allowed the Chinese state to initiate *perestroika* without *glasnost*, market reforms without political liberalism. The difference between the two constellations of "actually existing neoliberalism" is that whereas neoliberal technology has allowed China to evolve toward socialism from afar, neoliberal reforms in Russia have stimulated conditions for a recentralization of corporate socialism.[17] We thus view "postsocialism" not as simply a historical transition but as a situated process that, unevenly articulating privatizing mechanisms, produces different configurations.

Neoliberal Configurations

Anthropologists gather data through direct observations of situated practices and processes, and because we become entangled in these practices, we are tied to a form of mid-range theorizing. We are thus skeptical of high-flying claims that homogenize vast ranges of human experience and problems. In this volume the challenge for us is how to identify the conceptual space for investigating problems configured by particular alignments of privatizing and socialist rationalities. Specifically, how do we identify the emerging space of problematization crystallized by diverse logics and practices?[18] A broad-brush approach propelled by macro-level abstraction frequently sweeps away variable, particular conditions shaped by unstable mixes of global and situated elements.

For instance, although David Harvey describes global capital flows across multiple scales, he relies on the "neoliberal state" as the key unit of analysis. The neoliberal state has an "institutional framework characterized by private property rights, individual liberty, free markets, and free trade."[19] Thus, because he defines neoliberalism as a state apparatus, he views China in an era of market reforms as a deviant entity that does not quite fit the "neoliberal template."[20] Clearly for Harvey there is the standard neoliberal state, from which China deviates because neoliberal governance is combined with state authoritarianism. It appears that Harvey is drawing on the formulation of Wang Hui, a leading intellectual at Qinghua University, who has argued that after the Tiananmen incident, market extremism came roaring back under the guidance of state policy. Wang calls this post-Tiananmen phase "neo-liberalism with Chinese characteristics." The difference between Harvey and Wang is that for the latter, the combination of neoliberalism (radical privatization) and political repression is not a deviant form of rule but a characteristic of the new global order as a whole, with China perhaps an extreme case.[21]

Both observers, however, view neoliberalism as a universal structural condition. In their formulations, neoliberalism is an inexorable process that renders all national spaces intelligible or commensurable in accord with predetermined universal norms. Such perspectives assess whether particular nation-states are more or less "neoliberal" in terms of a preconceived collection of attributes, but they tend to give short shrift to the role of situated phenomena in shaping outcomes.[22] The concept of neoliberalism as a universal model proceeds by evaluating countries according to external criteria of globality rather than examining each globalized space as a configuration that is at once universal and particular.

Another homogenizing view of neoliberalism maintains that we are in an age of planetary transition "from disciplinary society to the society of control." Michael Hardt and Antonio Negri maintain that in this capitalist "Empire" the "carceral logics" of disciplinary institutions and technologies are being left behind as "mechanisms of command become ever more 'democratic' regulatory forms acting upon the minds and bodies of the citizens."[23] Such claims, of course, are not sustainable in the Chinese context, where, as we have argued, neoliberal practices of regulation coexist with illiberal forms of industrial and state controls.

In contrast to these views of neoliberalism as a universal arrangement, we advocate studying neoliberalism as a mobile set of calculative practices that articulate diverse political environments in a contingent manner. Any political regime can adopt a neoliberal technology of governing and self-governing without changing its entire state apparatus or character. Neoliberal strategies of governing for optimization can be taken up in any political environment—whether advanced liberal, postsocialist, or authoritarian—and deployed selectively in relation to internal spaces and populations.[24] Thus we note that the adoption of neoliberal practices in China does not thereby cancel out the legacies of central planning, nor are market-driven calculations uniformly deployed across the nation's territory, let alone have they come to define the political ideology of the Chinese nation.

Whereas Harvey's model sees a contradiction between neoliberalism and Chinese socialism, we view China's selective embrace of neoliberal logic as a strategic calculation for creating self-governing subjects who will enrich and strengthen Chinese authoritarian rule. Also, contrary to Hardt and Negri's assertions, we maintain that China is constituted through a mix of regulatory regimes and carceral logics, of market exuberance and sovereign restraints.[25] Finally, China's sovereignty is so central to its self-image that even so-called neoliberal hegemony must conform to its unyielding sense of sovereign power.[26]

Elsewhere, Stephen J. Collier and Aihwa Ong have proposed assemblage as a more appropriate space of analysis than the scale of the nation-state or empire.[27] An assemblage is not framed by preconceived political or social terrains but is configured through the intersection of global forms and situated politics and cultures. Neoliberal rationality can be one among other logics of governing in play in a particular situation without becoming the dominant feature of the environment itself. In other words, disparate global and situated elements co-produce a particular space, and this interplay crystallizes conditions of possibility and outcomes that do not follow a given formula or script drawn from a master model.

Each space of problematization cannot be determined in advance as having democratic or revolutionary outcomes. In China, market-driven practices are inextricably linked to state policies, so that self-enterprising activities frequently rely on political structures and relationships rather than opposing them. Instead of presuming that private freedoms would inevitably lead to state opposition, our approach investigates how the state and the private sphere, government and individuals, are engaged in the co-production of practices, values, and solutions that usually do not have a liberal democratic outcome. Instead of following the civil society model so beloved by outside observers, the contributors to this volume seek to give a sense of how privatizing needs, desires, and practices can be enhanced, deflected, or subverted by whatever else is going on under or around them. Each situation is configured by diverse elements—qualities of politics and place, of desires and bodily needs—that in combination produce unexpected outcomes.

This angle of ethnographic inquiry identifies a spectrum of situations that are emerging through the interplay of the micro-powers that correspond to a singular generality. Our ethnographic approach is thus diagnostic, an exercise in analyzing "the new social" by discerning the cross-currents, the spatial swerves, and the social discordances variously spawned by privatization. Ethnography thus problematizes a historical space by tracing the trajectories of values, practices, and events that come together to constitute a context in motion. In analytical terms, we identify the ensemble of global and situated elements—discursive and nondiscursive practices, technology and politics, ethics and identity—and examine how their interactions shape a particular milieu. This subversive approach responds to contemporary fluidity and flux by rendering the abrupt spatial shifts, the pulsating desires, ideas, and choices that converge and configure the cultural landscape. We stress the need for rigorous analysis alongside the humanism of anthropology. Because we recognize that these spaces of investigation are emerging milieus, we do not presume to know how things will turn out. In this "ecology of ignorance" our unknown future pivots on the contingent series of decisions made and not made, problems solved and not solved, in ever-shifting constellations of knowledge and politics.[28]

Accessing the New Social

Another universalizing assumption links the spread of market-driven reason to the rise of liberal individualism. Yet ethnographic investigations show that privatization in China promotes a minimalist kind of individual freedom shoehorned into an authoritarian environment. Neoliberal calculations and practices are focused on animating enterprising subjects who accumulate individual advantages rather than on liberal subjects who champion the rights of the governed and the self-limitations of "liberalism." The paradox of China is that micro-freedoms coexist with illimitable political power.

In China, privatizing strategies have undermined socialist notions of justice that are already difficult to enforce across the land. Socialist supports such as subsidies for housing, education, health, and food have been systematically stripped away, especially in the cities.[29] Meanwhile, in the countryside, peasants have to fend for themselves and their families as state supports for education and health care wither.[30] Furthermore, millions have suffered under conditions that can only be described as massive immiseration as a result of rampant land grabs by local elites. The manipulation of socialist beliefs and values by self-interested optimizers both in and outside the government has deepened and widened the gap between the new rich and the poor masses.[31] Secretive deals between bureaucrats and businessmen conceal abuses in the name of socialist ideals and nation building.[32] But only a tiny fraction of the most outrageous forms of corruption—the transfer of state funds, misuse of land resources, abuse of taxes and customs duties, and so on—have been punished by Beijing. So while privatization is ostensibly limited to specific domains, the remaining socialist protections have become embattled. As corrupt officials and the new rich have maximized private wealth with little interference, a new civil rights movement (*weiquan yundong*) is developing. Nongovernment organizations working for human rights, migrant rights, and environmental protection are proliferating in the People's Republic, and the discourse of human rights is beginning to be part of the Chinese public culture. Lawyers and advocates seek to defend the rights of the poor against official power, but they are increasingly hampered by the state itself. Rather than agitating for liberal individual rights, every year tens of thousands of exploited peasants and workers have been demanding social justice and restitution from the authorities. While the state has expressed its socialist commitments to the rural sector, it seeks to curtail the power of lawful collective complaints ("mass cases") in the name of the need for "social stability." Lawyers who handle popular disputes with state authorities now face severe restrictions on their ability to litigate on behalf of wronged citizens. Since late 2006 lawyers representing "mass cases" action have had to submit to the "guiding opinions" of judicial administrative bureaus and the government-controlled lawyers' association.[33] As these curbs on lawyers vividly illustrate, the powers of the self released by privatization do not include the right of political critique or representation against the state. Indeed, the intricate interweaving of state power with everyday practices means that there is no social realm that can be said to be "free" of state intervention.

Since self-interest is encouraged just in the realms of employment, private enterprise, and consumption, individual freedom of expression is authorized only in relation to the commodifiable and the marketable. One might say that officially, market reforms have introduced a limited conception of personal freedom as the actualization of self-interest, seen in the multitude of self-improving producers who have contributed to the advancement of the nation's economic power. Not surprisingly, the word "privatization" is seldom invoked, since it might give the mistaken impression of a systematic transition to Western liberal capitalism, a shift that the current Chinese government does not consider part of its future. In an environment in which economic liberalism flourishes without political liberalism, and market individuation thrives without political individualism, China is evolving a distinctive neoliberal configuration.

We therefore differ with those who claim that privatization in China has unmistakably produced a liberal public sphere. The rise of the bourgeois public is often traced to the birth of industrial capitalism in the West. Over time, powerful merchants created a free space where the feudal power of the state could be challenged. The public sphere as an ideal type in Western democracies is a site of unfettered individual expression, a space where citizens gather to publicly defend their inalienable rights and to fight state oppression.[34] This model of a structural opposition between the public sphere and the state has informed discussions of the "postsocialist transition" in Eastern Europe and in China. Many scholars have pointed to the literal gathering in public squares from Budapest to Beijing as a sign of the birth of a new civil society in authoritarian countries.[35] It is not clear, however, that vibrant entrepreneurial activities, property relationships, and self-governing practices are building the foundation of a Chinese civil society, although a new social space is being configured. Deborah Davis has observed that commercial freedoms have expanded a social space for "civil liberties" that may have political consequences, including the undermining of state authority.[36] Other observers view the spread of self-pleasing activities—consumer choice and satisfaction of individual desires—as carving a space of political autonomy within Chinese postsocialism. For Judith Farquhar, the new consumerism that stimulated "postsocialist appetites in the roaring nineties" were expressive of "a political and transgressive edge" in a daily life still conducted under overwhelming state power.[37] Meanwhile, Lisa Rofel is careful in noting that the rise of the "desiring subject" does not signal the development of "wide-ranging aspirations, hopes, needs, and passions" that are necessarily in opposition to the state.[38] Clearly the spectacular growth of self-interested activities cannot be easily accommodated within a model that opposes sociability to the authoritarian state, individual cultivation to political authority, or individual desires to socialist controls. How then do we access this new social space and rethink its relationship to socialism from afar?

Instead of locating the exercise of sovereign power and self-sovereignty in two separate domains, we propose a concept of "the social" as emerging through the complex interrelationships and interactions between the two. This interlacing of the public and the private, the political and the individual, requires that we problematize the notion of "society." It is common for China scholars to view "Chinese society" in terms of the socialities based on the interpersonal relationships (*guanxi*) that are created apart from or supplementary to the state apparatus.[39] As an alternative to this binary framework, our approach identifies multiple connections between everyday practices and state policies, so that the social milieu is conceived of not as independent of the state but as constituted through interrelationships with it. For instance, Nikolas Rose views "society" as a notion that is linked to the social contract with the state. He uses "the social" to refer to the political ideologies and institutional arrangements associated with welfare and security. The social is thus a historically variable and contingent form, dependent on particular types of thought and action that configure a particular horizon of the social.[40] Post–Tiananmen era governing from afar is producing a qualitatively different social from that of the earlier period, when "society" was produced by hegemonic socialist ideology and a variety of state-directed social benefits. With the institution of market reforms and a general opening up, much of this social support has withered away, to be replaced by privatization policies and norms of self-responsibility. Thus a new social is emerging from the interweaving of regulation at a distance with a broad range of self-interested practices. In other words, the current collective experience of the social has been thought about and acted upon by a constellation of "human intellectual, political, and moral authorities" from near and far, interacting within a delimited space.[41] We now turn to the specific steps and events that register the emerging contours of the new social in the Chinese configuration.

Postsocialist Biopolitics

Our emphasis on the role of the state in freeing up as well as limiting powers of the self is in contrast to other approaches that stress only the role of capitalism.[42] The immediate post-Tiananmen era marked a crucial break in socialist policies. In early 1992 Premier Deng Xiaoping made an inspection tour of southern China and called for the establishment of special economic zones. His speeches signaled a new, more friendly political climate for rapid capital accumulation and the development of mass consumption. This new biopolitical regime de-totalized socialist society by reconfiguring socialist power in relation to self-enterprising powers. Communities and individuals were urged to be self-responsible, to take care of themselves through commercial or other privatization activities. There was a dramatic shift away from the controlled disposition of social goods and the social determination of individual conduct toward, as the slogan goes, "socialism with Chinese characteristics."

In the new regime the population previously viewed as "ordinary people" (*laobaixing*) became a multitude of individuals now required to shape their own life chances. In the 1980s the state still maintained centralized control of the economy and claimed moral responsibility for the well-being of the citizens. Only some groups were expected to take the first steps toward individual initiative, as expressed in the call "Let some people get rich first" (*rang yibufen ren xian fuqilai*). But the new biopolitical thinking soon sought to universalize individual responsibility and initiative. Slogans such as "To be rich is glorious" (*fuyu guangrong*) encouraged self-enrichment schemes through private enterprise, thus launching the first wave of private entrepreneurs (*getihu*).[43] Meanwhile, poor and rural people were encouraged to seek their own livelihood by diving (*xiahai*) into the booming labor markets and competing for jobs on their own. A vast "floating population" (*liudong renkou*) now feeds the labor demands of burgeoning coastal cities and inland growth zones.

Alongside the encouragement to be self-reliant and self-enterprising, political control is exercised through the profiling of different groups perceived to be more or less aligned with new norms of competitiveness and profitability. The new biopolitics problematizes the quality of the population (*renkou suzhi*), as the corporeal value of the rural masses is increasingly found wanting in relation to the demands of expanding markets.[44] Antipoverty campaigns have recently sought to quantify embodied values in relation to profitable goals. Elite proponents stress the need of the laboring masses to improve personal attributes such as civility and self-discipline in order to sustain China's role as a global player.[45] Another line of differentiation separates those who focus on self-enterprising activities (businessmen, professionals, party hacks, workers) from those who pose a potential challenge to state power (Falun Gong followers, migrants, the dispossessed masses). This reconfiguration of good and bad subjects—from "red and expert" in pre-Tiananmen days to "self-enterprising" today—is based on a re-assessment of those practices that are aligned with market activities and loyalty to the state. Other risk-taking individuals (from some types of criminals to protest-ing peasants, dissident journalists, and human rights lawyers) come under sur-veillance and face strict discipline. In short, post-Tiananmen biopolitics requires a new kind of ethical training in order for self-promoting subjects to manage their lives through the pursuit of private interest, but within political limits set by authoritarian rule.

The new rich, in search of new lifestyles, have pushed aside hundreds of mil-lions of rural migrants, who must now provide for their own education, health, and everyday survival needs. Chinese cities are bursting with capitalists, profes-sionals, managers, and experts in various fields, as well as "hunters," fixers, and hucksters whose self-propelling conduct connects the different realms of social ac-tion. Dissidents and human rights activists are also growing in numbers, but their existence is precarious, and they are haunted by the authorities. This configura-tion of the new social raises questions about the future direction of ethical respon-sibility and political identity. While self-experimentation may exceed the limits of state control, the micro-freedoms of property ownership and ownership of the self are frequently aligned with patriotic fervor for China's emergence as an economic superpower.

Self-Practices

When governing depends on animating the freedom or capacities of individuals to act, politics becomes a matter of troubling the link between knowledge and ethics. In China there has been a widespread collapse of belief in socialist ethics (although diehard segments continue to occupy the nodes of political power) among ordinary people caught up in the feverish chase after moneymaking schemes. The breach between socialist logic and collectivist ethics is profound, even as socialist rule persists. In its place has come the return of a Confucian-inflected nationalism that stirs dangerous levels of passions and jingoism against perceived global enemies.[46] Such Confucian loyalty is directed mainly at the state and bends Chinese citizens to the will of their authoritarian rulers. At the same time, mass migration and the pursuit of individual wealth and power reduce the role of kinship and community networks as the sole arena of Confucian ethics, although such familial and *guanxi*-driven social ethics continue to be salient in many situations. Techniques for care of the self are recasting ethics in relation to the logic of risk in disparate spheres of life.

Michel Foucault argued that the "concept of governmentality makes it possible to bring out the freedom of the subject and its relationship to others—which con-stitutes the very stuff of ethics."[47] Self-possession and self-expression have become entangled with ethical questions about how to "know yourself" and how to "take care of yourself." Furthermore, self-choices and self-governing are linked to tactics for dominating others, thus creating an ethical problematization of people's relationships with others.[48] Techniques of the self configure a life worth living, putting into practice values that define a particular moral order.

We suggest that modernity as an ethic of "how one should live" is being proposed again in contemporary China, shaped by an unstable constellation of events: fading collectivist values, the compulsion to self-govern, and the heavy hand of authoritarian socialism. These disparate forces interact to create uncertain situations in which problems of living arise. For many Chinese, privatization creates an ethical dilemma about how the life of goods can be linked to the good life, or how the self-governing life can be linked to an emerging economy. New "regimes of living" emerge from the dynamic configuration of technical, political, and normative elements, provoking new ethical problems and dilemmas.[49] As subjects learn to make their own choices and plan their own lives, this remains the fundamental bewildering question at the heart of what it means to be Chinese today.[50]

The widespread commodification of things and persons opens up a new horizon of obligation for individuals to plan their lives by developing a reflexive attitude toward confronting a society in flux. It is important to stress that individuation (geren hua) in the Chinese situation does not necessarily mean the growth of liberal individualism, or Western values of individual rights which are influential only among certain sectors of the educated elite. Rather, we identify this individuation as an ongoing process of private responsibility, requiring ordinary Chinese to take their life into their own hands and to face the consequences of their decisions on their own. Individuation goes beyond making choices in consumer markets; it also extends to choices that shape one's tastes, habits, lifestyle, health, occupation, friends and networks in relation to a surfeit of forms of knowledge and practices.[51] Thus the reinvention of selfhood and personal privacy are embroiled with new kinds of knowledge and information that participate in shaping "the new social."

• • •

The chapters in this volume explore privatization not as system or hegemony but as techniques associated with neoliberal governmentality that unleash powers of the self. The proliferation of intimate self-practices work powerfully to intermesh the private with the public, posing questions about what it means to be Chinese in neoliberal times.

The book is organized into two parts. The chapters in part one, "Powers of Property," examine how the burgeoning private interests rooted in control over property, land, money, business, and labor power are involved in the radicalization of personal power over others and new norms of class and social privileges.

Ethnographic research captures the power of ownership to create dramatic class inequalities as well as new regimes of value. Li Zhang's study in chapter 1 of Kunming's upscale residents unveils connections between the cultivation of a villa lifestyle and exclusionary practices and the destruction of public space. Benjamin L. Read in chapter 2 examines how new homeowners have organized against landlords in order to acquire and protect property rights. In these cases, powers of the self in the midst of runaway development have given birth to a new class that defines itself in isolation from the less fortunate, as well as against real estate speculators, by means of the self-interested practices that are consolidating middle class-power in metropolitan China.

Meanwhile, privatization reforms have caused an earthquake on the periphery of cities and in the countryside. The socialist legacy has created a unique land regime based on an uneasy marriage between state ownership on the one hand and proliferating commercialized use rights on the other. It has become clear that market access to land requires constant negotiation with "socialist land masters." Youtien Hsing notes in chapter 3 that by permitting developers to "privatize" state land, these officials have betrayed their socialist obligation to protect the interests of the masses. The collusion between the power of the state and the power of property has contributed greatly to the dispossession of the poor. Privatization has led to another form of accumulation: fees and taxes levied by the authorities. In chapter 4 Bei Li and Steven M. Sheffrin give an account of how taxation reforms have given rise to a new arena of struggle between Beijing, local officials, and ordinary folk over the ownership of revenue and income. Market development has thus exploded the meaning of state protection and ownership by creating conditions for political and economic elites to form alliances against the masses.

Foreign enterprises are proceeding along different axes of privatization to gain access to China's labor power and cultural resources. Pun Ngai argues in chapter 5 that the adoption of transnational labor codes by multinational corporations in China is in actuality a ruse to deflect international criticism and a performance of a kind of corporate paternalism that disempowers workers. Following a different trajectory of capitalism, Louisa Schein highlights in chapter 6 the predicament of the Miao minority, who, having been bypassed by modern media, are being taken advantage of by Hmong Americans who appropriate their cultural image for transnational business. Foreign companies are thus a source of privatizing strategies that create new forms of market stratification among China's hidden populations. Such situations do not simply build on relationships from an earlier period but are formed through new articulations between neoliberal norms, situated politics, and cultural values. The different constellations of actors, property, and institutions engender specific milieus of social injustice, inequality, and marginalization. In some cases, self-practices promote the accumulation of private advantage at the expense of others; in other cases, powers of the self stir a new politics of civic involvement.

Part two, "Powers of the Self," explores the new postsocialist biopolitics of micro-ethical practices in diverse realms of the market, the home, the workplace, and public culture. These practices of self-care are constituting new kinds of self-conscious subjects. Some are experiencing the exhilarating powers of self-production by devising individual practices in relation to consumption and employment, while others are burdened by anxieties over self-management as they navigate the surfeit of information unleashed by marketization. The most basic care of the self involves care of the body. In the midst of the collapse of socialized medicine, Nancy N. Chen observes in chapter 7 how the new rich are practicing a novel form of self-care. They stock their medicine cabinets, visit the hospital, read media information, and adopt new health regimes. In chapter 8 Matthew Kohrman offers a contrasting picture of Yunnan, where men puffing on their cigarettes are increasingly viewed as unruly bodies incapable of self-care and self-reform. He finds that the male image is under assault from anti-smoking campaigns that seek to disassociate Chinese masculinity from the use of tobacco. The need to remoralize oneself is pursued along a different track in chapter 9 by Mei Zhan. In a time of SARS, she finds affluent urbanites coping in two diametrically opposed ways. Some Shanghainese reacted to the threat by defiantly feasting on wild animals. Others, meanwhile, have awakened to a new civic awareness of the need to combat the spread of the disease. Collectively, these chapters capture various ways in which caring for the body can, on the one hand, be deeply influenced by commercial values or, on the other, stimulate a new engagement with public issues.

Yet another mode of self-investment is evident among new professionals whose careerist practices are shaped through the nexus of market and political forces. In chapter 10 Lisa M. Hoffman observes that young urban workers in Dalian are being induced—through job fairs, employment criteria, and the media—to make self-responsible "correct" choices as "patriotic professionals." At least in this situation, the ethical constraints of nationalism mold the self-choices of managers. In Shanghai, Aihwa Ong in chapter 11 finds professionals self-consciously fashioning themselves as cosmopolitan workers who can mediate between capitalist and political interests. This role requires building up one's individual capacities so as to translate across multiple spheres of value. By illustrating different kinds of ethical self-training, the cases show that self-propulsion is not incommensurable with state interests, but in fact has become crucial in linking Chinese interests to global markets.

The final chapters exploring the powers of the self delve into the everyday dilemmas of the era of self-responsibility. The loneliness and disorientation associated with privatization are enhanced by the waning of socialities based on neighborhood communities, schools, and kinship. In some cases the search for answers to inner needs and desires has sparked a lively exchange of information technology that increasingly blurs the division between the private and the public.

Chinese turning toward the Internet should not be assumed, however, to be seeking freedom of information and of individual speech. Members of cyberpublics are mainly looking for data to fill gaps in their spiritual or fantasy life. In chapter 12 Dan Smyer Yü observes the growing numbers of "netizens" who seek guidance from digital Buddhas. He argues that their private anxieties and confusions are manipulated by religious charlatans who make money off the cyberconsumers. Zhou Yongming also rejects claims that the Internet is invariably a tool for spreading "democracy" in an authoritarian environment. He finds in chapter 13 that cybercafés are permitted to feed youthful desires and wild fantasies without the state losing control over the flow of information. These cases of state control of cyberspace should caution us against the assumption that more Chinese going online necessarily leads to the spread of democratic values. In an afterword, Ralph A. Litzinger reflects on the need for China scholars and observers to think "outside the Leninist corporate box."

Collectively the chapters present a diversity of situations in which the new powers of the self raise diverse questions about culture, ethics, and politics in postsocialist China. Our aim has been to diagnose a discordant set of conditions crystallized by neoliberal Chinese milieus that celebrate the staging of the self in tandem with the staging of sovereign power. New kinds of ethical practices emerge in these situations, and in their diverse ways they pose questions about the nature of neoliberalism without political liberalism: What does it mean to be both postsocialist and Chinese?

PART I

Powers of Property

1. Private Homes, Distinct Lifestyles

Performing a New Middle Class

Li Zhang

The post-Mao economic reform has brought about unprecedented wealth and remarkable economic growth, but the income gap and social polarization have soared in this rapidly commercializing society. A small group of the newly rich—including private entrepreneurs, merchants, well-positioned government officials, and managers of large profitable corporations—is taking up an enormous share of the new wealth and cultivating a luxurious lifestyle beyond the reach of the majority of ordinary Chinese. At the same time, millions of rural migrant laborers, laid-off workers, and other disadvantaged citizens (*ruoshi qunti*) are struggling to make ends meet, a situation leading to widespread discontent and even public protests.[1] Despite such rising social problems, neoliberal practices centered on the privatization of property and lifestyles are being increasingly naturalized and valorized in the urban public sphere.

Early versions of this chapter were presented at the 2004 Annual Meeting of the Asian Studies Association; the workshop on "The Social, Cultural, and Political Implications of Privatization in the People's Republic of China," Shanghai, June 28–29, 2004; the Department of Anthropology and the Center for Asian Studies at the University of Wisconsin, Madison, September 2004; the conference on "Class-sifying 'Asian Values': Culture, Morality, and the Politics of Being Middle Class in Asia" at the College of the Holy Cross, Worcester, Mass., November 4–6, 2005; the

One of the most important changes in China's urban landscape is the formation of a new social stratum—the "new middle-class" (*xin zhongchan jieceng*)—made possible by this privatization.[2] The demise of the public housing regime and the rise of the commercial real estate industry have opened up new opportunities for urbanites to seek differentiated lifestyles, status recognition, and cultural orientations. Thus, recent reconfigurations of residential space have proved vital to the formation of a new urban middle-class culture. My central argument here is that private homeownership and the increasing stratification of living space are not merely an expression of class difference or an index of status but also the very means through which class-specific subjects and a cultural milieu are being formed. Drawing from my long-term ethnographic fieldwork in the city of Kunming in southwest China, I analyze this dual cultural process of space making and class making by examining how, on the one hand, self-conscious middle-class subjects and a distinct "class milieu" (*jieceng wenhua*) are being created under a new regime of property ownership and living, and how, on the other hand, socioeconomic differences get spatialized and materialized through the remaking of urban communities.[3]

Rather than treating class as a given, fixed entity, I approach it as an ongoing process of "happening." As E. P. Thompson nicely put it, "I do not see class as a 'structure,' nor even as a 'category,' but as something which in fact happens (and can be shown to have happened) in human relationships."[4] This approach is particularly important to my understanding of class making after Mao because, as a private real estate developer pointed out, "one may be able to see the emergence of social stratification based on people's economic status, but it is still very difficult to speak of any middle class because there has not emerged a distinct class culture shared by those who have accumulated certain material wealth. Class making after Mao is still in its very early, amorphous stages; this is going to be a very long and confusing process." Thus it makes more sense to speak of the formation of middle-class subjects (oftentimes fragmented) than to assume a clearly identifiable class already in place. It is this cultural process of making and happening, in which a group of people attempt to articulate their interests and stage their dispositions, that I hope to unravel.

"Modern China" seminar at Columbia University, October 5, 2006; and the workshop on "Reclaiming Chinese Society: Politics of Redistribution, Recognition, and Representation" at the University of California, Berkeley, October 27–28, 2006. I thank Michael Burawoy, Mun Young Cho, Sara Friedman, Emily Honig, Rebecca Karl, Mark Miller, Kevin O'Brien, Aihwa Ong, Eileen Otis, Lisa Rofel, and the participants and audiences at these events for their helpful comments and conversations. The research was supported by the Wenner-Gren Foundation for Anthropological Research, the University of California President's Research Fellowship in the Humanities, the Davis Humanities Research Fellowship, the Institute of Governmental Affairs Junior Faculty Research Grant, and Faculty Research Grants from the University of California at Davis.

What is central in the formation of middle-class subjects in China is the cultivation of a distinct "cultural milieu" based on taste, judgment, and the acquisition of cultural capital through consumption practices.[5] In this open, unstable process, competing claims for status are made through a public performance of self-worth, while at the same time what is considered suitable and proper is negotiated.[6] Class making thus takes place not only within the domain of relations of production but also outside of it, namely, through the spheres of consumption, family, community, and lifestyle.[7] Although Marxist-inspired scholars have long recognized place as an important constituent of class, the emphasis has been on how the workplace serves as the primary arena for working-class politics. As a result, not enough consideration has been given to the cultural process that occurs within other social domains. The importance of community life in the formation of class is well illustrated by E. P. Thompson's seminal work *The Making of the English Working Class*, which delineates everyday practices of the working class in their community, family, church, school, leisure, and consumption.[8] For him, class is as much cultural as it is economic. Even though the situation of Thompson's (English working-class) subjects is very different from that of the middle-class Chinese I am writing about, and even though his notion of class is deeply rooted in the fundamental conflict between capital and labor, I find his willingness to locate class politics in a much broader social and cultural realm and treat it as a dynamic process extremely fruitful. This cultural and processual approach opens up a new space for rethinking class beyond economic terms and rigid structural divides.

I take the culturally oriented approach toward class further here by focusing on two social spheres *outside of* direct economic production—community-making and consumption practice—in order to shed new light on the cultural formation of the new Chinese middle class.[9] Drawing on Pierre Bourdieu's theory of "habitus," I argue that the emerging forms of living and everyday consumption play a critical part in constituting the social dispositions of class-specific subjects, and not merely in displaying their status.[10] It is in this sense that I see lifestyle choices and consumption as productive forces. More specifically, my ethnographic account demonstrates how commercialized real estate development and exclusionary residential space provide a tangible place where class-specific subjects and their cultural milieu are created, staged, and contested.[11] In delineating this mutually constitutive relationship among space, class, and consumption, I also consider how the rapidly expanding advertising of housing has become a vital engine in manufacturing and disseminating the dreams, tastes, dispositions, and images of the new middle class.[12]

In this chapter I frequently use the Chinese term *jieceng*, instead of *jieji* or the English words "class" and "status," for important reasons. Since the end of Mao's regime, Chinese people have largely avoided the term *jieji* in talking about social stratification because this concept was highly politicized and closely associated with the brutal and violent class struggle that caused pain and suffering for many under Mao. It is another term, *jieceng*, that is now commonly used to refer to socioeconomic differentiation. This vernacular term allows one to speak about various newly emerged socioeconomic differences without quickly resorting either to a set of preformulated, historically specific categories such as "capitalists" versus "proletarians" largely determined by one's position in the relations of production, or to the Maoist conceptualization of class as a form of political consciousness. But at the same time, *jieceng* refers to more than just status. The term is deeply intertwined with one's ability to generate income and to consume. It is most commonly used by Chinese today to refer to an emerging social group called *zhongchan jieceng* (literally meaning "the middle propertied stratum"). Although this group is still in a rudimentary stage of formation and thus lacks a shared identity, its members have begun to explore and cultivate a new culture of living as a way to articulate their economic and social location in society. Thus my intention in using the term *jieceng* (rather than "class" or "status") is *not* to erase politics and ideology from my account of the mounting socioeconomic differentiation in China, but to render a culturally and historically specific concept that mediates between the two distinct yet related analytical terms "class" and "status." The slippage between them is thus intentionally retained in the discourse of *jieceng*, which allows the simultaneous consideration of economic and cultural processes.[13]

In what follows, I first briefly trace the spatialization of *jieceng* as a result of a recent neoliberal move to privatize property ownership and lifestyle, and then turn to an ethnographic account of how different cultural milieus and class-specific subjects are cultivated within the stratified living space by focusing on consumption practices and a sense of social insecurity. I then briefly analyze the role of real estate advertising in shaping the cultural meanings of the new *zhongchan jieceng*. In the conclusion I reflect on some implications for rethinking the cultural politics of class, space, and consumption at a time when certain neoliberal strategies are being utilized by the state to transform Chinese society, and on their unexpected consequences.[14]

From *Danwei* to Stratified Living Space

Under the socialist regime the majority of urban Chinese could not own private property; instead they lived in state-subsidized public housing allocated by their work units (*danwei*).[15] In Kunming, a city of approximately 3 million residents and the capital of Yunnan Province, residential communities prior to the housing reform were largely organized into two forms: (1) mixed, non-*danwei*-based neighborhoods, under the control of the municipal housing bureau, which included mostly renters of diverse social backgrounds; and (2) *danwei*-based communities, which included relatively large housing compounds constructed, owned, and regulated by work units, which acted as de facto landlords and managers. In other words, it was *danwei*, not specific street names and numbers, that served as the most important spatial indicators for social mapping. Inequality in the public housing system was expressed mainly through the quality and size of apartments. Such differences were largely determined by the scale, strength, and status of work units and one's position within a given work unit rather than by private wealth. Such concepts as "poor working-class neighborhoods" or "upscale neighborhoods" were virtually nonexistent in most Chinese cities under socialism.[16]

Then in 1998 the State Council launched its reform to privatize public housing. Under the new policy, families were encouraged to buy their apartments from their work units at a discounted rate significantly below market value. Initially many urban residents were skeptical about the privatization scheme. Their main concern was whether private homes would be protected by law, since at that time the Constitution did not recognize private property ownership. Under these circumstances, the Chinese government launched several campaigns to ensure its urban citizens that privatized housing would be treated as a form of commodity and protected by the state. It urged people to abandon the welfare mentality and adopt a commodity-oriented perspective. As one slogan put it, "Housing is no longer a welfare item; it is a commodity." By 2000 most *danwei*-based public housing had been privatized in Chinese cities.

At the same time, there has been rapid growth in the construction of new private homes that have little connection with the *danwei* system.[17] The real estate industry centered on housing construction has become the primary engine of economic growth in China. The emerging new communities (*xiaoqu*, literally meaning "small neighborhoods" or "small quarters") are rapidly transforming the Chinese urban landscape into a highly stratified and socially segregated environment marked by income. The new homes offer many choices in price, quality, style, service, and location for consumers in different socioeconomic positions. In Kunming today, the striking differences between the wealthy and lower-income neighborhoods can hardly be overlooked.[18] Lower-income housing consists mostly of matchbox-like apartments in buildings that are poorly constructed and poorly maintained. There is little public space between buildings and virtually no green areas. The low-quality exterior paint is easily washed away by rain, making the surface of buildings look like "crying faces with running tears," as one informant put it. By contrast, the commercially developed upper- and middle-class neighborhoods feature a variety of architectural styles and high-quality construction materials, and are spacious, clean, and well protected. The colors of these new buildings are bright and cheerful. There are plenty of well-kept lawns, flowers, plants, and parking garages.

Factors that further differentiate urban residential space today include property values, community services, and the social characteristics of the residents. Let us take a closer look at the three kinds of communities into which the residents of Kunming are stratified.

"Gardens" and "Villas"

The newly constructed luxury neighborhoods are commonly referred to as "gardens" (*yuan* or *huayuan*). Most of the housing consists of spacious condominiums in high-rises or multistory structures in convenient prime downtown areas or the core urban districts (*shiqu*). There are also town houses and detached single-family homes, called *bieshu*, located in the developing suburbs. All of these are "commodity housing" (*shangpinfang*), which can be bought and sold freely by private individuals. Located in well-protected gated communities, each unit costs about half a million yuan or more, far beyond the reach of the majority of ordinary citizens. Some of the luxury single-family houses cost as much as 2 million yuan. Jade Garden, located near Green Lake in Wuhua District, is one of the upscale gated communities that I visited frequently. Because it is near downtown, adjacent to a beautiful park, and located in the best school district, Jade Garden is one of the most expensive properties in the city. It consists of a high-rise tower and several large six-story buildings forming a completely enclosed residential compound of some two hundred units. The sale price per unit ranges from 600,000 to 800,000 yuan, depending on the view. Each unit measures roughly 150 square meters, which is considered spacious by Chinese standards. This complex is run by a private property management agency that is known for its high-quality customer service, modeled on that of its Hong Kong–based parent company. It has an indoor swimming pool, gym, and clubhouse and meticulously maintained landscaping.[19] Like most other upscale compounds, this fortress-like complex is protected by surveillance cameras and private security guards. Residents use their own keys to open three sets of gates: the large metal front gate (which is closed at night), the building unit gate, and the house door. During the daytime the main gate is open, but the guard stops and questions anybody who does not appear to be a resident there. I was stopped twice and had to wait until the guard called my friends and confirmed that I was indeed their guest.

Mr. Zhao, who lives in Jade Garden, runs a specialty sports and leisure clothing business which is well-known among middle-class families and expatriates looking for high-quality Western-style clothing. Zhou, who is in his late thirties, graduated from a well-known college in 1987 but decided to give up his intellectual career for private business in 1991. He was able to pull only several thousand yuan together for startup, so in the beginning the operation was small. He rented a stall of less than 10 square meters on a street near a local university. Four years later the city government decided to widen several roads and thus demolished all the stalls and shops on them, including his. By then he was already making good money and was able to rent a larger store on a main commercial street. Between 1995 and 1997 his business took off, and he made about 1 million yuan annually. He attributed his success to three things: knowing how to select high-quality products in classic leisure styles, offering superior customer service, and starting

Figure 1. An upscale gated condominium complex. Courtesy of Li Zhang.

the business early. By the time I met him, his business had grown into a three-store chain operation with ten employees.

Zhou owns a spacious condo on the tenth floor with a sweeping view of Green Lake. I was greeted at the door by a young live-in nanny who did the cooking and cleaning and took care of his little boy. The furniture was good but not lavish. His family could easily live on the income generated from the clothing business, but his wife also wanted to have a career. She worked as a cashier at a major bank. I noticed a Bible on the coffee table and a statue of the Virgin Mary on the bookshelf—items not commonly found in Chinese homes. Zhou explained to me that informal Bible study groups are emerging among the urban middle class. The new private communities provide a safer space for religious activities because there is less direct governmental surveillance.

Although residents in the upscale neighborhoods have one thing in common—wealth—their occupational and educational backgrounds are diverse, and they are not considered "elite" by the larger society. As merchants, entrepreneurs, or what David Goodman calls "owner-operators," they tend to be lumped into one of two categories: *zuo shengyi de* (businesspeople), as opposed to those working in the state sector, and *da laoban* (big bosses), as opposed to the wage laborers in the private sector.[20] The secret of their success is that they started their businesses relatively early and thus were able to take advantage of the emerging private market for rapid capital accumulation before the competition intensified.

Mid-level Neighborhoods

The "middle-stratum neighborhoods" (*zhongdang xiaoqu*) consist of commercially developed housing, but the ways in which the families obtain them vary, and the social composition is complex. Over half of the units are sold as straight commodity housing to private buyers at prices ranging from 200,000 to 400,000 yuan, depending on the size, quality, and location. The rest are bought in bulk by large *danwei* which then sell them to their own employees at a subsidized rate.[21] *Danwei* are able to negotiate a better price than is offered to individual buyers. Communities of this type are also gated and protected by security guards, but the controls are not as stringent. A well-dressed person with an urban professional appearance is likely to pass without being questioned by the guards. Catering to emerging middle-class families, this kind of neighborhood attracts firm managers, independent business owners, and highly specialized professionals and intellectuals who earn substantial sideline incomes.[22]

Ms. Tang lives with her husband and daughter in a 110-square-meter condo in Riverside Garden, a large, newly constructed residential community in the northern part of the city. This area used to be farmland but is now covered by new gated communities. Prior to purchasing this home, they lived for over ten years in a small, rundown apartment assigned by her work unit. After graduating from college in the late 1980s, Tang became a high school teacher, bringing in a monthly salary of about 1,500 yuan. Her husband first worked for a state enterprise and then "jumped into the sea of private business" and went to work for a small firm selling personal therapeutic equipment. He soon became the marketing manager of this national distributor's regional office, earning 5,000 to 10,000 yuan a month, depending on sales. By the time they purchased this apartment in 2001, they had saved enough cash for a large down payment (50 percent of the 200,000 yuan total) over a ten-year mortgage. Tang was very happy with the additional space and her new living environment. But she also felt isolated and disappointed in her neighbors because, she claimed, "they are not well educated and their *suzhi* [quality] is low."

Gongxin Neighborhoods

Lower-income neighborhoods in China are usually called *gongxin jieceng xiaoqu*, which literarily means "salary/wage-based communities," because most residents there live on relatively fixed incomes (ranging from meager to moderate salaries or wages). There are varied types of housing constructed under different conditions, and the body of residents is more diverse. A large proportion of such housing is developed by commercial real estate companies under direct contract with specific *danwei*, and there is also some lower-cost yet reasonably nice commodity housing priced at just under 200,000 yuan per unit. The second type of housing is created by the city and provincial governments to house relocated families that were pushed out of the city core by several large-scale urban redevelopment projects in the 1990s.[23] The third type of housing is that built under the state-promoted "Stable Living Project" (*anju gongcheng*), which gives developers special loans, tax breaks, and other benefits in order to keep the costs down, but at the same time requires that these housing units be sold to qualified lower-income families at an affordable price. In recent years, as a result of the state-owned enterprises reform, many factory workers have been laid off (*xiagang*) and no longer have any stable income.

Jiangan Xiaoqu is a large lower-income community located in the northern part of Kunming. Until the early 1990s this entire area was all farmland. The first several buildings were put up at that time by the Panlong District Real Estate Development Company for some three thousand relocated families driven out of the inner city. Later on this company constructed eight more apartment buildings for a nearby university. Jiangan residents are mostly factory workers, clerks, service sector workers, migrants, schoolteachers, and university professors and staff. There are also local farmers who were given replacement housing when their land was appropriated for development. Initially the *danwei* assigned these housing units to their employees as part of their welfare allocation, but later employees were asked to buy back the ownership from their *danwei* at extremely low cost. In recent years social polarization within the community has deepened. Some residents were laid off by their failing state enterprises, while others have gained more consuming power and are able to move into better and larger commodity housing elsewhere by renting their Jiangan housing to migrants. Unlike the fortress-like upscale neighborhoods, Jiangan is more open and lively, without walls and surveillance cameras. Every day elderly men gather around small stone tables in open public areas to play chess and smoke pipes; retired women and men congregate to sing Chinese opera.

Theft, however, is a major problem in this rural-urban transitional zone as people of different kinds frequently flow in and out, while the police are virtually absent because this area is not fully incorporated into any urban jurisdiction. Although the property management agency is supposed to take charge of public security and community services, its manager claims that it is impossible to fulfill such responsibilities because of the lack of funding, as it has encountered strong resistance in its efforts to collect the regulation fees from the families. The security team is substantially understaffed and cannot afford any high-tech surveillance devices. Individual families are left to protect themselves by installing metal bars

Figure 2. A lower-income housing compound protected by iron bars. Courtesy of Li Zhang.

over their windows and balconies. Residents in the eight buildings initially owned by the university have organized mutual watch groups and installed metal fences and gates around their buildings. These gates are locked between 11 P.M. and 6 A.M. but are wide open during the day.

While urban residential communities have become more and more stratified along lines of personal wealth, it is far from clear whether people in the non-*danwei*-based neighborhoods share much in common. No longer "comrades" (*tongzhi*), residents in the new communities are merely "strangers" surrounded by walls and gates. Are they capable of developing any sense of common social and cultural identification beyond material wealth? Can we speak of any identity of interests, habitus, and dispositions, or even an emerging class consciousness among these "strangers"? Can shared spatial experience lead to a particular kind of class-specific subject? The next section seeks to grapple with these questions.

Figure 3. Social life and public space in a *gongxin jieceng* community. Courtesy of Li Zhang.

Cultivating *Jieceng* and Respect

One afternoon in the midst of a light summer rain, three of my former high school classmates came to pick me up in a silver Volkswagen Passat to go see a new upscale housing compound called Spring Fountain in the western suburb of Kunming. One of them, Ling, who was recently promoted to the head of a local branch of a major bank, had just bought a home there. The condo Ling purchased is spacious, about 200 square meters, with three bedrooms, a large living room, a dining area, and two bathrooms. This compound of 150 households is not considered large in comparison with other recent developments, but it is nicely designed with trees, grass, and plants. The center of the compound features a goldfish pond, a Chinese-style pavilion, a miniature stone mountain, water lilies, and fountain display accompanied by light Western music. These things are not merely an aesthetic veneer but are important in locating one's *jieceng*. Though impressed by the landscaping and generous living space, the other two friends began to feel uneasy. Both of them (and their spouses) worked for state entities, so they could not afford such a place. When I asked what they thought of it, one of them replied:

Envy! I wish someday I can live in such a community and be part of this group! But if I rely on my salary, I will never be able to afford a place like this. Look at the environment here—plants, water, flowers, and music. . . . This is where human beings should live. My place has none of these, but is surrounded by street noise, dust, and cooking smells from the street hawkers outside my window.

They then said in a semi-teasing tone that even though they still considered Ling a close friend, he really belonged to another *jieceng* now. The other friend, a woman who worked in the provincial health education office, explained to me:

Even though before I knew that he [Ling] made good money, I still felt he was one of us because he lived in a community not so different from mine. We could go knock on his door whenever we wanted. But now things are different. Every time I came here, the security guards would stop and question me, especially because I do not drive a private car. I would not want to come to visit him here as often as I did before. It just makes me feel inferior and out of place.

Their sense of exclusion and uneasiness derived mainly from their inability to acquire a place that demands consuming power beyond their reach, a place that so tangibly demarcates socioeconomic differences through concrete spatial forms. Furthermore, through much-enhanced new surveillance devices (heavy metal gates, closed-circuit cameras, laser sensors, professional security guards, and so on), upscale communities have heightened their social isolation and segregation as they exclude unwanted intruders outright. Such exclusion is often justified by the fear of urban crime and by a neoliberal rationale that valorizes private property, personal wealth, and the pursuit of a privileged lifestyle at the expense of public space and social intermingling.[24] Through such highly visible spatial demarcation, it externalizes and foregrounds previously invisible or less pronounced socioeconomic differences. Community is thus deployed as an active element in structuring class differences.

Places like Spring Fountain are generally perceived by urbanites as *furen qu*, a place where wealthy people congregate, yet those living within these places sense a lack of any social and cultural cohesion among the residents. One question I asked my interviewees was, "Do you find anything in common with others living here?" Nearly all answered no or not much. Many used the word *za* (diverse, mixed) to describe the social components of their community. As Ling put it:

People here have quite different social backgrounds and experiences. They are indeed a hodgepodge [*da zahui*]. The only thing they have in common is money and consuming power. But I guess a *jieceng* is much more than that. Perhaps after one or two decades of living together, these people will gradually form some sort of common lifestyle, tastes, and dispositions. But for now I do not feel that I share much with my neighbors.

Residents in these communities tend to have a strong sense of privacy and rarely interact with one another. Among some thirty people I interviewed, only two said that they had visited their next-door neighbors once or twice, and then only to see the interior remodeling before they and their families moved in. The rest said that they never visited. One elderly woman who lived with her well-to-do son's family told me that her son had specifically warned her not to invite neighbors in or to say much about his business because strangers were not trustworthy. I asked where they would seek help in case of an emergency. None of my interviewees mentioned neighbors. When I asked why, some said it was because they had their own car and did not need others to help with transportation. In case of a medical emergency, they would rather call a fee-based ambulance service. Others said that they would rather hire a *baomu* (caregiver) to take care of a sick family member than ask for help from neighbors because, as one woman explained: "I do not even know my neighbors. On what basis do I ask for help?" She continued:

> We used to live on a *danwei* compound and knew almost everyone. We paid visits to neighbors and friends in our spare time. But since I moved into this new community, things have changed. I have not been to any neighbor's home so far. They would not invite you. At best they say hello to you when running into you outside or playing with kids at the playground. I would not feel comfortable going to their home or chatting, as we really have little in common. After all, we are strangers to one another.

What we see here is a dual process at work: the spatial differentiation of people by community based on private wealth, and the atomization of individual families within each housing compound based on a heightened sense of privacy.

In upscale communities, residents tend to engage in conspicuous consumption. The ability to consume the right kinds of things is taken not only as the measure of one's prestige (*zunrong*) and "face" (*mianzi*) but also as an indication of whether one deserves membership in a particular community. If one's consumption practices are not compatible with the kind of housing or community in which one lives, one would be seen as "out of place." Such social pressure does not emanate from any identifiable organization or set of written rules, yet it is all-pervasive and embedded in the everyday cultural milieu. Although homeownership and community choice constitute the core of this new consumer culture, other realms such as private car ownership, interior design, children's schooling, leisure activities, clothing, food choices, and manners are also important spheres through which *jieceng* is performed and conceived. While China's newly rich get ahead economically, they share a gnawing sense of social insecurity and thus long for respect.

Ms. Liang and her husband had just bought a home in the luxury community of Jade Garden. Though only a high school graduate, her husband was able to make a substantial living from his small-scale gasoline and industrial oil trading business. She explained to me how they had ended up here and her perception of the lifestyle suitable for a place like this:

> A few years ago we had already saved enough money to buy a unit in another up-scale [community], but we eventually decided on a lower-level community. Why? Because even though we could afford the housing itself, we could not afford living there at that time. For example, when most families drive their private cars, I would be embarrassed if I had to ride my bike to work every day. Even taking a taxi is looked down upon there. If our neighbors see my parents coming to visit me by bus, they will be laughed at too. Since my rich neighbors go to shop for shark fins and other expensive seafood every day, I cannot let them see me buying cabbage and turnips. All the families there seem to be competing with one another. If you do not have that kind of consuming power, you'd better not live there, because you will not fit in well.

By the time I interviewed her, her family was in a stronger financial situation, and thus she felt that they were ready to reside in an upper-level community and learn to live like their well-to-do neighbors. They bought a car and completely remodeled the entire house with gleaming redwood floors, marble tile, fancy lighting, modern kitchen appliances, and luxurious furniture. She stopped working outside the home in order to devote all her time to her husband and toddler son even though they already had a full-time nanny. Her sense of readiness for community membership was closely tied to her family's ability to demonstrate a certain degree of consuming power in everyday life.

Like Liang, many other *zhongchan* residents I met also felt obliged to engage in the proper kind of consumption in order to validate their status and gain respect from their peers. But since everyone is learning to become a member of an emerging *jieceng*, what is considered proper and suitable is mutable and unclear. Oftentimes there exist competing notions of suitable consumption, which generate anxiety among the residents. They watch and compare their own activities with their neighbors' in order to get a better sense of what and how to consume. For example, it has become popular to join the exclusive fee-based club (*huisuo*)—a new site of prestige that sets *zhongchan* families apart from the mass of others. Children have become another focal point for cultivating the skills and manners deemed necessary to become true members of the affluent class. In Shanghai as well as other cities, for instance, affluent parents send their children for expensive private training in golf, ballet, music, horseback riding, skiing, and polo, even to finishing schools run by foreigners to learn how to become proper ladies and gentlemen.[25] I went once to a lavish, members-only golf club in Kunming with my friend Ling, the bank head, where he was teaching his twelve-year-old son to play golf.

Another distinct trend in middle-class consumption is the emergence of multiple pastime sites catering to a small group of "leisure women." Although the majority of urban Chinese households today are two-income families, this is not always the case for the newly rich. Women in some well-to-do families have quit their jobs to stay home and thus have plenty of free time. Since their husbands are usually preoccupied by business and entertainment away from home, these lonely women seek out such leisure activities as hair styling, manicure, and facial treatments, which have flourished in the wealthy *xiaoqu*. One of the most popular activities in recent years for both men and women with disposable income is to frequent "foot-soaking entertainment centers" (*xijiao cheng*). These are small, specialized salons where customers can soak their feet in warm fluid brewed from special Chinese medicinal herbs and then receive a long foot massage. Some of them are covert sites for sexual services catering to men. Such salons tend to be concentrated in the new private neighborhoods, where the residents have the time and money to patronize them.

In sum, new consumption practices have come to play a crucial part in reshaping people's tastes and dispositions, creating a privileged lifestyle.[26] As my ethnographic account shows, *zhongchan jieceng* is not a static thing one possesses, nor is it predetermined by one's position in the social structure; it has to be constantly cultivated and performed through everyday consumption activities. To be able to consume certain commodities in certain ways is a key mechanism in the making of *jieceng*. In this particular context, homeownership and one's subsequent spatial location in the city have become the most significant components of social differentiation and subject formation in the reform era.

Why is consumption so important in cultivating and performing *jieceng* in China? This is partly due to the difficulty nowadays of pinpointing the exact sources of personal wealth or gauging one's income simply by knowing one's occupation. In fact, it is a social taboo among the newly rich to ask how someone generates income because many business transactions take place outside the bounds of law and official rules. During my fieldwork, one of the most difficult problems I encountered was the reluctance of relatively wealthy people to talk about the source of their income or the nature of their business. When the production of wealth has to be kept secret and intentionally made opaque, then conspicuous material consumption serves as a viable way to assert and maintain one's status.[27] Another important factor to consider is the sense of social insecurity among the emerging upper and middle classes in their quest for propriety and respectability. The cultivation of habitus (or *jieceng wenhua*) through various consumption practices is in a sense a form of social experimentation in an uncertain cultural field and a strategy for getting ahead in an increasingly competitive society.

Advertising *Jieceng*

The making of the *zhongchan jieceng* goes beyond the spatial reconfiguration of communities and consumption practices. It is also realized through another closely related domain: mass advertising for new homes. Real estate developers in China not only manufacture homes but also construct and disseminate new notions of *zhongchan jieceng* and a distinct set of ideas, values, and desires. Through the powerful tool of advertising, these widely circulated ideas and images become a primary source of social imagination through which the urban public comes to understand what "the middle class" means and how its members should live. Advertisements for private housing frequently make explicit linkages between a particular lifestyle (embodied foremost in one's housing choices), a set of dispositions, and one's class location. In sum, they are not just selling the material product (houses) but are also selling the associated symbolic meanings and cultural packages. As a result, China's new "housing revolution" has not only made possible a comfortable form of luxury living but also provided new meanings and spatial forms for a new social class.

Let us take a closer look at one such advertisement published in a major newspaper in Yunnan Province. Titled "Town Houses Are Really Coming!" this advertisement, taking up an entire page of the newspaper, was sponsored by a real estate corporation that was building a large residential community of four hundred new homes. The lower half of the page is a picture showing a smiling young Chinese woman embracing rosy flower petals while standing on the seashore. The caption below reads: "The platform of the middle class's top-quality life: Though not villas, the Sunshine Coast Town Houses are a special, tasteful living zone that specifically belongs to the city's middle class." The upper half of the page contains a carefully crafted narrative explaining what town houses are, where they come from, and what they stand for. Since most Chinese people are unfamiliar with the history of the town houses and its social index in the West, developers can easily manipulate the symbolic importance of this kind of housing. The opening section of the text identifies the town house as a preferred way of life for the new middle class: "In the year 2000 a brand new living space called the 'town house' ignited the buying zeal of China's middle class. From Beijing and Tianjin to Shanghai, Guangzhou, and Shenzhen, town houses have caught the eye of all urban middle-class people and become their top choice in reforming their lifestyles. Town houses signify the beginning of a truly new way of life in China." It further claims that "town houses are extremely popular in Europe and America, and are becoming the classic residential space for the middle class. . . . They can foster unprecedented 'community culture' and a strong sense of belonging among a distinct group of residents." Such claims suggest that if one can afford this type of home and lifestyle, one will automatically become part of China's new middle class as well as of a privileged global social class marked by Euro-American modernity. What is so appealing about town houses to the Chinese is that they offer not only private property ownership but also extended private space (such as a small private garden) beyond the limits of the "bird cage"–like *danwei* housing. Developers can thus market town houses (with their small private gardens) as a "perfect independent space that allows one to touch the sky and the earth"—the true pleasures of the new middle-class lifestyle. The connection between private space and personal freedom is important here. Owning one's own home, spatially and socially detached from the *danwei* and from the neighbors, is taken as a sign of true liberation because it enables one to break away from the usual social constraints and surveillance. The crux of this advertisement is that to buy a home is to buy class status, and community membership is all about class membership.

• • •

As socialism is profoundly transformed by privatization, market forces, and consumerism, class politics takes on a specific contour that requires a closer look at the interplay of property ownership, space making, and consumption practices. While the shop-floor experience is central to the formation of a working-class identity and class consciousness among factory workers, laid-off state employees, and migrant workers,[28] this is not the case for the emerging upper- and middle-class subjects. Once spatially dispersed under the public housing regime, urbanites in China could not be easily identified as distinct social groups. But today, under the new commercialized property regime, individuals who have acquired personal wealth are able to converge in stratified private residential communities. Such emerging places offer a tangible location for a new *jieceng* to materialize through spatial exclusion, cultural differentiation, and private lifestyle practices. It is in this sense that residential space does not merely encode socioeconomic differences but plays an active role in the making of class and social performance.

As China increasingly embraces neoliberal reasoning and strategies, such reemerging class differentiation is portrayed as a natural and progressive move away from Maoist absolute egalitarianism. The sacredness of private property, the desire for privacy, and the possibility of pursuing personal freedom and happiness are deployed as the building blocks of a neoliberal way of life at the expense of equality, public space, and social responsibility for the poor. In this context, the political potential of the emerging middle class remains unclear. So far there is little evidence to suggest the formation of a meaningful independent political and civil space to counterbalance state power.[29]

The way that *jieceng* is increasingly spatialized and performed in the cities of post-Mao China reflects a global trend toward the privatization of space, security, and lifestyle in the neoliberal era as states are passing on more and more of their responsibilities to private entities and individual citizens. Increasingly, upper- and middle-class families in the United States and Latin America, for example, are being drawn into what Teresa Caldeira calls "fortified enclaves"—privatized, enclosed, and monitored residential spaces—to pursue comfort, happiness, and security.[30] As people retreat behind gates, walls, security guards, and surveillance cameras, spatial segregation and social exclusion are intensified.[31] The fear of crime and violence and the right to protect private property are often used to justify these moves. But social exclusion based on such spatial practices is not only eroding public space but also giving rise to new forms of social differentiation through the explicit act of living and staging.

2. Property Rights and Homeowner Activism in New Neighborhoods

Benjamin L. Read

The idea that private property forms a basis for freedom and empowerment is deeply rooted in the Western liberal tradition. John Locke famously believed that the right to property was so fundamental that government's primary purpose was to protect the individual's claim on his possessions; moreover, only the possession of land and goods ("estate") qualified people as full members of the political community.[1] Friedrich Hayek, in his critique of socialism, wrote that "the system of private property is the most important guaranty of freedom."[2] The British conservatives of the Thatcher revolution carried out privatization policies designed to expand individual households' ownership of assets, in part out of the belief that "possession means power, the kind of power that matters to ordinary people—power to make choices, power to control their own lives."[3] China's own liberals, epitomized by Liu Junning, embrace such ideas as well.[4]

While most passionately expressed by extreme liberals and libertarians, the basic logic of these ideas is so widely accepted as to be quite commonplace. Much analysis of China's transitional economy is unquestionably informed by the belief that expanding ownership is increasing citizens' autonomy and power vis-à-vis an authoritarian state. There are in principle a number of mechanisms through which private property might lead to this result. Secure ownership of assets could reduce individuals' dependence on the state, leaving them more at liberty to say no to it. It could legitimate resistance against state encroachments. Thatcherites (as well as American proponents of the "ownership society") would argue that the possession of property could inculcate new mentalities, such as "self-sufficiency, independent-mindedness, energy and adventurousness."[5] Property could create both literal and figurative spaces for open deliberation among asset owners, in contrast to state-organized hierarchies that expect obedience and leave little room for debate. Through such spaces, and by establishing sets of common interests, it could provide a basis for new solidarities with other property owners. But it is one thing to hypothesize all this in the abstract and another to observe it in reality. In the discussion that follows, I inquire into the empirical political effects of the expansion of private property rights and ask whether and how the rise of ownership brings about new forms of individual, or especially collective, empowerment.

To be sure, private property rights in commercial residential housing are but one of many bases on which groups and individuals assert claims. Others include the state's constitution, laws, and policies; expectations concerning pensions, health care, and other benefits; spiritual beliefs; collective property rights such as villages' control over land; and so forth.[6] It has become common in China for holders of stocks and other investments to engage in collective action when they feel they have been mistreated.[7] Consumer activism against fraud and other abuses has drawn widespread attention.[8] All of these are manifestations of what is now commonly called *weiquan*, popular action aimed at upholding rights.

Transitions from state-socialist to market economies inherently involve the creation of new forms of ownership. Yet such transitions typically leave the exact definition and implications of new rights unclear. Even in the abstract, laws and policies defining these rights contain substantial areas of ambiguity or silence. Specific cases in which rights are asserted are likely to be cause for disputes. Moreover, the holding of certain forms of property may, to some actors, imply corollary privileges that remain to be negotiated and specified.

When property owners strive to defend or expand their claims, they can choose many forms of action. Owners can pursue *individual* strategies by confronting rival claimants themselves, privately contacting government officials, or filing lawsuits that ask courts to uphold their personal claims over property. Alternatively, they may join together with other owners in launching *collective* efforts to protect what they feel belongs to them. Collective action, in turn, can also manifest itself in different ways. Property owners can hire third parties (lawyers, for instance) to represent their group interests. They may express their demands within state-sponsored organizations, submitting to and placing their hopes in a form of corporatist intermediation. Or they may form their own autonomous organizations through which to press claims.

These multiple forms of action have quite divergent political implications. Some of these possibilities, notably the path of intermediation, may empower property holders only in modest ways if at all.[9] Others have the potential to redefine the power relationship between citizens and state agencies. Collective action is of special importance within authoritarian political settings to the extent that it represents a departure from or a challenge to the established organizational structures within which the state seeks to shape, confine, or manage the expression of interests and demands.

Here I look at the specific topic of homeowner organizations within what are called "new neighborhoods" (*xinjian xiaoqu*). The emergence of this type of neighborhood is only one aspect of the tide of housing privatization that swept China's cities in the course of the 1990s. The other major components of this dramatic (though incomplete) process are the restoring of rights to preexisting homes that were expropriated after the revolution, and the massive sell-off of state-owned apartments to their occupants. A number of studies have presented the empirical outlines of housing policy change from the 1980s to the present, so I omit this background material here.[10]

Before continuing, I should note that the assertion of property claims over housing is by no means new in the People's Republic of China. Before the widespread privatization of housing, even apartments clearly *owned* by the state "work unit" (*danwei*) were subject to normative claims by employees. Those work unit members without their own homes often had (and continue to have) a set of expectations about when they deserve a housing allocation. Work unit members who had been assigned housing could often expect to live in it indefinitely, despite not owning it. Such claims are hardly confined to work units. Particularly in recent years, property rights over homes in older neighborhoods in China's cities have become subject to what can be intense disputes. Housing offices adjudicate ownership of homes that were once appropriated by the state, in some cases restoring them to the original occupants or their families. As large tracts of urban real estate are demolished and rebuilt, residents face the choice of accepting a buyout offer from state-backed developers or trying to push for a better deal, sometimes employing tactics of collective protest.[11]

But "new neighborhoods" have given rise to a panoply of distinctive rights claims. The central government has issued special policies that authorize a new form of homeowner organization for these locales, and provincial and city governments have set out their own guidelines for interpreting and implementing these central policies. In many cases, homeowners in these new housing developments have organized to mount collective claims and assert control over the administration of their neighborhoods.[12] In this chapter I examine the qualities of the organizations that homeowners themselves create and the kinds of collective action that they pursue. How should we assess these groups? Theoretical work on voluntary organizations and their political efficacy suggests three dimensions along which to assess China's *yeweihui*.[13]

First, we need to understand the nature of the organization and its relationship with powerful external actors. What kind of role does the state have in shaping the homeowner groups? Are they constituted independently from the state? Are they free to organize as they wish? Do they depend on state approval?

Second, we should investigate the internal practices of these organizations. To what extent do they employ democratic decision-making processes, for instance, in the selection of leaders? How cohesive and tightly organized are they, and how enduring over time? How widespread is the participation of ordinary homeowners in these organizations which are intended to represent them? In their meetings and other forms of communication, do they promote open and free deliberation on matters of common concern?

Finally, to what extent are these groups able to exercise power over their neighborhoods? What are the sources and limits of their power? Do they employ contentious tactics such as demonstrations or more quiet techniques of persuasion and negotiation?

Future research should strive to draw broad conclusions about the homeowner groups based on careful evaluation of large numbers of them drawn from representative samples. As of yet, such data are not available. This discussion attempts something much more modest by presenting four concise case studies of neighborhoods in Beijing and Guangzhou and assessing the organizations there along the criteria I have just outlined. The four case studies were chosen from the twenty-three new neighborhoods in which I conducted interviews. They were selected purposively, with an eye toward illustrating the diversity of organizational processes, conflicts, and outcomes that currently exist.

Origins and Development of
Homeowner Organizations

On March 23, 1994, the Ministry of Construction issued a document titled "Methods for the Management of Newly Built Urban Residential Neighborhoods,"[14] referred to hereafter as the Methods. For nine years these guidelines represented the central government's major statement on the way new neighborhoods were to be managed, and therefore they deserve to be examined in some detail. As of September 1, 2003, they were superseded by a new set of central regulations,[15] but the on-the-ground effects of the new rules have only begun to emerge as they are interpreted by local governments and tested by homeowners themselves.

The Methods stated clearly that they applied not to all residential neighborhoods but specifically to "newly built residential neighborhoods," further defined as "newly built residential neighborhoods that reach a certain scale, and that have relatively complete infrastructural arrangements." While somewhat vague, this designation was meant to apply to the residential complexes that at the time were just beginning to be built in large numbers in China's major cities, many of which are made up of commercially built and sold housing (*shangpinfang*). These neighborhoods, the document said, should be managed in a professionalized fashion by property management companies. In the process of creating a new neighborhood, developers should select and hire a management company prior to selling the homes. But at some (unspecified) point thereafter, a "residential neighborhood management committee"[16] should be established to oversee matters of property management.

Specifically, these committees were to be "formed of elected representatives of the residential neighborhood's property owners and occupants," and would "represent and uphold" their legal rights and interests, "under the direction [*zhidao*] of the real estate administrative authorities." Among the powers explicitly assigned to these organizations was the right to select and hire a property management company, to inspect and oversee its work, and to review and discuss "major matters of management service." The Methods thus illustrate how the Ministry of Construction envisioned the formation of a new type of local representative body to defend the collective rights and claims occasioned by the emergence of a new category of property holder. The way in which *yeweihui* came into existence has not followed directly from this central government document, however. City governments, as instructed by the Ministry of Construction, wrote detailed rules (*xize*) for implementing the Methods. These local policies, and the ways in which they have been put into practice, tend to diminish and restrict the homeowners' ability to organize.[17]

There are at least four general reasons for this. First, local governments often have a financial stake in the development companies. Second, even private developers are able to exercise informal influence over state decisions. Third, local authorities have reason to side with the property management companies to the extent that they rely on their help in administering new neighborhoods.[18] Finally, state officials are generally uncomfortable with and suspicious of independent organizations. They would prefer the government-managed Residents' Committees to remain the primary locus of urban governance at the grass roots. As will be evident in the case studies, homeowners in some neighborhoods have seized the initiative to set up their own representative structures willy-nilly. In others, developers and property management companies have taken advantage of restrictions built into local regulations to choreograph the installation of *yeweihui* that they control or that are disinclined to challenge them.

Just as important, the principal motor driving homeowner organization is not government policy at either the central or local levels but rather the ways in which homeowners feel their rights are being abused by the developers and property management companies. In most cases their main concerns are the following. First, they want the property developers to deliver the homes that they paid for and that are specified in their purchase contracts, or to compensate them for failing to do so.

Second, it is not uncommon for homeowners to pay for and move into their homes without receiving a legal deed (*chanquan zheng*) to the property. For those who have been denied these essential documents, obtaining them is an urgent demand. Third, they want to be free from price gouging, whether on property management fees themselves or on other items such as parking and utility fees. Finally, residents also seek special amenities to improve the quality of life in their neighborhoods, especially those that were featured in the advertising material which attracted them in the first place or were otherwise promised to them. These can include facilities such as parks, playgrounds, and kindergartens.

Power relations within new housing developments vary widely. Struggles unfold, in the first instance, on a neighborhood-by-neighborhood basis. In one *xiaoqu* homeowners may have organized effectively, while in another just down the road they may have failed to do so. The situation is thus analogous to a labor movement in which workers are primarily bent on winning better treatment from their respective firms rather than effecting broad-based institutional change or building class solidarity. The direct goals for most homeowners are tangible advances affecting their immediate circumstances: a reduction in fees, compensation by developers, or permission from the district or city authorities to establish a formal owner committee in order to achieve such things.

That said, links and communication beyond the individual neighborhood are becoming increasingly prominent. Informal contacts among owner-activists from different neighborhoods within the same city have existed in Beijing and Guangzhou since the late 1990s, and more recently the media have begun to give greatly increased coverage to homeowner activism; previously only the boldest, most pro-reform newspapers wrote about this topic. Finally, the transmission of information by the Internet has become more and more prevalent. Several large Web sites devoted to homeowner matters allow for general discussion, dissemination of, and commentary on government policies, and the perusal of "how to organize a homeowner group" guides written by experienced activists. This permits a transcending of the lines between individual neighborhoods, even though homeowners can also choose to confine their chat room commentary to neighborhood-specific forums.

In the years that have passed since the issuing of the Ministry of Construction document that was intended to authorize homeowners to form committees through which to exercise control over their neighborhood's property management, it still remains common for developers to dominate the *yeweihui*, or to stop them from forming in the first place. In Guangzhou one long-time activist estimated at the end of 2003 that only about a tenth of the owner committees there were fully controlled by the homeowners themselves. Informants in Beijing and Shanghai report roughly similar proportions in those cities as well. Investigation of individual neighborhoods allows us a better understanding of the circumstances that produce these outcomes.

Case Sketches

The brief sketches that follow cannot provide a full history of the struggle in their respective neighborhoods nor do justice to the complexities involved. They aim to give an overview of the case that allows for a preliminary assessment across the major outcomes of interest. As noted earlier, while the homeowner organizations have in some cases gone under different names, they are all referred to here as *yeweihui*.

This discussion draws mainly on interviews but also on written sources. Real names of neighborhoods are used in two cases that have received coverage in the Chinese media. In the other two cases, the neighborhoods are referred to by pseudonyms in order to protect their anonymity, as are individuals' names in all four cases. Also, in these instances certain unique details have been rendered less precisely than they could be (for instance, dates or numbers of housing units) though not altered.

Beixiu Huayuan

Cai Xiaoling moved into Beixiu Huayuan[19] in 1996, shortly after it was built. Containing 345 units, this development was priced at the high end of the Guangzhou market, with units initially selling for between HK$7,000 and HK$13,000 per square meter. It was in large part the discrepancy between the promised luxury of the apartments and their actual state that spurred the homeowners to organize against the developer and the management company. For example, floors were made of cheap wood instead of the contractually specified teak, and doors within some apartments did not close properly. Also, the developer attempted to charge the residents for electricity that was used not in their own homes but in the construction of another block of condominiums nearby. This is typical of the way in which seemingly minor grievances concerning privately owned homes can ignite formidable responses.

Cai and others began preparing to organize a *yeweihui*. The developer opposed this idea and attempted to obtain the cooperation of the police in stopping them. "It was not easy to organize. We had to have a secret, underground organization, with meetings at two or three in the morning," Cai recalls. She and her fellow homeowners held more than ten meetings in her home before the *yeweihui* was formally established. This was accomplished in 1997 at a gathering (*dahui*) that elected a slate of seven committee members out of four times that many candidates. At the insistence of government officials, the *yeweihui* was then expanded to include the manager of the property management company and her aide. These nine individuals elected Cai chair of the committee.

Beixiu Huayuan, as one of the very first neighborhoods to organize, was a pioneer among the city's *yeweihui*. Leaders established ties with organizers in other

developments and provided advice and encouragement to them. Beixiu thus illustrates how homeowner activism in one neighborhood can create a domino
effect in others by demonstrating what is possible. Cai noted, however, that the
government's stance subsequently shifted and that later owner groups have
found it more difficult to obtain government approval.

The property management company's two *yeweihui* representatives were unable to stop the owner organization from firing the company and hiring a new
one. The old management company initially refused to leave the premises. It finally vacated its offices in 1999 after the homeowner group pursued a lawsuit for
more than a year (which ended inconclusively) and after some of the residents
withheld management fees. Although the *yeweihui* did not change property
management companies for at least the next several years, it continued to exercise
authority over its new service providers. Though seemingly mundane, for a
group of individuals to wield this kind of power is no small accomplishment.
Over a period of four years the committee on different occasions fired three managers or vice managers of this company, in one case because of allegedly fraudu-
lent bookkeeping.

According to city government policy, the owner group is required to hold new
elections every two years. As of late 2003, Beixiu's group, however, had not held
any elections since the vote that established it. Cai stated that it would be difficult to obtain the participation of the required 50 percent of residents on any
given evening. Although the local Street Office told her that she should hold an
election, it had not insisted on this, and Cai noted that she still possessed the
group's official stamp (*gongzhang*). Like the other activists described in this chapter, she was not paid for her committee service. The owner committee had one
open meeting per year, usually attended by twenty to thirty people. (At the
yeweihui's behest, the management company also held parties for the residents
twice a year.) The nine members of the committee met only irregularly and handled most decisions through telephone consultation with one another.

Cai fielded a wide variety of requests and inquiries from both inside and outside the neighborhood; she received "lots of calls" every month. Other Beixiu
owners sometimes talked to her when they encountered problems with things
such as utilities. The nearby Residents' Committee occasionally asked for her
help on such things as keeping track of occupants' family planning status, but
Cai states that she paid little heed to such requests. "I don't want to hurt the
owners. I say 'I don't know' and dismiss them."

This case is thus an example of a homeowners' group that has established itself as an independent body, able to negotiate its relationships with other
actors—including the state—from a position of considerable strength. Yet it also
shows how this kind of autonomy does not necessarily mean that ordinary residents become closely involved in local governance.

Dingyuan

Dingyuan[20] is a *shangpinfang* neighborhood whose town house–style homes initially sold for 3,000 to 4,000 RMB per square meter. It is situated on former farmland more than half an hour's drive from the city. As of the summer of 2003, the local government had not yet established Residents' Committees in this or nearby developments; thus the state had no immediate presence. Only about one hundred of the three hundred total units were occupied. Just like in other neighborhoods, residents here were motivated to organize because of complaints about housing quality and about the fees they were charged. Owners cited excessive heating and electricity bills; leaks in the walls, ceilings, and door frames; and the use of low-quality building materials. The developer had also promised a certain amount of green space in the neighborhood for the residents' enjoyment but later built on this land. An advertised tennis court and playground never materialized.

In November 2002, when few people had yet moved into the neighborhood, a small group of organizers held a meeting at which they asked residents to sign their names on a document approving the establishment of an owners' committee. Half a year later, when the developer's contract for property management services was about to expire, these organizers hastily arranged another meeting to elect a *yeweihui*. This group successfully hired a new management company but was not (at least initially) able to gain redress for breaches of contract by the developer.

In contrast to neighborhoods in which homeowners maintained unity in the face of their adversaries, Dingyuan was wracked by paralyzing divisions among its residents. A particularly bitter split erupted in 2003 between the *yeweihui* and a portion of the residents over the issue of dog ownership. The committee's leadership sought to banish dogs from the neighborhood. It pointed out that some residents did not clean up after their pets and argued that the needs and preferences of people should come before those of animals. When a group of owners established a cordoned-off area of the lawn intended for dog-walking, the committee opposed this and took the provocative step of posting signs announcing that it had distributed poison inside this area. Letters posted on the *yeweihui*'s bulletin board attacked the organization's critics as "petty people" (*xiaoren*).

Differences had previously emerged on other issues as well. The *yeweihui* had taken a hard line against the former management company, calling on residents to refuse to pay their management fees; some of the residents who heeded this call were sued by the company, leaving them disgruntled. The SARS crisis of spring 2003 also led to a difference of opinion, with some residents asking the *yeweihui* to hold a meeting to discuss measures to keep the disease out of the neighborhood, while the committee, in contrast, told owners to stay focused on the struggle against the developer.

In the fall of 2003 the six members of the *yeweihui* jointly resigned, citing their frustration that, as they saw it, they had done a great deal of work and yet received nothing but complaints and recriminations from other owners in return. This took place shortly after the committee fired the managers on the basis of a ballot it had circulated throughout the neighborhood. For a while there was no staff to collect trash and provide security, until a small group of residents took the initiative and hired a new management company without consulting anyone else.

Dingyuan shows that even without state interference, there is no guarantee of achieving the kind of harmony and cooperation among property owners that is required to create functioning organizations. The division of ownership into household-based parcels, together with tensions arising from the necessity of collective decision making, can lead to atomization rather than unity.

Lijiang Huayuan

Lijiang Huayuan[21] is the largest of the housing developments discussed in this chapter. It is located about 15 kilometers south of Guangzhou on part of Nanpudao, an island lying amid the tributaries of the Pearl River. Construction began in the early 1990s, and as of early 2004 more than ten thousand housing units had been completed, grouped in at least nine distinct sub-neighborhoods that range from high-rise condominiums to town houses to unattached houses. The development company is a joint venture backed by both the Guangdong government and the government of Panyu, a former county-level city that became a district of Guangzhou and in which Lijiang is located.

As of 2004 the homeowner committee had been in existence for more than six years and had gone through four rounds of elections. In Lijiang's case, the *yeweihui* had been closely linked to the developer and its affiliated property management company, and had only a dubious claim to electoral legitimacy. In all four elections, the developer exercised considerable influence over the proceedings and went to great lengths to ensure that its favored candidates won. In the first two elections this was in part accomplished by doing little to publicize the balloting. (Only around 200 residents out of 4,200 households cast votes in the first election in 1997, and around 1,000 out of 6,000 in the second election in 1999.) Also, according to local regulations, the development company is permitted to cast votes for each of the unsold homes that still belong to it. This gave the company an overwhelming advantage. Finally, it was aided by the fact that many residents were reasonably satisfied with Lijiang's property management. Two major incidents over a period of five years, however, had resulted in large-scale homeowner mobilization and an attempt by disgruntled residents to win control of the *yeweihui*.

The first controversy arose when Lijiang announced in January 1999 that the price of a round-trip ticket on the commuter shuttle bus to downtown

Guangzhou would rise from 5 to 7 RMB. Several hundred residents gathered in front of the management company's offices to protest. In the days that followed, they held a demonstration march within Lijiang and also sought redress from the provincial government and People's Congress. They boycotted the Lijiang bus by arranging their own chartered bus service and by forming carpools with automobile-owning residents. The Lijiang bus service backed down and offered bulk-rate tickets at the original price.

The second dispute led to an even more prolonged period of resistance. It began in December 2002, when bulldozers appeared along the southern edge of Lijiang Huayuan and began clearing trees and grass. Unbeknownst to the residents, Lijiang's developers had cut a deal with another development company according to which a road more than 20 meters in width would be laid along that section of the neighborhood's perimeter in order to link a separate planned housing complex with the main highway. Many homeowners, particularly those with windows and balconies facing the road, were outraged, complaining that this directly contradicted the developer's assurances that the land would be preserved as bucolic green space shaded by peach trees. In the weeks that followed, several hundred residents staged a series of demonstrations in the name of *weiquan*, upholding their rights. On the night of December 31, participants camped in tents on the half-completed roadbed; on January 19 they planted a hundred saplings there. In the meantime, the homeowners (many of whom worked in Guangzhou's media and advertising industry) used their connections to attract publicity to their cause, and also sought help from provincial People's Congress representatives. Although the road was nonetheless built in the end, the developers compromised and agreed to reduce its width and relocate it farther away from Lijiang's homes.

For the owner-activists involved, the road conflict highlighted the illegitimacy of the official *yeweihui*, which had stayed quiet during this period and apparently failed to stand up for the homeowners it claimed to represent. Led by an insurance company employee in his early thirties, a group calling itself the "little homeowners' team" (*xiao yezhu tuandui*) organized a slate of fourteen candidates to compete in Lijiang's fourth round of *yeweihui* elections.[22] Ballots in this slow-motion election were cast between December 15, 2003, and February 16, 2004. On February 20, after employees of the property management company opened the ballot boxes, it declared that the roughly 2,800 votes failed to meet the required threshold of 50 percent participation by the 10,210 homeowners. The election was declared invalid, and no plans for a re-vote were immediately announced.[23]

Lijiang shows remarkable examples of collective action by homeowners and their ability to achieve gains through overtly contentious tactics. But it also illustrates the ways in which developers collude with local government to neutralize such efforts, and the challenges of organizing lasting and democratic forms of self-governance that can persist in such hostile circumstances.

Jiashan

Jiashan's[24] homeowners began organizing at the end of 1998. Their most urgent demand was to acquire deeds to the apartments for which they had paid and in which they were living. Four years after the sale and construction of Jiashan's homes had commenced, the city government retroactively declared that the developer had failed to follow proper legal procedures. The homes would remain illegal and ineligible for deeds until the developer paid a series of fines, fees, and taxes—especially the land transfer fee (*tudi churang jin*) that is incurred when village land is appropriated for urban housing construction. The population of Jiashan rose to around four thousand households in total after the neighborhood was fully built. The units were relatively inexpensive, costing between 1,500 and 2,200 RMB per square meter.

Local officials cited technicalities in declaring Jiashan to be ineligible to establish a *yeweihui* and would give their blessing only to the forming of a *yeweihui* "preparatory group." Limited in this way but otherwise unrestrained, owners held a series of large-scale meetings. At one gathering of around two hundred members, a preparatory group was elected, composed entirely of homeowners. As of four years later the status of the owner group remained unchanged, with no sign that it would be upgraded to that of fully authorized *yeweihui*. During its most active period, the preparatory group held meetings twice a month, usually attended by ten to twenty people. The group had no formal leadership, but one woman in her fifties with almost two decades of experience as a lawyer gradually emerged as its center of gravity, with others deferring to her as the "person in charge" (*fuze ren*).

The preparatory group adopted a mode of action that featured persistent and assertive lobbying of government officials. It avoided behavior that it feared might alienate those officials, such as demonstrations or lawsuits, although in at least one instance it did employ the threat of contentious behavior. The preparatory group leaders visited state offices to plead their case, sometimes repeatedly, often bringing a delegation of homeowners with them to add emphasis. The developer initially refused to talk to their organization. Its stance changed over time, in part owing to pressure from the homeowners. While the preparatory group never called on homeowners to withhold fees and utility payments from the property management company, many did so anyway. Both the government and the developer came to acknowledge informally the preparatory group's legitimacy as the homeowners' representative by negotiating with it and in some cases acting on its demands.

Despite not receiving official recognition, the homeowner group scored several major achievements. Its most significant accomplishment was pressuring government authorities at the city, district, and township levels to compromise on the penalties and taxes they were demanding from the developer, while also pressuring the developer to meet those reduced demands. This facilitated the process through which the owners received their property deeds.

The preparatory group also won a number of other victories. Jiashan homes had no telephone lines at the time that homebuyers began to move in. Moreover, its electricity came from inferior village-level lines that supplied power only during certain hours of the day. A group of owners went to the government complaints (*xinfang*) office to take up this issue, bringing a letter signed by members of more than two hundred households. The *xinfang* officials asked them to leave, but the homeowners stayed, threatening to come back in even larger numbers and to take their case to higher levels of government. This impelled the officials to work out a compromise with the developer that led to the provision of phone lines and more reliable electricity. In 1999 a manager of the property management company was involved in a physical scuffle with a homeowner that left the latter with a broken wrist. When the police substation declined to help the injured party win redress, a group of ten homeowners repeatedly took the case to the district police and government. Eventually the manager was detained by the district police for fifteen days, and an agreement was reached whereby the company apologized publicly for the injury and paid 35,000 RMB in compensation. All these events represented tangible gains won by the owners through solidarity and persistent action.

In the summer of 2002, the lawyer who served as the *yeweihui* preparatory group's principal organizer moved out of Jiashan into a newer development, citing her desire to live in a neighborhood with parks and other amenities. She continued to receive calls from homeowners in Jiashan asking for her help on various matters, but she was determined to leave her organizational work behind her. The stress was bad for her health, she decided, and she was tired of listening to people's bickering. Her departure proved to be a blow. No one wanted to make the effort to fill the role she had played. As of mid-2004, the informal *yeweihui* had lapsed into inactivity.

Here, as in the case of Beixiu Huayuan, we can perceive a weakness found in nonprofit organizations in many settings: excessive dependence on a single key organizer and lack of institutionalization. Yet this neighborhood also shows that local government sometimes responds to homeowner pressure by accommodating their demands.

Assessment

The reemergence of private housing, especially in newly built (as opposed to preexisting) neighborhoods, indeed makes a difference. Owners of property do acquire compelling new interests that can motivate the founding of new organizations and spur group action. Yet interests alone do not dictate outcomes; instead what emerges depends on a complex mixture of individual agency, group dynamics, and trial and error, played out against a shifting backdrop of possibilities and constraints. Homeowners' interests sometimes converge with one another and sometimes do not; moreover, owners face other actors whose interests are served by disempowering them. Elements of the state play contradictory roles, with the center authorizing an exceptional form of grassroots representative body while local governments often work to negate the stated purpose of these policies.

I have identified three sets of criteria by which to evaluate the homeowner groups: their degree of autonomy from and leverage over external actors; their internal practices and relationships with their constituents; and their exercising of power. As the case studies illustrate, in the application of these criteria it is necessary to differentiate among three general categories of groups currently found in China's "new neighborhoods." Some are both approved by the government and controlled by residents themselves, like that of Beixiu Huayuan. Others have official status but are under the sway of developers or management companies, like Lijiang Huayuan's incumbent *yeweihui*. Still others operate without full official sanction, whether as de facto owner committees (such as Jiashan's) or as groups that strive to challenge existing *yeweihui* (such as Lijiang's *xiao yezhu tuandui*).

Local governments hold power over the *yeweihui* in certain ways. They can grant or withhold official status, and in some cases this can crucially affect the organizations' ability to get things done. But achieving organizational autonomy from the *developer* is often even more challenging than achieving autonomy from the state. While some developers reconcile themselves to collective bargaining with their customers, they much more commonly strive to dominate or subvert the organizations that are intended to represent them.

In terms of the tactics they use to try to achieve their goals, as well as their internal practices and relations with constituents, the three types of organizations are quite distinct. Unofficial groups, understandably, seem most likely to employ contentious tactics. Lacking other forms of leverage, they try to become a thorn in the side of either their economic adversaries or local officials or both, in the hope that these other parties will compromise with or accommodate them in order to get them to quiet down again. This form of group also does the most to encourage broad participation, holding "big meetings" or rallies and trying to enlist the support of large numbers of fellow homeowners.

Especially during their early phases prior to achieving control, owners' movements are prone to disunity. Developers commonly try to suppress these movements, using tactics such as buying off individual activists through selective concessions or cash payments. In more extreme cases, they employ threats and even violence against organizers and their families. Even in the absence of suppression, homeowners can be difficult to coordinate. Many of them work long hours at demanding jobs that leave them little time for meetings. Sometimes there are internal disagreements over goals or tactics. Owners typically lack reinforcing social bases of solidarity, such as common work unit membership. The general problem of free-riding applies well to the *yeweihui* because the benefits of successful collective action (for instance, reduced property management fees) are shared by all, whereas the costs are paid only by those who take part. Therefore, organizers work hard to reach out to the neighborhood and try to win people's involvement and commitment.

Once established and recognized by the government, the *yeweihui* often switch from contentious tactics to less noisy forms of lobbying and negotiating. They also seem to lose some of their enthusiasm for gathering input from constituents through regular and open meetings. Leaders often feel that their mandate is beyond question, having been earned through hard work, and that winning the support of other residents is no longer necessary. In the case of Beixiu Huayuan, chairwoman Cai even felt comfortable dispensing entirely with the cycle of regular elections to which she was supposed to adhere. In Dingyuan, the *yeweihui* leaders' apparent disregard for maintaining the support of their constituents contributed to the unhappy, polarized situation found in that neighborhood. Still, even in places like Beixiu, where leaders do not particularly value elections, we need not conclude that the groups are unresponsive oligarchies. Though they may not be models of participatory democracy, they appear accessible to residents' requests and demands, and they maintain a latent capacity to mobilize broad-based collective action.

Developer-dominated owner groups, in turn, are especially quiet and low-key. They are typically formed through procedures that keep participation to a minimum. Their day-to-day affairs are often run by an administrator (*mishu*) who is in fact an employee of the developer or property management company. They at least give an appearance of being open to complaints and suggestions by the homeowners, and sometimes genuinely follow up on such requests. But it would be incorrect to describe them as collectively empowering the residents. Although they are controlled by companies rather than by the government, such groups resemble state-corporatist institutions in that they claim to represent a constituency yet act in large part to restrain its articulation of its interests and also block it from pursuing alternative channels.

In other cases, however, residents have clearly exercised collective power in remarkable ways. Even in the loosely organized, short-lived protest efforts that arose in Lijiang over the bus fare and the building of the road, homeowners were able to achieve all or significant parts of their demands. Ongoing, semi-institutionalized organizations like those in Beixiu and Jiashan are even more notable, both for what they were able to accomplish on their constituents' behalf and for the form of local self-rule they represent. In these neighborhoods, state agencies that hypothetically could challenge or negate the *yeweihui*—Residents' Committees, Street Offices, police stations—instead implicitly acknowledge the legitimacy of the organization. Here we observe, as well, that these groups assert the right to speak for the owners in many kinds of dealings with the outside world.

At the end of the day, the four "outcomes" in the neighborhoods described here are anything but final. Each surely represents just the opening scenes of a long drama. Property rights and ownership create a *potential* impetus for action. But what will steer and channel such action? In part, this depends on the state. It remains uncertain whether the authorities will continue to tolerate the essentially self-organized *yeweihui* that operate in some of the new neighborhoods. Another fundamental question is whether (or how quickly) homeowners' groups will be allowed to form in what might be called old neighborhoods, such as privatized work unit housing or areas managed by housing offices (*fangguansuo*). Yet the question is not merely one of relaxing the state's grip; it may even have a positive role to play in averting conflict and preventing the kind of meltdown that took place in Dingyuan. Translating the interests of a scattered assortment of owners into coherent, civil, sustained, and effective action is no mean feat. It will require activists to adopt and propagate organizational practices that channel the homeowner movement into constructive and sustainable patterns.

In short, the private ownership of substantial fixed assets in the form of residential property *does* have the potential to bring about substantial reallocation of power at the neighborhood level. But whether this power will, in effect, be wielded by the homeowners themselves, by development and management firms, or even by new state intermediaries will be the result of struggles still under way. The political effects of major upheavals in property ownership will thus take time to unfold.

3. Socialist Land Masters

The Territorial Politics of Accumulation

You-tien Hsing

Below the numerous construction cranes and behind the high-rises, a new type of urban politics has emerged in many Chinese cities. This new urban politics was triggered by radical changes that have taken place in the socialist regime of land rights as cities have expanded dramatically since the late 1980s.[1] In 1988 China's land leasehold market was formally established. It separated ownership from use rights pertaining to urban land. While all urban land is still owned by the Chinese state, as enshrined in the PRC Constitution and the Land Management Law, land use rights can now be leased for a fixed period of time.[2] This new regime has thus commodified land tenure but not privatized it. Although the land is officially state owned, it remains unspecified as to who within the state sector can represent the state, legitimately exercise the ownership rights, and profit from the land rent. As rapid urban expansion fueled an upward spiral in the commercial value of urban land in the 1990s, intrastate competition in the exercise of ownership rights became increasingly contentious.

From my fieldwork in China's large cities,[3] I have found that the competition and negotiation over urban land rights between agents in different segments of

This chapter was originally published in *China Quarterly*, no. 187 (September 2006): 1–18, under the title "Land and Territorial Politics in Urban China."

the state provides an effective analytical perspective on the political economy of urbanization in China.[4] The land-centered urban politics of the 1990s reflects the changing relationship between central and local state players in the city. Land also serves as the main vehicle for the local state to consolidate its territorial authority in the era of fiscal and administrative decentralization.

I have identified two sets of dominant statist players in this land-centered urban politics. The first set consists of the territorial local governments and their leaders. While the State Council has nominal ownership rights over all urban land in China, the territorial governments have the local knowledge and immediate access to state-owned urban land located in their jurisdictions. In this discussion I focus on the municipal governments, with occasional reference to district governments.[5] A second set of statist players come from vertically organized state units, which are a legacy of the *tiao-kuai* matrix in China's bureaucratic structure. Such players consist of central-level government, party and military units, and state-owned enterprises that are physically located within the jurisdiction of municipal governments but are mainly subject to the vertical administrative control of the *tiao*.[6] Also representing the state, they hold the exclusive use and management rights over the land they occupy. They have expanded such rights to de facto ownership since the 1980s, becoming what I call "socialist land masters."

China's new urban politics is unfolding as an intrastate struggle over land between these two sets of statist players, municipal governments and socialist land masters. In this chapter I make three interrelated arguments about their struggles over land rights.

First, the assertion of landed property rights is a power process. In urban China, the legality of state land tenure is a conditioning factor, but the actual exercise of urban land rights is contingent on political maneuvering by the two statist contenders to define and defend such rights.[7]

Second, for local states, urban politics is mainly organized around land development projects to consolidate and actualize the state's territorial power.[8] Local states may be empowered by fiscal decentralization and other central policies to regulate and control urban land. But their capacity to convert such delegated authority into the successful exercise of territorial power is not guaranteed by central policies.

Third, the success of local states in achieving land control and consolidation of territorial power depends on three types of capacities: the political capacity to maneuver the socialist land masters acting from above; the organizational capacity to discipline and coordinate various subordinate units from within; and the moral capacity as the legitimate market regulator and social protector to respond to the society below.

China's land-centered urban politics in the 1990s is new in comparison with that in other capitalistic cities. The capitalist "urban growth machine" in U.S. cities is driven by a coalition of local politicians, private developers, and local media and professional groups.[9] This coalition is built on the bedrock of the ideology and institutions of private property ownership. In Chinese cities, under the state land tenure system the engine driving the urban growth machine is the competition and coalition between different segments of the state, while other sectors remain much less prominent than their American counterparts. This state-centered urban politics is new also in comparison with that in Chinese cities during the pre-reform era. Under the planned economy, urban politics was played out mainly around the competition and bargaining for state budget allocation. State budgets were allocated through the vertical *tiao* system by economic planners in distant political centers in Beijing or provincial capitals. But land, as the new object of competition over urban resources, is immanently local. The immobility of land and its physical attachment to the territory make the competition for land ultimately a local affair. Land gives local state actors an incomparable leverage in this new round of resource competition.

In the discussion that follows, I first examine the competition between the municipal government and socialist land masters for premium urban land, then look at the municipal government's strategies and limitations involving land control and territorial consolidation. In the conclusion I show that, when seen from the point of view of the local state, decentralization involves more than the levels of central control and local autonomy; it also extends to the territorial process of exercising local state power that is both granted and earned.

Socialist Land Masters' Challenge to Municipal Authority

In June 2000 a district chief in Changsha municipality took me on a tour of the city. He kept referring to the land under the direct proprietary control of the district government as "my land." He also asked me for suggestions on developing "his" five hundred *mu* here, and "his" twelve hundred *mu* there.[10] Before the city tour I attended a luncheon with him and two urban planning officials, a government banker, a businessman, and a local commercial developer. The district chief tried to persuade the developer to give up a projected high-density residential/retail complex on a corner lot in the city core because the district government had plans to build a landmark government office tower surrounded by a public plaza on that site. But the developer, who was connected with the military, said there was no way for him to change the plan now that the foundation work had already started. The district chief was clearly disappointed. So as he ticked off his prized list of land in his possession after the lunch, I realized that his control over urban land nominally under his jurisdiction was far from complete.

Many municipal government officials I meet in China nowadays share a similar sense of personal proprietorship over the land under their jurisdiction. They all agree that territorial governments should be made the "real landlords" in order to assert full regulatory control over land use and transactions and to secure rent payments in China's fragmented urban land system. During interviews I often feel that their sense of power seems to derive from the measurable, usable, and tradable land parcels in their jurisdiction. They move tactically to expand their control over the growing urban land and real estate markets.

Revenue from land is one primary consideration. As central revenue transfer has been drastically reduced in the new budgetary regime, which also promotes fiscal decentralization, municipal governments look to locally generated revenue to cover urban infrastructure, social welfare, education, and other government expenditures. In this context, land-related revenue streams become especially important as they make a direct and increasingly significant contribution to the local state's coffers. It is estimated that land-related revenue accounted for 30 to 70 percent of the total revenue of all subnational-level governments in various municipalities in the late 1990s.[11]

Land-related revenues come from two sources. The government as regulator derives revenues from taxes and surcharges on land appreciation and transactions from various development projects; the government as proprietor has receipts from the direct sale of land leases and from rents on government-built industrial and commercial structures. The latter source of revenue is more stable than the former because the former is too often subject to tax evasion and avoidance. It also costs the government less to collect revenue from direct sales or rents than from taxes and surcharges. Most important, revenue from land lease sales is outside the formal state budgetary system, and is thus fully retained in the local coffers.[12] As a result, local budgetary autonomy has come to depend on land-related revenue, especially receipts from the sale of land leases.

In addition to contributing revenue, land lease sales serve to demonstrate the municipal government's territorial power. In a way, that power is measured by the area of land that is under the municipality's direct and exclusive control. Land connects tangible resources that are of fiscal importance to the intangible and symbolic display of power associated with various urban landmarks. Since the early 1990s, local government leaders have competed with one another to build extravagant public projects such as new city halls, central plazas, statues commemorating local legends, office towers, and luxury hotels. These towering modern structures visibly demonstrate local leaders' achievements. But to build these symbolic projects in strategic locations, municipal officials must move to establish full regulatory and proprietary control over land parcels in the city centers. Parcels of land under the control of the municipal government also serve as a political resource that can be exchanged for favors or other resources, such as investments in industry and urban infrastructure.

Among the main challengers to the municipal government's control over premium urban land are the socialist land masters. Under the socialist land tenure system in the pre-reform period, various urban land users such as state-owned enterprises, military units, hospitals, universities, research institutes, utility providers, and government agencies were allocated land through administrative channels according to central capital investment plans. These institutional land users not only held rights to the use and management of the land they occupied but also acted as de facto owners who could make decisions about exchange and transfer of the land they occupied. These socialist land masters have inherited several legacies that give them two major advantages in the competition for control over urban land in the post-reform era. The first is the advantage of location. The socialist land masters, especially the industrial enterprises, occupy some of the land in the heart of the city. This came about because, motivated by the idea that the socialist city should be a production center instead of a consumption center, economic planners had allocated centrally located land to many high-ranking and high-profile industrial state-owned enterprises (SOEs) in the 1960s and 1970s. By the early 1980s, industrial enterprises and warehouses occupied about 30 percent of the core area in Chinese cities, a percentage that was much higher than in most capitalist cities.[13] For example, about 5 percent of the total area that made up the urban core of Beijing was home to 55 percent of the state-owned factories in the city.[14] In Shanghai, nearly 60 percent of the state-owned factories were located in the central part of the city, and almost 70 percent of the industrial workers worked and lived there by 1982.[15] As a result, ten industrial bureaus in Shanghai controlled more than a quarter of the city's industrial land in the 1980s and established themselves as super–land masters in the 1990s.[16]

A second advantage these socialist land masters enjoy is simply the quantity of land they control. In the past, because work units (*danwei*) also functioned as the channel of welfare distribution for the socialist state, land was allocated not only for the factories, warehouses, and office structures but also for employee housing, health clinics, day care centers, and schools for the employees' children. The logic of soft budget constraints also meant that the SOEs and other state *danwei* had bargained hard for more land than they could use because land came at little cost.[17] Each *danwei* was subject to a vertical budgetary and personnel system (*tiao*) that was largely beyond the reach of territorially organized local governments. Physically, they may occupy as large an area as several city blocks combined. On the eve of the establishment of the land leasehold market in 1988, much of the core areas of the large cities in China was occupied by these vertically linked but horizontally fragmented *danwei* compounds.[18]

As long as the pace of urbanization was slow and land rights were rarely transferred for profit, such fragmentation of urban land control was not a problem. But the rapid industrialization, urban expansion, and economic diversification in China since the late 1980s have intensified the competition over urban land. In 1988 a leasehold market for land was formally established, which effectively separated land use rights from ownership rights. While the state ownership of land remains unchanged, land use rights can now be legally transferred as land leases;

they are tradable in the market by negotiation, tender, or open auction.[19] Urban land has thus become commodified even if de jure privatization of land is still outlawed. By creating market-like competition for land rent, the commodification of land has set the socialist land masters in motion. They form their own land development companies and expand their use rights to include the right to transfer and profit from land under their control.

The large land reserves that the socialist land masters have accumulated in the central part of the city are now paying off. As a low-risk strategy, many of them simply transfer land use rights to commercial developers and then profit by collecting rent. One Chinese analyst estimated in 2001 that only a minority of the land development companies in Beijing, about 1,200 out of 4,000-plus, actually engaged in development projects themselves.[20] The rest actively sold their land use rights to commercial developers who did not otherwise have access to the premium land parcels. An informal network of land brokers has emerged to facilitate the circulation of landownership in many cities. Among the successful brokers are former staff members from landowning state units and officials with connections to relevant government agencies.[21]

The enterprising and resource-rich socialist land masters have further expanded their land reserves by consolidating parcels belonging to many different work units under the same administrative system (*xitong*), or by purchasing additional land from other state units on the verge of bankruptcy through insider connections. Strong financial backing by the vertical *xitong* organization has made such ambitious land purchases possible. Thus, throughout the 1990s, ambitious socialist land masters built up an even larger land reserve by leveraging the *xitong* system's financial power and by assembling large tracts of premium urban land parcel by parcel through intrastate transactions.[22]

As a result, nominal state ownership of urban land coexists with a highly fragmented pattern of land use and management under various socialist land masters. The fragmentation of land control has its roots in the planned economy. But it has made a much greater impact on the urban land system in the post-reform era. In the 1990s the socialist land masters would become the most formidable players in the urban land market and major challengers to the consolidation efforts of municipal governments.

Municipal Governments' Territorial Consolidation Projects

Pressed by fiscal urgency and motivated by political ambition, municipal government leaders are eager to assert their territorial authority and gain the upper hand in the struggle against the socialist land masters over premium urban land. Since the early 1990s, many urban governments across China have adopted numerous strategies to consolidate and reinforce their control over land. Their strategies include promoting capitalist urban land use doctrines over socialist ones, setting up new government agencies to rationalize land management, embarking on urban redevelopment projects in the name of modernization, and establishing institutions such as land banks in an attempt to monopolize urban land supplies. In this section I discuss these strategies within the categories of "city rational," "city modern," and "city monopoly" projects.

City Rational Project

A horizontal, territorially oriented urban land management regime started to emerge in the late 1980s, symbolized by the establishment of the new Ministry of Land Management in 1986. Local bureaus of land management were established in ensuing years. The fact that they were placed under the supervision of municipal governments added to the municipal government's authority over land management. The local bureaus of land management at the municipal and district or county levels were granted the authority to prepare annual land use plans, allocate quotas for conversion of farmland to non-farm uses, issue permits for such land conversion, and monitor land lease sales.[23] By 1998 a revised land management law stipulated that all administratively allocated land parcels would have to be transferred to the municipal government before they could be leased out to the developers. With these provisions, the municipal government is formally recognized as the exclusive representative of the state in exercising the right to transfer land and to profit from its commercial use.[24]

Such legalistic and administrative recognition of the municipal government's authority over urban land is only the first step toward consolidating its territorial power. It does not guarantee success in exercising such delegated authority. The central government–level contacts of many socialist land masters make it politically risky for the municipal government to confront them directly over illicit land deals. So the municipal government has sought doctrinal legitimation from Western urban planning guidelines. It uses the argument that urban planning is fundamentally about realizing the exchange value of land on the market and about allocating land in market-efficient ways. Accordingly, the land that yields the highest rent should be used for activities that generate the highest market value. Since there is a rent gradient from the urban center to peripheral areas, centrally located land lots should go to the highest bidders, who can generate the highest value from the land.[25] High rent–generating projects are usually real estate ventures such as luxury hotels and condominiums, retail boutiques, and office-retail complexes, not large Leninist factories with smoking chimneys.

Since the late 1980s, Chinese urban planners have been trained in schools using American city planning textbooks.[26] Since the principle of efficiency in urban land use has dovetailed with the development discourse in urban China since the

1990s, the new generation of city planners has enjoyed the political support of municipal government leaders. Together, municipal officials and city planners argue that profit-losing state factories and nonprofit institutions such as schools and hospitals should be relocated away from the city center to make room for banks, hotels, retail shops, high-end commercial housing, and office complexes. The rapid growth of the service sector in many large Chinese cities has added urgency to addressing the problem of suboptimal use of urban land.[27] China's city planners often compare New York, London, and Tokyo to large Chinese cities to drive home the idea of inefficient land use patterns in socialist cities, echoing the municipal officials' call to correct the problem with a more efficient use of urban land based on its exchange value.[28]

Chinese city planners make yet another point against the traditional socialist land masters who preside over a mixed-use pattern of land utilization. The planners promote the idea of zoning, which calls for separate, specialized patterns of land use for different categories of urban activities. City planners argue that the mixed land use pattern in socialist *danwei* compounds makes it costly to provide adequate public facilities, which often require a large area of land devoted to relatively uniform uses in order to achieve economies of scale. As large *danwei* compounds mix industrial, residential, commercial, and service uses of land in their own cells, it is impossible to establish a proper land rent gradient for the city as a whole. The planners argue that the *danwei*-based land use pattern fragments land and wastes precious resources. They urge tearing down the walls of the *danwei* compounds and integrating them into a unified urban land planning and management system coordinated at the municipal level.[29] In short, with the city rational project, the municipal government adopts the doctrines of rationality and efficiency embodied in capitalist land use planning to strengthen its position against socialist land masters in the competition for premium urban land.

City Modern Project

Armed with arguments for rationality and efficiency, municipal officials started to take the city back by initiating redevelopment projects in the old neighborhoods of the urban core. For decades, many old neighborhoods in Chinese cities have suffered from a host of problems, including high residential density, deteriorating and increasingly unsafe structures, inadequate facilities such as flush toilets and kitchenettes, and nonfunctioning neighborhood sewage systems.

But *danwei* compounds in the urban center are off-limits to municipal urban planners. Municipal officials are blocked from entering the gated and guarded compounds. They find it difficult to conduct land surveys, not to mention gathering updated information about land use and land transfers. Residents in such compounds, most of whom are also employees, form a tight-knit community, and they are often reluctant to cooperate with municipal officials and planners. The socialist land masters answer to vertically higher authorities and resent what they perceive as unwarranted outside intervention from lower- or equally ranked municipal and district government officials.

So municipal officials start with neighborhoods that are not attached to any particular large state unit. Under the banner of improving the living environment for residents and modernizing the city, municipal governments across China have launched massive urban redevelopment projects in urban core areas since the early 1990s. They have established their own land development companies and/or used land as equity shares to partner with commercial developers in undertaking such projects.

As the developers, supported by the municipal government, tear down old structures and build new ones, the municipal government redraws the physical boundary of its authority and reclaims its proprietary and regulatory power over valuable urban land. Redevelopment projects usually start with land surveys and official designation of "unsafe" buildings (*weifang*). Then follows the demarcation of "redevelopment zones," land value appraisal, title verification, and cadastral registration. Detailed plans for land use and redevelopment are made for each redevelopment zone. Licenses are issued for land use conversion, real estate development, construction, marketing, and sales of the projects. Each of these seemingly mundane administrative procedures serves to reinforce municipal government's control over the marked land and the process of its commercial development. It does not change the nominal ownership rights of the land by the state. Yet it does affirm the municipal government's proprietary and regulatory authority over designated urban space and defines the reach of municipal authority. Through this process the municipal government attains proprietary rights over specific, clearly marked urban land parcels. One immediate consequence is that it becomes a signatory to all land leases with developers. Through land surveys and cadastral registration, it not only updates the records about individual land parcels but also legally incorporates them into the urban land management system. The claim of proprietorship, more accurate information, and regulatory authority reinforce one another in establishing the municipal government's firm control over the urban space. By the end of the redevelopment process, if everything goes smoothly, the municipal government will have a clearer inventory of the land it "owns." It can then decide which parcel can be sold to or exchanged with whom, at what price, and how much is to be charged and taxed for the transaction and development.[30]

For the municipal government, urban redevelopment is about demolishing the old urban spatial structure and installing a new one under municipal management. It is both a spatial and a sociopolitical project. Through this process of modernizing the city, the municipal government tries to reclaim its control over valuable urban land.

City Monopoly Project

Urban redevelopment can be an effective way of reclaiming urban land parcels in a piecemeal fashion. But the ambition of municipal government leaders is for the government to become a super-landlord in the city: a landlord that owns, plans, sells, develops, and regulates all land in the city. In this endeavor they were helped by a real estate crisis in the mid-1990s. After Deng Xiaoping's historic visit to Shenzhen in the spring of 1992, a wave of "development fever" swept the country. As the battles for land in urban core areas became increasingly furious, much farmland on the urban fringe was converted to non-farm development. The simultaneous and rampant construction booms in both urban core and fringe areas in turn created property oversupplies. By the end of 1993, it was estimated that 30 to 50 million square meters of built floor area were vacant nationwide. Another 50,000 hectares of land were vacated but not developed.[31] In 1994 Premier Zhu Rongji announced an austerity policy, which severely reduced the sources of real estate financing. Many booming cities on the east coast were left with skeleton hotels and office towers and half-finished condominiums.

This crisis in the real estate market provided an excellent opportunity for municipal governments to launch a new campaign of urban land control. Municipal government officials blamed development companies sponsored by socialist land masters and the fragmentation of the land market for causing and then bursting the real estate bubble.

Municipal policy analysts reported that the oversupply of property and the real estate bubble of 1994 were created by "too many suppliers without a central coordinator in the market."[32] The first step toward achieving a solution is to identify a coordinator. The municipal government, as the newly designated manager of the state-owned landed property in the city, so the argument goes, is eminently suited to play such a role.

In order to coordinate effectively, it is necessary for municipal and district government to centralize land supplies. In 1996 Shanghai's municipal government established the Center for Land Development, which was to function as a land bank for the city. This land bank would purchase land use rights from land users, negotiate a profit-sharing plan with them, and then put the land parcels in its reserves for resale on the market in open auctions or through public tender. A successful land bank could facilitate the efforts of municipal government to centralize land supplies and become a super-landlord in the city.[33] By opening up the process of land lease transfers through auctions and tenders, the municipal government also hoped to reap a larger share of the land rent and establish systematic bookkeeping practices for land management, land use planning, and taxation.

The municipal government's attempt to centralize coordination was in alignment with central policies in the early years of the twenty-first century. The central government began to impose more rigorous land control policies. In 2001 the State Council made the land bank a national policy.[34] In May 2002 the Ministry of Land and Resources issued Ordinance No. 11, which made open land auctions and public tenders mandatory for commercial development projects. In the land auctions and public tenders organized by the municipal land bank, developers would have to pay the official rates for land leases, which are on average eight to ten times higher than the privately negotiated price.[35]

Open auctions also meant higher compensation rates for relocated residents, larger down payments, and fixed payment schedules.[36] In addition, developers would have to comply more strictly with land use regulations such as the density measure called the Floor-Area Ratio (FAR), which is critical to developers' profit margin. Because of the potentially heavy impact on land price and development costs, real estate circles came to call Ordinance No. 11 a "land revolution."[37]

Municipal Governments' Capacity Tests

Ordinance No. 11 indeed created much controversy. Socialist land masters and large developers criticized the new policy of mandatory open land auctions as municipal government's abuse of administrative authority and excessive interference in the market. In the meantime, because of the abundant land reserves they had built up in the first ten years of the land lease market, the land masters and large developers did not feel the need to bid for additional land at open auction. As a result, few large land development companies participated in the auctions.[38]

Another source of constraints on the municipal government's ambition to control land comes from within the municipality itself. The municipal government is hardly an integrated organization with a unitary set of agendas. There are numerous bureaus, committees, and offices in the government and party systems of a municipality. Under the pressures of fiscal independence, many municipal agencies have established their own development companies. For example, the Beijing municipality boasted 623 development companies; in 1995, 108 of them were owned by state *danwei* and 485 by various municipal agencies.[39] Individual agencies control the operation, and hence the profits, of these development companies; their internal coffers (*xiao-jinku*) are inaccessible to municipal-level officials. In some cases the very agencies that regulate the land market and urban development make their own real estate development deals.[40] When individual government agencies seek to profit from land deals, the municipality-wide consolidation project suffers as land under the control of individual governmental agencies circulates outside the land bank, escaping the control of municipal leaders.

Internal fragmentation of land control becomes worse when we take into account the different and sometimes contradictory mandates of various municipal agencies. One classic divide falls between the bureaus of land management and urban planning. The two bureaus belong to two different vertical chains of command, or *xitong*: the land management bureau takes orders from the Ministry of Land and Resources, while the urban planning bureau answers to the Ministry of Construction. The land management bureau has a mandate to preserve farmland and control growth, while the urban planning bureau is under constant pressure from municipal leaders to plan for growth. The land management bureau produces annual land use plans and allocates quotas of farmland conversion accordingly. The urban planning bureau produces yet another set of plans for urban expansion, with often exaggerated growth projections.[41] Both sets of plans are legally binding. While the two agencies share the authority to approve land conversion and development at different stages of a project, contradictions in their mandates often lead to inconsistencies in land use regulation.[42] Sometimes their disagreements prolong the process of project approval and create legal and administrative gaps in land regulation. Developers play one bureau off against the other in their bid for unlicensed construction and illegal projects.[43]

The municipality is also a hierarchically structured bureaucracy. Below the municipal government are district governments in built-up urban areas and county governments in rural areas. Almost all sub-municipal governments have established their own development companies, and many have more than one. Shanghai, for example, is well known for the powerful and active district governments that hold premium land in the city center. The Shanghai municipal government delegates to districts the authority over land use, including the right to make land use and urban development plans, approve development projects, negotiate land lease sales, and sign leases directly with developers. The district governments are allowed to retain as much as 85 percent of the total revenue from land lease sales.[44] As a result, district leaders have embarked on ambitious projects of turning old neighborhoods into new commercial complexes. They have also aggressively taken on new development projects. Each district has tried to create its own downtown for the sake of charging premium commercial land rents. Thus Shanghai and other large cities now boast multiple "Central Business Districts" (CBDs) initiated by competing district governments, some of which do not reflect the development plan of the municipality as a whole.

The internal organizational conflicts within the municipal government make compromise necessary. In order to maintain growth momentum and GDP performance, most municipal leaders allow some *kouzi* (exceptions) in implementing the demands of Ordinance No. 11 for open auction and public tender of land parcels for commercial development. For example, the Beijing municipal government leaves open four such *kouzi*, which allow nonpublic negotiations for four types of projects that involve land lease. Such projects include building in the greenbelt zones, construction of small towns on farmland in the urban periphery, the reconstruction of dilapidated housing (*weifang gaijian*), and the development of high-tech industrial parks. As it turns out, most of the development projects fall into one of the four categories and are supported by suburban counties or municipal districts. Thus, most land leases in Beijing continue to proceed through individual negotiations rather than open auction.[45] Shanghai has observed similar *kouzi* in its implementation of the ordinance.[46] Municipal leaders' ambitions for territorial consolidation are thus dampened by the internal fragmentation of the municipality.

Finally, the relentless pursuit of accumulation in the 1980s and 1990s exposed municipal governments to mounting challenges to their legitimacy as social protectors and market regulators.[47] Since 2000, increasing numbers of residents affected by urban redevelopment projects have protested unfair relocation compensation, violent and forced eviction, and official corruption in land lease sales. Politically skillful urban residents employ socialist slogans and demand justice and social protection from the Communist Party. Discontented residents send letters to higher-level governments or visit their offices to lodge complaints against municipal and district governments.[48] In many large cities the amount of litigation over unjust and unlawful relocation has increased sharply since 2002. One such lawsuit in Beijing represented more than ten thousand plaintiffs against Beijing's planning committee and government-backed developers.[49]

With increased attention from the media and central leadership on social conflicts generated by urban development, and the cadre evaluation system that takes into account the number of petition cases from each jurisdiction, municipal leaders became alarmed. And it is not just the weakest members of society who are protesting against land-triggered social problems. A growing number of owners of private homes in the newly built residential areas have organized themselves into homeowner associations.[50] These young, well-educated and well-informed, Internet-connected homeowners, many of them white-collar professionals, have launched litigation against developers for complaints such as false advertising, breach of contract, violation of housing density regulations, and insufficient public facilities in the new complexes. Some homeowners go further and take the municipal government and its urban planning bureau to court for issuing development permits that violate zoning regulations and urban development plans, such as for building additional residential towers on the community green.[51]

The role of the municipal government as an impartial market regulator is also being challenged by the development industry, which has undergone restructuring since 2000. In recent years many large socialist land masters have transformed themselves into shareholding companies, identifying themselves as private firms. Some small- and medium-sized private developers have also become more visible. Members of the new private sector, consisting of the former socialist land masters and smaller developers, now complain about the municipal government's active involvement in land and real estate markets. They argue against charges of conflict of interest as the municipal government assumes a dual role as market participant and market regulator at the same time. Among other things, municipal governments have been accused of violating the "natural law of the market."[52] Municipal leaders who have been obsessed with urban expansion projects now find themselves confronting questions about their capacity to protect the society and regulate the market.

• • •

Municipal leaders' territorial consolidation projects are integral to the state- and land-centered urban politics of large Chinese cities. In their competition with the socialist land masters to control urban land, the success of municipal leaders depends on their political capacity to deal with the land masters above, their organizational capacity to discipline the fragmented sub-municipal units from within to achieve accumulation, and their moral capacity to maintain legitimacy. In the process, municipal leaders face both challenges and opportunities to define and defend the boundaries of their territorial power, and in this way their governing capacity is tested and built.

These contingencies and constraints on the capacity of local states make it necessary to reconsider the connection between decentralization and local state autonomy. In the literature on local states in post-reform China, their autonomy is often treated as a natural outcome of top-down fiscal and administrative decentralization policies.[53] But the question of whether and how the centrally granted authority is translated into the actual exercise of territorial power has yet to be clarified. I have shown that decentralization as a grand policy scheme does not guarantee local state power. While municipal governments enjoy the delegated authority of urban land management and land market coordination, it remains an open question whether and how municipal governments are able to convert such delegated authority into the effective exercise of territorial power. When one "sees like a local state," decentralization becomes not just an issue of the level of central control and local autonomy but also a matter of local states' capacity to operate with power that is both granted and earned. The process of exercising state power, therefore, is not a zero-sum game between the central and local states but an open, endless project of strategic maneuvering and negotiation among heterogeneous state players.

4. Tax Tensions

Struggles over Income and Revenue

Bei Li and Steven M. Sheffrin

Shortly after the Chinese New Year of 2000, when spring planting season arrived, the government officers of Qipan Township, Jianli County, in Hubei Province, central China, found that over 90 percent of the township's arable land had been left uncultivated.[1] Despite their best efforts to encourage the peasants, about 16 percent of the farmland had been abandoned by the end of March. In the meantime, more than 40 percent of Qipan's total population of 33,000 had left home to search for work in towns and cities, a figure almost double the out-migration for 1999.

Why did people choose to work far from home when there was so much idle land? Kaimin Li, a sixty-year-old man from Jiaohu Village in Qipan, said that he earned only a little money by growing rice in 1998 and suffered a loss in 1999. In 1999, each *mu* (0.067 hectares) of middle-season rice yielded an income of only roughly 320 yuan. But the total cost per *mu* of land was over 352 yuan, 185 yuan of which was for all kinds of taxes and fees, including the agricultural tax, slaughter

Support for this project was provided by the Center for State and Local Taxation at the University of California, Davis. The authors would like to thank Li Zhang, Aihwa Ong, and participants at the workshop for their valuable comments. We also thank Jean Stratford for providing excellent editorial assistance and insights on the project.

tax, special products tax, village levies, township levies, and other taxes. Thus Li's estimated loss amounted to 32 yuan per *mu*, before taking into account his own labor cost.

The problems caused by unregulated and nontransparent taxation are no better in urban areas. In the Yuci District of Jinzhong City, Shanxi Province, after being laid off from their jobs, a middle-aged couple opened a small shop to sell braised pork with soy sauce. The shopkeeper husband complained to a journalist that with more and more taxes and arbitrary charges, he could make hardly any profits.[2] In addition to central and local taxes, the major fees they paid in the year 2001 included a sanitation fee (60 yuan per month), a wastewater treatment fee (over 300 yuan per year), an anti-epidemic testing fee (480 yuan per quarter), a property-leasing administration fee (30 yuan per year and 10 yuan for the certificate), as well as a road-blocking fee (60 yuan per month and 5 yuan for the stamp on the receipt). Moreover, there were other informal charges. "Each year when I went to the local trade and industrial bureau to renew my business license," the shopkeeper said, "they would force me to subscribe to some newspaper." He showed the journalist a few poorly printed and unread copies of *Jinzhong Economic News*, which had cost him 100 yuan for twelve issues. He had been required to spend 72 yuan on another journal, *Taxation Announcement*, while turning in his payment at the local tax bureau. In addition, he paid 90 yuan to join a consumer association, 150 yuan to the trade and industrial bureau for a computer management fee, 12 yuan for an iron band to hang up on the shop door for "sanitation and social order responsibilities," and so on. His wife complained that the tax collectors came from so many different government departments that she became very nervous whenever she saw anyone with an official-style large-brim hat coming around.

While China has experienced remarkable economic growth in recent decades, the fiscal system supporting this booming economy remains far from efficient. Arbitrary and nontransparent local taxation increased along with the new economic activities; this widened regional inequality and gave rise to corruption and rent-seeking behavior, which in the long run will not only harm economic development but also weaken social stability.

This chapter examines the main problems in the current tax-sharing system in China and their causes, with a focus on financing local public services. Despite the reform measures that have been adopted by the government, we argue that improvements cannot be sustained without a substantial restructuring of the tax system and intergovernmental fiscal relations. A robust tax system is needed to minimize corruption and to ensure the efficiency of the public finance system. A long-term solution would be to grant local governments more discretion and to develop a more efficient local taxation system. The property tax is a potential candidate for a stable and growing source of local taxes.

How do these issues relate to privatization in China? Over time, Western market economies have developed barriers between private actions taken in the private or nonregulated sector and actions taken by government officials. The logic of fiscal policy in modern market economies is that payments made to government bureaucracies need to be carefully spelled out in formal law, public statutes, and regulations. This practice limits rent seeking on the part of government officials and provides necessary clarity to the private sector. In the current Chinese setting, a formal tax system coexists with essentially "private" or, more accurately, self-interested actions taken in the name of public entities to raise funds for state activities. These self-interested actions on the part of state actors undercut the growth of private sector actors and also undermine the potential for the growth of a modern tax system, which is needed to provide public services. Ironically, as China embraces market logic and privatization, it must limit the self-interested actions of government bureaucrats in order to effectively "privatize" the private sector.

In the next section we present an overview of the current tax system and recent major changes and explore several problems that have arisen with the current system, including the growth of excessive and arbitrary fees and taxes. We then examine aspects of the land-leasing system and the system of real estate taxation, and discuss possible transformations of the current system. We also discuss the problem of corruption in relation to the design of the current tax and revenue system. Finally, we highlight some of the challenges to reform within the current structure and practice of privatization in China.

A Brief Overview of the Chinese Taxation System

Between 1980 and 1993, China implemented a fiscal system characterized by its practice of contracting, which was also known as "eating from different kitchens." Not only could the revenues shared between central and local governments be negotiated, but also income taxes could be imposed on enterprises by local governments through contractual agreements. This complicated and uncertain tax structure led to a huge loss of revenue. As a result of this system, as well as the shrinking profits of state-owned enterprises (SOEs), the main source of taxes, the total government revenue–GDP ratio dropped significantly from 31.2 percent in 1978 to 12.6 percent in 1993. The central government's share of total fiscal revenues declined from 38.4 percent in 1985 to 22.0 percent in 1993, creating concerns for the central government.

The 1994 tax reform constituted a comprehensive package of measures that substantially changed China's tax structure and intergovernmental fiscal relations. Its main features were:

1. It increased the central government's share of budgetary revenue. In the new system, taxes are of three kinds: central taxes, local taxes, and shared taxes. Central taxes consist of the consumption tax, customs duties, income taxes from

central enterprises and from banks and non-bank financial intermediaries, and so on. Local taxes include business taxes, individual income tax, income taxes from local enterprises, the urban construction and maintenance tax, all agricultural taxes, real estate tax, and the land use tax. Shared taxes include mainly the value-added tax (VAT), of which the central government obtains 75 percent of the revenues and the local government gets the remaining 25 percent.[3]

2. It simplified the tax structure and equalized the treatment of enterprises with different ownerships. The new system extended the VAT to all turnover processes, eliminated the product tax, and combined and consolidated other taxes.

3. Taxation power was recentralized and tax administration was decentralized. The central government determines tax bases and rates, chooses the revenue-sharing formula, and sets the amount of transfer payments to each province. Tax contracting between local governments and enterprises was prohibited. Two separate tax administration systems were established, with the national tax bureau collecting central and shared taxes and local tax bureaus collecting local taxes.

The tax-sharing reform successfully increased total fiscal revenue and strengthened the central government's control over the macro-economy. The government revenue–GDP ratio stopped declining after 1995 and gradually increased to 18 percent in 2002. In the meantime, the central government's share of total budgetary revenue increased dramatically to over 50 percent in 1994 and has been maintained at around that level since then. As the new tax system left expenditure assignments untouched, the central government's share of total budgetary expenditures remained around 30 percent, with slight fluctuations.

As a direct result of the revenue centralization, almost all provinces fell into budget deficit and had to rely on transfer payments from the central government to finance public services. Without formal taxation power, subnational governments faced with financial difficulties turned to collecting extrabudgetary revenues (EBRs). These are the funds collected by the administrative and institutional units of government which are outside the normal budgetary process. In addition, "self-raised" funds and other nonbudgetary resources are collected by local governments and their administrative departments.

To a large extent, this vast array of charges is a legacy of bureaucratic socialism magnified by the perceived need for local government revenues. All bureaucracies, including socialist ones, have a tendency to emphasize a distinct mission for the components of an organization, even at the expense of fulfilling broader goals. According to this logic, each unit would seek support from its own fee or charge in order to sustain its operations. This natural tendency was magnified by the quest for new revenue sources for local governments following the national reforms.

The exact scale of EBRs is hard to estimate, as local governments are neither required nor willing to report them, but EBRs are believed to account for 8 to

10 percent of GDP, or even more.[4] The rampant expansion of EBRs in rural China has resulted in an especially heavy tax burden on peasants, which we discuss in detail in the next section.

The fiscal difficulties of local governments under the current system, especially the heavy rural tax burden and widening regional disparity, have drawn extensive social and academic concern. Since the late 1990s, the Chinese government has issued a series of important reform measures in an attempt to regulate and curtail EBR collection and to equalize the tax burden. These have included several measures to bring off-budget items into the budgeting process and to eliminate more than 21,000 separate charges and fees by converting them to taxes. In addition, in March 2000 the central government launched a rural "fee-tax-swap" reform intended to relieve the peasants' tax burden. In Anhui Province and several counties in other provinces, most agriculture-related taxes and fees were consolidated into a unified agricultural tax with a higher rate. Then in April 2002 the State Council announced the implementation of a comprehensive rural "fee-tax-swap" reform in twenty provinces, autonomous regions, and municipalities, accompanied by a central transfer of 24.5 billion yuan for the year 2002.

The assignment of income tax revenue was also the subject of another important reform. Since January 2002 the revenue from the local enterprise income tax and individual income tax, which used to be local tax sources, has been shared between the central and local governments.

Difficulties with the Tax-Sharing System

In this section we examine a number of problems that have arisen in connection with this system of sharing tax revenues.

Large Extrabudgetary Revenues

As noted, extrabudgetary revenues of the central and especially local governments have increased dramatically since the 1994 tax reform. Although the collection of EBRs requires approval from the central government, local governments often bypass this rule and claim great discretion to levy informal fees and arbitrary surcharges. This has resulted in problems of taxation such as those mentioned at the beginning of the chapter. Another famous example is that of the McDonald's restaurants in Beijing.[5] Only fourteen of the thirty-one fees paid by McDonald's were formal taxes; the others included a wastewater treatment fee, a management fee for the food and beverage industry, a traffic safety fee, a sanitation fee, a "greenification" fee, an air raid shelter maintenance fee, a river dredging fee, a family planning fee, a fire protection fee, and others.

Revenues of approximately 383 billion yuan in EBRs were raised in 2000, about 70 percent of which came from administrative and institutional units. These revenues were mostly user charges collected for government-provided goods and services: charges for IDs, passports, driver's licenses, vehicle licenses, patents, various business and professional certificates, and supervision fees for construction projects and for environmental protection, among others. Another 10 percent, or 38 billion yuan, stemmed from certain government-raised funds, for example, funds for railway and airport construction, electricity and other municipal utilities, forestry and fishery management, welfare for the disabled, and so on. Revenues from fund-raising programs of township governments accounted for another 11 percent, or 40.3 billion yuan, which were basically for five purposes: schools, family planning, veterans, militia, and road construction and maintenance.

In terms of expenditures, the majority of EBRs were used for operating and administrative expenses. Approximately 12 percent, or 42.6 billion yuan, went to capital construction projects; 11 percent, or 38.7 billion yuan, was spent on expenditures by township governments; 10 percent, or 3.4 billion yuan, went to cover other expenses; and a mere 4 percent, or 14.6 billion yuan, went to urban maintenance projects. Very little of the funding (perhaps 16 percent) is spent on items such as capital construction or local infrastructure that may be apparent to taxpayers.

Nontransparency and Corruption

It is evident that the array of charges collected by different departments not only increases the level of taxation but also introduces an unhealthy level of nontransparency and inefficiency into the taxation process. A common complaint from taxpayers is that they have to deal with collectors from various government agencies, each of which may require a different accounting statement, and taxpayers never know how much more they will need to pay tomorrow. The level of uncertainty of this way of doing business is certainly harmful to economic growth in the long run.

Since EBRs are handled outside the normal budgetary process, it is very hard for the government to track or forecast their collection or plan for effective allocation of the revenues. Each level of local government collects a variety of informal fees and levies. And since these fees are "informal," quite often there is neither consistent treatment of taxpayers, consistent calculation of fees, nor effective supervision of authorities.

Furthermore, the high levels of nontransparency and the informal nature of EBRs have led to significant corruption and tax evasion, both of which result in huge losses of fiscal revenue and public welfare. Local officials who take bribes can easily bypass the rules and grant exemptions or reductions to enterprises or individuals while pocketing revenues meant for the provision of services. Although there is little systematic information on the level of corruption and lost revenue in the local government finance system, anecdotal evidence abounds. In August 2003 China's auditor general reported that over a five-year period, some 710,000 national audits had been performed, recovering some 86.4 billion yuan in funds owed to the central government, with 108 billion yuan in embezzled funds still missing. Over 6,100 cases were forwarded to the police for criminal investigation, and 4,242 party cadres were disciplined.[6]

Widening Regional Disparities and the Heavy Rural Tax Burden

The current arrangement of central transfer payments has widened regional disparities. Under this system, even the richest provinces and municipalities such as Beijing, Shanghai, Guangdong, and Jiangsu have experienced budgetary deficits and have had to request central transfers. The transfer payment system has favored the richer provinces rather than being used for purposes of equalization. This is because transfer payments consist partly of taxes received by each provincial government according to the taxation revenues of each in 1993, and are therefore strongly correlated with economic strength. In addition, earmarked grants are generally for specific infrastructure projects, which require matching funds from the local government. As a result, they are more likely to be obtained by richer regions. Since the taxes returned to local governments and earmarked grants make up a significant share of total transfer payments, the equalizing function of central transfers is weakened. Compared to the more developed provinces of the eastern coast and to the autonomous regions in the west (which are heavily subsidized for political purposes), the agricultural provinces of central China have been least favored in the current fiscal arrangement, despite their poor economies.

Given the present system of transfer payments, as subnational governments raise off-budget funds to finance their expenditures, the poorer ones are even more reliant on these revenues than those that are prosperous. As a result, an increasing tax burden has fallen on the peasants. The rural tax burden is notoriously heavy in China, and the array of formal and informal exactions on peasants is an expression of the financial difficulties faced by local governments. Table 1 summarizes the formal and informal exactions on peasants according to a survey in 1999.

An empirical study based on data covering 120 villages in ten provinces of China from 1986 to 1999 shows that rural taxation is quite regressive not only across provinces but also across income levels.[7] From 1993 to 1999, in two rich provinces (Guangdong and Zhejiang) the share of a peasant's total income that went to pay taxes and fees increased from 6–7 percent to around 9 percent, whereas the share in the three poorest provinces (Hunan, Sichuan, and Jilin) increased from 10–12 percent to 17–21 percent. The data show that on average, peasants with the lowest annual incomes spent 17.5 percent of their total income

TABLE 1
Peasant tax burden

Types of charges	Items and explanations
State taxes	Agricultural tax, special products tax, slaughter tax, farmland tax, contract tax, animal husbandry tax, and education surcharge
Township and village levies	Village levies are for three purposes: collective investments, welfare, and cadre compensation; township levies are for five purposes: schools, family planning, support for veterans, militia, and road construction and maintenance
Corvée labor services, often monetized	5 to 10 days of labor on flood prevention, afforestation, road or school construction; 10 to 20 days of "accumulation labor" on state water conservancy or afforestation projects
Fees, apportionments, and fundraising	For road or school construction and other local improvement projects; newspaper subscriptions, purchase of insurance, marriage certificates, and so forth
Fines	Collected by numerous government agencies for infractions such as birth control violations
Burdens connected with peasant sales to state ("hidden burdens")	Compulsory grain sales to state at below-market prices; scissors differential between industrial and agricultural prices; local abuses such as payments in IOUs, not cash

Source: Thomas P. Bernstein and Xiaobo Lu, *Taxation without Representation in Contemporary Rural China* (Cambridge: Cambridge University Press, 2003), 50, 77–78.

Note: IOUs (*baitiao*) are paid to peasants in lieu of cash for their sales to the state. Often this was the result of local officials' diversion of state procurement funds to more profitable undertakings. During the rural rioting in 1992–1993, in which IOUs were targeted, the central regime sought vigorously to eliminate IOUs, but scattered reports of payments in IOUs continued to appear.

on taxes and fees (excluding education fees), while those with the highest incomes paid only 5.1 percent of their income on taxes and fees.

Another study by Shuming Liu states that the root cause of rural taxation problems is China's discriminatory taxation policy toward peasants in recent decades.[8] In China, urban residents pay individual income tax only if their annual income is over 9,600 yuan. But peasants even in very poor regions have to pay rural taxes and a variety of informal fees and levies. The urban-rural per capita annual income ratio increased from 2.7:1 in 1995 to 3.1:1 in 2002. According to a senior official from the State Development Planning Commission, the estimated ratio for 2003 was even higher, by far exceeding the worldwide average urban-rural income ratio of 1.5:1.[9]

With the extension of the rural "fee-tax-swap" reform to twenty provinces in 2002, the central government demonstrated its willingness to alleviate the problem of the rural tax burden. The main aspects of this reform were: (1) the elimination of the slaughter tax as well as fees and levies collected by village and township governments, and the abolition of the education fee and other administrative fees exclusive to the peasantry; (2) the phased elimination of corvée labor services over a three-year period; and (3) the adjustment of agricultural tax policies and agriculture-specific products taxes. New agricultural taxes are calculated on the basis of arable land area, with an upper limit of 7 percent. Several investigations conducted in Anhui Province have shown that average taxes and fees imposed on peasants have significantly decreased since the reform, and the simplification of the tax structure stimulated incentives of peasants to pay their taxes on time.[10] The relations between peasants and local officials have also improved. Evidence from local surveys, however, shows that the current central transfer system has not eliminated the revenue shortfall of local governments.

Urban Land Leasing and Local Revenues

To gain a better understanding of China's property taxation, it is important first to have an overview of the current land use system. According to the Chinese Constitution, all land is owned by the state. The 1982 and 1988 amendments to the Constitution separated land use rights (LURs) from ownership and clarified the legality of LUR transfer. Local governments, empowered by the state, can assign land use rights to users and charge them a lump-sum leasing fee. The lease terms range from forty to seventy years.[11]

With strong economic growth and development of the private housing market, transfer of LURs and land-leasing activities increased rapidly. Land-leasing income became a primary source of revenue for local governments. From 1988 to 1997 the Shanghai municipal government raised, on average, 11.2 percent of its annual revenues from land leasing.[12] The comparable figures are as high as 25 to 50 percent in some cities.[13]

Local authorities, especially municipalities, have much incentive to promote the transfer of land use rights. First, since the land-leasing revenue need not be shared with the central government, local governments in serious financial difficulty are always eager to use land leasing to finance infrastructure construction projects. Second, under China's unitary political system, local officials are generally appointed by the central government. GDP figures and fiscal revenues are a key gauge of their performance. City leaders are able to "show capabilities" to the central government through their large-scale development projects.[14]

Recent literature has studied the similarities and differences between China's ongoing urban development and the U.S. urban renewal of the 1950s and 1960s.

One study suggests that local governments have formed pro-growth coalitions with local nonpublic sectors (such as real estate developers) to stimulate economic growth and to enhance their political legitimacy.[15] Other authors argue that China's inner-city redevelopment "has been propelled by emerging local elites using decentralized state power to pursue fast growth in rising real estate markets."[16]

While these coalitions help to ease local government's fiscal tensions and to accelerate urbanization, there are potential social costs. Driven by the high returns, local governments have expanded the transfer of LURs very quickly, which encourages overheating of the urban real estate market and an unsustainable boom in private housing prices. Also the large-scale redevelopment programs have been "transformed into a speculative type of development involving massive demolition and ruthless displacement."[17] In the meantime, corrupt activities and the misuse of land leasing by local government are rampant. According to a news report, some 168,000 cases of irregularities were disclosed nationwide in 2003, almost double the number in 2002.[18] A total of 687 people involved were punished, including 94 who were held accountable for criminal offenses. These striking facts demonstrate the lack of supervision and other shortcomings inherent in the current land-leasing system.

The Property Tax System and Possible Fiscal Transformations

The property tax is commonly viewed as an appropriate source of local government revenue throughout the globe. Local governments are in the best position to identify ownership and changes in ownership, to track changes in properties that might affect their tax status, and to develop collection systems.[19] Also property owners are less reluctant to pay taxes when they believe that the revenue will be used to finance local services, enhance the regional economy, and thus positively affect property appreciation. The property tax has been the main source of local revenues in many Western developed countries. But in China it remains a minor source of fiscal revenue. Data from the *China Statistical Yearbook* show that in 2002, two major real estate taxes, the property tax and the urban land use tax, accounted for only 3.3 percent and 0.9 percent, respectively, of local governments' tax revenues.[20] In Western economies the comparable figures could range as high as 40 percent. Obviously there is an opportunity for greater reliance on property tax revenues to finance local government. China's recent urbanization and booming housing market have created an important window for further development of the property tax.

As previously discussed, landownership is separated from ownership of structures in China, and different kinds of taxes are imposed on land use rights and properties. We nevertheless refer here to all property- and land use–related taxes as real estate taxes.

Under the current real estate tax system in China, there are various tax categories. One important characteristic is that many of the major taxes are based on transactions rather than on holdings of property, as would be typical in a Western property tax system. Table 2 shows the major taxes and fees related to land use rights and property transactions in China. Some of them (for example, multiple taxes and fees on land appreciation) are duplicative and were presumably instituted purely to increase government revenue. This complicated tax structure increases collection and

TABLE 2
Main taxes and fees related to real estate transactions in China

Tax and fee items	Brief descriptions
Related to structures and other improvements	
Contract tax	3 to 5% of the transaction amount, paid by the purchaser
Stamp tax	0.03% of transaction amount, paid by both parties
Business tax	5% of the transaction amount
Urban construction and maintenance tax	There are three applicable tax rates: 1%, 5%, and 7%, according to the location of the taxpayer
Additional education charges	3% of business tax
Property tax	1.2% of discounted original value of property, or 12% of rental value
Process fee	1% of the transaction amount shared equally by both parties
Property ownership registration fee	80 yuan for each dwelling unit; and a fixed amount for each transaction of non-dwelling unit set by provincial governments
Certificate fee	For property ownership certificate and other related certificates
Related to land	
Fee for the assignment of land use rights	Payable by enterprises and individuals obtaining the land use rights
Land appreciation tax	Payable by all units and individuals receiving income from the transfer of state-owned land use rights, buildings, and their attached facilities. A four-level progressive rate
Land appreciation fee	Payable by land use rights owners selling or leasing land use rights to a third party. Calculation is based on the transaction amount
Urban land use tax	Payable by units and individuals using land within the limits of cities, county sites, administrative towns, and industrial and mining areas. Calculation is based on actual land use area, measured by local authorities.
Arable land occupation tax	Payable by units and individuals occupying arable land for nonagricultural use

Source: Translated from and based on Dongwei Zhang, "The List of Taxes and Fees Related to Real Estate Transactions," *Tianxia Real Estate Legal Service Network*, December 2003, http://www.law110.com.

administration costs, introduces inefficiency, and unduly influences the development of the urban housing market.

As the general period for land use rights is from forty to seventy years, and Chinese laws do not specify concrete measures for implementing lease renewals, it is hard for governments to benefit from future increases in land or property value once the land use rights are sold. Lacking sufficient long-term taxation revenues from property owners and land users, local governments put more emphasis on extracting one-time payments from urban housing developers and dealers, which are ultimately borne by the purchasers of housing units. As a result, consumers are actually paying the real estate taxes for the next forty to seventy years at the time of purchase, a situation that creates a significant barrier to ownership. A survey shows that in the year 2001, average household income in Beijing was 34,000 yuan, but one medium-sized (80 square meter) apartment cost from 360,000 to 380,000 yuan.[21] The house price–to–income ratio was 11:1, much higher than the average level in Western developed countries (from around 3:1 to 6:1).

In contrast, there are only two major taxes on real estate holdings: the property tax and urban land use tax. These taxes have a relatively limited base and low rates. The property tax is calculated according to the formula:

$$\text{Annual property tax payable} = (1 - \text{discount rate})$$
$$* \text{original value of property} * 1.2 \text{ percent}$$

where the discount rate is determined by the local government within the range of 10–30 percent.

Since the property tax is based on the original value, new enterprises usually pay much higher taxes than older ones. As a result, some old and poorly run state-owned enterprises located in central urban areas keep paying very low property taxes although their properties have appreciated considerably, which is a distortion of market resource allocation. In addition, properties owned by military units, government agencies, social organizations, schools, temples, and parks and the like, and privately owned properties for nonbusiness use (for example, residential property) are also exempted from the property tax. The exclusion of urban dwelling units significantly limits the tax base.

Those subject to the urban land use tax include units and individuals using land within the limits of cities, county sites, administrative towns, and industrial and mining areas. The amount payable is calculated on the basis of actual land use area, as measured by local authorities. The applicable tax rate varies across cities and across districts within each city, a situation that captures to some extent the disparity of urban land value. Given the small scale of the urban land use tax (less than 1 percent of total local taxation revenue), however, its effect remains trivial.

To enable the local government to benefit continuously from the appreciation of land value driven by economic growth, the experiences of Hong Kong and some other regions with well-developed public leasehold systems could provide some lessons. A comparative study of the public land-leasing system of Canberra and Hong Kong suggests that the government can retain a portion of the land value appreciation by asking a lessee to pay a lump sum of money (called an initial land premium) at the beginning of the lease, an annual land rent, a premium when the lessee modifies lease conditions to acquire additional rights for land redevelopment, as well as a premium for renewing the land rights when the lease expires.[22] In this way, from 1970 to 1991 the Hong Kong government recaptured, on average, 39 percent of increased land value from selected sites through land leasing. Owners of residential properties also have to pay annual rates equal to 5 percent of the estimated rental value of their flats, while owners of commercial real estate pay a 15 percent property tax on income earned from their rental premises.

To develop a more efficient and revenue-generating property tax system, it will be necessary to simplify the tax structure and broaden the tax base. First, all land users and property owners should be required to pay the property tax except for explicit exemptions (such as for military, educational, and other selected social purposes). Second, taxes and fees now imposed against the real estate transaction process should be simplified and subject to lower rates. Third, the property tax payable should be based on the market value of properties and land use rights so as to optimize resource allocation.

The problems underlying the current property tax and land-leasing system have attracted considerable social and academic attention in recent years. In 2003 the central government issued a directive to improve the property tax system. Government researchers have begun to discuss the advantages and viability of introducing a unified real estate tax.[23] A 2005 news report suggested that a consensus seemed to be emerging among experts that it would be better to shift the taxes on real estate and land partly away from the initial construction and sale of homes to the period of maintaining and using the homes.[24] A clearer understanding of property rights, an appraisal system, and a full real estate management system need to be in place, however, before a modern property tax can be adopted.

Of course, there are important administrative challenges to reform. Given the rapid pace of urbanization in China and the lack of long-term recordkeeping, it will be a challenge for local governments to develop and maintain up-to-date records of land use and property ownership. It will require coordination among the municipal bureaus and other local services. The establishment of consistent and scientific criteria for evaluation procedures will also be crucial to the effectiveness of property taxation. Nevertheless, such administrative reforms will be necessary if the local government system is to keep pace with private sector development and support privatization in areas that are now suffering economically.

Minimizing Corruption and Promoting Compliance

Corruption, defined as "the sale by government officials of government property for personal gain," is commonly believed to be detrimental to development.[25] The structure of government and political institutions is a key determinant of the level of corruption.[26] The illegality of corruption and the need for secrecy make these activities very distortive and a leading cause of economic welfare loss. For example, the necessity to keep corrupt activities hidden suggests why so many poor countries would rather spend their limited resources on infrastructure projects and defense—where there is scope to engage in corrupt activities—as opposed to education and health, which offer fewer opportunities for illegal profit.

Tax-related corruption has been prevalent in China because of its complicated administrative system, the huge amount of off-budget funds, and weak supervision. Moreover, with bureaucratic controls weakening as the economy incorporates increased private enterprise, there are additional opportunities for rent-seeking behavior and corruption. Private actors have wider scope to pursue their own interests under the cover of a government bureaucracy. The structure of the system also matters. Under the current public land lease system, the entire payment for land use rights over the duration of forty to seventy years is charged in full by the local government at the time of assignment. There is no annual rent afterwards, and the property tax and land use tax payable are trivial compared to the amount of the land use fee. Therefore it is more like a one-time transaction between land users and the local government. This results in high marginal benefits to bribers and bribe takers, giving birth to an increased level of corruption and misbehavior.

One common way to reduce corruption is to raise the marginal costs to bribe payers and corrupt officials. This can be achieved by providing generous remuneration and benefits to government officials (as in Hong Kong and Singapore) or by strengthening the internal control over the operations of land leasing. Another solution that would be practical in China is to reduce the marginal benefit of corruption by splitting the one-time payment of land use rights into a series of smaller (perhaps recurring) transactions. Following the practice of Hong Kong's public leasing system, in addition to the initial payment, the local government could levy an annual rent on land users. Or the period of land use rights could be shortened, say, to ten or twenty years instead of forty to seventy years, coupled with a priority on lease renewal for land users. Both measures can significantly reduce the payment involved in a single transaction and thereby decrease incentives for corruption.

One reasonable concern is that local governments may be reluctant to lose the high returns of LUR transfer through the one-time arrangement. Indeed, this is a key source of revenue for local governments. But in the long run, the decrease of such land-leasing revenue can be offset by continuous land rent income and an increase in tax revenues led by broadening the real estate tax base. The property tax can be imposed on all land users and property owners, accompanied by periodic reassessment of property values. The adoption of a wider base and higher rates for property taxes will not only enable reduction of the taxes on transactions but also help to minimize and strengthen the detection of corruption. Assessments on property should also be made publicly available. Although a movement toward this system would not eliminate corruption—some corruption in the form of bribes for underassessment does occur in Western property tax systems—it would tend to reduce it.

The role of taxpayer is also critically important in an effective tax system. A significant challenge is to create a "tax culture" conducive to voluntary compliance. This is a long-term project for all tax systems and will require time to develop. While there are no panaceas in this area, transparency of the tax system is the first step; without transparency, there is no hope of developing a culture of voluntary compliance. Making assessments publicly available and permitting the government to place liens on property in the face of delinquent payments is a necessary tool that is used in economies, including Hong Kong's, that utilize the property tax. From the point of view of increasing compliance, the property tax is one of the most efficient taxes, because it not possible to "hide" real property—that is, land and improvements—from the authorities.

To develop a culture of compliance, citizens must also feel an important psychological connection to expenditures in any tax system. If local fees or charges are perceived as feeding the central government in Beijing, there will be a natural resistance to paying them. If, however, they are seen as contributing to the provision of local services, the psychological dimension changes. How money is raised and where the public perceives it to go is an essential aspect of public finance.

Final Thoughts on Local Taxation and Privatization

China's rapid modernization and need for central budgetary revenue have put a tremendous strain on local governments. These governments have retained an antiquated revenue system ill equipped to cope with the challenges of social modernization. The structure of local taxation and land leasing is also highly conducive to corruption. Unless a more flexible and modern local tax is introduced, China's local governments will face increasing stress and inefficient social outcomes. The current system allows too many local officials to make deals on their own behalf without sufficient constraints imposed by laws and administrative practice. As the private sector develops, it also becomes necessary to constrain the self-interested behavior of state officials with respect to revenue collection. Effective privatization in this context means developing a legal environment in which private sector transactions are able to flourish as well as diminishing rent-seeking behavior on the part of state officials.

Current reform movements such as the "fee-tax-swap" system implicitly recognize the need for curbing arbitrary fees and simplifying the base of taxation, particularly in rural areas. Unless additional revenues are made available for local governments, however, the underlying pressures of the fiscal system will remain.

There are a number of challenges in moving to a new fiscal system for local governments. First, it is necessary for the public to understand the conceptual basis for property taxation in the Chinese socialist state. Although land is owned by the state and leased to private parties, the state can still tax the bundle of rights associated with the land lease. Other countries (New Zealand and Israel) and some states in the United States (for example, Hawaii) combine leasing systems with property taxation. The value of the lease subject to taxation is dependent on the term of the lease and the underlying market conditions. The value of improvements on the land (property and other improvements) can be calculated separately and added to the value of the leasing rights to determine the total value of all property subject to taxation. Although there are administrative costs associated with moving to such a system, it is not inconsistent with the ideological basis of the Chinese state in its new enterprise environment.

Second, as previously discussed, local officials and entrepreneurs in major cities have become comfortable with the political and economic dynamics associated with one-time land-leasing fees. From the point of view of local governments, these fees provide an immediate cash flow as well as opportunities for bribes and kickbacks. From the developers' point of view, up-front leasing fees are a one-time cost that does not increase over time as the value of urban land increases. Unfortunately, the developers' gain is precisely the governments' loss. Shorter lease terms that are subject to renegotiation could mitigate this problem, but only at the expense of costly lease renegotiations and an increase in uncertainty with regard to property rights. An annual property tax based on market value could accomplish the same goal but at a lower social cost.

5. "Reorganized Moralism"

The Politics of Transnational Labor Codes

Pun Ngai

The period since the mid-1990s has witnessed a surge in the practice of intro-ducing transnational corporate codes of conduct, labor standards, and labor rights in China. In tandem with the role of the Chinese state in regulating labor condi-tions and enforcing national labor laws, transnational corporations (TNCs), often big brand-name American and European retailers, have increasingly advocated corporate codes of practice for their Chinese production contractors and subcon-tractors.[1] This gives rise to a series of puzzles about postsocialist Chinese labor politics: Why has transnational capital taken the initiative in protecting Chinese labor? What is the role of global capital vis-à-vis the Chinese state in regulating la-bor relations in a period of rapid labor reform? How are these novel practices of corporate codes shaping the changing Chinese factory regimes into a form that is truly global? What will be the possible effects on workers' power and politics in the face of these globalized factory regimes?

I am grateful to Anita Chan and John Unger for reading the earlier version of this chapter. An earlier, shorter version of this article was published in *China Journal* (July 2005). The field studies were financially supported in part by the Hong Kong Research Grant Council for a re-search project titled "Living with Global Capitalism: Labor Control and Resistance through the Dormitory Labor System in China" (2003–2005).

What is influential, and thus worth investigating, in this race to implement corporate codes is the increasing penetration of global capital into Chinese society in the form of providing "good" governance in relation to labor conditions and labor standards. This process can be understood as an active projection of global capital into labor relations by proactively infusing labor standards with new business ethics and institutions. I conceptualize this tendency of capital to regulate Chinese labor politics as a form of reorganized moralism in an increasingly globalized Chinese context. The principle of reorganized moralism involves reworking neoliberal principles operating at the micro-workplace level not only to rearticulate labor rights practices from the corporate point of view but also to move into the sphere of labor rights and labor protection, a domain supposedly belonging to the role of the state and civil society. Hence this practice creates the impression that transnational capital is protecting the rights of Chinese labor from a despotic regime in postsocialist China. In this chapter I study labor codes in two Chinese workplaces and try to demonstrate how the moral imperative of these codes results in the penetration of capital into the sphere of labor rights in China. Contrary to the argument that these workplace practices advance the normalization of employment relations and improve the working and living conditions of laborers, I argue that despite certain improvements of limited scope, this reorganized moralism aims to "remarket" business ethics and thus results in privatizing labor rights through the managerial practices that are further justified in a global business environment. This leads to a rapid process of "soft" institutionalization of labor rights in the workplace in terms of the procedures and systems erected for governing codes of conduct, thus constituting a form of labor containment devoid of worker participation and empowerment.

Over the past few decades, time and again the international media and academics have published reports and data supposedly showing that Chinese labor rights have been seriously violated in many private and foreign-financed enterprises.[2] In reaction to these notorious labor practices, transnational capital has worked actively to reorganize factory regimes by adjusting labor conditions and reshaping labor relations as well as regulating the managerial practices of its producers. As Reebok International Proclaimed in "Toward Sustainable Code Compliance: Worker Representation in China" (2002):

For over a decade, Reebok International Ltd. has implemented its code of conduct—the Reebok Human Rights Production Standards—in the independently owned and operated factories that make its products. We do this to:

1. benefit the lives of the 150,000 workers who make our products;

2. ensure that workplace conditions meet internationally recognized standards and local law;

3. honor our corporation's commitment to human rights; and

4. protect our brand reputation.[3]

A moral façade for capital was thus created. Reebok's experiment in instituting general workers' elections and forming factory trade unions, as well as the emphasis of other TNCs on encouraging production workers to participate in monitoring codes and workplace decisions, creates a nuanced picture for understanding the implementation of corporate codes and their influence on labor politics in China.

This chapter highlights a fundamental paradox of global capital in shaping production regimes: the "economic" aspect of global capital, as revealed in "race to the bottom" production strategies and global just-in-time factory regimes, will still tend to produce systems characteristic of "disorganized despotism," and yet the "political" aspect of transnational capital, under pressure, is forced to keep a check on the dark side of these production regimes in order to constrain the tyranny of management at the expense of labor rights. Global capital is thus inherently conflict-ridden, and its contradictory nature continuously shapes factory regimes in China within the global system of production. On the one hand, the improvement of working conditions as a result of implementing corporate codes serves as an alibi for the "rationalization" discourse, which argues that the practices of transnational companies in China are greatly enhanced and rationalized when they compete to meet international standards.[4] On the other hand, rather than leading to labor power and resistance in the workplace, labor politics becomes co-opted by the "political" side of capital. The result is at best managerial paternalism, with labor rights, if granted at all, originating from above.

This chapter begins, first, with an investigation into the "why" and "what" of implementing corporate codes in China, including the international anti-sweatshop campaigns, in an attempt to disclose the "logic" of transnational capital. Second, it offers a micro-focus on the workplace level, and code of conduct practices are assessed not only from the perspective of TNC representatives in China but also from that of rank-and-file staff, mainly production workers in the factories. Third, it shows that through the implementation of company codes within the production regime, global capital achieves hidden controls over labor relations. Systematic procedures such as documentation, filing, and reporting systems with regard to labor issues bear witness to this process of the corporate shaping and monitoring of labor standards. This is reorganized moralism with the purpose of achieving the institutionalization of labor relations in the workplace by forcing Chinese factory regimes to meet international standards. The consequence, however, could be the shrinking of labor autonomy and collective power if labor protection mechanisms are defined, regulated, and constrained by capital.

The Corporate Codes Movement, the State, and TNCs

The regulation of factory regimes by capital is occurring at a juncture where there is a "vacuum" vis-à-vis the state in regulating new labor relations in Chinese society. By "vacuum" I do not mean that the state is rapidly retreating from a regulatory role in shaping new labor relations—far from it. Rather the state is intentionally reforming its role via a process of labor legalization and reinstitutionalization.[5] Conspicuous examples include the promulgation of the Labor Law of 1995 and the setting up of labor arbitration committees for channeling disputes arising under the new conditions. But the limitations of the state's role in regulating the new management-labor relations and providing labor protections in the rapidly transforming socialist economy are well known, and hence the Chinese state has often failed to forestall labor protests and resistance.[6] The disarticulation between state politics and production politics in postsocialist China provides a role for global capital, which, interestingly, acts as a "world policeman" in enforcing legal and moral standards in the workplace. In this sense, "rule by law" is not only a state project, put forward by Ching Kwan Lee (2002) to explain the role of the state in accelerating labor legalization in China, but also a project of capital, using "soft law" to govern new and increasingly globalized production regimes.

This proactive role of transnational capital in providing labor "law" and protections perhaps runs counter to our understanding of the logic of capital in expropriating Chinese labor. Why have these transnational corporations with a moral façade suddenly appeared in China? The logic of this practice has to go beyond the internal capital-labor relationship.

Global consumer movements and public awareness of corporate social responsibility in North America and Europe led to the rise of anti-sweatshop campaigns in developing countries. Under pressure, transnational corporations, especially in the textile, clothing, and footwear industries, started to introduce company codes of conduct regarding labor standards in China in the early 1990s.[7] The adoption of corporate codes became a trend for TNCs such as Levi Strauss, Nike, Reebok, The Gap, and others. The introduction of codes became part of these companies' strategic policies in securing the sale of their goods and services on the global market. Variations in applying corporate codes and policies were noticed, as some TNCs created specific codes concerning forced labor and human rights for their suppliers and subcontractors in China.[8] Internal monitoring of subcontractors or suppliers by the companies' representatives on a regular basis is the usual case, although sometimes independent monitoring involving invited academics, auditors, and/or NGOs is used to enhance credibility.

The trigger for this ethical codes movement in China was a striking piece of news released in 1992 by the *Washington Post* about the production of Levi's jeans with the use of Chinese prison labor.[9] Worried about its corporate image worldwide, Levi

Strauss immediately reacted to the public's concern by drawing up a code of labor standards titled "Business Partner Terms of Engagement and Guidelines for Country Selections," and demanded that their suppliers and subcontractors in China and elsewhere adopt and implement the code.[10] Other major TNCs in retail industries followed suit, competing to set up their own codes of conduct as part of their global production strategies.[11] The race to apply ethical codes in China reached its climax when, in 1999, the CEOs of Phillips–Van Heusen, Reebok, and Levi Strauss wrote a joint open letter to President Jiang Zemin requesting an urgent meeting to explore the possibility of "working together" to improve labor rights in China.[12] This attempt failed when the Chinese government showed no interest in talking to the CEOs of the three companies and continued to consider labor rights protection to be an internal Chinese affair.

It is apparent that the parties involved in code of conduct practices in China include not only global consumers, TNCs, suppliers, and company shareholders but also the Chinese state and workers. The Chinese central state, which is reluctant to confront labor standards issues in a serious way, readily resorts to references to "external intervention in Chinese affairs," particularly when those forces are indeed from outside. Provincial, municipal, and lower-level governments, however, display a variety of attitudes. As evidenced by my studies in the Pearl River delta and the Yangtze River region, they may take ethical codes to be simply a matter of individual business behavior. No official government departments, including the Labor Bureau, have seriously considered company codes of conduct, assessed their influence on labor rights protection, or monitored or enforced the process. The human rights representatives of TNCs have openly criticized the incompetence of the Chinese government in regulating labor standards. One told me: "The government is useless here; no labor law is actually enforced. We take up their role of providing labor protections."

The companies' concern is of course for their public image, which is a decisive factor in determining whether the public buys their products and hence in determining their survival under conditions of extreme global competition. Critics argue that these company codes and actions are public relations ploys, since the TNCs are judge and jury of their own regulations,[13] and that the relationship between the TNCs and their suppliers in applying company codes is never equal.[14] Nevertheless, suppliers and producers for TNCs in China have no choice but to implement company codes and accept in-house TNC representatives' supervision of working conditions, as well as allowing workers' committees or trade unions to be set up. This has resulted in a substantial impact on the reorganization of Chinese factory regimes in terms of company size, production facilities, management practices, and the working and living conditions of laborers.

The continuing pressure for an ethical codes movement in China comes also from international anti-sweatshop campaigns, notably the No Sweatshops campaign in the United States, Labour behind the Label in the United Kingdom, and the Clean Clothes Campaign (CCC) in Europe. Many trade ethics organizations working on a worldwide scale, such as Social Accountability International, the Fair Labour Association, the Worker Rights Consortium, and the Ethical Trading Initiative, have also been established. For decades these international campaigns, labor organizations, and trade ethics associations have launched campaigns calling for the establishment of an agreed-upon international code for transnational companies regarding their offshore production facilities and widespread use of flexible and cheap labor. For instance, CCC produced a unified international code for all its affiliated companies and interested parties.[15] In 1998 it developed a model, called the "Code of Labour Practices for the Apparel Industry Including Sportswear," for the entire garment and sportswear industry (including athletic shoes). It has attempted to apply this model code to China.

Field Study of Globalized Factory Regimes

It is within this context that the various international campaigns launched their pilot projects in China, and within which my colleagues and I took the opportunity to join one of them. The field study is based on an eighteen-month observation of a pilot project launched by an international campaign to promote fair labor and business ethics in China. In addition to some general surveys, NGO documentation, and mass media coverage, staff and workers' views from two factories—one in the Pearl River delta and the other in the Yangtze River region—were solicited in order to assess the labor codes practices and their influence on the politics of production. Interviews were conducted in the workplaces as well as in workers' dormitories between 2002 and 2003. These two enterprises were provided with systematic studies and in-depth interviews. They were chosen because they had signed an agreement with a brand-name European TNC to implement and monitor the corporation's code.

The two enterprises we studied in detail are China Miracle Garments (China Miracle), in the Yangtze River region, and China Galaxy Apparel (China Galaxy), in the Pearl River delta.[16] In addition to frequent exchanges with the directors, the production managers, the personnel secretaries, the social compliance officers, and the trade union chairs, the interview research focused mainly on the production workers. They were selected on the shop floor by our own research team, taking into consideration factors of gender, age, marital status, position, and department. We chose a total of fifty workers at China Miracle and thirty-two workers at China Galaxy for in-depth interviews covering work units of departments including the design, cutting, production, quality control, and packaging departments.[17] Night visits to the factory dormitories were also undertaken to check information provided by the workers while in the workplace.

The Goal Is to Be Global

The race to implement codes has led to the rapid establishment of globalized factory regimes in the newly industrialized zones in China. Enterprises in the two deltas were under pressure to enhance their companies' profiles by upgrading their production facilities, reviewing management practices, and improving workers' living conditions to varying degrees. To them, the adoption of corporate codes was an additional burden accompanying just-in-time production and high quality requirements, but these enterprises hardly had a choice. Severe competition among enterprises in China resulted in the loss of company bargaining power with the TNCs in the global production system. Global leverage on TNCs with respect to labor standards put pressure on manufacturers in China and elsewhere. Many directors complained that while production order prices continuously dropped, the requirement for labor codes had remained stringent over the previous few years. They took the need to implement these codes as market pressure and emphasized: "What we can do is to let our enterprise be global and live up to the international standard of codes. It is the only way to secure production orders from our clients, especially those from America and Europe."

Thus China Miracle, a joint-venture enterprise owned by Taiwanese and mainland capital, had injected a huge investment to build a new forty-acre compound in 2000. The investment of RMB 20 million had not only enlarged the size of the enterprise but also improved the facilities and working conditions. The factory's strategy was to build a model enterprise in the Yangtze River region so as to attract more production orders. The new compound, which went into operation in March 2001, consists of a three-story production building with an attached administrative block, a separate one-story canteen, and a detached utility room.[18] Surrounded by a rectangular wall with gates policed by armed security guards, China Miracle is one of the most spectacular enterprises in the high-tech development zone. In addition to the heavy emphasis on product quality, meeting the company codes and international standards such as ISO 9000, ISO 14000, and SA8000 were also goals set by the management team.[19] The company director remarked: "The code practice required by the European corporation is a 'market behavior.' We are lost at the moment, but we hope to get a return in the long run. It's the way to survive in the world market."

Like China Miracle, China Galaxy had the ambition to establish itself as a model factory in the Pearl River delta. Established in 1993, the enterprise, belonging to a Hong Kong corporation, was mainly under the control of a Hong Kong director and five Hong Kong managers, supplemented by twenty mainland supervisory staff members who were in charge of the daily management and operation of production. In addition to production orders received from the European TNC, China Galaxy also produced sportswear for American brands. The Hong Kong corporation was well aware of code of conduct issues and hence laid down strict guidelines for China Galaxy as well as its other factories in Shenzhen to follow. Even when first established in Dongguan, China Galaxy already aimed at building an advanced and modern enterprise in the delta, outshining the thousands of other plants in the same sector. It expanded quickly to a workforce of 1,500 in the mid-1990s. The company was able to introduce modern management models and international labor standards. Directors and managers were proud of having built up a new "factory empire" on the mainland, one that not only was physically magnificent but also was equipped with advanced production facilities and rationalized managerial practices.

To upgrade its company facilities to meet the code requirements, China Galaxy made another investment of RMB 5 million to build a new dormitory in 1999. The dormitory compound was like a modern boarding school, with facilities including two canteens, a dancehall, a reading room, a shop, and a small clinic. Surrounded by trees, the compound offered an open area for workers' recreational activities such as badminton, basketball, and the like. The dining hall was also filled in the late evening with workers watching television programs and film presentations. It was just like a small community with everything basically sustainable. Typical of a model factory in China, however, there was a hierarchy of accommodation, serving to segment the labor force. The managers were provided with flats consisting of three bedrooms, a dining room, kitchen, toilet, and bathroom. These flats were well furnished with TV sets, refrigerators, air conditioners, and modern cooking and bathing facilities. The production workers, by contrast, were housed in dormitory rooms with a shared toilet, and with a common room for provision of hot water on each floor. Each dormitory room accommodated six to eight workers, with storage space for their clothes and personal belongings.

All the dormitory facilities, providing comparatively better living conditions for workers at China Galaxy than at other factories in the region, strictly follow the European corporation's codes, which require that

1. Dormitory facilities meet all applicable laws and regulations related to health and safety, including fire safety, sanitation, risk protection, and electrical, mechanical, and structural safety.

2. Sleeping quarters are segregated by sex.

3. The living space per worker in the sleeping quarters meets both the minimum legal requirement and the local industry standard.

4. Workers are provided with their own individual mats or beds.

5. Workers are provided their own storage space for their clothes and personal possessions.

6. Dormitory facilities are well ventilated. There are windows to the outside or fans and/or air conditioners and/or heaters in all sleeping areas for adequate ventilation and temperature control.

7. Sleeping quarters have adequate lighting.

8. There are at least two clearly marked exits on each floor, and emergency lighting is installed in halls, stairwells, and above each exit.

9. Fire drills are conducted at least every six months.

10. Hazardous and combustible materials used in the production process are not stored in the dormitory or buildings connected to sleeping quarters.

11. Sufficient toilets and showers are segregated by sex and provided in safe, sanitary, accessible, and private areas.

12. Hot water or facilities to boil water are available to dormitory residents.

13. Dormitory residents are free to come and go during their off-hours under reasonable limitations imposed for their safety and comfort.

These meticulous regulations are an attempt to address the criticism of Chinese factory regimes as despotic and authoritarian. These detailed corporate codes also push Chinese factory regimes to become global and modernized. The economic aspect of capital, however, often clashes with its political aspect, resulting in an inescapable ambivalence of capital practices in the workplace, and these discrepancies in circumstantial contexts predetermine the extent to which corporate codes are implemented. As one production line leader at China Galaxy asked: "Who cares about labor rights? Do they [transnational corporations] really care about our working conditions? In times of rushed production outputs, we still have to violate the code." Another company manager in Dongguan frankly explained to us: "We are forced to apply the Disney labor codes, but we can judge from our intuition that when production and codes are in conflict which side we can cling to. Once I phoned their production department and asked, 'Do you still want your products in time?' The monitor left our company alone."

Reorganized Moralism: "Paradoxical" If Not "Hypocritical"

One characteristic of these globalized factory regimes is that the reorganized moralism which has emerged since the early 1990s is by nature fraught with paradoxes and contradictions. The moral face of capital proved illusory when workers' views were solicited. While the managers of China Miracle and China

Galaxy claimed that every worker had been provided with a written copy of the European corporation's code when they signed or renewed their contract, all but two of the workers interviewed informed us that they had not received a copy. When we asked whether the code had been introduced in their morning meetings or other settings, most of them responded with hesitation. Only a few workers had some knowledge or understanding of the code's provisions. One worker mistook the code as China Miracle's own regulations. She asked me in reply: "What is a code of conduct? Do you mean company regulations? Yes, we have very strict regulations, and if we make a mistake, we will be fined. Quality control is very high in this company."

Even though the management of the two enterprises had introduced the code during morning meetings before the workday began, they did so in order to "train" the workers by repetition how to answer the monitors, especially as to working hours, rest days, and wages. Uniform answers with wording as identical as in a recital, however, raised doubts about these responses: "We work eight hours each day. No compulsory overtime work. We have Sunday off. We get time-and-a-half pay for evening work, double for weekends, and triple for public holidays." The mystery of the workers' compliance in giving standard answers to certain questions was solved when we visited the' dorms at night, where the workers were relatively free to express themselves. "You know we are afraid of losing production orders," said one. "We also don't want to give wrong answers and get into trouble." The workers had been indoctrinated with the idea that if they gave the wrong answers, they would damage the profitability of the company, and thus, in the long run, their own jobs and salaries.[20] The workers' consent to management hegemony was traded for a tale of profit.

Supervisory staff, by contrast, saw the code of practice more critically as a hypocritical act by the TNCs to assuage the "inner sins" of rich Western countries. Severe global competition for low-cost products and just-in-time production demands structurally constrained implementation of the code and resulted in a "paradoxical" if not "hypocritical" role for company practices specifically, and for the moral façade of capital in general. The two terms "paradoxical" and "hypocritical" were often used, not only by the production managers to comment on the corporation's code at China Miracle and China Galaxy, but also by senior staff in other companies in the Pearl River delta. One production manager said: "The foreigners, *laowai*, do not understand the situation of China. We are an overpopulated country and we need development, you know. If they want good and cheap products, they have to trade off human rights. It is quite obvious."

Nevertheless, the working conditions at enterprises with code practices are better than those without such codes in the same region. At China Miracle and China Galaxy we witnessed no cases of forced or bonded labor. All workers were provided with a contract to sign at the end of a probation period, although it was not a standard contract drafted by the local Labor Bureau; the contract was much simpler and included fewer clauses than the European corporations' codes required.[21] Neither company kept the identity cards of workers, which other enterprises in China often do to prevent workers from quitting. Disciplinary penalties were replaced by a system of rewards and compensations. The standard working day was ten hours, from 8:00 A.M. to 8:00 P.M. with a two-hour break for meals. Workers often had a rest day on Sunday unless pressing production orders required overtime work. This is a core provision of the European corporation's code, which stated that all workers should have at least one day off in seven.[22]

Another important provision of the code, often the most contested terrain, concerns excessive overtime work. The code states that "the factory shall not require, on a regularly scheduled basis, a work week in excess of forty-eight hours without overtime work and sixty hours with overtime." This provision is obviously incompatible with the Chinese Labor Law, which stipulates that the norm is forty hours a week and thirty-six hours of overtime a month. Most of the TNCs are aware that their code provisions on working hours are illegal and exceed Chinese law. Few of them, however, have revised their codes or stated clearly that the national standard would apply. Many enterprises violated the Chinese Labor Law in regard to working hours. The workers at China Galaxy and China Miracle had to work as long as twelve hours each day, six days a week. Even where the Reebok or Disney codes were adopted (and these codes claimed to uphold the standard set by local laws), we did not observe genuine differences with regard to working hours.

The controversy over working hours often provided justification for the TNCs and their representatives to argue that it was the Chinese workers who opted for overtime work and pay. We paid particular attention to this issue and repeatedly asked the workers to express their views. Most mentioned that if they did not work overtime, the basic salary would be too low to support their daily living expenses. A nineteen-year-old woman worker at China Miracle said: "With overtime work in the evenings and weekends, then we could earn about 600 to 700 yuan [US$75–90] each month. Without overtime work, we could earn only 300 to 400 yuan [US$50]. That is not even enough for my expenses in the city." Another said: "Yes, you may say we prefer long working hours. What's wrong with that? We sell our own labor to earn money. We travel a long distance in order to work. If we can't feed ourselves, what's the use of having a holiday on Sunday?"

The wages of production workers at China Miracle and China Galaxy were still a bit higher than at many other companies in the same regions. Failure to meet the legal minimum wage requirement, however, was noticeable when overtime hours were deducted and wages were calculated on the basis of an eight-hour workday.[23] Overtime work on weekdays, including Saturday, was counted at the normal piece rate, though Sundays and public holidays paid double, which was still not a common practice in China. No pay was given, however, for annual leave or statutory holidays in either of the two enterprises. The workers were off for ten days during the Chinese New Year in 2002 without any pay. When we questioned this practice, the personnel secretary of China Galaxy said that it was not realistic to expect the company to comply with the Chinese Labor Law. She said sarcastically, "If we did so, each worker could have a salary higher than mine."

All in all, in putting such codes into practice, the political aspect of capital finds itself trapped in a quandary in shaping labor standards and working conditions. Pressure on the factories to meet international codes of conduct came from the outside, directly from global buyers who were in turn pushed by the international anti-sweatshop campaign. The rationale behind instituting the code of conduct practices thus was a business consideration leading to the quasi-obligatory effect of capital's regulation of labor rights issues in the workplace. This top-down process of granting labor rights nevertheless had its drawbacks stemming from the contradictory nature of capital. The code of conduct practices in the workplace looked "rationalized" enough, but also "paternalistic and benevolent," condensing two dichotomous processes—one rational and the other despotic—as the two sides of a single coin. But the goal of implementing "rationalized practices" in the workplace did not necessarily result in changing despotic factory regimes in China. The implication of code of conduct practices is not that they are about the potential dilution of despotic or paternalistic factory regimes but rather that the reaction to them may, paradoxically, lead to a politics of containment of capital in Chinese labor relations.

The Process of Institutionalization

The politics of containment of capital—a process of co-opting labor rights by capital assisted by the principle of reorganized moralism, is further substantiated via a process of institutionalization and formalization of labor standards and regulations in the workplace. Many enterprises create new positions, such as social compliance officers, to enforce code implementation and raise workers' awareness of code provisions. Social compliance officers were employed at China Miracle and China Galaxy under the requirements of the European corporation in mid-2002. These social compliance officers understood the code implementation as requiring nothing but systems of documentation and filing. They were keen to show us their newly constructed files and records demonstrating the institutionalization of advanced management and labor standards as claimed. Thus there were files on "Code of Conduct Training Procedures," "Code of Conduct Test Records," "New Workers' Assessment Form," "Workers' Complaint and Handling Records," "Guidelines on Admission and Dismissal," "The Management of Dormitory Guidelines," and the like. One social compliance officer told us: "The most important aspect of code implementation is about documentation and filing. How can you prove [compliance] to your buyers and their monitors? You have to show figures and data. The more details in your files, the better it will be."

The need for official documentation systems was applauded by the auditors, who played an indispensable role in advising on the code's implementation in the two enterprises. The role of the auditors was also particularly important in the process of institutionalization in that almost all the recommendations they made centered on the setting up of registers and filing systems. For instance, on the issue of compliance with the code relative to child and juvenile workers, the auditors meticulously suggested that the companies create three registers: the first one for recording copies of the IDs of juvenile workers (ages sixteen to eighteen), the second a register of physical examinations given those workers, and the third for recording and evaluating the training program for juvenile workers as required by the code.

The example provided was only the tip of the iceberg of a vast process of documentation. Much more energy was devoted to designing record systems on code training, wages, working hours, contracts, and nondiscrimination employment policies. Training sessions on the code's provisions were organized for new workers, who had to pass a test covering basic information about the company and the provisions of their contracts but mainly about the code. Sample test papers were shown to us, and everyone had received full marks. Interviews with workers, however, continued to indicate that they did not actually understand the reasons for having such a code and the benefits they could receive from it, although some of them did mention "human rights," "labor rights," nondiscrimination, and the prohibition of compulsory work. In fact, except for the new workers, training sessions were provided only to upper- and mid-level managerial staff, such as supervisors and line leaders, who in turn disseminated information on the code to their work units or production lines.

Despite obvious actual nonconformities, the directors of the two enterprises were particularly satisfied with the improvements they had made in institutionalizing code practices, and especially with suggestions given by the social compliance officers and auditors. The director of China Miracle remarked: "We now have a clear direction about what to do. Paperwork is time-consuming, but it's a must to show our commitment. It is good that we now have a lot of records for your inspection." Thus the contradictions between the code practices and production practices seemed to be resolved in this rapid process of "soft" institutionalization. Documentation, registers, and filing were seen as a must in order to implement the code, or at least to demonstrate the facility's compliance with it and the Chinese Labor Law.

But the principle of reorganized moralism requires something more solid in addition to the process of "soft" institutionalization. "Solid" institutions such as labor complaint mechanisms and trade unions were to be set up in the workplace to demonstrate the willingness of the enterprises to implement the code provisions. For China Miracle and China Galaxy, creating labor dispute mechanisms and trade unions could enhance the reputation of the companies and their management-labor relations in terms of improved "supervision, communications, and guidance." Three mechanisms for dealing with labor complaints were thus devised: a labor dispute committee, a complaints hotline handled by grievance supervisors, and face-to-face meetings for workers with the social compliance officer. A detailed three-page-long complaint-handling procedure states that its mission is to "guarantee unimpeded internal company information flows, figure out problems, solve them, and effectively contain potential troubles in time." The procedure stipulates three ways to file complaints: written reports could be placed in suggestion boxes placed on each floor, and oral complaints could be made either through hotlines or in person to the social compliance officer or the labor dispute committee (set up by the trade union, the social compliance officer, the personnel secretary, and the production manager).

Notwithstanding that these complaint mechanisms had been established in the workplace, few of the workers paid much attention to the changes or thought of making complaints through these processes. Only one of the workers interviewed claimed that she had used the suggestion box to suggest improvement of the food in the canteen. Workers fully understood that no matter how transparent and effective, these grievances mechanisms had been set up without their participation. They were used by the management, for the management. Interestingly, one worker pointed out: "There are a number of names posted on the wall for hotline complaints. You can see, but we never use them." Why not? "We see these so-called grievance-handling supervisors every day on the shop floor. They are our superiors. What's the point of going outside the company and phoning in if we have grievances?" Look at those phone numbers painted on the wall, workers told us; they were simply for purposes of decoration. While none of the workers interviewed reported ever having made a complaint, records of complaints and grievances were shown to us by the social compliance officer at China Miracle, who failed to recount clearly the circumstances relating to any of the complaints.

Both China Miracle and China Galaxy had a trade union as a exhibit for their international buyers. China Galaxy set up its trade union in 2000, but it was barely functioning when we interviewed the union chair in May 2002. China Miracle had one that was newly established in June 2002. In spite of the union requirement by the European corporation's code, which states only that "workers are free to join associations of their own choosing,"[24] management from above had nevertheless helped workers exercise "their own choosing" by setting up a union according to the China Trade Union Law. The union was formed without the initiation and participation of workers, under the guidance of the city-level Garment Industry Federation Trade Union, which sent a representative to serve as the union chair at China Miracle. The union committee consisted of five representatives from management, including the social compliance officer. The two described as "worker representatives" were actually a shop floor supervisor and a line leader.

There were three main reasons for setting up the trade union at China Miracle: to show extra commitment in complying with the code; to meet the requirement of SA 8000, which was believed to be important in gaining production orders from big American retailers; and to enable the company to sign a collective contract for all workers through the union, which was granted the right by the China Labor Law. Manipulating the collective contract was particularly important in that once the pro-management trade union took over, the company did not have to offer individual contracts to workers. In addition, the company could further contain collective bargaining power through a trade union that was under its control. The union chair, a party member in his mid-forties, said: "Why do we need to set up a trade union? It's not because of a state request or regulation. Ours is a joint-venture company, and we still have the option to do or not to do it. It's solely a market consideration. Nowadays we believe in market forces, and only market forces can effectively ask the company to set up trade union. . . . A trade union can help communication between the company and workers, and it's good for the company's development."

The trade union was thus considered a business institution working to meet international code requirements, to facilitate management control over the workforce, and to enhance company productivity through workers' consent to the production regime. In spite of the hopes held by management, the workers were notably lukewarm toward the union, and it had difficulty recruiting members on the shop floor. The union began with sixty-seven members in June 2002 and had increased to ninety-five members by late December of the same year. Most of the union members were managerial, technical, and supervisory staff; fewer than ten were production workers, who had been strongly persuaded to join. Most of these ten were local residents of the region who had been working there more than two to three years and were thus often considered the "old workers" (*lao yuan gong*) of the company. This meant that these workers had a deeper sense of loyalty to the company than most other workers, who were typically migrants, transients who stayed for a shorter time at the factory. One member who was a production worker explained to us: "Oh, yes, I know a lot of workers did not join the trade union. Why did I join? I didn't think about that much, and there is no particular reason. Our supervisor mobilized me to join and said it's good for organizing activities for the workers. She said I was a *lao yuan gong*, so I should be supportive of the trade union." As far as the ordinary production workers were concerned, this union had been mobilized and established in a top-down way, and most of them obviously lacked enthusiasm for it. The election was only a formality without any real sense of workers' democracy. It could only be a co-opting of labor autonomy and labor power from above, as the labor protection mechanism was defined as well as regulated by management.

•   •   •

This discussion has striven to unravel the principle of reorganized moralism, a micro-concept of the new managerialism which works through capital to privatize labor rights at Chinese workplaces. Our study of codes of conduct practices in Chinese workplaces has demonstrated that the moral imperative of such codes results in the penetration of capital into the sphere of labor rights in China. It is true that many rationalized practices have been put in place, including expanded investment to upgrade company facilities and the normalization of employment relations through the provision of labor contracts requiring one day off in seven, the ending of deposit systems, and the like. Regardless of these improvements of limited scope, the whole idea of a code of conduct was to demonstrate the companies' commitment to complying with internationally required labor standards, and thus for the companies to secure a firmer place in the global production chain by gaining more production orders and expanding into new markets. This has resulted in a rapid process of "soft" institutionalization in the workplace in terms of procedures and systems for governing codes of conduct. As the two factories in the Yangtze River delta and Pearl River delta showed, the companies had devoted huge resources to setting up systems and procedures, but they demonstrated no genuine concern for labor rights, less still for workers' representation or participation. In particular, the numerous labor complaint mechanisms looked like business gloss, and the trade union was a mere formality set up without workers' support. The grievance mechanisms and trade unions further demonstrated the trend toward business "co-opting" labor rights, which should be an element of civil society.

The cardinal concern of this study has been to let the voices of staff and workers be heard at a time when most of the big TNCs such as Reebok, Adidas, Levi Strauss, and The Gap are competing to implement codes of conduct in China.[25] Derived from staff and workers' views, this study has argued that codes implementation represents a process of capital-defined labor rights in Chinese workplaces, and hence generates a politics of containment from the side of capital in shaping Chinese labor politics in a global context. The politics of containment is squarely reflected in three issues: first, the rapid institutionalization of labor relations by the capital imperative at the workplace level; second, the turning of labor mechanisms and trade unions, newly established in the factories, into business institutions for facilitating the production and business goals of capital; and third, the appropriation of workers' autonomy and labor power, deliberately defined in the company codes of practice as a top-down regulatory process. In replacing the role of the Chinese state in regulating labor standards in the workplace, this top-down process of granting labor rights could result in advancing typical authoritarian factory regimes in which the management plays a paternalistic role in "protecting" the workers from labor exploitation.

6. Neoliberalism and Hmong/Miao Transnational Media Ventures

Louisa Schein

This chapter compares two discrepant but articulated moments that concern the use of media and China's Miao minority. In juxtaposition they reveal how the apparent remoteness of the Miao from centers of Chinese economic change is matched by a rival form of connectedness, to intraethnic circuits of transnational media production. In one moment, that of reception, the Miao are targeted as audiences for national media that promulgate marketization; in the other, that of production, Miao enter into media production ventures with their co-ethnics, Hmong Americans. Such strategies position Miao at the juncture of two neoliberal state programs—of the United States and China, respectively. Both programs seek to fashion autonomous entrepreneurs who will relieve the privatizing state from the burden of responsibility for their welfare by choosing instead to plunge into the turbulent sea of the free market to make their own economic way. In the course of my discussion, it should become clear that while the United States and China represent two quite distinct aspects of contemporary neoliberalism/privatization, the subjects who are the focus of this chapter reveal ways in which these forms come to knock up against each other as entrepreneurs, peasants, diasporic subjects, and other small-scale actors envision and pursue modes of transnational connectedness.

Articulated Neoliberalisms

In the discussion that follows, I mobilize a notion of discrepant but interlocking neoliberalisms in part to talk back to any homogenizing, all-encompassing sketch of globalization that might strip the specificity from instances—of media reception in China and of transnational ethnic media production—discussed here. The particular configurations I relate might be well described by Stephen Collier and Aihwa Ong's counter-notion of "assemblages" which may be characterizable as global in scale but are also always "heterogeneous, contingent, unstable, partial, and situated."[1] In the two moments I sketch here, we see the enveloping significance of state retrenchment in the area of social welfare, but on the part of two distinct states, one postsocialist and privatizing, one vehemently and hegemonistically capitalist. The Miao in China and the Hmong in the United States are related to these respective states in ways that are both similar and different.

The United States

Hmong in the United States hail from Laos, where they participated in the CIA's "Secret War" during the Vietnam era and then fled their country after 1975 as political refugees. The figure of the refugee forces a contradiction in the practices of a neoliberal state such as the United States. International exigencies, particularly those of maintaining ideological alterity from undesirable or threatening regimes, militate toward the (often spectacularized) provision of asylum to political exiles, who—at least initially—may not be economically viable in U.S. society. Arriving in the United States, then, refugees, typically with limited language, job skills, or capital, must be, by definition, wards of the welfare state. Yet this status is ultimately an unsustainable one, since the shifting America they find themselves in is one that, as Pierre Bourdieu and Loïc Wacquant have put it, is characterized by "the generalization of precarious wage labor and social insecurity, turned into the privileged engine of economic activity."[2] This economic milieu into which they are inserted premises their membership in society, their good citizenship, on swift "autonomization," on taking responsibility for themselves as a verification of their "freedom."[3] Hence they immediately become liminal and in flux, since their host's agenda, even as it initially extends to them a charitable safety net, is, from the moment they set foot on American soil, to remake them into "self-sufficient" contributors to the U.S. economy.

As Colin Gordon, condensing Foucault, suggests, the promotion of autonomy has come to be imbricated with educational investments which serve to increase the value of individuals, and this too becomes one's own responsibility; in other words, "the individual producer-consumer is in a novel sense not just an enterprise, but the entrepreneur of himself or herself."[4] The figure that has come to be the disseminator of this revamped notion of selfhood is that of the social service provider, who, as Ong has pointed out, not only serves the function of delivering economic and social supports but also educates and works "to cleanse newcomers of the perceived backward or immoral aspects of their antiquated culture, to govern their everyday behavior, and to make them individually responsible subjects of a neoliberal market society."[5]

Since 1975, many Hmong have come to support their own resettlement through undertaking this refashioning. They have, on the one hand, accomplished economic self-sufficiency through language and employment programs that channel Hmong into low-paying jobs in manufacturing and service. But on the other hand, more appropriately, they have remolded themselves into desirable neoliberal subjects through the cultivation of ethnic entrepreneurship. Independent ventures have become the ever more inexorable solution to burgeoning underemployment, especially in the context of a Hmong poverty rate of 38 percent, compared with 13 percent for all Asian Pacific Americans, and an average per capita income of $6,613 versus the $20,719 earned by Asian and Pacific Islander Americans.[6] Canny as they are about the contraction of the welfare state, and acutely conscious of the betrayals that the United States is capable of ever since its precipitous withdrawal from Laos in 1975, many Hmong immigrants have not waited for their social welfare safety net to be pulled out from under them or for the tenuous security of their menial jobs to be shattered by continued offshore relocations.

Harking back to the anticommunist era which turned them into refugees through U.S.–Southeast Asian military engagements, Hmong Americans display their history of subjectification as aggressors against socialism and defenders of autonomy: they champion their freedoms and their good fortune in having accessed such liberties as a consequence of their transnational migration to the center of valorized ostensible self-determination. Some then proceed, as entrepreneurs, to refuse dependency on the state and instead assume their appropriate roles as archpractitioners of economic "freedom." That they "choose" entrepreneurial paths accrues to their performance of Americanization. As Jamie Morgan has suggested: "The autonomous rational human is the rationale of the neoliberal ideology of the minimal state. . . . The neoliberal individual is free to be different so long as he or she acts the same."[7] For new immigrants this sameness is rendered, in part, precisely as economic conformity through autonomy, by which good citizenship is in turn measured.

These "good citizens" have, then, adopted what has been portrayed, especially by critics of Thatcherite Britain, as the hallmark of neoliberalism: "enterprise culture."[8] More specifically, they have found means to generate income *within their own communities*. Their alternate strategies include small businesses such as restaurants, groceries, video shops, chiropractic clinics, auto repair shops, and laundromats. They also include the purchase of real estate, which Hmong landlords in turn rent to other Hmong.

It is, however, those who have carved a less conventional and less local path who are my focus here. A number of Hmong, following a trajectory identified by Ong as one of the fast tracks to legitimation within the American economy, have developed *transnational* enterprises.[9] Although they did not arrive with the assets—capital, skills, and so on—that are typically so valuable to the development of flexible or transnational citizenship, they have, with their meager earnings in U.S. cities, developed a host of strategies for capital accumulation abroad, especially in those parts of Asia where they can activate kin or pseudo-kin connections. These Hmong transnational ventures demonstrate features that are well known in the neoliberal era, such as flexible production and a privileging of market rationalities over the constraints of national boundaries. Working as they do with co-ethnics in multiple Asian sites, these new Americans might, in some ways, take their place among the paradigmatic transnational citizens Ong described when she asserted that "the new Westerner is an Asian figure who submits more readily to the governmentality of fraternally based network capitalism than to the political sovereignty of a democratic nation."[10] As we shall see, for the Hmong/Miao, the narrative of fraternity comes to transect almost any construction of the impersonal "free" market, evidencing what the sociologist Nikolas Rose deems the quintessence of "advanced" liberal rule, which "govern[s] through the regulated and accountable choices of autonomous agents and . . . through intensifying and acting upon their allegiance to particular 'communities.' "[11]

China

Meanwhile, the shifts in the Chinese economy have positioned Miao there to angle for the attentions of increasingly world-traveling Hmong entrepreneurs who seek both roots and earnings. The decentralization of governance and of budgets has left interior provinces whose revenues were already comparatively low increasingly less able to take care of the basic needs of their populations. Meanwhile, state sector institutions, including schools and industries, have been privatized. As we have seen, market activity is proffered as the most obvious solution for peasants who are ever more tightly squeezed to make the basic payments for amenities such as electricity and tuition under conditions of inflation and rising costs.

It is this involuting cycle of poverty that the ostensibly redistributive Xibu Dakaifa (Opening the West) policy, inaugurated in the late 1990s, was intended to arrest, or at least curb.[12] The policy, however, instead of constituting a systematic provision of social welfare or development aid to those who had been marginalized during the decades of economic reform, was instead structured primarily in terms of what might be called "development neoliberalism" or "neoliberal developmentalism." The multipronged initiative sought to combine spectacular development projects with forms of opportunity for extraction that would draw enterprises to the western region of China. A curious hybrid of command and market economies, it remains a state-orchestrated, and in some cases state-mandated, effort to shift responsibility onto the private sector, and to get the more easterly provincial offices and coastal businesses to team up with western ones for wealth-generating projects such as hydropower production, mineral resource extraction, manufacture of regional commodities, and the promotion of tourism.

For most of the more needy peasants in the western regions, the Xibu Dakaifa initiatives have been irrelevant to their livelihoods. The projects and investments that do take place tend to be recruited by major *danwei* (work units), whether state, private, or a blend, and are virtually inaccessible to small-scale villagers. This extends a policy of "betting on the strong," described in Yunnan by Jonathan Unger and Jean Xiong as early as the late 1980s, in which small business and agricultural development loans were reserved primarily for the wealthiest villages and households, those that stood the best chance of repaying the funds once their ventures were launched.[13] Additionally, some of the larger industrial projects have also fallen short of providing extensive employment, since they brought their own skilled labor from the coast. For those isolated from the more spectacular development projects, the only conceivable way to participate in the ostensible redistribution has been to concoct a tiny tourism development plan which they might use to solicit loans. Ultimately the implementation of Xibu Dakaifa emulated a kind of "trickle-down" model in which the presence of large-scale projects was calculated to generate tax revenues that would eventually ease the burdens of local governments.

In the following sections I sketch two outcomes of the isolation of the Miao from the circuits of neoliberal activity that have come to organize and differentiate the Chinese economy.

The Mediated Remote

One night in the Miao mountains of Guizhou, I revisited a middle-aged woman whom I had interviewed previously as a returnee from garment labor in the nearest city. She was staying at home now, doing needlework alone in a bare room under a dim bulb with the flicker of a television set shifting the light about the space. She was sewing to make money for her sons' education, but, she confessed, sometimes she would get distracted by the television shows. Volunteering a succinct phrase, she made clear that television served as a vehicle of fantasy transport for her and others like her who were otherwise confined by the limited possibilities of their class position. With a resignation mingled with discontent, she said with a sneer, "The rich travel; the poor watch TV."

The quest for TV in Miao villages is not simply a grassroots effort on the part of media-hungry villagers. It is also a very deliberate policy aimed at orchestrating change in a region that has for the most part lain fallow through the postsocialist transition. Their compound status of peasant/remote/non-Han has made the Miao of the southwest mountain regions quintessential targets for the central media strategy of disseminating market mentalities (*shichang sixiang*). Since liberalization of the economy has been extremely slow to generate small businesses, cash-cropping, or township and village enterprises in these regions, the state, hoping to relieve its social welfare burden in impoverished rural areas, has turned toward striving to constitute a desiring media audience whose eventual market activity, it is hoped, can be spurred by a recognition of the disparity between their actual material lives and the consumption riches displayed on television.

Midway through the 1990s, as the story goes, some of China's leaders visited Miao areas and, shocked at the abject level of poverty, decided to intensify development of communications and transport. As Hairong Yan puts it so pointedly, "The party state and the elite is unable to grasp how continuing poverty is integral to the process of marketization and how coastal cities and enterprises of all capital forms build their economic success on the back of interior rural areas that supply cheap resources and labor."[14] Hence policies of economic privatization, responsibility, and decentralization remained untouched, and little actually changed in terms of economic development in the villages. What *was* changed, under a policy initiated by the central government in 1994 and abbreviated by the term *cun cun tong dianshi* (every village connected to television), was the priority placed on getting media hookups installed. At that point, 81.3 percent of China's population was already receiving TV, including parts of Tibet.[15] Mountainous Guizhou, then, was one of the last outposts of media isolation. To remedy this, community satellite dishes and cable into homes were to be installed in as many villages as possible. Eighty percent of the costs would be absorbed by the central government.

Connectedness, whether through the paved roads being constructed all over the countryside or the cultural signals transmitted through space, was meant gradually to modernize minds and in turn enrich villages. Among the five top priorities of a poverty alleviation and development plan for the Mashan area of Southeast Guizhou, for instance, were not only improvement of basic living conditions, economic development, and population control but also connecting every village by satellite and by road.[16] By the end of 1999, according to one estimate, 9,500 minority villages in Guizhou had satellite dishes; of these, 4,000 were Miao villages, 2,000 of which were in Southeast Guizhou. The goal was to have every village equipped with satellite reception within five years.[17] Indeed, as Junhao Hong explains, as early as 1991 the Chinese government had already been giving permits to households in remote, rural, or mountainous areas to purchase their own dishes expressly for the reception of *Chinese* television. So great was the push for media connectedness that the state effectively looked the other way at the rampant reception of foreign programming and at the resale of satellite permits by cash-poor peasants to urban viewers.[18]

But other forms of standardization were also being schemed about in the promulgation of television. Miao elites, passionate and nationalist researchers of their own *minzu* (ethnic group), described to me some of the effects they envisioned TV would have on their communities. In the process, they conveyed their regard for the medium as an instrument of social incorporation that could bring minority peasants into the fold of state-promulgated modernity. In answer to my query about why the big push for television, one explained:

First, backwardness is a problem of sensibility [*guannian*]. Television encourages Miao peasants to be civilized, orderly, developed. It makes their outlook [*sixiang*] more advanced. It introduces law and prevents economic disturbances. It advises them and teaches them. Second, minority officials have been demanding television for their people in the countryside. Third, since it is necessary for the state to govern the minorities, television serves to win people over. Fourth, in China the peasants are so isolated that TV may be their only access to the outside world. They long to know more about the outside. Their minds are empty [*kongbai*], and TV fills the void.

Another Miao scholar described more concretely both what TV should do and how peasants watched it:

Television is an educational tool. It helps to publicize the policies of the Communist Party and it unifies the people. What peasants want to watch is news, legal education programs, technical agricultural programs, and shows about how to get rich. They aren't interested in pornography, or in serials and stories. They know they are untrue. What happens when peasants watch TV is that their horizons are broadened, and their closed minds are opened up.

Nonetheless, the content to be received on Chinese television was largely promotional, purveying an array of consumer products that Miao were to learn to desire. Aware that much of what these ads proffered was economically out of reach for most Chinese audiences, authorities framed the function of advertising as "educational and informational" instead.[19] In a manner so resoundingly critiqued in the West by Max Horkheimer and Theodor Adorno,[20] this fledgling culture industry tutored Chinese consumers-in-training to live in the space of ever-renewed desire, one in which goods may not be materially available but are increasingly ubiquitous as spectacles.[21] For the time being, until they could eke out more income, Miao and other peasants were to embrace consumerism without goods, with only tantalizing spectacle to spur them to action.

Eventually included under the broader rubric of Xibu Dakaifa, the effort exerted by the state to bring television and roads to minority villages was at least in part, then, intended to accelerate the overhaul of peasant consciousness toward market mentalities. In a discussion of the central notion of *suzhi,* or "quality," in contemporary China's neoliberal discourse, Hairong Yan gives the following characterization: "Suzhi marks a sense and sensibility of the self's value in the market economy."[22] It is precisely this sensibility, a "consciousness of development," that is viewed as lacking and in need of cultivation on the part of peasants and minorities in remote regions.[23] Yan goes on to describe the way in which this *sixiang*—so desirable to a neoliberal state seeking to evade accountability for rural poverty—comes to be emphasized: "The phantasmatic production of suzhi is a new valuation of human subjectivity specific to China's neoliberal reforms. Its specific deployment as a form of value coding inscribes, measures, and mobilizes human subjectivity as the powerhouse for productivity and development."[24]

TV, like the public address system that had bellowed throughout the villages before it, was to have an educative function, but now it was gradually to socialize remote peoples to the consumption desires and profit-making schemes deemed essential to the market transformation. Indeed, it was to individualize their desires and schemes, replacing the much-touted collectivism of the Maoist era with a kind of self-interest inculcated, it was hoped, through the promise of a better life. Now that cable had been laid to every home in many Miao villages, a desire on the part of individual households to purchase television sets was itself conceived as a potential spur to development: with cable access so close at hand, Miao were envisioned as more likely to experiment with private economic schemes to raise the cash that would enable them to bring "the world" into their households. And consistent with marketization discourse across China, the transformation of personal desires, despite being a program of the state, was to be glossed as a movement toward "freedoms" of lifestyle, choice, and self-fashioning so maligned under Maoism.

Permeating such discourses about the pedagogical potential of television are the distinctly spatialized notions of opening up, of breaching the closed boundaries of the retrogressive minority peasant mind, cross-cutting it with wider knowledges. A burgeoning internationalization of viewing content, of the type described by Arjun Appadurai,[25] Mayfair Yang,[26] and others, holds the potential for this type of translocal social imagining, an imagined cosmopolitanism that exceeds not only locality but also Chinese borders.[27] Consuming media, then, could be seen as a means to participating simultaneously in Chinese reform *and* in "linking up with the world," even if only in fantasy fragments meted out by a narrow sampling of television stations.[28]

In this light, the needleworker's comment that "the rich travel; the poor watch TV" can be seen as inadvertently defying the top-down portrayal of television's pedagogical effects. She narrated another volition: to, in the words of Neil Smith, "jump scales"—to transpose herself symbolically through her media consumption into the practices of a more mobile and prestigious class. As Smith puts it: "Jumping scales allows [persons] to dissolve spatial boundaries that are largely imposed from above and that contain rather than facilitate their production and reproduction of everyday life."[29] Such a vision, on the part of a rural Miao television consumer, despite having no immediate economic ramifications, can be seen to reverse conceptually the directionality of scalar flow. In other words, rather than being seen as a medium for the downward flow of educational content, television becomes a vehicle for the imagined upward flow of peasants into the cosmopolitan whirl of the "global subject," dismantling, however chimerically, the picture of local constraint contained in the dominant stereotype of the "closed mind" and the bounded village.

Transnational Ventures

The foregoing discussion sketches the Miao peasantry as objects—or neophyte subjects—of the state's pedagogical project of marketizing *sixiang*. In this formulation they appear, but for their fantasies, primarily as immobile, even inert recipients of state intentionalities and of media messages. They are lacking (*cha*) in *suzhi*, as Yan stresses, because they fall short of appropriate subjectivities with relation to self-improvement, development, enterprise, and consumption.[30] For a few, however, this immobility is contravened by an unusual transnational link that connects Miao in China to their co-ethnics, the Hmong in the United States. Hmong Americans still revere China as their ultimate homeland, especially since the Hmong of Southeast Asia were migrants out of China only in the last two centuries. Despite the difference in ethnonym, most Miao within China and most Hmong beyond its borders recognize their historical kinship as members of a single ethnic group, dispersed southward over millennia, crossing the space of what is now China and entering what is now Vietnam, Laos, and Thailand.

The Hmong of Laos, refugees from the Vietnam era, regard their exodus as involuntary, and because of the horrific extent of loss during the war, Hmong Americans have a particularly acute nostalgia for their homelands. Since the 1990s, some have begun to travel back not only to Southeast Asia but also to China to search for connections with their roots. Their journeys have dovetailed with strategies of the Miao in China, encouraged to court the funds of Chinese overseas who felt some connection to their homeland and wanted to help out. In a strange historical twist, as their far-flung dispersal intensified their interest in China as their ultimate homeland, the Hmong of Laos came to occupy for the Miao this category of overseas emigrants who might possess resources to be returned to their ancient lands.

Hmong Americans have given money to Miao in China for such projects as the building of schools or of cisterns for storing water, and they have given scholarships to their compatriots and fellow clan members. Miao elites have been vigorous in their efforts to recruit all manner of funds. They have offered courses with steep tuition fees and customized tours to Hmong returnees seeking deeper familiarity with their culture and history. International conferences have become a flashpoint for tensions over cultural unification versus economic exchange. Hmong Americans still talk about their shock and disappointment when their delegation of about fifty were the honored guests at a 1994 conference in Hunan. They were thrilled to be going to meet their co-ethnics in China for the first time, but complain that the conference ultimately placed too much emphasis on soliciting investment for joint ventures and too little on cultural exchange.[31]

The bids by Miao in China for Hmong Americans to enter into transnational economic ventures have a kind of ethical charge, addressing these relatively moneyed kin in terms of their communal obligations to Hmong and Miao worldwide. These ethics are in keeping with the strategies of neoliberal states that, as Nikolas Rose has pointed out, foster a political subjectivity which replaces state responsibility for economic welfare with a cultivation of a community sense of duty. Rose calls this approach "government through community," in which "the subject is addressed as a moral individual with bonds of obligation and responsibilities for conduct that are assembled in a new way—the individual in his or her community is both self-responsible and subject to certain emotional bonds of affinity to a circumscribed 'network' of other individuals—unified by family ties, by locality, by moral commitment."[32] And indeed, a range of such partnerships *has* been established with Hmong capital in China, Laos, and Thailand, creating a rhizomic network of business ties across the Pacific.

These schemes, minuscule as they may be within the scale of the Chinese economy, satisfy at least three related exigencies of the new reform era's valorization of privatization and opening up. First, they serve to recruit transnational revenues, which have proved especially difficult to draw to remote minority regions. Second, they generate local entrepreneurs, persons who have risen to the increasingly promoted challenge of generating wealth without relying on the state. Third, the ventures have provided a handful of jobs, or piecework income, which in turn relieves some of the pressure on labor-rich unproductive lands from which reform policy has long encouraged an exodus in favor of the *dagong* solution of temporary menial labor.

Media as Transnational Strategy

The remainder of this chapter concerns Hmong and Miao media practices in relation to the U.S. and Chinese economies in which dislocated Hmong/Miao are becoming or seeking to become players. Dozens of the primarily male Hmong travelers to Asia are involved in the production of videos that constitute diverse representations of the lands they call home. These tapes—shot, edited, and marketed entirely by Hmong—take their place in the context of a huge Hmong media scene in which hundreds of newspapers, magazines, audio cassettes, CDs, music videos, and videotapes are produced and sold, all within the Hmong market. Videos are made by a range of amateur and semiprofessional producers, many of whom have established companies with names such as Hmong World Productions, Asia Video Productions, Vang's International Video Productions, and ST Universal Video. The tapes are in the Hmong language and are targeted exclusively for intraethnic consumption. Shrink-wrapped and usually copyrighted, they sell for $10 to $30 apiece. Although typically produced for profit, they are not backed by corporate or other outside advertising interests. They are marketed at Hmong ethnic festivals, through Asian grocery stores and video shops, and by mail order.

Among this panoply of videos are dramas, martial arts thrillers, documentaries on important events, performance or "music" videos of singing and dancing, historical reconstructions, and Asian feature films dubbed into Hmong. A large proportion concern Asian homeland sites, and it is this exilic passion for the homeland that has produced openings for Miao in China to participate in ventures for the overseas market. The vast majority, of course, have played the role of cinematographic objects, colorful adornments on the screens viewed nostalgically by Hmong abroad. But a few have had the opportunity to join Hmong Americans in transnational networks of media production. I turn now to several accounts of Hmong/Miao media makers.

Transnational Ventures as Solidarity

A refugee from Laos, Bee Vang, now in his forties, has parlayed his unusual background into a complex transnational venture. When he was in Ban Vinai refugee camp in 1984, he did medic work with a Chinese doctor from San Francisco and began learning Chinese. After coming to the United States, he continued his Chinese language studies and translated for Miao visitors from China. He developed some contacts there and made his first visit in 1993. In 1997 he opened a shop in St. Paul, where for five years he sold Miao clothes imported from China.

Meanwhile, in 1996 Bee had already begun a video business. He had met some Miao media professionals at a radio and television station in a small city in a densely Miao county in southern Yunnan Province. They devised a plan for a joint venture which would help the local Miao association send children to high school. Bee would acquire Chinese movies, pay copyright fees, and send the videos to his associates in Yunnan. They hired six people, paid by Bee, to translate and dub the films into the Hmong language, and then converted the products to the U.S. NTSC video system. They then sent the master copies to Bee, who duplicated and sold the tapes alongside the clothing he was importing. The videos he chose were dramas and love stories, especially those set in minority areas, and documentaries about minorities in China. In addition to helping out some Miao locals by providing wages, Bee saw this as an educational venture: "I wanted people here [in the United States] to know more about Miao there, so I only chose videos that taught people about China and the Miao." Later he also hired Miao associates to shoot original movies. For a dubbed tape he paid $300, while an original production earned his employees in China $1,800.

Bee's production model is uncannily resonant with transnational corporate outsourcing strategies that have become ever so familiar in the post-Fordist era. On the one hand, through his video venture he effectively moved the work of translating and dubbing offshore, to a site of rock-bottom labor costs. On the other hand, in this impoverished minority region of southwest China, merely providing a wage—any wage—was also readable within his own subjectivity and within the Hmong/Miao community as a charitable act. And here his economic practice meshed seamlessly with the policy shifts undertaken by China in reform. With privatization, as we have seen, marginal peasants have been asked to throw themselves into independent economic activity. But in remote areas, rural enterprises and cash crops have failed owing to the lack of startup funds and a poor infrastructure for marketing. Left responsible for themselves, most have turned to selling their labor, especially in more urban and productive areas, either in service or in manufacturing. Bee's enterprise, then, managed to be consistent with what has been called the "double move of autonomization and responsibilization" in advanced liberalism,[33] in that it comprised both autonomous economic actors and also an ethical responsibility to others less fortunate in society. Notably, this responsibility operated at a transnational scale of community.

Partnering to "Open the Door"

Chanhia Yang, now in his fifties, is widely credited with making one of the first strong cultural links between Hmong Americans and their Miao counterparts in China.[34] In 1992 he was among the earliest Hmong to travel to China. His wife had brought home a videotape of a Miao professional singer, Mee Hang, based in Kunming. He thought, as he now recounts, "that's my family in China; I want to make a connection." He went to Kunming, but had great difficulty getting connected with Mee Hang. People kept telling him that she wasn't in town. Finally he was able to meet her. Her Hmong was not very good, but he told her: "I saw you in a movie, and I came to see you. I think you are the key. You and I will be the key to open the communication between China and the United States. Are you Hmong? Do you love your people? If you do, then you need to do something."

Chanhia's narrative proceeds to reveal a strong ethic of individual initiative. "We shook hands and promised to do something for the Hmong community worldwide. I told her: 'You and I don't need others to help; we two can do it. We must open the door.' " Referring to his own trek to China to find Mee Hang, connect with her, and establish a transnational link, he then recounted: "I knew that if we went to the leaders, we couldn't open the door; we had to go to the people. The United States uses the church to open doors, but as Hmong we use our culture." He proceeded to go to the Foreign Affairs Office to propose a cultural exchange program, knowing that anything other than cultural exchange would be looked upon with intense suspicion by the respective governments involved in granting approval. When he returned to the United States, he persuaded his local senators and congressmen to write letters in support of Mee Hang's visiting America. He went to the Chinese consulate to assure the officials that nothing would go wrong if a delegation were to visit. "I made them aware that we were Hmong," he says, "and invited them to come join our celebration."

Chanhia tells a tale whose protagonist is the border-crossing transnational agent who circumvents and/or manipulates state borders and agencies to bring about what he calls a people-to-people connection. The results were not modest. The first time he brought Mee Hang to the United States, in 1992, she had an entourage of fourteen, and it cost $100,000, money that was raised from donations garnered through Hmong voluntary agencies and individual contributions. Twenty thousand tickets were sold for the performance that Mee Hang gave in a public park. She visited several more times, in 1993, 1995, and 1996, each time at great expense.

In the meantime, he continues to import Hmong clothing and retails a unique line of videos under the company name Hmong Traditional Video Cassette of China and U.S.A. Most are tapes of performances with titles such as "Famous Hmong Chinese Singers, Parts I–IV," which he markets on the strength of Mee Hang's popularity. The tapes are not only shot in China but also edited there. Chanhia pays for the costs of production and reproduces the finished tapes from a master that is sent over to the United States. He also markets companion products such as posters and calendars featuring glossy shots of Mee Hang smiling winningly in colorful Miao costume. Although he hasn't been back to China since 2000, he is still able to make money at Hmong flea markets and festivals by selling his imports.

Miao Women's Self-Marketing

The market for gendered homeland culture has spurred other types of transnational business within the Hmong music scene. Several Hmong Americans based in Fresno, California, have "sponsored" young women from Thailand and Laos, meaning that they have put up money to produce them as singers, created tapes and CDs of their work to sell in the United States, and sometimes brought them over for special tours to cities with large Hmong populations. Recording of albums is done in Asia, where costs are low, while duplication and distribution are mostly done in the

United States. There is a double return for commodification of homeland "human resources." First, the costs for production and remuneration of actors and performers are held down by virtue of their being situated in Asia. Second, the homeland is particularly marketable. We turn now to two cases of Miao women who have entered the market themselves, as peddlers of their own gendered commodities.

Ying Yang hails from a small village on the border of China and Vietnam, but had come to the city of Kunming and was making her way as a singer. She had a Hmong sponsor in Fresno, and had issued five well-received pop albums for the U.S. Hmong market. An uncle introduced her to Yeng Tha Her, a Hmong college graduate who had acted in two Hmong movies. They began communicating by phone and e-mail and, as they tell it, "fell in love" without ever having seen each other. Given her reputation in music and his in film, they decided to make a movie together, and she scrapped all relations with other Hmong American sponsors. She and Yeng Tha hammered out a script via long-distance phone based on her story and his Hmong writing skills. Then he traveled to China, they met, and began shooting a semiautobiographical video called *Overseas Romances* (*Nplooj Siab Hlub Hla Ntuj*)—in which they played two young lovers, she from China and he from the United States—about their adventures in making a long-distance romance work. They traveled to Beijing and Shanghai and engaged the services of professional studios in both places, and they traveled to Ying's small hometown for picturesque rustic images. Shooting took two and a half months. Yeng Tha paid all the expenses and continued to support Ying in her everyday life in Kunming while they waited to see how the video would sell. It was released in the summer of 2005, and for the debut Yeng Tha rented a local theater to show it on the big screen for three nights. By early July it had sold two thousand copies. Ying's homeland cachet meant that she could woo not only a transnational lover but also a transnational venture and a future in a joint business.[35]

Mee Vang is a particularly unusual entrepreneur. She is a Miao woman from China, where she worked as a professional performer. Originally from a village in the mountains along China's southwest border, she had been recruited and trained for a small song and dance troupe that performed in the prefectural capital. There she had met a Hmong American man at least a decade her senior, who was traveling in China after going through a divorce. They decided to marry, and she came to the United States to make a new life with him. Unfortunately, this new life was shattered when her husband was imprisoned not more than six months after they had settled in Minneapolis. When I first met her in 1999, she was living a miserable life with her in-laws, childless and caring for other relatives' children, not having learned to drive or speak English, homesick and not knowing when her husband would get out of jail. She *had*, however, been given an opportunity to use the skills she had imported from China: a couple of times a week she went to a Hmong community center to teach dance to Hmong American youngsters.

By the time I met Mee again in 2003, her life had completely changed course. Her husband had won an appeal and had been out of jail for three years. She had two children and was pregnant with a third. And she had taken her occasional employment as a dance teacher and transformed it into a full-blown business run by her and her husband. In a large basement room rented in a building full of Hmong businesses in the heart of the Hmong district of St. Paul, her husband had constructed a dance studio. Mee offered classes in dance, in singing, and in Chinese language to Hmong children ages nine to sixteen. The language of instruction was Hmong, the local dialect of which she had only become proficient in during her years in the United States. Her instruction was in high demand, not only because of the tremendous desire of Hmong immigrants for things imported from Asia but also because she had had the good fortune of being chosen for rigorous professional training before she emigrated. Instead of Asia serving as the inert object of Hmong American commodification, in Mee's case it was a young, newly arrived woman from Asia who was selling her own cultural expertise, and with great success. When her groups of dancers entered contests at the Minnesota Hmong New Year's celebrations, they routinely won first, second, and third prizes. In a stark reversal of the usual Hmong American gender roles, Mee is supporting her family with this business. Her husband does not work separately but instead devotes himself to assisting her enterprise, watching their children when she is in class, maintaining the space, and so on. By 2005 she had four children and so many classes to teach that she had delegated some to two early trainees. She had hired a martial arts teacher to enhance the class instruction, and her husband had built a recording studio so that her singing students could make products from their songs.

Articulation and Assemblage

It is no accident that the first section of this chapter is composed of more general comments about a shifting media landscape, while the latter section presents agentive individuals and their strategies. The former section sketches a purportedly passive populace being acted upon by concerted efforts of pedagogy and marketization, a populace whose putative inertness is framed as an ideological problem to be addressed. These people are constructed as always only media *receivers*, even though their reception is thought to be a vehicle that should animate them toward increased market participation. The latter section, by contrast, portrays actors who seek wealth and transnational connectedness through enterprises involving media and performance arts. Not surprisingly, these are the media *producers*.

A more binarized structural account would emphasize the activism of the state in the former moment and the contraction of the state in favor of the market in the latter. Likewise, it would draw attention to the Chineseness of the kind of state-orchestrated vision of television's instrumentality while noting that it is American actors who come to the forefront in the description of media producers. My aim, however, is not to affirm these binaries or to reproduce an alignment of China with state power and the United States with market liberalism. Rather it is to ask what forms of neoliberal governmentality emerge in each instance and, more important, whether there is work to be done in thinking this environment in and beyond China as one field. It might be more productive to think not in terms of a unitary field that encompasses China and the United States, but rather in terms of an articulation of neoliberal rationalities that gives rise to the transnational flows and particular partnerships that are chronicled here.

This "tension," identified by Collier and Ong, between the genericized global and the specific assemblage also allows us to speak to some of the widespread tropes of post-Fordism in looking at the transnational relations of media production recounted here. While the characterizations "footloose" and "flexible" have become stock motifs in both dominant and more deconstructionist accounts of the paradigmatic post-Fordist subject,[36] they are not so straightforward as depictions of Hmong American ventures overseas. To be sure, these entrepreneurs are footloose in the sense that they readily board planes to cross international borders. And they are flexible in the sense that they have risen to the challenge posed by contractions in the U.S. economy and in refugee assistance and have generated alternative means of livelihood, with media production being only one of many self-devised strategies. But at the same time, such ventures are eminently constrained by the particularities of geography and ethnicity. What makes money in the world of transnational Hmong media is the kind of content that is "close to home," that is set in Asia, and that satiates the nostalgia of reluctant migrants remembering their lost lands. Media entrepreneurs, in other words, cannot go just anywhere in search of a favorable production environment but are, on the contrary, creating highly localized commodities that are contingent on their geographic situatedness. Likewise, what makes for low production costs in these Asian sites is the presence not just of any cheap labor but rather of co-ethnics who are *both* underemployed or marginalized by their remoteness from Chinese economic change *and* versed in culture and capable in Hmong language.

The investigation of market practices here also reveals tensions and contingencies concerning the parts played by the state. That neoliberal governmentality and the rollback of state supports has meant retooling both subjectivities and economic strategies toward autonomy in the "free" market might be thought of as a constant on both sides of the Pacific, but the instantiations are highly disjunctive and asymmetrical. Hmong American media producers operate independent of state institutions except for the passports they must obtain to shuttle back and forth to Asia and the marriage papers they must process for their brides. By contrast, their partners in China, far from being allergic to state power, operate in an environment characterized by what David Wank has called the active "commodification" of state resources.[37]

These accommodations between state and market call for a more nuanced conceptualization of the relationship, and for refusing any facile binarization of state power and individuated market practice. In the case of the Hmong/Miao we encounter a field of ostensibly spontaneous entrepreneurial practice that is constructed through extranational solidarity and across transcontinental distances. In the instances we have seen here, what emerges is a set of relations, asymmetrical and in one sense extractive, that take form at a transnational scale and as a consequence of geopolitical inequalities. Yet at the same time, these engagements are highly informed, as a precondition to their happening at all, by the drive to foster a trans-Pacific Hmong/Miao community, complete with a kind of ethical duty placed on those more mobile and more privileged members who hail from the United States. These projects may be thought of as assemblages of market rationalities conjoined with community ethics and policy concerns. Emerging out of privatization—a foisting of responsibility on individual economic actors— transnational ventures end up being at once autonomously initiated and highly consistent with larger state designs on both sides of the Pacific.

PART II

Powers of the Self

7. Consuming Medicine and Biotechnology in China

Nancy N. Chen

The first decade of this century has pointed to an ever-growing embrace of science and its technologies as the key to national and global prominence. What *Fortune* magazine has referred to as twenty-first-century megatrends—China's emergence as an economic colossus and the global rise of commercial life science— are coming together. Since the post-Mao economic reforms, laboratories— especially those in the biosciences—have been retooled as sites for commercial enterprise, while scientists have had to become entrepreneurial in order to head such entities. Yet ongoing concerns for the public's health and well-being will continue to surface as reminders that the expansion of the life sciences in twenty-first-century China is pressing up against dire basic human needs. In this there are important

Special thanks to Li Zhang and Aihwa Ong for organizing the workshop in Shanghai and for their comments on revisions. Feedback on earlier work from colleagues at the Laboratory for the Anthropology of Social Institutions and Organization (LAIOS); the MIT Science, Technology, and Society Program; the University of Nevada at Las Vegas Department of Anthropology; the Center for Chinese Studies at the University of California, Berkeley; and the Institute for European Ethnology at Humboldt University have been invaluable for this ongoing project. I am grateful to Marc Abeles, Jiemin Bao, Stefan Beck, Don Brenneis, Joe Dumit, Michael Fischer, You-tien Hsing, Michi Knecht, Emily Martin, Annemarie Mol, Paul Rabinow, Rayna Rapp, and Rosalind Williams for their insightful suggestions.

continuities with socialist policies and leaders. Science remains a critical platform for state strengthening and nation building. The notion of science as critical to nation building reflects a particular ethos that pervaded most of the previous century. The alliance of officials with scientists facilitated the embrace of expert knowledge as the basis of governmentality. Science became especially integral to state formation and nation building during the socialist era. In the present century, late-socialist campaigns rely heavily on discourses of scientific rationality and civilization. Therefore being attentive to certain formations allows us to trace the Chinese state through its practices. Government leaders are currently using biotechnology and the market as a double helix for economic and political might. With market expansion, shifts in time and space have made the Shanghai minute briefer than ever. Feelings of disruption and uncertainty have frequently been voiced by both official media and citizens as state services become downsized.

As the philosopher Giorgio Agamben has suggested in his study of sovereign power and "bare life," modern politics and juridical rule facilitate an intimate relation between mass democracies and totalitarian states. When states focus on the "care, control, and use of bare life" as political agendas, familiar categories of public and private fall away into "a zone of indistinction."[1] Such blurrings or displacements lie at the heart of new formations which have the power to determine life, death, and even the in-between states of living entities not classified as human In this chapter I suggest that an anthropological study of biotechnology enables a crucial mapping of the new China and of familiar inequalities. Despite the aim of biotechnology to address the needs of a growing nation and the widespread availability of pharmaceuticals, new lines of exclusion also emerge with these industries. Though more mobile and with better access to urban goods than ever before, rural residents and poor citizens face deepening inequalities which characterize a bare life marked by increased exposure to contagion, counterfeit medicines, and the spiraling costs of health care. In what follows I trace the rise of biotech as a seeming solution to modern life in the context of a burgeoning market in drugs and health-related goods.

Mapping Chinese Biotech

The Chinese state has much at stake in promoting biotechnology research and industry. It is hard to avoid survivalist accounts in which science and technology rescue China from the Malthusian fate of too many people and not enough food. The widespread starvation in the aftermath of the Great Leap Forward and other famines remains deeply etched in personal and institutional memory. Such stories locate biotechnology as the savior, not the problem, as in Euro-American accounts. Biotechnology has been touted as the best solution for meeting the needs of the world's largest population, ranging from food shortages to health care concerns. It is estimated that by 2040, China's population will have increased to 1.6 billion, and that food production must increase by at least 60 percent to match this growth. The aggressive promotion of this new science is deemed crucial not just for material resources but for the well-being of the entire nation. A corollary of the survivalist account is the concern about intellectual property in the race to the GMO (genetically modified organism) patent finish line. Socialist bureaucrats are determined not to become dependent on foreign aid or food crops. Such pressing issues outweigh the concerns for safety and the anti-GMO ethos voiced in Europe and the United States.

Partly in response to the Asian financial crisis and lessons learned from "Big Pharma" in the mid-1990s, biotechnology has emerged as the new engine for economic revitalization in the twenty-first century. It is necessary, however, to acknowledge how recent outbreaks of SARS and bird flu (H5N1 virus) have radically altered daily life. The epidemics have been a particular boon to the pharmaceutical industry. Panic buying of traditional medicines, herbs, antiseptic cleansers, antibiotics, and disinfectants such as vinegar has extended to, and boosted sales of, most drugs. There has been a resurgence of folk remedies and spiritual practices despite perennial state campaigns against superstition. Such consumption, and the desire for miraculous healing, form the backdrop to the cultivation of the biotech industry as a growth engine by the state.

Rather than envisioning fixed boundaries between agricultural, genomic, and pharmaceutical biotech, it is important for us to acknowledge the interrelatedness of techniques, practices, and production in each area and how together these have formed a platform for the Chinese state to develop modern life after entry in the World Trade Organization (WTO).[2] Parallel to Bowker and Starr's analysis of the work of classification and the politics of categories, the content of biotech, especially the extensive products, becomes distilled into what the government would like to classify as "Chinese biotech." It is crucial to note the different trajectory of the biotechnology industry in China compared to that of its counterpart in the United States. The biotech boom in Silicon Valley was driven by the marriage of venture capital with university research. The biotech private sector in China depends on several players: investors (including foreign multinationals, Chinese banks, and state-owned companies), scientists, and consumers. A constant refrain heard from the Chinese media and from scientists is the lack of resources (both material and human) for properly launching a biotech market. Scientists have to be trained, and labs have to be adequately funded. One way the government sought to reverse the brain drain of the post-Mao period was to set up the "Hundred Scholars Project" (recycling the "Hundred Flowers" campaign of the 1960s), a program in place since 1994 to woo talented scientists. The average start-up package includes about 250,000 Euros, three years' salary, housing, lab costs, and equipment.[3] "These days, the ideal is to have a Ph.D. in molecular biology from the United States and to be thirty-five years old," confided Dr. Shan, an M.D.

who had decided to return to Shanghai in his late forties. "The government has a policy to support younger scholars these days. I missed out, as I'm nearly fifty now. It's a good time to be young." Dr. Shan's remark pointed out generational issues that will persist as younger scientists are promoted to administrative positions over their older colleagues. Scientists, like other citizens, have to be molded into proper recipients of state capital in order to create the Chinese biotech market.

When I returned to Beijing Medical College during the summer of 2002, numerous signs for biotech firms were sprinkled all over campus. One colleague noted that "these are a dime a dozen" when I mentioned the ubiquity of such signs in lieu of political slogans. At a state science fair in 2001, sensational items such as transplanted human ears on mice were on display. Visitors could also view the results of projects under way such as "transplanting silkworm genes into goats, producing human organs through a stem cell bank, cloning corneas as a treatment for glaucoma, and studying gene pools of some of the nation's 56 minorities."[4] China is among the world's top three producers of amino acids and enzymes. Bioprospecting among Chinese medicinal plants and isolated minority groups has been undertaken by Big Pharma as well as by national research centers. Zhu Chen, director of the National Human Genome Project in China and vice president of the Chinese Academy of Sciences, spoke of the "great leap forward" in biosciences and technology. The genome project, which began in 1994, consisted of a consortium of labs which addressed resource conservation, technology and informatics development, and disease-causing genes.[5] By 1998, twenty-two genomic centers had been established in Beijing and Shanghai, in addition to thirty laboratories engaged in genomic and cloning research.

It is easy to be dazzled by the new technologies and the promise of a better future through biotech. Biotech offers a potent field of meanings in the production of both knowledge and subjects. The zones of inclusion, however, tend to be based in urban sectors or among well-to-do citizens with sufficient purchasing power to participate in this new economy. In what follows I trace how the biotech industry emerged in Shanghai as part of a national consciousness in which public and private interests merge to shape modern life.

Consuming Medicine and China's Pharma Valley

Shanghai's ascent in the late 1990s after the handover of Hong Kong is literally embodied in its urban landscape. Dazzling new buildings on the Pudong side of the Huangpu River face colonial banks of the Bund "reclaimed" from socialist drabness. At night, both sides of the river are lit up in neon for boat tours and strollers. A visit to the planning museum where the city plan of Shanghai is displayed offers real estate speculators a chance to check their investments. With the opening of the stock market in 1991, "stock fever," as Ellen Hertz found during her ethnographic research, became a part of daily life for most Shanghainese, even for those who did not even own stocks.[6] Shanghai is the cosmopolitan center of China, with over a million resident foreigners and more than 300,000 Taiwanese. This is the bubble economy in which the latest new thing of biotechnology has arrived. Since the mid-1990s, all major pharmaceutical firms have opened their main offices in Shanghai. The government and media have proclaimed Shanghai to be China's Pharma Valley (*yaogu*). This is the center for R&D, and research activities have focused on developing cardiac and cerebral-vascular, anti-infective, anti-cancer, fertility-regulating, anti-aging, digestive, and nutritional preparations. Most drug production actually takes place outside the city, where there is more space and where workers accept lower wages. Suzhou, the former imperial garden city with a history that spans several dynasties, has been reshaped as the center of production for the pharmaceutical and biotech industries. As in Shanghai, whole neighborhoods and streets have been demolished to make way for modern thoroughfares.

The reach of pharmaceutical capital extends far beyond Shanghai and other major cities. Even Lhasa, the capital of Tibet, is not immune to bioprospecting and "casino capitalism," which Vincanne Adams uses as a framework for understanding the ways in which "market interests become wedded to, and in some cases undergirded by, scientific knowledge practices."[7] The casino image reflects both the level of risk and the players' fervent desire to strike gold, despite the fact that ultimately the house—in this case Big Pharma—always wins. The political adage "follow the money" offers another important strategy for illustrating casino capitalism at work.

Medicine is big business in China. Since the mid-1990s the pharmaceutical industry has made tremendous profits in mainland China. The decline in state support for hospitals and subsidized medical care has had a huge impact on access to health care. As in other countries with for-profit medical systems, practices of self-medication abound. In addition to the two official systems of medicine—Western biomedicine and Chinese traditional medicine—numerous popular alternative healing practices are available. Tonics, vitamins, and injections are frequently sought as therapeutic measures for a wide variety of illnesses. Not all forms are state approved, and many are highly questionable. The widespread consumption of new pharmaceuticals in China dovetails with deeply embedded beliefs and traditions of self-management of health care. Practices of self-medication can be found throughout China. In urban areas, consumption is undertaken through a range of widely available medical practitioners. The nouveaux riches and the newly emerging middle class in urban China have hospitals, clinics, and medicine close by. Pharmacies, both state run and private, abound on the streets. Even with the decline in state support of health care, urban workers have access to many kinds of insurance coverage for medical expenses. In rural and poor regions, however, even with local pharmacies nearby, most uninsured families must choose between paying for medical care and medication or other basic necessities such as food, clothing, or shelter. Access to affordable health care has been drastically reduced with the decline in numbers of rural doctors (formerly referred to as barefoot doctors) and clinical outstations. Moreover, access to the goods of biopharmaceutical companies is overshadowed by exposure to contaminated foods and counterfeit medicines, another danger of consumption in the present era of privatization.

Stocking the medicine cabinet is one strategy of self-medication and care in the era of privatization. Whereas North American families frequently store medications in the private space of a bathroom cabinet, many Chinese families keep medications by the bedside or elsewhere in plain sight for easy access. In home visits I paid to several families with elderly parents, the prominent displays of prescription and over-the-counter drugs on bureaus and tables were almost altar-like. On one such visit to Shanghai during the summer of 2004, Mrs. Zhang surveyed the rows of medications that surrounded her bed, the sum of which could easily have cost half a month's salary. She referred to the massed bottles as a sign of her adult children's concern for her. She would take a handful of prescription tablets and over-the-counter pills with each meal. Bedridden with diabetes for over two decades, she was quite adept at describing the different uses of each drug, reflecting how one becomes in a sense a good consumer in the management of one's symptoms and health care. Self-medication does not always occur as the singular act of an individual. Consuming medicine is also steeped in an extensive network of social and kinship bonds. Mrs. Zhang's family members and their domestic workers were intimately involved in maintaining her rigorous schedule of consuming medicine, in both pill and tonic form, several times a day. Such a health regimen reflects not just the family's ability to afford the medications but the ways in which health care has become a privatized rather than a state expenditure. Health, including the ability to consume health-related products, is increasingly a mirror of wealth and inequality in the new economy.[8] For many Chinese, however, whether rich or poor, the underlying fear of illness and the exorbitant accompanying costs of health care fuel the consumption of pharmaceuticals and over-the-counter drugs as preventive measures.

Bioethics for Bare Life

With approval of its entry in the World Trade Organization, the development of biotechnology in China has been viewed by foreign and local investors as the next gold rush. Biotechnology offers much promise, and yet also ambivalence and concern, in this context. In the wake of market reform, most provincial governments have taken an entrepreneurial interest in biotech. Many bureaucrats and entrepreneurs do not wish to be left in the dust when there are imagined lucrative gains to be made. Toward this end, hybrid public-private enterprises such as

"Bio-Island," a research and manufacturing biotech facility on an island in the South China Sea, and special economic zones for pharmaceutical firms have been spawned.[9] The government has invested 1.26 billion Euros so far. While the goods of biotech and Big Pharma are presumed to be available to all, access is nonetheless determined by differential forms of consumption and exposure to risk. Rather than presuming a unified body politic under socialism, late-socialist forms of privatization have fostered multiple and often contradictory bodies of citizen-subjects. Affluent urbanites utilize biomedicine and new technologies to enhance their daily life and self-management. By contrast, rural Chinese bodies are exposed to dangerous contaminants, and thus the state utilizes the biosciences as forms of defensive management against them.

Until recently, the Chinese state vigorously pursued new biotechnologies and genomic research without much questioning of whether scientific practices would prove ineffective or, worse, detrimental. Such intensive research and capital investments do not come without a price. Despite robust exports and access to new goods and job opportunities, the domestic economy has produced not only nouveaux riches but also vastly poorer individuals without a familiar net of state welfare or services available. Ordinary Chinese, especially in rural and extremely poor regions, are increasingly the subjects of drug studies and new GMO crops.[10] The challenge of asserting questions of justice as integral to the examination of structural violence rather than as an afterthought is also critical. Rural communities face a vast spiral of environmental degradation, regional inequality, and poverty. The specter of HIV/AIDS, SARS, and avian flu looms dangerously. Officials only recently admitted that the government had a problem with HIV/AIDS and acknowledged that at least 1 million Chinese were infected. The World Health Organization estimate was double this figure, and at an annual growth rate of 40 percent, the European Molecular Biology Organization (EMBO) estimated in 2003 that by 2010 there could be as many as 10 million infected individuals, the largest number for any country in the world.[11] In this context of limited goods and great hopes, the emerging discourse of bioethics includes the call by Chinese scientists and officials to ban cloning and genetic piracy.[12] A sea change has been under way in which the state has deliberately slowed down research and even adopted bioethics guidelines. In 2002 the Chinese representatives to UNESCO outlined guidelines for stem cell research that restricted reproductive cloning. These guidelines were initially formulated by the Department of Ethical, Legal, and Social Issues of the Chinese Human Genome Center in Shanghai.[13] In addition, British guidelines on the manipulation of embryonic material up to fourteen days have also been addressed.

The recent epidemics have helped foreground not only the biotech industry but also the evolving Chinese nation-state in the early twenty-first century. The national and global responses to these epidemics will have ongoing consequences for social and political life in China. Beyond the focus on death tolls, the reportage has detailed the shifting political and social landscape. There has been an ever-increasing assertion of state scrutiny, such as the monitoring of e-mail and text messages to prevent rumors from spreading. Moreover, any person viewed as wantonly passing along the viruses can be charged with a crime and given the death penalty. Such surveillance is accompanied by the acknowledgment that the rural health care system is in chaos and that a new order, embodied by the appointment of a new health minister, is necessary. At the same time, there has also been a return to early socialist practices in which informers, especially neighborhood committees, were utilized to identify potential carriers who were not practicing self-quarantine. Wild game and domesticated poultry have been targeted as a vector for transmission of viruses, and many animals have been confiscated from sellers.

Even more breathtaking are the accompanying social changes. The donning of masks and enforced physical isolation have transformed the sociability of daily life. Rumors, conspiracy theories, and origin myths concerning SARS spread as rampantly as the disease itself. Rural villagers, who already bear the brunt of the inequalities of a market economy, have responded to the pandemic with violence and blockades of roads that bring urbanites to the countryside. The SARS pandemic has triggered memories of contagion and exclusion both in China, which has a long history of epidemics,[14] as well as outside the country. In such times, revisiting Albert Camus's novel *The Plague* has been instructive. Toward the end the narrator notes that "whereas plague by its impartial ministrations should have promoted equality among our townfolk, it now had the opposite effect, and . . . exacerbated the sense of injustice."[15] Following Galen and many subsequent scholars of medicine, anthropologists have seen disease never simply as a biological event but ultimately as a way to map inequality. Although the growth of biomedicine and its technologies have been made possible in China by privatization, access to the benefits of these developments remains limited and has had different effects for differently positioned bodies in the market economy. While the middle classes in urban China are becoming adept consumers, the options for peripheralized migrant workers, the rural unemployed, and the elderly are rapidly disappearing, as they become shut out from the newly privatized zones of consumption and membership. Health regimens and public health programs promoted during the socialist era as building strong bodies for the nation have become differentiated into forms of self-medication that reflect deep inequalities.

Cultivating Biocitizens

This examination of the emergent biotech industry in relation to the consumption of medical goods and services illustrates the roles that science plays in nation building. In this case science is a modernizing force which relies on boundary formation and regulations to contain official knowledge. Biotechnology is viewed by bureaucrats as a rational engine for conjoining technological innovation with economic reform, but not social or political reform. In the case of new biotechnologies, scientific knowledge becomes engaged as a form of entrepreneurial promotion for scientists, bureaucrats, and investors. Science is not so much a regulatory force but instead a generative force for new possibilities of self-determination and national legitimacy. Biotech matters because it frames the Chinese state and its desires for self-making. As Warwick Anderson has suggested, postcolonial technoscience is one way to map the changing political economy of capitalism and science.[16] Tracing biotechnology in China helps to anchor the broader issue of how the Chinese state is reconfiguring itself in the twenty-first century. Moreover, tracing the production of "Chinese" biotech illustrates key formations of market and state logic. Yet consumer practices, particularly in the consumption of pharmaceuticals, reveal an underlying context for the urgent embrace of biotechnology.

In an age of epidemic contagion and contamination, the state bureaucracy still faces the recurrent issue of how to maintain the social order in the midst of ongoing market reform. Old tensions and concerns about the social order remain, while the challenge to provide for a younger and highly transformed population has become much more complex. Discourses about psuedoscience have been used to distinguish between, on the one hand, practices that undermine the credibility of scientific knowledge and national progress and, on the other, state-sanctioned forms of enterprises which embrace the scientific spirit that cultivates the nation-state. In sum, the dichotomy between science and psuedoscience effectively creates boundaries that can be invoked to regulate science and its would-be practitioners. Science, and in particular biotech, is embraced to articulate and frame nationhood in China. Biotech promotes the dream world of mass consumption and the good life of modernity. Epidemics reveal an alternate image in which the production and consumption of such goods are based in the deep fear of being left behind and vulnerable to the violence of new economies.

If anthropologists and science technology studies scholars are to see bare life clearly as an arena for powerful acts of inclusion and exclusion rather than a zone of indistinction, our task is to continue documenting how life itself can be shaped, and even obscured, by the convenient frames of old comforts and new technologies. In that spirit, new consumers in China are being produced in an environment that envisions the market and biotech as conjoined. In the same way, we can situate the work of biotech as a means to cultivate biocitizens through forms of consumption by means of new regimes of order, both private and public. In such a politics of biotech governmentality, conventional meanings of nature and ethics are displaced to allow for new practices and forms of knowledge that do not necessarily make a better life possible for all. Moreover, the blurring of the line between public and private funding for such projects indicates how modern life, particularly in the context of the biosciences, is being reconfigured for nation building with the rubric of market consumption.

8. Should I Quit? Tobacco, Fraught Identity, and the Risks of Governmentality

Matthew Kohrman

One day during the fall of 2003, I was sitting at a table on the second floor of a teahouse, busy with the sorts of activities that often occupy anthropologists during early stages of a new field project. I was writing up interview notes, making journal entries, and phoning people who might help move my research along. The teahouse is in Kunming, the capital of China's southwestern Yunnan Province. It sits inside Kunming's Green Lake Park, the former home of Yunnan's provincial library and today seemingly a hub of all things ideally urban: planned gardens, paddleboat rides, and finely designed stone pathways for recreation, romantic walks, and views through foliage of the surrounding high-rise buildings.

At first, on that afternoon, I paid little attention to the fact that the college-age couple sitting next to me were smoking. I was in Kunming, after all, a city that for decades has been the capital of China's "Tobacco Kingdom," so called because of Yunnan's inordinate involvement in cigarette production. If anything about the smoke wafting my way that afternoon caught my attention initially, it was the fact that much of it was being produced by the young woman. Smoking among women has been relatively rare in much of China over the last fifty years

This chapter is a revised version of an article published in *Urban Anthropology* 33 (2004): 211–45.

and remains noticeably uncommon in Kunming.[1] As minutes passed, what struck me most about this young couple, though, was less their cigarette use than the reflective, languid expressions on the man's face. Whenever I happened to look his way, he seemed to be staring glumly, at times tearfully, into his hands or his partner's eyes. In subsequent months I came to learn of common challenges facing many Kunming smokers, but I never had an opportunity to befriend this man individually and learn what was vexing him that day.

By four o'clock, my tasks complete, I prepared to leave the teahouse. As I stretched and looked up, my line of vision rose past the couple and through their swirling smoke and the fumes rising from two men who had just occupied a table farther beyond, who were deeply involved in the distinctively male Chinese custom of cigarette exchange. I could only chuckle. How had I not registered earlier this familiar piece of public media hanging over everyone's head, seemingly as fraught with contradiction located in this teahouse as the young man across from me was fraught with distress? There, a short distance from me, just beyond where the newly arrived men were sitting, was a bright white, red, and black sign prominently displaying a circle with a line through it. At the bottom the sign stated *Jinzhi Xiyan*, "Smoking Is Prohibited."

Abiding Questions of Biopolitics

Like tobacco consumption, tobacco control is not a new phenomenon, in China or elsewhere. For centuries, in many parts of the world, there have been people using tobacco and there have been interventions to control that use. The control of tobacco, however, has undergone highly visible transformations of scope and intensity since the early 1990s. These transformations stem in part from the fact that cigarette smoking, more so than almost any other "hazard" in our current era, has become a bête noire of public health.

Although regulatory efforts to control tobacco have been expanding recently, they have not been expanding everywhere or with the same intensity from place to place. Emergent forms of biopolitics, like transnational capital today, are selective. They skip around and take noticeable root in some places while skirting others. One setting both inside and outside China where public health interventions have long found footing and which they thereby have often helped define is the city.[2] Such interventions have been fundamental to the conceptual and practical framing of cities and their denizens as either generating unique health dangers or as being centers for sanitary certainty and medical progress, as juxtaposed to an untamed, unwashed, underdeveloped rural periphery.

Yet if the problematization and promotion of health, as a set of practices, has been important for defining the urban as modern and vice versa, this raises a set of analytical and substantive questions. By what means should one explore how these practices (as they become instantiated through and *as* the modern) shape everyday experiences of city life? How are these practices understood and framed by local urbanites who are not simply "culturally embedded," so to speak, but enmeshed in distinctive sociopolitical assemblages that include state institutions, entrenched regional economies, and discourses pertaining to class, residency, gender, and desire?

In this chapter I explore these broad analytical and substantive questions vis-à-vis male urban subjectivity by simultaneously interrogating two issues: (1) the relevance of risk society and governmentality theories to the current regulatory regime of tobacco control in China, and (2) how some media shape that regime's effects in one city in the country's southwest.

Several scholars have examined the rising prominence of tobacco control in various global locales as being emblematic of the new roles of risk in the making of modernity.[3] They assert that tobacco control can be understood in terms of the most widely circulating sociological framework for analyzing risk, what the theorist Ulrich Beck has come to call "risk society."[4] Inasmuch as I demonstrate analytical value in applying Beck's framework to assessing changes under way across the PRC, I agitate for something more here, because when it comes to studying the regulation of cigarette smokers in contemporary China, risk society theory has noticeable limitations. To overcome those limits, what is needed is an application of other analytical tools, designed along different lines, for understanding more deeply specific sociopolitical processes, in particular historical interactions between governance, knowledge production, and the problematization of self. In this chapter's latter pages I deploy such tools, ones informed by Foucault's ideas about governmentality.[5] I illustrate ways that, in Kunming recently, tobacco-related media have become part of unique sociological transformations, wherein local regulatory practices together with ideas relating to urbanism and modernity have been promoting an emergent type of fraught subjectivity among male smokers.

Risk Considered

According to Beck, major shifts have been under way in recent decades across much of the world in the ordering of certainty and uncertainty, and these shifts mark a movement to a new age of modernity, one dominated not just by risk but by representations of risk, both of which increasingly defy easy calculation and management.[6] These risks come in numerous stripes, everything from environmental problems involving water and air, toxins in food and other consumer products, and terrorism to cancer, infectious diseases, and computer viruses.[7] Not only are risks more significant in magnitude and more de-territorialized than in previous epochs, Beck says, but also their causation and controllability today is understood to be quite different from what was the case in the past.

Mass media play particularly pivotal roles in this transition, what Beck has called the movement from a "first" (i.e., early) to a "second" (i.e., late) stage of modernity.[8] By increasingly trafficking in bloody reportage and actuarial statistics about human-made hazards, mass media fuel the expansion of risk awareness and also sow doubt about former solidarities and science. And in turn, by reporting on debates among experts about how individuals might manage and reduce risk, mass media encourage the *citizen as media judge*, in juxtaposition to the erstwhile more passive model of the citizen as recipient of superordinate directives designed to lead one down a clear path to risk avoidance. Moreover, by incessantly marketing lifestyle options, mass media feed the notion that the healthy and responsible individual is one who is capable of exercising rational thought to produce a distinctive self-narrative or personal biography, to navigate wisely the choppy seas of risk and uncertainty and produce a unique existence.

A key feature of all these transformations, Beck argues, has been a fundamental change in notions of self. Dovetailing with other processes of late modernity, most notably those associated with globalization, risk proliferation intensifies expectations regarding self-conduct. The combined force of risk and globalization corrodes traditional, communal, and regional solidarities; erstwhile bonds of class, family, and nation are weakened. People are expected to become more *reflexive*, more self-assessing of how they should live and how they should rationally avoid, if not control, risk.

Risk Society in China?

In what ways does risk society theory resonate with transformations under way in China's sociopolitical landscape? More specifically, how might a risk society framework help us understand the quickly changing and highly variable lifeworlds of Chinese citizens today?

With little effort, one could say that the trappings of risk society have been increasingly at play in many parts of China, especially urban landscapes.[9] As part of its expanding embrace of neoliberal economics, the party-state has withdrawn from much of its earlier Maoist commitment to social provision, thereby heightening many people's sense of vulnerability. Various processes, what numerous China studies scholars have referred to as globalization, have been reconfiguring features of governmental control, raising the expectation that individuals will be more self-regulating in areas such as job creation, education, and health management. Actuarial products have become a major growth industry in cities in recent years, with a wide variety of insurance, lottery tickets, and home loan programs being heavily marketed. Large segments of China's swelling urban populace complain that aspects of everyday life are becoming increasingly unanchored from previously well-understood ethical and social principles and that community and family ties are not as dependable as they once were.

Mass media in post-Mao China likewise seem to follow, if not fuel, trends highlighted by risk society theorists. After two decades of relatively tranquillizing news reporting, more recent years have witnessed a growing stream of sensationalist accounts (not only about murder, mayhem, and sudden reversals of fortune, but also about environmental catastrophes, traffic accidents, and air pollution) flowing from both older (print, TV, radio) and newer (the Internet, text messaging) forms of media. These, together with DVD/VCDs, billboards, and hand-distributed advertisements, are awash in messages about lifestyle diversification and conflicting expert advice on how to manage risks, which are often represented as wrought by modernization. These include everything from marital infidelity to food toxins, crime, market fluctuations, consumer fraud, and medical charlatanism. City bookstores today, including the "New China" outlets, are creating ever more shelf space for newly demarcated sections on self-help, career advancement, health improvement, popular psychology, and connoisseurship. China's advertising industry is growing at a record pace; in forums such as city newspapers, much of this growth is being fueled by health care marketing to individual consumers.

Public health seems to resonate with risk society precepts in other ways. People across many segments of urban China today hear and fret about new communicable diseases, attributing their presence to processes often associated with globalization and modernization. They lament that such diseases are emblematic of worrisome erosions of state health care financing and the consequent necessity for most families today to bear the burden of nearly all their own medical expenses. Community members, public health officials, and producers of mass media are not just becoming more vocal about contagion and cost, however. They are also expressing concern about how to manage what they view as being ineluctable modern health threats such as chronic diseases (for example, hypertension and diabetes), counterfeit drugs, tainted blood supplies, agricultural toxins, and carcinogens.

Risky Theory

Between October 2003 and August 2006, I lived in Kunming conducting fieldwork and archival research on smoking and tobacco control for a total of fourteen months. This research affirmed that, while risk society theory may hold promise for making sense of sweeping changes ongoing in China or elsewhere, one must be quite cautious in applying such theory, always questioning its relationship to long-term political-economic and cultural specificities.[10]

Close attention to risk society theory's notions of first and second modernity, for example, could easily lead one to assume that warnings about smoking-related harm and interventions to reduce tobacco consumption are new phenomena for China. That is clearly not the case. Health warnings against tobacco in written Chinese well precede any declarations by the World Health Organization or, for that matter, any other institution emblematic of our modern epoch. Although well into the twentieth century many a medical expert in China and elsewhere regularly trumpeted tobacco's medicinal elements, some Chinese experts as early as the fourteenth century were issuing health warnings.[11] For instance, the authors of the Ming Dynasty canon of herbal medicine, *Shiliao Bencao*, admonished that smoking tobacco should be avoided because it "consumes the blood and decreases life years."[12] Chinese experts were also warning by the eighteenth century of potentially harmful concentrations of yang elements in tobacco, and evidence suggests that those warnings influenced usage patterns, especially among women.[13] Government authorities in the late-imperial epoch also intermittently tried to reduce the public's exposure to tobacco, sometimes by radical fiat. The last emperor of the Ming Dynasty, Chong Zhen (1627–1644), issued one of the most profound anti-tobacco edicts that has ever appeared anywhere, one that came with the threat of decapitation to those who ignored it. Albeit to little effect, Chong issued an outright ban on tobacco. His rationale was that smoking greatly harmed youth.[14]

Thus when one looks at issues of tobacco regulation from a long-term historical perspective, threads of continuity with the present are plainly visible. Nevertheless, one cannot overlook the fact that circumstances have changed dramatically for tobacco-control in China since the late-imperial period, especially during the last twenty years. Efforts to educate a public regarding scientific findings on diseases that are induced by tobacco smoking and to regulate multiple aspects of tobacco are now both present and expanding areas of practice in China. What has caused this recent transformation? Clearly, of great importance have been processes of empirical inquiry and globalization (notably the ongoing growth of international biopolitics and the proliferation of information-delivery media).

Still, inasmuch as such processes have been quite significant in the rising stature of tobacco control in China over recent years, what we have been witnessing is certainly not the story of a shrinking state, as strict application of risk society theory might suggest. This may not be immediately apparent to some observers, in part because many members of the international media and public health community have bemoaned the inadequate efforts of the post-Mao state and other entities to stem cigarette consumption. Be that as it may, when one examines closely what has actually been done and how much of the knowledge that has been produced in the anti-tobacco field has come about in recent years, it is patently clear that China's party-state has been pivotal. More to the point, the party-state has been the central node through which anti-tobacco efforts nationwide have been promoted, shaped, and coordinated, including the proliferation of mass media messages.

When analyzing current anti-tobacco efforts in China, however, one must be vigilant not to swing too far toward a state-centric model, particularly one that depicts the state as a monolith. For it is clear that the party-state has not been acting alone when it comes to anti-tobacco efforts, nor has it been working as a unified entity. With tobacco, as with so many other administrative areas, the party-state today has been working as a multilevel, porous, highly diversified apparatus, one that contains innumerable internal contradictions. And perhaps nowhere has the notion of the party-state as an organization riddled by contradiction been more apparent than with tobacco. At the same time that the party-state has been the central node for managing anti-tobacco efforts in recent years, it has also been the central node for developing and managing China's tobacco market. In spite of the fact that many economic sectors in China have been significantly influenced by processes of privatization, the production, marketing, and distribution of tobacco have remained under the watchful control of China's government leaders. One reason why control of the tobacco sector has been so much slower to experience market reform is no doubt that the industry has been such a cash cow for taxation. Most years since the mid-1990s, tobacco has been the top contributor to China's tax coffers by industry. In 2006 alone, tobacco taxes nationwide totaled more than $36 billion.[15]

Listening to Smokers

How are we to make sense of all this activity in terms of the lives of cigarette smokers? At present, how are these contradictory forces being expressed through and shaped by local forms of experience? One way to begin plumbing this terrain is by listening to some of the most significant consumers of tobacco in China today, that is, urban men.

I have in recent years spent a good deal of time talking to men in Kunming about smoking.[16] In my first few months of research during fall 2003, something that caught me by surprise was the sizable number of men of various socioeconomic backgrounds who professed to have experienced personal struggles with cigarette smoking. These struggles take a variety of forms, including efforts to avoid starting smoking, to reduce the number of cigarettes smoked, or to initiate or maintain a quit.

Such struggles were surprising for several reasons. First, because cigarettes have been such a significant part of male social and economic life in post-Mao China,[17] possibly nowhere more so than in Kunming, I assumed that most men

I would meet while conducting fieldwork in 2003 would be uninterested in avoiding or giving up cigarettes. Second, during a previous visit to Kunming, a relatively brief stay in the summer of 2000, the vast majority of men whom I met not only smoked but also expressed little desire to stop.

Because of the dearth of longitudinal data on the topic in Kunming, I have no way of assessing if there is indeed rising sentiment among its residents to avoid cigarettes. What is clear, and what I have found particularly intriguing, is that many men who have paused to describe for me their personal struggles over cigarettes have used language similar to that of Kan Libo, a thirty-seven-year-old Kunming taxi driver:

> I've smoked for eighteen years now. I started when I left school and began to work. It was fun at first, just something I played with. Everyone did it. It was about being manly, being a real man [*nanzihan*], and it seemed important to success at work. What's the [Chinese] phrase? "Men who don't smoke will work in vain to ascend to top of the world." I still like smoking. I like opening a new pack of cigarettes, exchanging them with [male] friends. I like that smoking helps me get through the tedium of work. And I like that I'm making enough money now to buy good brands.
>
> But I've also tried to quit several times, each time to no avail. My willpower just isn't strong enough. Cigarettes are like so many other things these days; they're easy to buy, but better to avoid. It's all a matter of willpower [*yili*]. I'd like to be free of cigarettes, but I'm just not strong enough. Those who can do it, I respect them a lot. They've got willpower, and that means they're strong and have cultural quality [*wenhua suzhi*].

Kan's monologue, like others I have heard from men in Kunming, strikes me as less the articulation of a rational choice-making figure fashioning his lifestyle than that of a man confronting a sense of personal weakness and working through fraught issues of identity. Kan's is a distressed language of failed self-management and desire regulation in the face of immense demands made by an addictive, pleasurable, and common form of consumption. His is also the distressed language of place, distinction, and status, in particular of membership in either a modern and civilized urbanism *or* a socially and politically salubrious world of masculinity.

To what social practices should we look in order to understand how this fraught form of existence (which seems to echo Kunming's and the party-state's contradictory relationship with tobacco) is being informed?

Risk society theory would lead us to believe that the mass media, particularly in the communication of expert knowledge, is key. And nothing would seem to fit Beck's argument more than publicly disseminated forms of expert knowledge falling under the rubric of self-help.

Self-Regulation

A trademark text for smoking cessation in many parts of the world is the self-help quitting manual. A small number of such manuals have recently been published in China and posted on Chinese Web sites. After five months in Kunming, I finally found my first print copy, high on the upper floors of a bookstore.

This manual is worth our consideration not just because it startlingly reflects ways that tobacco-control media have been framed by and are framing the notion of the angst-filled urban man but also because of how it illustrates a specific limitation of risk society theory.

With a significant nod toward the humorous, the manual outlines the tumult for men caused by both smoking and trying to quit, framing the former at times in terms of male erectile dysfunction and the latter in terms of nicotine withdrawal. It also clearly associates these two sources of tumult with a third cause, that of becoming more engaged with, if not in control of, the tribulations of modern urban life. To grasp this third feature, one needs to consider the unique format in which the manual is printed. The book is actually an anthology of two manuals, both translated from British publications. One manual begins on one of the book's covers, the second on the other cover. Moving inward from each side, the two manuals end in the middle of the volume. One manual is titled *Stopping Smoking: A Survival Guide*; the other is titled *The Office: A Survival Guide*.[18]

I have shown this self-help anthology to dozens of Yunnan smokers. After a good deal of laughter about the cartoons, most expressed dismay. The comments of Xu Bo, one of my Kunming neighbors, seem particularly poignant:

> This manual is great for a laugh. But how does it really help me quit cigarettes? It seems like it gives more advice on how to become a stronger and more civilized man. What I get from this book is that to enjoy sex more, I need to quit, and to quit, I need to depend on my individual will [*geren de yili*]. But you know what? I'm sad to say, my willpower probably isn't strong enough. I wish it was. But it's not. I've tried to quit before. I just get irritable. And then I start again. That leaves me feeling angry and even more uncertain of what to make of all these messages that smoking is bad for me and that I'd be a better person if I didn't smoke.

While one might say that this narrative betrays a growing sense of reflexivity in Xu's life, as Beck would predict, it certainly does not betray rational choice in action, rational choice working to help someone produce his own biography, rational choice acting to accommodate risk. Instead it comes across as a narrative about troubled manhood, expressed in terms of flawed competency and failed self-management.

This returns us to a significant problem for the application of risk society theory, or for that matter any other decontextualized, rational choice–oriented

Figure 4. Covers of two texts, *Stopping Smoking: A Survival Guide* and *The Office: A Survival Guide*. Credit: Baxendale, Martin, 2003. *Bangong Shi Shengcun Zhinan/Jieyan Shengcun Zhinan* [Office: A Survival Guide/Stopping Smoking: A Survival Guide] (Beijing: Yukong Press).

approach, to the terrain of tobacco control.[19] Decisions about if, when, and where to smoke cigarettes involve far more than rational choice, or at least they do in much of China.

To be sure, tobacco companies in the PRC, as elsewhere, have been striving to frame whether or not people smoke today as an issue of individual choice and freedom. I was provided that narrative quite matter-of-factly during a brief conversation with one of the top managers of Yunnan's largest tobacco company: "People should have the right to choose whether or not to smoke. That's a basic freedom. If I want to keep smoking, or if I want to quit, that's my decision."

Not only are cigarettes intensely addictive, however, but also in a social landscape like China's, there remains enormous pressure for people, particularly men, to smoke. Again, as Kan Libo and many others like to quip, *nanren buchouyan baizaishi shangding* (Men who don't smoke will work in vain to ascend to top of the world). Room for rational choice is further eroded by the fact that few effective smoking cessation drugs are sold in China. Briefly in the 1990s one of the most efficacious drug treatments, nicotine replacement therapy (NRT), was sold in various forms at exorbitant prices by its patent holder, GlaxoSmithKline Pharmaceutical. A few enterprising Beijing-based drug companies are now in the early stages of manufacturing NRT as well as bupropion, taking advantage of expirations in GlaxoSmithKline's patents, but so far the distribution of the medications is limited, particularly beyond the nation's capital.

Against this sociopolitical and pharmacological backdrop, it seems less analytically productive to examine public media pertaining to smoking for how they create the effect of a rational choice to avoid cigarettes. Instead a more valuable tack is to examine how and why, in dialogue with local forms of power, such media come to be produced and how they promote other effects at the level of subjectivity.

In what follows I examine two additional forms of tobacco-related media that are far more visible in Kunming than quitting manuals, and I explore how the local histories of these media relate to the production of distinctive and indeed problematic effects for Kunming men. Because of the state's considerable role in shaping these media, and in light of the analytical limitations I have outlined, my analysis taps a different line of scholarship from Beck's, that of governmentality.[20] This line is useful because it directs us to examine risk less in terms of a rational actor model and more in terms of the multiple ways that state and non-state practices, including media production, problematize people's lives, their forms of conduct, and their selves.[21] It is useful because it draws our attention to how, owing to multiple state and non-state forces, "the relation between the *forms of truth* by which we have come to know ourselves and the *forms of practice* by which we seek to shape the conduct of ourselves and others" may be influenced by media.[22] This is especially important in the context of contemporary China, where, in close dialogue with forces of the market and globalization, mass media are so often filtered through and generated by government agencies.

In the remaining pages of this chapter, much of my focus is on how a specific state office's involvement with tobacco control and mass media has been helping to generate what Mitchell Dean would call a "critical ontology of self."[23] In particular, I show that this office's management of two forms of media with regard to cigarette smoking has been especially significant in reconfiguring the understandings and experiences of the Chinese smoker in terms of a problematic embodiment, one centered on the shortcomings of cosmopolitanism, modernity, and masculinity.

Signs and More Signs

The first of the two forms of media to be discussed here is highly proscriptive. It is the most overt type of anti-tobacco symbolism found across Kunming: the slogan printed in bright colors and bonded to the wall behind the young couple in the Green Lake teahouse, the message on cellophane affixed with glue to the inside of Kan Libo's taxi. "No Smoking" signs are an increasingly prevalent sight in Kunming. Their presence stems in large part from one state institution. This is the Kunming Patriotic Health Office (KPHO). An arm of Kunming's Public Health Bureau, the KPHO has approximately a dozen employees and has been the city's representative to the larger national Patriotic Health System, which is run under the auspices the Ministry of Health.

In 1985, in response to directives from Beijing, the KPHO began distributing "No Smoking" signage, initially on mimeograph paper. The scope of the distribution was quite narrow and indeed ephemeral, since the paper decomposed quickly. All this changed in the late 1990s, when the Kunming government hosted the 1999 International Horticultural Exposition, the city's largest and most important international event to date. This exposition was a consummately urban phenomenon. The Expo was informed by and expressed a spate of transnational discourses, aesthetics, and practices of urbanism. It was designed to showcase Kunming as a modern, sanitary, cultured international metropolis, open for business and boldly progressing into the twenty-first century. It was also designed to showcase Kunming residents as progressive and sophisticated urbanites.

Toward both ends, in anticipation of the Expo, the KPHO applied to the city finance bureau for funds to cover a significant upgrade in "No Smoking" signage. Since receiving those and subsequent funds, the KPHO has produced signs in burnished brass, with the hope that they would be more durable and far more welcomed by target destinations as objects of worldly sophistication and cultural quality (*wenhua suzhi*). Also, in coordination with the Horticultural Exposition, the KPHO began issuing "No Smoking" stickers to taxi companies, and conducting intermittent checks to ensure that they received placement in prominent positions, specifically on the Plexiglas dividing the driver from the rear passenger compartment.

The choice to target taxis is an interesting one to consider in terms of men's identity formation. A profession that across the PRC is predominantly male, taxi driving is closely tied to China's longstanding androcentric gendering of public space and ongoing engagement with both modernist patriarchal ideas about mobility and authority creation.[24] In the spring of 2004 I heard the following from one taxi driver about the effects he has felt since his profession was selected as a governmental target for tobacco control:

> Since these stickers started going up in taxis, Kunming police have become very strict about drivers smoking, especially when we have passengers. I've been pulled over twice and fined. As a consequence, my wife has been pushing me to let her drive [our taxi] more during the day. She doesn't smoke, so the new laws are not such a problem for her. I agree that Kunming needs to become more civilized, but it's so frustrating that I'm not allowed to smoke. I need cigarettes to make it through my workday. Driving a cab is stressful and exhausting. Not being able to smoke only makes my work harder. Also, I'm in this little space all day with passengers who are always smoking, and the police don't care about them. Am I to tell them not to smoke? That'd be rude, and it'd hurt my income.

The second form of media to be discussed—the cigarette billboard—is far more visible across Kunming than "No Smoking" signs. Whether driving a cab or involved in other pursuits, most citizens see cigarette billboards innumerable times each day. These large ads appear in vivid colors atop big buildings, blazoned along sky bridges at major intersections, as a backdrop to bus stops, and peppered around innumerable other city sites. In smaller allied formats, less under the supervision of the KPHO, cigarette advertising can be seen in magazines, on television and Web sites, and at times on ephemera such as plastic bags, lighters, and ticket stubs. In Kunming, all such advertising usually promotes Yunnan's major cigarette brands, including names such as Yunyan, Honghe, Hongtashan, Xiaoxiongmao, Yuxi, Fu, and Ashima.

How did the KPHO become involved in the management of cigarette billboards? How have these billboards been communicating messages about tobacco control? And what do they have to do with the formation of a conflicted and decidedly urban ethos? The KPHO has been drawn into shaping tobacco billboards by two regulatory regimes. The first began to develop in the 1990s largely as a consequence of pressure put on the Chinese leadership by various international organizations. Owing to that pressure, an increasing number of directives have been created by central government branches which restrict the form and content of tobacco advertising nationwide. The earliest directives prohibited tobacco advertisements from showing people actively smoking, displaying cigarettes, and communicating overt messages about cigarettes. They also required that the words "Smoking Harms Health" appear on all ads. Since the beginning of this regulatory process, the burden of ensuring that these directives are enforced has been largely shouldered by China's network of Patriotic Health offices.

I visited Kunming for one month in the summer of 2000 and again in October 2003. The transformation in tobacco billboards during that three-year period was patently clear. Gone were many of the billboards I had seen earlier, including most of the meter-long packs of cigarettes that used to hang every 15 meters along many of Kunming's major roads. Filling some of the gaps left by these earlier forms of tobacco advertising was a spectrum of tobacco signage heavily focused on brand identification and much more influenced by graphic art techniques. For instance, the manufacturers of Yunyan and Fu (Good Fortune) were now simply displaying their names, elegantly laid out in subtle yet vivid graphics. Other billboards had tapped a decidedly hypermasculine trope. The previously staid Honghe billboards were now replaced by ones depicting a group of digitally enhanced bulls charging across an open field or a close-up image of a Formula One racing car. Hongtashan was in the early stages of launching a new billboard campaign showing rugged expedition mountaineers, ice axes in hand, scaling snow-covered peaks.

Not only had the form and content of tobacco billboards changed during this period, but so too had their number. Moving around the city when I returned in 2003, I found myself confronted by far fewer large cigarette ads. This thinning of billboards caught me by surprise. I was well aware of the new regulations flowing forth from Beijing covering tobacco advertising. I had read about the regulations in the United States. Still, little did I expect the numbers of billboards to decline dramatically, especially not in China's tobacco kingdom. It is hard to overstate the political-economic weight that Yunnan's tobacco corporations wield in the provincial capital, Kunming. In recent years tobacco has not just been the largest industrial sector in Yunnan; it has been responsible for approximately 70 percent of the province's tax revenues.

Keeping Clean, Being Urban

As it turns out, the obvious transformation in Kunming's tobacco billboards owes as much to overt attempts by Beijing and global organizations to curtail tobacco advertising as it does to an altogether distinct regulatory regime, one informed by discourses about risk and, even more, modern citizenship. Through this regime, the central government is prodding participating cities to become more modern and well regulated, and it is prodding those cities' body politic, the local population, to embrace lifeways that are less risky and, more to the point, reputedly clean and advanced.

This regime is called the National Clean City Program (Guojia Weisheng Chengshi Biaozhun). The National Clean City Program (NCCP) is a standardization and certification mechanism. Its criteria, some of which are present in previously promulgated PRC codes and regulations, are a kind of smorgasbord of sanitary and urban planning standards. Like tobacco advertising legislation, the NCCP has been closely tied to the Patriotic Health System. In the 1990s it was developed by the system's Beijing headquarters, and since then the task of implementing it has rested on the shoulders of the system's local offices.

There is something particularly interesting, indeed quixotic, about Kunming's involvement in the NCCP. From the outset, Kunming's leaders have known that the city would likely never be certified as a Clean City, since Kunming would never meet all of the program's standards. Stated another way, since 1999, when the national Clean City apparatus was launched, Kunming has been actively pursuing an administrative course of planned failure. The main glitch is a clause found at the end of Article 2, Section 6, of the "National Clean City Criteria." That article begins by stating that candidate cities must comply with supraordinate rules covering tobacco control work, including rules about creating smoke-free public spaces. It then goes on to state that participating municipalities must also establish tobacco-advertisement-free city districts.[25]

In April 2004 I discussed this program with a senior staff member of the Kunming Patriotic Health Office. We talked for several hours. He was dressed neatly, sporting an energetic demeanor as well as the distinctive smell of cigarette smoke on his breath. He explained the logic undergirding how and why Kunming has participated in the Clean City program:

> Kunming had little choice but to join the program. To be a modern city, one attractive to foreign investment, Kunming has to become cleaner. So, even though they knew we'd probably never get certified, our city leaders figured that joining the program would be good for Kunming. We'd be showing respect to the central government, and it would make us a more modern city. . . .
>
> From the start it was clear we probably couldn't fulfill all the tobacco-control aspects of the program. Distributing No Smoking signs, no problem. We've done it for years. The city's leaders are okay with that. No Smoking signs in public spaces—all modern cities have that, right? But tobacco-advertisement-free zones? We could anger lots of important people if we tried that. . . . So my office has decided to take a different tack in implementing the Clean City program. We've focused on existing tobacco billboards. We've pressed hard to get tobacco companies and their ad agencies to follow the rules about content, and we've pressed them to reduce the total number of billboards in Kunming.

It hasn't been easy. We've had to push every step of the way. Most of our own government officials are smokers. So at times we've had to make threats that we'd go to the press or that we'd put up anti-tobacco billboards. But slowly, everyone has come along. They've come to understand that if we want to have a modern city, and be able to compete for investment with cities like Beijing and Shanghai, we've got to make changes. The public image that so many people in Kunming love cigarettes has got to change. . . .

After his trip to Paris in 2002, our office's director started to press hard for the big ads here to be more artistic. He argued with everyone that, if these ads were more artistic, like what he saw in Paris, like what Honghe is now producing, fewer ads could serve the tobacco companies' goals, even ads without images of cigarettes.

The outcome has been positive; we've got fewer billboards in the city, we're following the rules more closely, and Kunming is looking more modern and civilized.

Although we can decry the fact that this interview betrays the egregious extent to which tobacco company interests have been diluting the strength of tobacco control in Kunming, I find the interview far more interesting for what it tells us about the broader workings of tobacco governmentality in China over recent years. First, it lays bare the significant role that mass media have played within state decision making regarding tobacco. Second, it displays that struggles are under way within regional governments over how best to handle tobacco in terms of internal and external economic pressures. How much should Kunming pursue external investment? How much should it protect its current tobacco revenues? Can it do both? Third, the interview affirms that cross-cutting pressures having to do with the creation of a "wealthy" yet "civilized" urban populace have been at once confounding and fueling officials' regulatory efforts to manage Kunming's largely cigarette-addicted male citizenry. And finally, it indicates that, in much the same way that many Chinese men are increasingly struggling to break their addiction to cigarettes but often not succeeding, Kunming's leaders are increasingly compelled to struggle over their polity's dependence on tobacco money, and with a similar lack of success.

To highlight these multivalent struggles further and once again give voice to the emergent "ontology of self" that I am trying to outline here, consider the words of Yang Ru, the father of one of my daughter's Kunming nursery school classmates. This is what Yang had to say when I brought up the topic of tobacco billboards:

I look at those big ads and I see how much this city is struggling with tobacco. The ads have all changed so much lately. There are fewer around Kunming, and they're all so much more beautiful. Why the change? Because tobacco is bad, because it's backward. It says it right there along the side of each ad, tobacco is bad for you. But how can

Kunming quit [*jieyan*]? This city is addicted to tobacco money. We need cigarettes to become modern. But cigarettes are so backward. What to do? No one knows. . . .

Still, I'm committed to trying to quit. Lately I often quit for a while, but rarely does it last very long. It's frustrating. Sometimes it gives me such a headache. That's okay . . . at least I try, and I'll keep trying. One has to eat a little bitterness [*chi ku*] once in a while. As frustrated as it makes me, it's important to keep trying. I need to keep trying for my family, but also for me, to prove to myself that I've got the willpower to stay away from cigarettes, even if only for a little time each month.

• • •

When I describe statements like this to public health colleagues inside and outside China, a common response I hear is a lament that is doubly remedial. Many a colleague complains that China has much to redress before becoming fully modern, and that in order to curtail smoking rates there, more information about the hazards of tobacco needs to be disseminated to the general public.

Inasmuch as dissemination of risk information can aid smoking cessation efforts, those who allocate health promotion resources in China should also consider several points highlighted in this chapter. First, there are people who are already striving to quit smoking in China. Even in a highly pro-tobacco city such as Kunming, a desire to quit can be found among many long-term male smokers. Second, this interest in quitting is being fueled by a distinct and powerful blend of regulatory impulses visible within mass media production. For many male smokers, what has been most pivotal in driving their interest to quit has been less a self/societal mandate to evade the risks of disease and improve life expectancy and more a potent normalizing urge to fend off backwardness and become modern. Third, because most people who are addicted to tobacco in China have little access to effective smoking cessation tools and smoke-free environments, the blend of regulatory impulses that they are facing leaves growing numbers of them wanting to quit yet feeling distraught that they are unable to do so.

In light of this situation, it seems that public health personnel interested in curtailing smoking-related suffering in China must consider acting not just remedially but nimbly. Rather than trying simply to cultivate citizens more fully versed in the details of tobacco-related risk, with the aim of creating "rational" decisions against, it might be equally if not more effective (1) to understand better the unique blend of normalizing impulses already militating against tobacco in China, and (2) to leverage those impulses shrewdly, integrating them with new efforts now nascent within the PRC to provide greater access to well-proven smoking cessation techniques (for example, quitting clinics, drug therapies, socioculturally matched manuals, hotline-based counseling), and smoke-free workplaces.

There is no time for laments, as any visit to a PRC hospital today makes patently clear. Tobacco-related suffering is already ravaging the country, and its arresting effects are growing daily. Men and women in China are increasingly aware of this suffering. And more and more would welcome better tools and policies to help them avoid cigarettes.

9. Wild Consumption

Relocating Responsibilities in the Time of SARS

Mei Zhan

At the height of the outbreak of Severe Acute Respiratory Syndrome (SARS) in spring 2003, the civet cat, a ferret-like animal, became an overnight international media sensation. Eaten as a delicacy in southern China, the civet cat was identified as potentially the original animal host of the SARS virus. In response to laboratory developments and to mounting international criticisms of its "irresponsible" attitude toward SARS, the Chinese government quickly implemented a comprehensive ban on marketing and consuming "wild animals." This emergency intervention was aimed at curbing urban citizens' unhealthy appetites for such animals, thereby nudging them away from seemingly senseless and irresponsible choices in consumption.

The civet cat, however, was not the only "star" of the SARS outbreak. Around the same time that civet cats and those who consume them came under intense scrutiny of various levels and branches of the Chinese government, Chinese and international media, and research scientists and medical professionals in and outside

I am indebted to Aihwa Ong and Li Zhang for their insightful comments and support which helped mold this chapter into its current shape. I am also very grateful for Ralph Litzinger's fabulous suggestions and encouragement. Leo Chavez, Susan Greenhalgh, Matthew Kohrman, Dorie Solinger, Lisa Rofel, and Sylvia Yanagisako offered valuable comments along the way.

China, another cluster of stars also burst onto the SARS stage: on May 11, 2003, the *STARS vs. SARS* telethon, the first television fund-raiser ever held in Shanghai, was simulcast in China and the United States. Organized by the Shanghai-born basketball star Yao Ming, the *STARS vs. SARS* telethon featured sports stars from China, Europe, and the United States, including Yao's colleagues from the National Basketball Association. The telethon invited private citizens as well as Chinese and foreign businesses to take responsibility in the battle against SARS through private donations. In particular, it intended to channel a large portion of the donation to better equip and protect medical professionals who were not only on the frontline of fighting SARS but also under public suspicion for being potential "contaminants." In doing so, the star-studded telethon crafted ambivalent narratives of "humanized" doctors that bore little resemblance to the images of self-sacrificing, invincible, superhuman doctors that used to dominate the socialist government's campaigns against infectious diseases and other medical crises.

I suggest that both events—linked through an emergency that was at once medical and sociopolitical—threw into sharp relief and even precipitated emergent middle-class discourses and practices in urban China. I approach my discussions of middle-class identity from two intersecting angles: the explosion of middle-class consumption, and the emerging middle-class consumer-subjects as bearers of privatized responsibilities. Writing against narratives of transition and transcendence, and highlighting the entanglements of Orientalist and "neoliberal" socialist and postsocialist imaginaries, I suggest that neither consumption nor privatization is a transparent or uniform process. Rather, in the discourses and practices of responsibilities during and after the SARS epidemic, the right to be "human" and the definition of an "individual"—not to mention the *proper* sort of individual—did not emerge as stable, self-explanatory points of references where social responsibilities could be easily relocated, but were themselves contested—sometimes very fiercely—in everyday life and across discrepant sites.

To do so, I first highlight the complexities and ambiguities of identity and subject formation through consumption. I explore consumption as eating and consumption as spending, while understanding both as visceral *and* discursive practices. In particular, I am interested in the proliferation of both bodies-that-consume and bodies-as-consumables as a means of critically examining entangled Orientalist and neoliberal discourses in and about China. I suggest that, first, rather than being emblematic of China's participation in global capitalism or its transition to ubiquitous neoliberalism driven by market rationality, consumption as a set of visceral and discursive practices at once refigures persistent Orientalist tropes and conjures up discrepant "neoliberal" imaginaries of market rationalities and consumer choices.

I am, therefore, interested not only in bodies at large but also, specifically, in both human and nonhuman bodies as "consumables."[1] Nevertheless, rather than assigning the consumables to "the world of goods" that shapes the consumer-subject within "the sphere of self,"[2] I mean to understand consumption as heterogeneous discourses and practices that problematize the assumption of the market as an unambiguous site for the production of choice-savvy and self-regulating individual consumer-subjects. I suggest that the bodily encounters and proliferating practices of consumption during and after the SARS outbreak provide occasions for the production of a set of contested hybrid identities and subjectivities. At stake in the production and representation of Chinese bodies of human, nonhuman, and superhuman sorts are not just imaginaries of China's past but also visions of cosmopolitan futures—futures that depend not so much on the transition to a new stage of consumption, market rationality, or globalism as on situated, contestatory discourses of cosmopolitan "humanity" and the places of various humans, nonhumans, and—as I will discuss—superhumans in it. Rather than focusing on how human beings become "individuated" consumers,[3] then, I am interested in the ways in which "human beings" as a category was opened up to intense contestation through practices of consumption; that is, I want to understand how, through consumption, we become or fail to become "human beings." In other words, this essay is concerned less with "market type" than with the actual articulations and practices of consumption.[4]

Second, I suggest that a set of discrepant cultural imaginaries also shaped translocal discourses of "human" action and responsibility during the course of the SARS epidemic. International and especially European-American media accused the Chinese government of not being a "team player" among the international community, and blamed the Chinese people for their exotic tastes and irresponsible patterns of consumption—especially their appetite for wild animals that were suspected of being the original hosts of the SARS virus. I contend that, in focusing exclusively on the Chinese party-state as the agent of (ir)responsibility and (in)action, and on the exotic tastes and culinary traditions of the Chinese as origins of SARS, these popular discourses of responsibility failed to account for the complex discourses and practices of particular bodies, subjectivities, and responsibilities that took center stage during the course of the SARS epidemic—especially the emergence of middle-class discourses and practices in urban China. In contrast, I suggest that the SARS outbreak pushed aspiring cosmopolitan, urban middle-class individuals into the foreground as an important and yet ambiguous locus for responsibility and human action. It was *their* choice of consumption that came under intense scrutiny from the state and mass media in and outside China, and it was *they* who, from the standpoint of the state and mass media, needed to be molded into savvy consumers capable of bearing privatized social responsibility. I in no way suggest here that the state has disappeared in China; rather, I want to understand the ways in which the Chinese state is being transformed through discursive forms of power and shifting discourses of responsibility. To explore further the ambivalences within consumption and what counts as responsible consumption, I now turn to the story of a banquet and the unruly human and nonhuman bodies it brought to the table.

Consuming the "Wild" and Wild Consumption

My research on SARS was itself the result of interrupted circulations and unexpected encounters. I had planned for a field trip to Shanghai in summer 2003 to conduct follow-up research on traditional Chinese medicine. My aspirations for transnational travel, however, were thwarted by something else's travel: the Severe Acute Respiratory Syndrome that first broke out in mainland China and Hong Kong in spring 2003 and spread to thirty countries on all continents except for Antarctica within a few months. I had no option but to postpone my trip until late August—after the World Health Organization (WHO) and the U.S. State Department lifted their cautions against traveling to China.

Upon my arrival in Shanghai, I was overwhelmed by the post-SARS "feeding frenzy," whereby, in the words of my friends in Shanghai, people felt as if they had just been released from prison and returned to consumption with a vengeance. Tourism again became a favorite weekend and holiday activity after the government lifted the ban on interregional traveling, once empty shopping malls were filled with bustling crowds scouring the shops for commodities to purchase, and restaurants were busy making up for the business lost during the SARS outbreak. I also found that SARS, still fresh in people's memories, was a recurring theme in my conversations with medical professionals, as well as other friends and acquaintances who had lived through the epidemic. Even the most mundane daily activities somehow turned into a conversation about SARS. While we were passing by a tollbooth on the highway leading to a nearby town, the driver of my car pointed out to me a small house about 200 meters away, telling me that, until a month ago, it had been used as a temporary quarantine station to check the body temperature of everybody who had to come into or go out of Shanghai on business trips, few as travelers were during those days. Acutely aware of the lingering presence of SARS throughout the fabric of life, and fascinated by the ways in which the SARS epidemic seemed to have sharpened people's appetites for consumption, I felt compelled to follow up with more research on the events surrounding SARS.[5]

A few days after my arrival in Shanghai in August 2003, I joined some friends from high school for a sumptuous dinner at a recently opened restaurant. It was located in the Hongqiao area, which used to be a suburb but is now an affluent and bustling commercial area. The restaurant was on the third floor of a commercial high-rise; in recent years an increasing number of new, upscale restaurants have been set up within commercial complexes such as shopping malls, rather than stand-alone buildings. We took an elevator to reach the restaurant.

The interior of the elevator was spotless. The carpet read "Monday," indicating that it was changed daily. Next to the pushbuttons on the wall was a large sign that read "Has Been Disinfected Today"—a new practice in Shanghai's public buildings beginning during the SARS epidemic.

At the entrance of the restaurant, we were greeted by a wall-to-wall fish tank containing a stunning school of red tropical fish, which were intended for viewing rather than culinary pleasure. There were so many fish that they effectively formed a fluid red screen shielding the interior of the restaurant from the visitors. Once the beautiful *qipao*-clad hostess conducted us around the fish tank, I found myself in a spacious "exhibition hall." In the middle was a large table, where vivid plastic replicas of key dishes were displayed, complete with price tags. A deli-style counter was set up on the left side of the hall, where various cold appetizers were showcased. The other two walls were lined with tanks that contained a wide variety of live fish, shellfish, crabs, and shrimp—most of which I had never seen before. Unlike the fish in the tank at the entrance, these were destined to be eaten. Taking notice of my awed expression, my friends told me that they had selected this restaurant because of its dazzling array of live freshwater and marine animals.

As we sat down to order, I noticed that there were no snake dishes on the menu. Although not a big fan of eating snake, I was nevertheless puzzled by its absence because snakes—fried, braised, or stewed—had been ubiquitous in Shanghai's restaurants during my visit in 1999.[6] My friends told me that snakes were no longer sold in restaurants because they could not be "farmed"—that is, humans cannot regulate the reproductive activities of snakes while keeping them in captivity—and were therefore listed among the "wild animals" that the Chinese central government banned as food during and after the SARS outbreak.

Snakes were not the only "wild animals" that disappeared from the dinner table because of SARS. Among competing explanations for the origin of SARS, the hypothesis of *zoonotic* (meaning "animal-borne") origin was most strongly favored by research scientists in and outside China and, furthermore, was the theory most widely spread through mass media, the Internet, and rumors.[7]

In late April 2003, at the height of the SARS outbreak, the Chinese government also came under mounting international criticism—especially from European and North American scientists and mass media—for its "lack of action" and "irresponsible attitude." Many North American and European scientists and media criticized the Chinese government for its "authoritarian" and "secretive" approach to the epidemic and urged more "democratic" ways of handling the crisis. They questioned whether China could become a responsible "team player" in the international community.[8] Others, by contrast, worried that government interventions in fighting SARS could halt China's progress toward democratization and bring it back under the communist style of state control.[9] Still others were so committed to the idea of a closed communist China that they seemed altogether oblivious to China's deep enmeshments in the world, or its transformations in the previous few decades. The April 26, 2003, issue of the *Economist*, for example, featured on its cover a portrait of Chairman Mao wearing a mask, and the lead article was titled "Can SARS Become China's Chernobyl?" The *Economist* was not alone in portraying a uniform, timeless, and isolated communist China on the verge of collapse because of its irresponsible handing of the SARS crisis.

In response, the Chinese Forestry Administration and the Chinese Industry and Commerce Administration announced a ban on the hunting, selling, purchase, transportation, import-export, and marketing of all "wild animals," with the exception of those necessary for scientific research. The term "wild animal," however, was both vague and all encompassing. Without any clear definition of which animals were considered "wild" and why, the "farmed tiger frog"—another delicacy and one of the best sellers at live animal markets—was singled out as the only "wild animal" exempt from the ban.[10] Moreover, although land animals—including most amphibians—were strictly banned, the status of freshwater and marine animals was less clear. Restaurants in Shanghai, for example, stopped serving "drunken seafood"—a method of preparation in which small, live freshwater or marine animals such as shrimps and clams are dumped into a pot of rice liquor and then eaten almost immediately. Whether an animal was "wild," it seems, also depended on whether it was consumed raw or cooked.

In May 2003 research scientists working on civet cats in Hong Kong and Shenzhen, Guangdong Province, isolated viruses similar to the human SARS virus and suggested that the civet cat was the likely animal host of the virus.[11] It is noteworthy that although some of these civet cats may have been captured, most had been commercially farmed. Almost all were destined to be eaten, at restaurants rather than at home. Nevertheless, the isolation of the civet cat as the animal host of the SARS virus did not ease the ban on—or lessen people's fears of—other "wild animals." It was only in August 2003, well after the last SARS patient was released from the hospital, that the ban was relaxed to exempt Chinese deer, African ostriches, turkeys, scorpions—a total of fifty-four assorted land animals. Most of the animals on the list were commercially farmed. Many were exotic or novel food items. The Chinese Forestry Administration explained that the rationale for its exemption was that the technologies for farming these animals were "mature" enough so that they could be domesticated and bred "for *commercial* purposes," even as the administration admitted that there was no guarantee of control of germs that could potentially jump from one species to another.[12]

The ambiguity of the term "wild animal" was also one of the topics at my dinner with my high school friends. We argued over which animals were "wild" and therefore banned—and whether the banning of "wild animals" indeed made much difference in dealing with SARS. Our discussion ended not in a consensus but with the arrival of our food, along with white towels soaked in disinfectant to clean our hands (only at the end of the meal did I find out that we were to pay for these towels, even though they were mandatory at restaurants in Shanghai). In spite of the absence of snake, our dinner did not suffer from any lack of exotic food. In addition to novel varieties of shrimp and shellfish, I had my first taste of sturgeon—commercially farmed and braised to perfection.

In subsequent weeks the topic of "wild animals" kept crawling back in various forms into my interviews with medical professionals in Shanghai, as well as my conversations with other friends, whether we were eating at restaurants, debating the origin of SARS, or talking about football. Even though the "wild animal" was at the center of everyday conversations and government regulations of SARS, the meaning of "wild" was by no means reductively "natural," nor could it be structurally defined in opposition to "domestic" or "farmed." I do not imply here that anything goes as far as the meaning of "wild animal" is concerned. To the contrary, I suggest that, through the act of banning certain animal foods and markets during the SARS outbreak, the "wild" was marked with a set of heterogeneous meanings specifically and intimately related to, if not produced by, human consumption—consumption in its visceral and discursive dimensions. The wildness of the civet cat came under scrutiny when research scientists, the Chinese government, and international media identified it as the likely animal host of the SARS virus and, at the same time, an item on the Chinese dinner table.

These human entanglements in the production of the "wild animal" suggest that what needs to be analyzed in understanding SARS is more than the physical body of the civet cat or the generic sequence of the SARS-like virus it carried. We also need to pay critical attention to the enmeshment of civet cats and other "wild" creatures deep within everyday life. In what follows, I argue that it was during a medical, social, and political crisis of potentially global scale that the "wild" took on contingent and contested forms through a variety of actions that were at once biological, political, legal, historical, social, transnational, and visceral. Elusive and heterogeneous, the "wild" emerged as a temporary point of convergence in discourses about SARS and, as I will show, at the same time resisted any identification as the readily accessible point of origin of the SARS epidemic.

Alternative Origins and Entangled Consumption

SARS was indeed a very bad disease for biomedicine. Between November 2002 and the end of the epidemic in June 2003, an estimated 8,422 people in over thirty countries were infected with various strains of the virus, and 916 died as a consequence.[13] Given that the 11 percent mortality rate of SARS is only slightly above that of influenza, however, SARS was nowhere near a plague, and the panic over SARS seems to have bordered on paranoia. This panic was compounded by the fact that, even as more and more people fell sick and died, biomedical science was late in coming up with an authoritative explanation or effective treatment. Scientists were not able to identify the virus as a novel coronavirus until April 2003,[14] five months after the appearance of the first clinical cases. Even now there are no effective treatments, definitive prognoses, or reliable preventive measures against a potential future outbreak.

The "inadequacy" of biomedicine was not the only factor that fueled the anxiety and paranoia over SARS.[15] It is noteworthy that speculation over the origin of SARS did not simply originate in the lab or in the Chinese government but had entangled roots in the repercussions of recent world events. The sudden explosion of media coverage of SARS in and especially outside China coincided not with the outbreak of the epidemic but with the U.S. invasion of Iraq at the end of March 2003. Although some earlier speculations in and outside China suggested a natural and nonhuman origin of SARS, others spoke of biological warfare: Was SARS a mysterious biological weapon? Rumors that SARS was a "foreign" biological weapon spread through Chinese Web sites; some even claimed that the novel and highly unusual virus was designed to target "Chinese" genes.[16] Debates about the origin of SARS continue today—for example, as to whether the virus jumped from animals to humans or the other way around—long after the story of the civet cat as the animal culprit prevailed in research communities and mass media.

Even as competing origin stories abounded, medical, sanitary, and everyday practice in China targeted multiple routes of transmission, especially respiratory transmission, which was emphasized by several different sources. In May 2003 the WHO released a conference report claiming that the major mode of transmission of SARS was respiratory, although the potential for infection by ingestion must also be considered. Medical professionals on the ground noted, too, that infection rates were much higher at high-tech locations such as hospitals with centralized ventilation systems.[17]

Although medical and everyday practices—such as wearing masks and frequent cleansing of surface areas with disinfectants including vinegar—worked against multiple and especially respiratory routes of transmission, it was the civet cat that became the most infamous creature in the origin stories of SARS. In what follows I focus on the one origin story that became ubiquitous and dominant in discourses of SARS—that of the civet cat and China's so-called wet markets.[18] Why, among all the competing origin stories and suspected routes of transmission, did the civet cat draw the most intense scrutiny from researchers and media in and especially outside China? Why does the civet cat, along with other "wild animals," continue to be the target of aggressive government regulation and media controversies even after the SARS outbreak? Why, while images of masked faces on magazine covers became symptomatic of the spread of SARS,[19] did scientific and popular discourses zero in on the practices of China's wild animal markets in their narratives of origin?

I suggest that underlying the fear of the civet cat was the assumption—

popularized by research scientists and mass media in and outside China—that it was only when humans came into physical contact with the wild animal that the virus jumped species and started a deadly epidemic. The story of the "zoonotic origin" of SARS got a boost not only from the identification of the SARS virus as a coronavirus similar to flu viruses but also from the speculation that the initial site of the outbreak was either Hong Kong or Guangdong Province in southern China, both famous for their bold appetites for exotic animal foods. Moreover, the first identified SARS patient was reportedly an animal handler who worked in the wild animal food markets of Guangdong Province.[20] The argument about the link between human appetites and the nonhuman origin of the virus was further consolidated by reports of the discovery of large quantities of SARS antibodies among animal dealers in Guangdong.[21] In May 2003 research scientists in Guangdong and Hong Kong identified the civet cat, a delicacy in southern China, as the original animal host of the SARS virus.[22] In the meantime, the same scientists pleaded for the immediate closing of wet markets in China and other Asian countries as a measure to stop SARS in its tracks and prevent future outbreaks. These pleas were quickly and widely publicized in scientific and medical journals as well as through mass media in and especially outside China. As discussed earlier, the Chinese government responded by banning the consumption of almost all wild land animals.

At play in the frenzy surrounding the "zoonotic origin" is the translocal scientific and media representation that the Chinese, in indulging their appetites for exotic "wild animals," transgressed proper barriers between human and animal, the domestic and the wild, culture and nature. In other words, the story of zoonotic origin did not blame nature itself for the SARS outbreak; what was wrong was the Chinese people's uncanny affinity for the nonhuman and the wild. This affinity was symbolized not only by the highly mutable virus that was crafty enough to move between Chinese bodies of both human and nonhuman sorts but also by the visceral act of consumption.

In fact, in both media coverage and scientific origin stories of SARS, the civet cat and the wet market in which it was sold were often conflated. European, North American, and many Chinese newspapers and Web sites were replete with narratives linking the "age-old tradition" of eating wild animals with SARS. These sensational reports portrayed the strange entanglements of human and animal bodies, and the deadly filthiness of such entanglements.[23] The following is a vivid description of wild animal markets in Guangdong by Reuters:

> Two little boys giggle as they play hide and seek among hundreds of filthy cages packed tight with civet cats, dogs, porcupines and squirrels. . . . Amid the stench of death and decay, traders of exotic animals—a culinary delight for many southern Chinese—haggle over prices with customers, occasionally turning their attention to their children, pinching their cheeks or tousling their hair. Narrow

passageways are strewn with animal dung, urine, entrails and grimy fodder. "What's there to be afraid of?" asked Mrs. Huang, carrying her three-month-old daughter on her back. "We have been working and living here for years and we have had no problems." A few steps away, men with iron pipes clubbed a dog unconscious and slit its throat. Others squatted around another dead dog, plucking it clean of hair with their bare fingers. Virologists believe that such markets in China and farms where people live in very close proximity to animals are fertile breeding grounds for disease and viruses.[24]

Littered with interspecies bodily entanglements, these voyeuristic images of the "local culinary tradition" were then contrasted with and condemned by the sanitized, authoritative voice of an abstract "virologist": Unnatural interspecies encounters breed disease and viruses. And the unnatural affinity with animals through eating, the stories go, lies in a Chinese way of life "that has existed for as long as anyone can remember."[25] As a logical consequence of this kind of reasoning, many scientists cautiously recommended the eradication of wet markets, while at the same time identifying Chinese people's wayward culinary taste as both a public health hazard *and* a deeply rooted cultural tradition that needed to be "respected."[26]

This accusatory ambivalence and voyeuristic curiosity toward visceral entanglements involving Chinese bodies of both human and nonhuman sorts underscores the viscerality of racialized Orientalist tropes that produce various exotic Others through their excessive pleasures and enjoyments. In the case of scientific and popular discourses of SARS, we witness the recurrence of a familiar narrative strategy that visceralizes the traditional and the uncanny as the origin of a culturally specific disease that—if not contained—threatens to destroy the globe. The civet cat, in particular, became a protagonist in the origin stories of SARS because it conjured up familiar Orientalist representations in which the wild and exotic character of Chinese bodies—of both human and nonhuman sorts—emerged out of visceral acts of consuming. Although these tropes are nothing new, I am fascinated, first, by their obsession with the viscerality of consumption, and second, by the effectiveness of the visceral in producing racialized bodies and identities. Moreover, I suggest that, while mass media and scientific representations constructed a visceralized "ancient" Chinese epicurean tradition as the "real origin" of the SARS outbreak, they also did so by locating narratives of excess squarely within the sphere of the market and mass consumption, which is not an emblem of "ancient Chinese culture" but a product of recent economic, social, and political transformations.[27] The market, rather than the site that invariably produces self-fashioned consumer-subjects, is already saturated with racialized bodies whose very humanity is at stake.

Doctors at the Edge

Civet cats, or rather those who consume them, were not the only ones whose place among human beings was cast into doubt in the story of SARS. In mainland China and Hong Kong, many of those who came down with SARS were doctors and nurses who worked at high-tech institutions such as the Prince of Wales Hospital in Hong Kong and the People's Hospital in Beijing, both of which remained quarantined for months during and even after the outbreak.[28] Some doctors and nurses who risked their lives fighting SARS declined to be interviewed on television; others agreed to be interviewed on the condition that the interview would not be conducted at their home and that their faces would be obscured so that friends and neighbors would not recognize them and decide to avoid them. Medical professionals became tragic heroes, potential victims, as well as sources of contamination.

In Shanghai, where there were only eight confirmed cases of SARS, "fever clinics" for anyone who had a temperature higher than 37.5° Celsius (99.5° Fahrenheit), and quarantine wards for potential SARS patients, were nevertheless set up in all major hospitals. A doctor who worked on one of these wards told me that, upon entering the quarantine ward, he did not know whether he would get out again. He explained:

> I volunteered for the squad [to treat potential SARS patients] in April, and stayed in the ward without going home for more than four weeks. The top floor of our hospital was quarantined for potential SARS patients. There were fifteen beds in there. We had no idea how many beds we would eventually need. At one end of the ward were the patients' beds, at the other the beds for doctors. There were three beds in between that were kept vacant. When I checked on my patients, I wore two protective suits, three pairs of disposable surgical shoes, three masks, and a pair of goggles. Even so, I knew that I was still exposed to air when I used the stethoscope. I tried to use it as infrequently as possible. Otherwise I just had to take the risk. Luckily none of the patients in the ward had SARS, although some turned out to have measles.
>
> It was such a relief to be home eventually. While I was inside [the hospital], I heard stories about taxi drivers refusing to take people coming out of the hospital. One of our nurses had to call us from her cell phone so that we could tell the driver that she did not have SARS. So it was just as well that I did not leave the hospital for four weeks.

This was a narrative of anxiety, uncertainty, and vulnerability—an edgy narrative, really—that formed a stark contrast with the former image of doctors as glorified, superhuman socialist heroes who sacrificed themselves for the collective good and who were literally invincible regardless of the difficulties they faced.[29] The disappearance of these superhuman doctors did not happen overnight. As noted by a number of anthropologists and other social scientists, in the 1950s and 1960s the rural poor—and eradicating infectious diseases afflicting them—were among the main focuses of socialist China's health care policies.[30] Indeed, government-dispatched proletariat doctors led the "people's war" against various epidemics. The Chinese government took on disease prevention as its responsibility and provided low-cost health care to almost its entire population. The WHO lauded the "China model" of health care, which became famous worldwide.

Since the economic reform of the 1980s and especially the comprehensive health care reform which began in the 1990s, however, health care in China has become rapidly privatized: health care has become a commodity, patients have become consumers, and hospitals find themselves having to transform themselves into successful profit-making enterprises. A 2004 study by Shaoguang Wang suggests that the large-scale commodification of health care has led to a widening gap between rural and urban areas and to increased class disparities. Market reform, according to Wang, actually resulted in the waste of medical resources, market inefficiency, and worsening health care coverage for the general public.[31]

Medical professionals bore the brunt of this drastic transformation, and their image suffered greatly. Having fallen from the pedestal of the socialist hero, they are now often viewed with suspicion as greedy moneygrubbers. On the one hand, during my fieldwork in Shanghai's hospitals at the end of the 1990s, I routinely encountered patients who complained about doctors trying to sell them expensive medication, asking for "red envelopes" (containing extra payment to the doctor), or refusing to perform necessary procedures when patients were not able to make a payment right away. Some of these stories were the result of conflicting policies at each hospital which were subject to constant change. On the other hand, the doctors I worked with complained constantly about being caught between having to make a living, or even preferring to become a successful entrepreneur, and sticking to their training as virtuous socialist doctors whose top priority was serving the people and saving lives.

Thus, even before the SARS crisis, medical professionals had ceased to be seen as superhuman heroes, and their image was in need of extensive repair. The SARS outbreak, then, was both a challenge and an opportunity to reinvent a new kind of doctor—a humanized doctor. And the short film *Going Home* did just that:

> *A row of brick houses of a distinctive 1930s Shanghainese style stands against the silhouette of skyscrapers. A grandmother enters the door with groceries in both hands. She announces, "I'm home!"* . . .
> "I'm home!" a grandfather calls out as he ascends the stairs of his house.

"I'm home!" a young man assures his lover as he steps off a bus. Both he and his lover have been wearing white surgical masks, and he removes his lover's mask to gaze at her lovely face.

"I'm home!" A little girl in school uniform runs through the schoolyard, down the streets of a beautiful neighborhood, and into a warmly lit upscale apartment building. Her father opens the spotless stained-glass door as she announces her arrival. She runs to the kitchen window, gets up on a small stool, looks out, and fixes her gaze expectantly on the alley outside. No one comes. The phone rings. She rushes over to pick it up and yells into the mouthpiece, "Mama!"

At the other end of the phone, in a hospital, the girl's mother, in doctor's uniform and with a surgical mask hanging from one ear, holds the phone with a gloved hand. The glass door behind her is painted in conspicuous red characters, "Quarantine."

The little girl rambles on excitedly about her grades at school, how she is learning to braid her own hair, and how her father burned the rice while he was cooking. . . . Her father, wearing an apron, hovers over her and begs her not to tell her mother about his blunder.

As she continues listening to her daughter, the mother is helped into a bodysuit, and then a pair of goggles. Finally she puts her mask back on. Her daughter asks: "Mama, when are you coming home? Dad and I will wait for you. . . ."

The woman murmurs longingly, "Soon, soon," as she prepares to step into the quarantine ward. Her bodily transformation from a mother to a doctor on duty complete, the mother/doctor disappears from the screen and is replaced by a deeply emotional voiceover: "Loved ones are expecting. The motherland is waiting."

Going Home was written by the novelist Wang Anyi and directed by Huang Shuqin. The actress Pan Hong played the role of the mother-doctor. All three were famous, enterprising Chinese women—and mothers. The film was aired on television on Mother's Day, May 11, 2003. Mother's Day, which has become increasingly popular in the United States as a consumer holiday celebrated with cards, flowers, presents, and family lunches or dinners at restaurants, is also enjoying rising popularity in urban China, and especially cosmopolitan centers such as Shanghai. Yet *Going Home* was not just about the celebration of universal motherhood or middle-class consumption and lifestyle. May 2003 was also the height of the SARS outbreak. *Going Home* was in fact aired as part of the *STARS vs. SARS* telethon.

In emphasizing the familial life and maternal sentiments of the doctor and highlighting both her professional courage and her bodily vulnerability, *Going Home* conjures a doctor who is a far cry from the invincible proletarian heroes whose images and stories used to dominate government campaigns against infectious diseases and other medical crises in socialist China. Whereas the socialist heroes were portrayed as larger-than-life superhumans whose chief goal in life was to sacrifice themselves in the cause of combating diseases that plagued the Chinese people, especially the rural poor, *Going Home*, in contrast, skillfully crafts a "humanized" doctor—not just any kind of human being, but an urban middle-class mother and professional. It does so by immersing the doctor in images and narratives of emergent middle-class lifestyles: shopping, upscale neighborhoods, a cozy middle-class family. Moreover, the doctor is also a human at the edge and under threat: she is not just a protector and a savior; she is necessary if others are to be protected, saved, and loved. She has become the individual bearer of responsibility in fighting SARS—her body weary from intense work and her spirits heavy under constant danger. More important, through the figure of the mother-doctor, *Going Home* and *STARS vs. SARS* invited other middle-class subjects to share the responsibilities of an emerging medical crisis through monetary donations, and in doing so, as I discuss in the next section, to become "human."

Relocating Responsibility

At 2 A.M. on May 11, 2003, in Irvine, California, I began watching the live Webcast of the telethon at the Chinese Web site www.sohu.com.[32] A few months later, in Shanghai, I watched it again on a video I obtained from the Great Sports Channel. The *STARS vs. SARS* telethon began with a montage of disaster footage in recent history from different parts of the world: the *Challenger* explosion, scenes of hunger and the AIDS epidemic in Africa, the flood of the Yangtze River in 1998, firefighters at the scene of the imploding World Trader Center, nurses helping the wounded (presumably during the First World War), crowds of people wearing masks from fear of SARS. . . . The montage was followed by screens that read, in both Chinese and English:

> We know for sure that
> The bonds of mankind strengthen in crises
> As dignity arises from disaster
>
> When everything has come to pass
> We look back and see
> What a great place we have attained
>
> The wise act with calm
> With love we can conquer fear

Rejecting origin stories of SARS that identify the epidemic with China and the Chinese, and narratives of excessive Chinese appetites and dangerous entanglements with animals, the opening scenes of *STARS vs. SARS* located the SARS epidemic squarely within other disasters suffered by "mankind." This strategic practice of location redefined and elevated SARS into a global disaster and crisis of humanity, and the fight against SARS became a human battle fought calmly and lovingly, especially by doctors, nurses, sports stars, and the general public in the person of TV viewers. Yao Ming himself reiterated this participatory discourse of the responsibilities of humankind. Appearing on the TV screen near the end of the telethon, Yao concluded that SARS was humanity's "common enemy."

In *STARS vs. SARS*, the "bonds of mankind" were not represented by any individuated human being. Yao Ming, the host of the telethon, was a successful international athlete and entrepreneur. Most of his guests, who appeared through live interviews or pretaped video footage, were also famous athletes and sports personalities familiar to the Chinese audience: Yao's colleagues at the NBA and the commissioner of the NBA, soccer stars from European clubs such as Real Madrid and AC Milan, members of the Chinese women's national soccer team, and so on. Since the end of the 1990s, NBA games have been broadcast live on Chinese Central TV and eleven local channels. Likewise, soccer games from the English Premier League, the Spanish La Liga, and the Italian Serie A have all been broadcast live on central and provincial TV channels. Millionaire sports stars such as Shaquille O'Neal, Michael Jordan, Ronaldo, and Maldini are household names in China today.

From the very beginning of the telethon, the TV hosts emphasized that they wanted to use the "viewpoint" and "strength" of sports to deal with disease and disaster, and to overcome fear. What are the viewpoint and strength of sports? Sun Wen, the beloved captain of the women's national team, spoke of her attitude toward SARS: "The most important thing is to maintain a healthy and calm state of mind. The more nervous you are, the more attention you pay to this thing [i.e., SARS], the weaker your immune system becomes." Other sports stars echoed her comments.[33]

Healthy lifestyle, self-discipline, and entrepreneurship. The emerging urban middle-class was not only the targeted consumers of corporatized sports but also the bearers of responsibility in humanity's fight against SARS. On the one hand, the urban middle class was personified in the images of doctors, nurses, and sports stars; at the same time, the middle class took on its responsibilities through "voluntary" monetary contributions and self-disciplined health practices. By the end of the three-hour program, the telethon had raised 504,440 RMB and $280,000 from individuals and private companies in China and the United States.[34]

In *STARS vs. SARS*, the distinction between the world of goods and the sphere of human identities was again called into question. This time the Chinese human body was not aligned with the civet cat but was included in the fold of "humanity." Yet not any Chinese body or subject is eligible for the status of being part of humanity; it is the members of the cosmopolitan middle class who have emerged as potential savvy consumers and responsible private citizens. Even for this emerging middle class, it takes humanizing maneuvers to make them "human." In conjunction with Orientalist and neoliberal imaginaries surrounding the question of the Chinese people's appetite for civet cats, the relocation of responsibility in *STARS vs. SARS* articulates an alternative vision of humanity, represented by an aspiring middle class that must now bear its responsibilities and tame its wild appetites.

Becoming Human?

In recent years, various parts of the world have borne the brunt of several epidemic outbreaks: mad cow disease, West Nile virus, avian flu, and SARS. These new emergencies brought back into focus other ongoing epidemics such as AIDS, as well as more distant memories of the bubonic plague and other "plagues." At one point or another, all these pandemics threatened—and in some cases continue to threaten—to reach the global scale. But geographic and national boundaries are not the only boundaries they traverse: the radical unruliness of the human, nonhuman, and superhuman bodies in these dangerous encounters challenges any attempt to divide the world neatly into humans and animals, culture and nature, Us and Them. These entangled bodies and things challenge the naturalness and wholeness of humanity by highlighting how some bodies, whether human, nonhuman, or superhuman, are always already marked.[35]

Recent discussions about neoliberal governmentality in Europe and North America have often assumed an already existing rational market that operates by predictable codes of conduct, and responsible consumer-subjects whose state of being human goes largely unchallenged. In China studies, celebratory popular and academic discourses have invoked images of lively markets and mass consumption as convenient tropes for China's transition from a production-based, planned economy toward economic and social progress. Some are even hopeful that China's market economy, in producing enthusiastic consumer-subjects and cultivating horizontal relations of consumption, will create a more democratic everyday sociability similar to, if not identical with, that of European and North American liberal democracy. Even as these discussions can help bring neoliberal discourses into focus in understanding China's transformations, I suggest that they also run the risk of privileging consumption as an unmistakable sign of modernity and globality, and that they perhaps too readily translate consumption into the (anticipated) production of neoliberal subjectivities and identities. Without problematizing the linkages between the market, consumption, privatization, and neoliberalism, we may inadvertently reproduce narratives of transition that relegate to the background other kinds of translocal networks and encounters by which meaningful bodily practices and subjectivities are produced while at the same time leaving these networks and encounters relatively immune from critical analyses.

It is necessary, I think, for us to talk about transformation through consumption without falling back on narratives of transition that oppose tradition to modernity, local to global, production to consumption. With that in mind, I hope that the unruly human and nonhuman consumables and those who consume them challenge us to rethink critically the ways in which nature and culture, wild and domestic, traditional and modern, past and future are invoked and refigured in diverse and meaningful ways. Before we can assume that humans have become individuated through market rationality, we need to examine how the right to be human is negotiated and contested, and how it sometimes has to be fought out.

10. Post-Mao Professionalism

Self-enterprise and Patriotism

Lisa M. Hoffman

On a cold December morning in 2003, a colleague and I visited the new modern office building near Liberation Square that houses Dalian's Talent Service Center (*rencai fuwu zhongxin*) and Talent Market (*rencai shichang*). When we arrived, guards at the main entrance checked our credentials and allowed us to pass without buying a ticket. We wound our way around people in the lobby who were reading newspapers listing jobs and company promotions, and past a small bookstore with materials about how to find an appropriate job, develop one's management skills, and study for an M.B.A. This marble-floored building was a far cry from the city's first talent market, which I had visited ten years earlier. That office was in a set of small rooms next to an entertainment and antique store complex on the edge of a city park.[1]

For helpful comments on multiple drafts and sustained engagement, I thank Aihwa Ong, Monica DeHart, Jennifer Hubbert, Stephen Collier, and Ann Anagnost. The chapter has gone through a number of drafts and conference presentations between 2002 and 2005, and I am grateful for participants' comments, particularly those of Jeff Maskovsky and Wing-Shing Tang, as well as the anonymous reviewer and editors of this volume. A longer version has been published in *Economy and Society* 35, no. 4 (2006): 550–70 (see http://www.tandf.co.uk/journals), and I thank Taylor & Francis Ltd. for permission to reprint parts of that piece here. Elaine Jeffreys offered helpful comments on that article.

The Talent Service Center, run by the municipal government's personnel bureau, offers a number of services to people with post-secondary degrees and marketable skills who are looking for new jobs. In addition to hosting regular job fairs and providing a computer database system for employers and employees, the center helps professionals manage their employment and insurance records outside their workplace. Such centers opened across China during the 1980s and early 1990s, with the first established in Shenyang in 1983. Weekly and seasonal (for example, spring graduation) job fairs held by the centers have grown dramatically in size since the early 1990s, although their structure has not changed much over the years. Company representatives station themselves at tables, posting announcements on the wall behind them that advertise the company, open positions, and the desired credentials for each job, including degree, years of experience, and sometimes even age, gender, and height. Those looking for work read the posters and approach the tables to ask questions and participate with employers in the now commonplace practice of "face-to-face interviewing."

The opening of talent exchange centers and the establishment of job fairs are important phenomena to note in discussions of new forms of governing and emerging private lives and autonomous selfhood in China. The lack of labor markets and planned labor distribution were key features of high, or traditional, socialism.[2] In the planned economy, college graduates received job assignments in line with five-year plans and then moved to where they were needed for national development. Since these work unit positions traditionally were for a lifetime, the assignments came with the guarantee of a steady salary and the benefits of the socialist welfare package, known as the "iron rice bowl" (housing, medical care, retirement, ration coupons, and so on). Getting into college and graduating into a work unit assignment thus denoted lifelong employment and stability.

Challenges to this system were apparent by the early 1980s, when the Education Commission initiated a series of reforms in the assignment system, university enrollment policies, and curriculum that aimed to develop the kind of "human capital" deemed necessary for China's new "open door" policies.[3] Economists and foreign investors accused state units of monopolizing educated workers and blamed the units for "wasting" talent through overstaffing, the poor utilization of their skills, and labor hoarding. The failure of the assignment system to let talent "flow" to where it was most needed and into positions where the workers would be "satisfied" and develop their talents were newly identified as serious problems. Deng Xiaoping argued, for instance, that if talented personnel did not move around, then their ideas would become rigid and inflexible (*rencai bu liudong, sixiang jiu hui jianghua*).[4] Further accelerated in 1992 after Deng's tour of southern China and the Chinese Communist Party's official acknowledgment of "the conceptual framework of 'the market' as a mechanism of government . . . [at] the Fourteenth Party Congress,"[5] assignment system reforms made reference to both new logics of supply and demand and the critical role of educated personnel in building the nation.

To address the "problems" of wasted talent, the lack of personnel flow, and poor job satisfaction, new technologies of labor distribution—job fairs, face-to-face interviews, and career counseling—emerged in place of direct assignment and local implementation of state plans. Universities learned what it meant to "guide" graduates into appropriate positions without assigning them. They also had to help both students and work units become familiar with the new world of "demand-meets-supply" exchanges and "mutual choice." Graduates and working professionals started writing résumés and asking questions about a potential employer's business plan. And in the new marketplace, state-owned work units as well as private enterprises presented themselves to applicants as places that valued talent, used talent efficiently, and did not waste the skills and knowledge of their human resources. The notion of human capital surfaced as an important category of development and prosperity for companies as well as cities, fostering new kinds of competition among locations as well.[6] Thus by the mid-1990s, rather than anticipating a job assignment, college graduates across the country expected to earn an entry-level position in either the state or non-state sector, to make their own career decisions, and to manage their own professional development. "Employees," who also could be unemployed, emerged in place of "assignees," those who had had no choice but to accept their new assignment.

In other words, various actors have problematized the command economy, and even since the early days of the reform era, new questions have been raised about "what should be ruled, by whom and through what procedures."[7] In light of reform era reassessments of the planned economy and job assignments as containing inefficiencies and contradictions, it became both *reasonable* and *practicable* in the post-Mao era to think that market exchanges would "rationalize" the distribution and flow of educated labor power. In numerous interviews people suggested that the market mechanism—and not the planned economy's job assignment system—was the best way to distribute these talented workers. That is to say, the market has become a kind of "test"[8] or "regulative ideal"[9] of good or efficient government in China.

In this chapter I analyze this problematization by examining the new technologies devised to foster the development of desirable human capital and to regulate the distribution of educated workers—including choice. I argue not only that "neoliberal" techniques of governing (such as marketization of labor, calculative choice, and the fostering of an ethos of self-enterprise) have emerged in place of state planning, but also that these neoliberal techniques are linking up with Maoist era norms and values of serving the country, challenging many analyses which argue that nationalism has been overshadowed with globalization. This phenomenon is apparent in the formation of the new professional, a self-enterprising subject who also is decidedly concerned with, and has an affinity for, the nation—what I call patriotic professionalism.[10] Professional subject-hood, in other words, exhibits neoliberal elements, Maoist era ideals and expressions of patriotism, and periodic authoritarian measures—a configuration and social formation not accounted for in many definitions of neoliberalism. Such definitions presume an opposition and perhaps an incompatibility between neoliberal projects of "individual" improvement and self-enterprise, on the one hand, and notions of national or "social" progress, solidarities, and values, on the other.[11] Thus the emergence of patriotic professionalism draws our attention to the diverse and contingent nature of "neoliberal" governmentality, pushing us to reflect not only on emerging forms of governing and professional subject-hood in late-socialist China, but also on what we mean by neoliberalism itself.[12] By arguing that individual choice is indeed a *form of governing*, I also offer a conceptual framework for analyzing the emergence of "privatized" social acts and forms of selfhood.

Governing through Choice

An important component of the change inspired by Deng Xiaoping has been an official shift from a reliance on politically "red" cadres to a preference for those with expertise and talent, recasting the role of educated and talented personnel in China.[13] Talent, human resources, and human capital have been touted in official and popular discourses as important sources for development in the new century. As a young man from a state-owned securities enterprise explained: "We need talented people for development. It doesn't matter what kind of enterprise it is. Everyone needs them. Talented people solve difficult problems. You can train them, and they help guarantee an enterprise's future development." Professionals and credentialed staff have become important actors in—and sites of—national development. The phasing out of the assignment guarantee and the phasing in of autonomous decision making may be understood as important devices in fostering this desired human capital and national strength while also shaping what is meant by privatized self-actualization in contemporary China.

Many analyses of reforms in socialist planning, however, represent choice, autonomy, and private life as freedom from the state and as an opportunity for people to be who they "really" are. The growth of labor markets and employment options is one arena of reform where narratives of freedom are especially strong and to which people often point as proof of the retreat of the state and the decline of governance in everyday affairs in China. Yet such narratives assume that personhood exists prior to force relations, and thus that "freedom" from state intervention means that true agency may be restored. Rather than measuring the degree to which people "really" are or are not free in the reform era, here I ask how choice and autonomy are *a part of* the governing and subject-formation processes. Freedom, then, is not indicative of the absence of power or governance, but is a technique of governing whereby the regulation and management of subjects happens "through freedom."[14] This analytical orientation shifts questions of autonomy and privatization away from state-society power struggles and toward an examination of job choice as a mechanism of governing and sub-jectification.

Analyzing employment choice as a form of governing thus means that Dalian's job fairs resonate in interesting ways with technologies of rule in advanced liberal regimes such as the United States. Advanced liberal rule governs "at a distance," "through the regulated choices of individual citizens," and speci-fies subjects of "responsibility, autonomy and choice."[15] New practices of choice in late-socialist and postsocialist societies also work through the "autonomization" of social actors, establishing new norms of behavior and relations to the self. Employment markets for college graduates, for instance, pivot on a re-specification of social actors as autonomous in ways not possible under the centrally planned system of direct state job assignments, what David Bray describes as the transition from the "traditional employment mentality" to the initiative to "create your own rice bowl."[16] Traditional socialist governing through structured "dependency" seems to have given way to rule through new degrees of autonomy from planning organs, and through choices handled responsibly, echoing descriptions of advanced liberal regimes.

Yet there are important differences in neoliberal governmental forms in socialist China and advanced liberal rule in the United States, particularly in the way patriotism, which draws on Maoist notions of loyalty and a strong nation on the world stage, is infused into practices of choice and an ethos of self-enterprise. Thus, before we turn to an analysis of professional subjectivity in contemporary China, some clarifications are necessary.

Neoliberalism and Socialism in China

The extensive privatization and marketization of everything from health care to insurance in advanced liberal regimes such as the United States and the United Kingdom highlight the particularly *de-statized* aspect of these domains and the kinds of decisions that are made within them. Provision of goods and services and decisions about them have been pushed outside the bounds of the formal government bureaucracy. In China, however, the late-socialist state, along with other actors, continues to condition the meaning of post-Mao autonomy through regulation of the domains and ways in which choices are made. This conditioning is apparent in the consistent use of moral education to get graduates into certain positions, specific rules about where graduates may settle their household registration, university interventions into what is called an "unbalanced" marketplace, and the use of fines and scholarship points to encourage socially responsible but autonomously made decisions. The state, in other words, remains an active participant in neoliberal governance—and what we may call emerging privatized lives—in China.[17]

Comparing disparate regimes such as the United States and China allows us to highlight parallels, but also to note variations, so that we may "think about different versions of neoliberalism"—ones that govern through freedom and prioritize the market mechanism but adopt other measures as well.[18] The taking up of neoliberal practices in China references the Western liberal tradition in important ways, but it does not mean that certain forms of personhood, for instance, will necessarily emerge. Patriotic professionalism is such an instance of the integration of neoliberal practices with other, even authoritarian social norms. Moreover, as Gary Sigley reminds us with his provocative term "liberal despotism," "authoritarian and illiberal measures are constitutive of the way in which a liberal arts of government operates," depending on the segment of the population being targeted.[19]

We may then approach neoliberal governmentality "as a practice, which is to say, as a 'way of doing things' oriented toward objectives and regulating itself by means of a sustained reflection," rather than as a particular, already formed ideological or social formation.[20] These diverse sites are linked in terms of how things are done, "a common set of technical mechanisms,"[21] and the "means of sustained reflection." Such an approach to the study of neoliberalism allows us to investigate what is generalizable across different sites without being forced to identify a particular form of subjectivity, for instance, as emblematic of neoliberalism. It is helpful to think of neoliberalism, then, as a "global form," where "global" refers not to an all-encompassing universal but rather to "a distinctive capacity for decontextualization and recontextualization, abstractability and movement, across diverse social and cultural situations and spheres of life,"[22] opening the conceptual space to recognize the wedding of neoliberal techniques with a reform era patriotism that links contemporary self-development with state strengthening.

Choice, Self-enterprise, and Professionalism

Here I turn explicitly to the intersections between practices of choice, notions of self-enterprise, and the emergence of professional subjectivity in contemporary China.[23] At the same time that rationalities about good government and modes of national development changed in post-Mao times, mechanisms for regulating and governing the citizenry also shifted, resulting in the emergence of new forms of personhood, or subjects of government. Through the examples that follow, I illustrate how post-Mao practices of choice and ideas about career success have helped establish new norms of respectability and professional subject-hood. Employers, for instance, often told me that recent college graduates were a distinct cohort with notions of self-development and enterprise incorporated into their working lives. Referring to such workers, the personnel manager at a large Sino-U.S. joint venture said: "These young people are not the same as the white-collar workers in state units, in terms of their lifestyle, their behavior, and their thinking. They are younger and better educated. They will develop, and we don't want them to leave our company."

Young professionals also have adopted reform era rationalities, drawing on norms and values outside the party-state, "rendering reality thinkable and practicable" in terms of market competition, individual achievement, and self-managed development.[24] Thus their talk of finding positions that matched their majors (*duikou*), where they could get good experience (*duanlian ziji*), and where their abilities could flourish (*fahui nengli*) is more than just descriptive of their dreams, for these narratives of the self exhibit a "style of reasoning" about the self and about governmental interventions.[25] Job seekers spoke, in other words, as human capital, talented employees—not assignees—who wanted opportunities for personal and professional development in their work.

Liao Meili, a young Dalian University of Technology (DUT) graduate, for instance, who found a position with a tourist agency in Beijing, explained her plan for career development:

> I have this plan—to go into a stable corporation, get experience, and then go to a joint venture or a foreign company . . . because there the competition is more severe, and I will be able to develop myself more. . . . I want to devote myself to [the new job] and see what I can do for it. Sometimes people complain the [state] units are too old and the habits can't change, but this is a new unit [where she will work]. I think I will stay longer than five years. I want to develop in the same corporation and do it from the grass roots. It is better for personal development. Now I have this plan, but I don't know about the future.

A schoolmate of hers, Zhang Long, said he wanted, first, to use his major; second, to make a good salary; third, to find a place where his potential for development would be good; and fourth, to be able to stay in the city of Dalian. "I don't care if the work is stable," Zhang said. "I want to use all of my abilities and have a good salary—well, at least a reasonable salary. If that means I have to change jobs a lot, I don't care." Listing priorities for a new job as Zhang did and constructing career plans as Liao did are new devices that frame a personal sense of self through practices of choice and experiences of autonomy from direct state planning.

Not surprisingly, other students were anxious about the reforms, the pressure they felt to find a "good" job, and the very real possibility that they could remain unemployed. Many looking for work expressed anxiety over the search process, while at the same time they professed the desire to be self-reliant and to use their training and skills in their work. This suggests the emergence of an increasingly commonsensical attitude about choice, autonomous decision making, and career possibilities, even as it produced worry and insecurity for many.

Interviews and experiences of "mutual choice" at job fairs are particularly salient moments of subject formation for the graduates. They afford both the company representatives and the applicants an opportunity for deliberate self-presentation. Tang Liping, who found a position in a Sino-U.S. joint venture, described her experience:

> I heard they needed an assistant [to the manager] from a friend so I sent my materials to the manager. Then I went for an interview. They introduced the company, and I introduced my major, my hobbies, and myself. . . . They asked me what I thought about salary and working conditions, and I told [them] that working conditions and development of the company are more important than salary. Also, it is very important if I can use my knowledge and improve myself. . . . I think the company will develop and grow. . . . [In five years time], if I am still at this company, I will not be the assistant to the manager. I want to be the manager or a business professional, or maybe have my own trading company and be an independent company.

Tang also claimed that she wanted only one-year contracts with the company in case she decided to leave. She had confidence that her contract would be renewed if she worked hard at her job. "If the work is suitable for me and the personal relations are good, then I will stay; if it is not suitable and I am not happy, then I will go." The focus for these young graduates was squarely on their individual career plans and their autonomy from state planning. As they experienced interviews and résumé writing, they faced, and constantly talked about, opportunities (*jihui*), choices (*xuanze*), and insecurities not existent in the planned system. Their desires also resonated with work units that tried to distinguish themselves from the "inefficiencies" of the planned system, which "hoarded labor" or "disregarded" skills.

In contrast to what these college graduates were experiencing, under the planned system of high socialism, labor power and skills were not "owned" by the individual.[26] Rather they were a national resource and part of the means of production owned by the state;[27] returns on one's labor power "were realized only in the state's production, but not on the individuals."[28] As part of the assignment system, work positions also embedded the college graduate in the urban welfare system of work units and redistributive economics that granted the unit immense control over its members. Rather than referring to a student's personal interests or abilities, something that would have been considered selfish and bourgeois, the assignments aimed to equalize development across the country (deemphasizing coastal areas) and eliminate exploitative labor markets and unemployment. The acquisition of skills, then, was "for the improved performance of the organization or the fulfillment of political objectives of the central or local party leaders" and not for individual fulfillment or personal career advancement.[29] Labor power, in other words, was not an individual resource to be sold in the marketplace or even to be developed for personal growth, nor was it about the "efficient use" of labor power.[30] Job assignments under the centrally planned system were issues of *national duty* and expressions of socialist nation building. Career planning and skill development to fulfill an individual's professional goals were politically unacceptable, exemplified in Liu Shaoqi's statement that "it is the worthiest and most just thing in the world to sacrifice oneself for the Party, for the proletariat, for the emancipation of the nation and of all mankind, for social progress and for the highest interests of the overwhelming majority of the people."[31] After the reform era began, however, new technologies of rule displaced state planning and established the market mechanism as a "tool" to evaluate governmental effectiveness and efficiency and as a way to reform a governmentality "whose abuses one tries to limit."[32] This led to the opening of job fairs and new practices of professional career planning.

The young people I met focused on their own potential professional achievements—and insecurities—often contrasting them with the experiences and attitudes of their parents. A young woman from Wuhan, Cai Li, who hoped to work in Shanghai is a good example. Her parents had had the opportunity to return to Shanghai, their original hometown, in the early 1990s. But as she explained:

> They said no because the job would have been harder than what they had. . . . They don't want to change. . . . If I were them I certainly would move to Shanghai. If life is OK, then it is OK, but there is no chance for more improvement. They are used to this, and their children are grown up, but to my brother and me, there still are a lot of opportunities available that we can try. I am not afraid of failure. I may have failure in Shanghai, but I am ready to face my possible failures. I don't know what I will confront. This is the main difference between the generations.

She continued that if the institute where she would be working as a translator gave her a good chance to improve herself, and her abilities and knowledge were used effectively, then it was likely that she would stay there for many years. If not, she would go. Unlike her parents, who came of age in the era of traditional socialism, Cai believed in the idea of career mobility as a source of individual and social growth. "I don't know what I will confront," she said, but "I am ready to face my possible failures." She embraced the idea of individual choice, even if it meant that she had to face the possibility of "failure" which she could blame on no one but herself. That she did not fear the shift of accountability from the state to the individual exemplifies how neoliberal rationalities of self-responsibility may be embedded in reforms in the job assignment system as well as everyday forms of self-governance.

Similar to, though not the same as, prevailing rationalities in advanced liberal regimes that encourage people to "enterprise themselves," these reforms govern at a greater distance and through persuasion rather than coercion, specifying autonomous and responsible subjects.[33] It is through the very practices of making choices and feeling (relatively) free in these decisions that the post-Mao professional subject emerges—an active and responsible subject (and one who often feels quite insecure) deemed necessary for China's late-socialist development.

Autonomy, Responsibility, and Patriotism

As these young people made more privatized decisions about where to work, they did so in relation to statements about being "responsible" with their autonomy. An emphasis on responsible choices is rooted in neoliberal regimes of appropriate forms of self-enterprise, while also echoing Maoist demands for service to the nation and duty to one's fellow citizen. Throughout the research process, I heard people say that young workers should not only think of themselves as they made decisions about where to work. Their employment choices had to be informed by a sense of social and national responsibility too, melding a more privatized self-actualization and post-Mao patriotism in interesting ways.

A guide designed to help college graduates choose a profession, for instance, listed several characteristics of a career, including its being a way for each individual *to serve society* as well as his or her position. Other items identified a profession as a way to develop each individual's ability, a stage for realizing life's worth, and a significant part of any person's life.[34] University personnel, especially those in the newly named employment guidance offices (*jiuye zhidao bangongshi*), understood that they had an active role to play in this process of choice, steering graduates into appropriate positions that also met state needs. No longer implementing mandatory plans, school administrators have been encouraged to "guide" (*zhidao*) students to learn about themselves as individuals while also being "aware of their social responsibilities."[35] An administrator at DUT echoed these sentiments when he said that in addition to thinking "about their personality, their uniqueness, what kind of work is appropriate for them . . . and the conditions of the company . . . [students] must also think about what the country needs and what the situation is like in that local place. They cannot only think of their own ideals." Reinforcing such a perspective, President Hu Jintao said in 2006 that the young should learn to "love the motherland" as a key virtue of "socialist honor" (harming the motherland being a sign of "socialist disgrace").[36] Moral education that promotes feelings of nationalism should not be equated with "propaganda," however, a pejorative term in the English language that likens state ideology to brainwashing.[37] Instead the kind of patriotism expressed by educated urbanites helps establish standards of respectability for professionals in society at large. As norms, they are important techniques of self-formation, though of course under continual negotiation in everyday life.

Wen Shubang, a senior at DUT, is a good example of how human capital exchanges framed the educated citizen as a potential source of national strength. Wen began by proudly stating that he had a position in a state-run foreign trade office. "I heard they needed someone in this office, but the application period was already closed," he explained. "I went to talk to them anyway, and because my scores and accomplishments in college are better than others', they were still willing to hire me." Many of his classmates coveted this type of position, for it offered him training opportunities, help with transferring his household registration to Dalian, and some degree of security, as it was part of the state system. The salary, however, was just average. "A high salary helps a lot, but it is not that important now," Wen said, as he rationalized why he should be satisfied with the pay he had been offered:

> I am just starting to work. I hope I will get a lot of training, and wealth, but it is not practical to want too much because I am a new worker. If you go to a private company the salary may be higher, but there are not as many opportunities for training there. What I need to see is if my salary meets my accomplishments after a year or two. . . . Many units wanted to hire me, including a foreign company. I could have chosen a job with a much higher salary, but I didn't because the jobs weren't related to my major. If I go too far beyond my major and my knowledge is too broad, I won't be able to advance my career. I won't know enough about anything, so what does it solve if only your salary is high? Going to a state-run unit is *my own choice*, and anyway, I should work for the country [*yinggai dui guojia fuwu*]. Later I can go to a private or foreign company.

His assertion that he had a responsibility to work for the country is reminiscent of old slogans such as "Long Live Mao." Yet contemporary decisions that graduates like Wen made are quite different from those of the cohort before them. Wen and his classmates struggled with the *choice* of working in a state, private, or foreign enterprise. While patriotic duty is not a new device for encouraging certain activities and behaviors, making choices in these fields is. Graduates also had to maneuver between wanting to fulfill individual dreams, confronting the reality of possible unemployment, and managing family pressures and duties—all while meeting their sense of social responsibility, such as supporting the nation. Seeking career development and acquiring newly desirable skills in the marketplace does not mean these young professionals identified themselves as separate from or in opposition to the nation. Many, like Wen, are patriotic professionals, that is, young people who harbor neoliberal ideas of self-development as well as late-socialist patriotism. Wen embodied this responsibility in his rationalization of his average wages and in his conviction that he should serve the nation. Responsibility in post-Mao China denotes both patriotism and individual interests.

College students heard about the intermingling of individual development and competition with national strength and identification from a variety of sources, including school officials, local papers, popular publications, and even parents. When I first met Mr. Wu at Dalian's Talent Market, he had recently returned from Germany and was looking for a new job. At that time Wu lived with his parents in their small apartment almost an hour's bus ride from the center of town. He longed for the chance to go abroad again, or at least to work in a foreign company. The German assignment, however, had been disappointing, as the company had failed, and he was not able to fulfill the dream he had established for himself. Immediately after returning to Dalian, he found a job with a large Sino-U.S. joint venture. His father strongly opposed the long commute this job required and the thought of another failure for his son in a "foreign place." In fact, Wu's father told him that if he worked for a foreign company, he would not be permitted to take time off to care for him if he got sick, or if he died, resonating with what Vanessa Fong calls "filial nationalism" and with what Zhongdan Pan and colleagues refer to as "the master frame of 'family-nation'" in China.[38] In other words, if Wu worked in a foreign company, his father feared that he would not be able to fulfill his filial duties. "I had to think of what my father said. I couldn't hurt his feelings." So Wu declined the position and returned to the market. He eventually found work in a tax service company officially registered as private, though in reality it relied heavily on the subsidized labor of government employees.

Responsibility—to one's family, one's country, and even one's own professional development—could take the form of sentiments about China on the world stage or it could be expressed in terms of actually working for the state, indicating that there is a dynamic and complex interplay between the party-state and "popular nationalism" (*renmin minzu zhuyi*).[39] A *Time* magazine article reads, for instance, "Even as they [urban youth] sip Starbucks lattes or line up at the U.S. embassy for student visas, they bridle at what they view as an attempt by the rest of the world to suppress a budding superpower. 'America wants to keep China down,'" one young entrepreneur is quoted as saying.[40] In this configuration, a young person could sip lattes and work for a foreign company while also standing up for China in the world. Thus it is not required that one work directly for the state or that one proclaim an explicit allegiance to the party to appear patriotic, also evidenced by Laurie Duthie's interviews with executives in multinationals in Shanghai.[41] Caring for the nation in contemporary China does not demand that one *sacrifice* one's future for the nation. In the reform era, patriotism is about fulfilling one's potential through responsible choices, thus fostering national development.

The notion of patriotic professionalism I am developing here allows us to see how ideas of autonomous self-development and patriotism are being incorporated into a single subject position without causing great personal turmoil. The dreams of recent graduates and young professionals of going abroad to work, studying for an M.B.A. in the United States, or even just getting the opportunity to train in a foreign company's office often are embedded in conversations about China, national strength on the world stage, and modernization. Pan Qing, a young graduate who found a job with a large Korean trading firm, explained that she wanted the position because the company was "world famous" and she could "get experience" there. When I asked how long she thought she would stay, she answered: "In fact, I don't like this company because I think I am a traitor to my country. When people are young, they think their goal is to get money from foreigners for China, but now it is the other way around," that is, foreigners are taking money out of China. Her long-term plan was to go to the United States for an M.B.A., then she would find work in trade. Announcement of this plan rolled off her tongue immediately after she criticized foreign companies in China, though she avoided any mention of the "foreignness" of the M.B.A. "I want to do something to prove that Chinese people deserve recognition," she said. "This is another reason why I want to go to the United States. They have better education there, and I want to compete with them." For young women like her, these are not contradictions.

One of Pan's classmates told me that "young people should go overseas to open doors, study modern things, and come home to build our own country." Noting that a classmate of hers went to the Unites States in their junior year, she said: "She told us about the United States. She can't stand the discrimination in America. There are misunderstandings. In your own country, you can help your country. She wants to come back; being in your own country is better." Another of Pan's classmate who had found a position in a state unit, and with whom I spoke several days later, explained why her "destiny" was to work for the state and not for a foreign company:

> The foreign company can provide good conditions and comfort, but you give your talent to a foreigner, and they earn money from China. Maybe in five years I will work for [a foreign company], but in ten years I will be working for the state. Maybe I will continue studying as a postgraduate in five years. . . . I will definitely work for a foreign company for two to three years, but not for a long time.

She admitted that many of her classmates did not agree with her argument that people should ultimately work for the state rather than foreign companies. Yet her narrative was filled with contradictions about what was most important—working for the state, finding the best career opportunities, or earning a high salary. In fact, she had been looking for a job in a foreign company but could not find one. It is precisely this combination of ideas about self-managed development and expressions of patriotism, either by working for the state or by making one's self and thus the nation strong, which offers evidence of a new ethics of subjectivity—specified by the wedding of neoliberal governmentality with Maoist notions of duty recast in terms of reform era economic goals.

• • •

In arguing here that choice and freedom are *forms of governing,* I do not mean to discount the very real and tangible changes in Chinese citizens' everyday lives. Rather I wish to highlight that the arena of choice in contemporary China is a complex and sometimes contradictory process of subject formation. It includes practices as diverse as "mutual choice," in which employees and employers, not state functionaries, make decisions, engage in negotiations over the meaning of competence and success, hold gender-specific opinions about appropriate positions and careers, and debate issues of familial stability and social mobility.[42] The form of professional personhood that emerges in these negotiations may be understood as engaging neoliberal rationalities of self-enterprise and privatized practices of self-actualization, as well as a sense of caring for the nation that strongly references the Maoist era. Thus, this new regime of professional self-development suggests a self-enterprising subject who is at once autonomous from state planning agencies yet is still tied to the nation through strategic expressions of patriotism, whether in the form of working in a state unit or in the form of protesting the NATO bombing of the Chinese embassy in Belgrade or the more recent controversial revision of textbooks in Japan.

It is important to recognize that this is not merely a reappearance of high-socialist nationalism in contemporary times. Rather it suggests that new understandings of what it means to be patriotic are being formed in everyday practices such as job seeking or family negotiations over career development in the context of transnational labor markets. Job choices are infused with Maoist era values of loving the nation *as well as* reform era views on economic development, self-enterprise, material gains, and potential social mobility. Thus it does not make sense to equate patriotic professionalism with the nationalism expressed by high-socialist cadres, in other words, even as it clearly builds on that tradition.[43]

Moreover, I have argued in this chapter that examining the formation of patriotic professionalism highlights a particularly valuable conceptual space for recognizing and making sense of a neoliberal analytic in socialist China. While the analysis of China generally, and of new employment markets more specifically, provides an opportunity to recognize "neoliberalism" in a non-Western site, it also offers a moment to reflect on the contingent and diverse nature of neoliberal governmental forms. Emerging forms of personhood do not necessarily follow assumed ideological lines of "neoliberal" political projects. Recognizing this allows us to understand how neoliberalism and socialism may intersect and produce unexpected configurations—for example, the wedding of neoliberal "ways of doing things" with socialist norms of building the nation. At the same time, such an approach offers a potentially useful analytical stance for discussions of *private* social worlds and self-care in contemporary China.

11. Self-fashioning Shanghainese

Dancing across Spheres of Value

Aihwa Ong

I am a dance girl and I am a [Communist] party member. I don't know if I can be counted as a successful Web cam dance girl. But I'm sure that looking around the world, if I am not the one with the highest diploma, I am definitely the dance babe who reads the most and thinks the deepest, and I'm most likely the only party member among them.

Blogger, pseudonym Mu Mu, in Shanghai

In 2005 a hot Chinese Web log displayed the saucy comments, accompanied by the come-hither images, of Mu Mu, CCP party girl cavorting in her underwear. The *New York Times* reporter Howard French prudishly interprets this "on-line revolution" as political evidence of a growing challenge to China's ever-vigilant on-line censors.[1] He claims that Mu Mu the dance girl is "giving flesh to the kind of free-spoken civil society whose emergence the government has long been determined to prevent or at least tightly control." The journalist cites a Berkeley-based lecturer who remarked on Mu Mu's "highly ironic commentary about sexuality, intellectual and political identity" as "undermining the

This article draws on research in American corporations and their employees in Shanghai in June 1998, June 1999, and June 2004. The interviews quoted here took place in 2004. I thank Song Ping of Xiamen University for her assistance in making local contacts.

182

ideological basis of power." This interpretation is highly questionable, but U.S.-based observers are easily seduced by the political promises of these corporate-like, private pleasure–seeking bloggers. Such interpretations should give one pause. Can China's fluid integration of capitalism, authoritarian rule, and the pleasures of self-fashioning be so starkly framed in terms of diametrically opposed forces? Clearly a more nuanced understanding of the political infiltration of the new exhibitionist subject is needed here.

Mu Mu's own remarks make this American reading of the inevitable rejection of communism rather questionable. Instead of finding evidence of an anti-state protest, an alternative reading of Mu Mu's blog is that it represents the crystallization of new possibilities sparked by the interplay of capitalist markets and communist rule. The cyber-chattiness and sexual display appear to be an adventurous reconfiguring of the lines between the private and the public. Mu Mu herself understands this. She remarks that "in China, the concepts of private life and public life have emerged only in the past ten to twenty years. Before that, if a person had any private life, it only included their physical privacy—the sex life, between man and woman, for couples. I am lucky to live in a transitional society, from a highly political one to a commercial one, and this allows me to enjoy private pleasures, like blogging." In this world of intertwined economic and personal privatizations, one can be a CCP member as well as a sexy woman indulging private pleasures before the wide-open eyes of the cyberpublic. This risqué conjoining of pious socialist officialdom with prurient self-display transforms blogging from a personal diary into public musings about the disjunctures between disparate domains of everyday life. I view Mu Mu's Web log as a form of cyber-reveling in the new conditions for straddling the public and the private, the political and the personal, party politics and personal escapades.

Privatization as a Technology of the Self

Urban professionals in Shanghai are taking on new attitudes and behavior best described as self-fashioning. Whereas many Chinese are still accustomed to being told what to think or do by the state or party, a select few are encouraged to develop a new kind of reflexivity in relation to market reform and personal destiny. This radicalization of self-reflexivity among elite urban subjects, I argue, represents a particular engagement with neoliberal values that promote self-initiative, self-investment, and self-enterprise.

This Chinese version of self-proprietorship, however, is not the product of political liberalism, but is fostered by conditions produced at the intersection of market freedom and political authoritarianism. Other observers have examined privatization as a set of enterprising activities that will eventually erode the socialist state. In contrast, I draw attention to self-ownership expressed in innovative actions that improve one's life chances and optimize individual power that paradoxically enhances the power of Chinese sovereignty.

This new focus on individual fate marks a dramatic departure from the pre–market reform era, when the state "owned" citizens' bodies, exacting enormous sacrifices in the name of the socialist revolution. State directives controlled every aspect of bodily care and conduct, including the body's feeding, laboring, and performance of prescribed roles. The current shift toward self-management, at least for select educated classes, is an opportunistic moment sparked by the conjoining of Chinese authoritarianism and neoliberal rationality. I conceptualize neoliberalism as a migratory logic that fosters practices of self-enterprise and self-reflexivity in the face of market uncertainty.[2] Neoliberal reason articulates Chinese socialist politics in a very specific way, creating conditions for a self-revolution among the professional elite, yet casting the personal as political in a solely commercial matrix.

Self-ownership as a neoliberal value thus expands and transforms the meaning of the private. I view "privatization" as fundamentally an ethical relationship to oneself, in the sense of one's relationship to the self, to others, to things, and to one's fate. Hegel links private property with power over oneself, and the expression of one's will in relation to one's body, to other things, and to other people. One may argue that privatization fundamentally pivots on control over one's property, including one's overall existence as an individual person.[3] This self-possession is governed by ethical values regarding questions of what it means to be human, or how one ought to live. This array of self-practices Foucault calls "technologies of the self." By "technologies" he means "a matrix of practical reason," or the various means through which human beings develop knowledge about themselves. "Technologies of the self" refers to the practices through which individuals work on "their own bodies and souls, thoughts, conduct, and way of being in order to attain a certain state of happiness" and well-being.[4] This is a process of ethical self-training that ponders the problems of being in the world, of what one is, what one does, and how one should live.[5]

In contrast to the stereotypical "free subjects" of Western liberalism, the Chinese urban milieu promotes a radicalization of the personal without the radicalization of political freedom. CCP politics is being soft-pedaled when it comes to the privileged sons and daughters of the ruling elite. A shift in political thinking increasingly encourages risk taking, especially among the business and professional classes. So slogans about privatization, such as "Doing Business" (*jingshang*) and "Making Money" (*zhuanqian*), are more than about creating wealth. The slogans give official permission to make oneself over by developing one's capacities and accumulating private sources of power. Encouragements to self-reform, individual freedom, and self-reflexivity are entirely driven by commercial interest and discourse, skirting the question of individual political freedom.

As the personal has become radically commercialized, downsized politics now runs through conceptions of the stylized person as a form of commodity. New practices of market-savvy personhood are not independent of the state but are an expression of self-will that reflects a socialist transformation of the neoliberal technique of "governing at a distance."[6] Because new modes of being and acting depend on building up individual capacities, the exercise of individual powers is inseparable from exercising power over others.

The radicalization of self-reflexivity mutates the practice of *guanxi*, or the exchange of personal obligations and favors to maximize personal gain. China scholars tend to fetishize *guanxi* as the ethical foundation of Chinese cultural authenticity which has survived millennia of social change.[7] Yet they miss or seem to dismiss how *guanxi* itself has been mutating rapidly. Elsewhere I have observed that employees of American corporations in Shanghai explain that their forms of *guanxi* are more "horizontal" than the structures of exchange in the pre–market reform era.[8] But here I stress the aspects of self-care and private accumulation of wealth and skills that have become a dominant aspect of the elite *guanxi*-spinning subject. The can-do Shanghainese is someone who is constantly tweaking her individual talents in order to maximize her capacity to proliferate connections and access to power. Self-knowing *guanxi* subjects no longer concentrate on opportunities to trade favors with more powerful others. Beyond developing social acuity and opportunism, they also work on themselves, stylizing their personalities and honing their skills, at once obvious and obscure. There is also a difference in the way they elicit and control exchange relationships. As will become clear, the new professionals build their individual power by creating relationships that span diverse spheres of values. Besides self-cultivation and self-reflexivity, what is called for is nimbleness in relation to globalized milieus, people, and knowledge.

Self-fashioning as Knowledge Practice

By self-fashioning, I refer to the unscripted, self-reflexive thinking and action that are continually shaped and transformed by the diverse kinds of knowledge that circulate in the dynamic and globalized Chinese environment. This mode of self-enterprise is not practiced in a segregated realm of privatization but rather requires the constant translation of values between market and political spheres.[9] Through acts of self-fashioning at the nexus of competing economic and political information, the new professionals promote their sense of ownership over their own lives.

A major aspect of elite self-enterprise involves the micro-politics of translating values across competing spheres of power that shape Shanghai's emergence as a world city. Among young professionals, self-fashioning goes beyond accumulating the right certification, jobs, or social contacts to be a successful player in the fast-changing market. Beyond new relationships to things and to others, privatization among the urban elite includes an ethical self-transformation into a translator of values, a mediator among the surfeit of forms of knowledge that is circulating in contemporary China. This mode of self-formation entails a radicalization of reflexivity in planning one's life in the face of new contingencies. Ulrich Beck uses the term "individuation" to describe the political obligation to the private self in a Germany contemplating a risky post-welfare future. By individualization he does not mean atomization or anomie but rather "a compulsion for the manufacture, self-design, and self-staging of not just one's own biography but also its commitments and networks."[10] A similar set of expectations is being experienced by urban Chinese as everything that used to be guaranteed by the state has been redefined as personal decisions, choices, and risks. Among elite Shanghainese, this requirement of self-responsibility and self-enterprise is viewed as an open-ended opportunity for the accumulation of wealth and power. While others have dwelt on the amassing of riches, my focus here is on individuals who gain ownership of themselves by adjusting swiftly to a changing environment. Specifically, I consider new professionals working for foreign businesses whose self-fashioning is derived from a translational ethos, or the compulsion to develop capacities to translate across competing value regimes.

Thus "self-fashioning" rather than "self-management" is the more appropriate term for capturing the individualizing logic of Shanghainese yuppies. British theorists have considered the proliferation of self-practices within the context of advanced liberalism. Nikolas Rose recasts Foucault's technologies of the self as an ethico-politics that concerns itself with "the self-techniques necessary for responsible self-government and the relations between one's obligation to oneself and one's obligation to others."[11] Rose is mainly concerned with self-management as a technology for developing patterns of social accountability. Marilyn Strathern takes a similar view by maintaining that the "best practices" of audit and self-monitoring instill in people the need to measure themselves against ethical codes establishing good management practices or economic efficiency.[12] Finally, going beyond the United Kingdom, Nigel Thrift notes that global business knowledge has been key to the adoption of reflective practices among Asia's new professionals. In his view, "reflexive management" refers to thinking that reflects on business and is fed back into business practice through self-management.[13]

Self-fashioning, I want to stress, goes beyond the kind of self-management frequently associated with submission to social obligations, to management norms, or to "best practices" for creating an culture of accountability in a particular institution. In Shanghai, the self-practices among professionals seem less encumbered by concepts of professional responsibility, procedures, and norms. Instead the neoliberal promptings inspire extremely individualistic strategies that are fundamentally about self-advantage and self-propulsion through the turbulent mix of risks and opportunities created by global markets and China's emergence.

We have here an interesting permutation in self-reform which is triggered by the encounter with neoliberal values but is not reined in by broader norms that speak to some vision of the social good. The invoking of China and Chinese culture gestures toward patriotism. The phrase *xia hai* (plunging into the ocean) aptly captures the sense of living by your wits, of diving into the sea of market competition and surviving through entrepreneurialism and risk taking. The concept of self-fashioning thus captures the self-inventive and self-reflexive manner in which individuals tailor their practices in the light of disparate knowledges and daily challenges yielded by the hypercapitalist milieu.[14]

Translating across Spheres

Shanghai today is dominated by a new class of white-collar professionals ready to hustle, fix, and massage relationships among the worlds of global capital, communist politics, and *guanxi* ethics. It is clear that what these people do is put knowledge into circulation in order to produce new value. Arjun Appadurai has noted that special codes and actors control the flow of goods and information between different "regimes of value" (or different cultural orders for judging value). The diversion of valuable goods "from an enclaved zone to one where exchange is less confined and more profitable . . . is frequently the recourse of the entrepreneurial individual."[15]

I take the formulation further by arguing that self-enterprising actors exploit discrepancies between zones of value not only by controlling flows but also by actively converting knowledge in one zone into value in another. Translation implies iterative change, relating elements that were previously distinct and existing in different realms. To paraphrase Barbara Czarniawska and Guje Sevon, it requires enterprising individuals to abstract ideas and goals into objects that can be shifted into another context, from which they emerge, "translated" into new kinds of objects and actions.[16] Self-fashioning involves the astute defining and mixing of different knowledges and the capacity to convert information in one zone into a new value in another. Fashioning implies acts of steering, of directing the movement of ideas and action across multiple spheres, and the ensuing transformation.[17] Self-fashioning thus implies not only fine-tuning oneself but also steering oneself through diverse networks of knowledge and value. Such vigilant self-practices induces an openness to contingency, and possibilities for both strategy and play.

My focus is on men and women who work with foreign firms in Shanghai, the crucial self-fashioning figures who make global business function and China's markets boom. The self-reflexive tactics displayed by professionals exploit breaks between the corporate sector and the local authorities, or between international players and the Chinese public. To these New Yorkers of China their greatest personal value to themselves (and to foreign capital) lies not in having technical knowledge or in submitting to the norms of Western management but in their individual capacity to convert value across economic, cultural, and political fields. Soft performance, rather than sheer technical expertise, is central to Shanghainese yuppies as they fashion and stage themselves at the very nexus of situated and global networks of power.

Self-reflexive practices invariably involve gendered symbols and the symbolization of gender in conditions of possibility sparked by the international scene. With their masculine power rooted in Chinese patrimony and institutions, ambitious men learn to play the game of mediating between foreign interests and Chinese political bodies. Decentered from the tangle of political institutions, ambitious female professionals turn their translational skills toward businesses in the international realm. Clearly there are male executives involved in transnational arenas and female officials who control keys that unlock political influence. Such notable exceptions include the sons and daughters of former political leaders such as Deng Xiaoping and Zhao Ziyang, the so-called princelings who have capitalized on family connections to open doors for foreign companies. My claim is that the gendered pathways of self-empowering careers are not mutually exclusive. Rather I wish to highlight the contrasting vectors of self-fashioning that orient male professionals toward using situated political power and their female counterparts toward developing cosmopolitan social skills. Such professionals would seem to be China's proponents of liberal individualism, but do their self-enterprising activities dis-embed or reinforce their embeddedness in the Chinese political context?

Political Fixers

Some observers note that the "successful person" (*chenggong renshi*) in China today is represented by "a married middle-aged businessman," or the entrepreneur (*getihu*) who has acquired some glamour by exercising personal freedom (*ziyou*) and developing a respectable style (*qipai*) that displays aesthetic judgment.[18] Against such self-made men, I wish to draw attention to employees of multinational corporations. While seldom as rich as local businessmen, the new professional is in my view a more radically reflexive figure on the Shanghai scene. The knowledge worker does not simply define success by amassing wealth, political connections, and mistresses. Rather, he solves the problem of self-directed masculinity by constantly converting technical and cultural knowledge into different circuits of value. This border-crossing skill is so crucial to their self-image that professional men often refuse to submit to corporate rules of compliance and team play.

But the logic of self-direction is not simple expressive individualism immediately recognizable to foreign employers. This is the crux of a profound misunderstanding among Western managers, many of whom maintain that Chinese employees have been trained to follow orders. "Chinese employees are well-educated but do not think in terms of problem-solving. They cannot solve new problems and have no integrative learning," said the German director of a cutlery firm that has relocated its entire production operation to Shanghai. In the view of other Western managers, what Chinese workers need is a healthy dose of American individualism.[19]

Such discourses of American individualism versus Confucian hierarchy are a stereotypical representation that misrecognizes the thinking and action of Chinese professionals. Male employees tend to distinguish between investing in their own careerist goals and investing in the company. Instead of prioritizing problem-solving for the firm, many focus on solving problems of acquiring individual power. Their strategy is to consistently exploit gaps between knowledge and value regimes. This personalistic agenda is often opaque to Western managers who work hard to break through what they perceive to be worker impassivity instilled by authoritarian norms.

Not surprisingly, Chinese men feel that American individualism and spontaneity, while entertaining and fun, are short-sighted and misguided. At a famous digital company, an American manager was viewed as a friendly and likeable guy who interacted with subordinates through a constant barrage of jokes and informal comments. But his subordinates pointed out that his "style is an obstacle in communicating with the Chinese." The locals remarked that his personal style was different from theirs, though they appreciated his energy. "But when things go bad, he should control his emotions." In another context, a customs official remarked disdainfully, "American culture is too spontaneously subjective and willful" and "is not suitable for firms in China." At the same time, such thinking does not constrain Chinese professionals from being quite individualistic in their handling of social knowledge and relationships. This seeming paradox between a rejection of American-style individualism and a Chinese self-interested instrumentality is further compounded when set against the stereotypical view that Confucian norms constrain self-interested behavior. As we shall see, Confucian norms of social rank and deference can in fact become mechanisms for self-serving strategies of mobility and advancement.

The self-fashioning of professionals is reinforced by a sense of entitlement as highly educated Chinese men, that is, individuals who embody Chinese culture and prestige in a way that Westerners cannot understand and will never share. Chinese men have *guanxi* power at multiple levels which foreigners can never achieve. At the same time, the authorities implicitly trust only Chinese men, thus intensifying the importance of male professionals as intermediaries with foreign firms. At the same time, foreign companies rely on Chinese men to deal with officialdom. Without these bridging figures, it is no exaggeration to say that global business in China would grind to a halt. So let us take a closer look at two of them.

Chen is an import-export (*wu liu*) manager for the German cutlery company mentioned above. "It is a question of appropriate position. Most men always think about the next position in another firm. After one year, they want to leave because it seems a waste of time already invested. They always want to expand their salaries. They do not think they can take risk within the ranks; they want to be hired as managers right away. Men think they ought to have the top position in a company." Short of that, male professionals want to hold key positions that involve wielding personal and political power. Thus "many men want to work for joint ventures because there is the need for *guanxi* to deal with top government officials." In his view, then, the value of Chinese men to foreign companies lies not in their technical skills but in their access to the world of Chinese officialdom.

In his own case, he had accumulated vital contacts as a businessman up and down the coast before going to work for the German company. In his current job he negotiates on behalf of his foreign bosses with suppliers and customers. More strategically, he deploys his connections with old school chums and friends now employed in institutions that control the flow of goods in and out of China. In this murky sphere of officialdom, a cadre of male bureaucrats tightly limits political access, sanctions, and permission to elite Chinese men. Because of his *guanxi* connections, Chen can handle the firm's needs for foreign currency conversion, transfer shares, and ensure on-time delivery to various local authorities. "Some think that time is money. But you have to have a relationship with the relevant person. There is a short cycle time for products. So there is the need to call the relevant person to take care of the cargo, or it may end up [stuck] in shipment." His role includes not only converting technical needs into political obligations but also exercising the capacity to identify, in the maze of bureaucracy, the "relevant person" to push the button that will set desired objects or actions into motion. "Government connections are best for shortening times for handling things. It depends on how important it is in [officials'] thinking to do something." Chen's translation of the firm's needs into a political priority for the government official concerned is a necessary conversion in order for foreign capital to realize its investment in China.

Chen's crucial role is repeated in many foreign firms that rely on a well-connected male employee to spring the mechanism for circulating the flow of commodities and services. Another such player is Wu, who is employed in a Fortune 500 company that manufactures equipment for health and security uses. Wu sees himself as a critical link between "the company and the customs house." He has made himself indispensable by becoming a very flexible resource, dealing with all aspects—ordering, processing, and exporting materials—that require translation from the global business realm to the customs authorities. His translation role is absolutely necessary, because as he sees it, Americans are hampered by their lack not only of contacts with bureaucrats but also of the necessary cultural finesse. "Chinese people have this concern with self-esteem and feel very strongly about it. If Americans don't give face, their business won't succeed in China. They cannot deal with our official culture but must let Chinese employees manage social relationships. The stress on individualism is a major problem in cultural understanding. For instance, at Kodak, the Asian American manager for the Asia-Pacific [region] is more effective than whites in dealing with customs officials." An ethnic Chinese representative of a foreign company is more likely than a foreigner to earn the trust and respect of Chinese officials. Besides knowing how to handle foreign business affairs and managers, the flexible Chinese professional must learn to penetrate and activate the bureaucratic networks.

The China customs tower (Hai Quan Lou) in Shanghai is a beautiful green structure built in the 1920s to control the maritime trade with Western merchants. Today the slightly shabby exterior cannot conceal its strategic power in operating the switch that regulates the flow of goods and profits in and out of China. Despite official discourses insisting that there is less need for *guanxi* as China gains in economic power, Chen maintains, "Officials on the ground think that *guanxi* is a good thing, not corruption." Chinese authorities consider *guanxi* a way to preserve something that can only be called "Chinese national value," a domain of enclaved political power that is severely restricted, and can be pried open only by self-enterprising men like Chen, who can mediate and control the flows of value to global markets. Asked to describe his "work," Chen says: "I visit bureaucrats and conduct talks during dinner. If a problem is handled smoothly, we will have more dinners. A lot of gifts are presented."

While others may view such behaviors as merely the continuation of *guanxi* business as usual, I view them as translational practices that participate in a mode of self-fashioning that constitutes a new ethical regime of self-reflexivity and self-valuation. Practices that daily convert value across separate spheres are political acts that allow the new professionals to oscillate between being company men and bureaucratic men without becoming completely one or the other. By abstracting information about institutions and inscribing them in practice, self-fashioning mediates among potentially competing systems of value. Meanwhile, the circulation of these self-practices reconstitutes networks that allow value to be converted back and forth between economic and political domains, thus also reconstituting the social in metropolitan China today. Professional fixers and operators are shaping a new kind of politically innovative masculine subject. Self-confident, politically connected, and risk taking, he wields technical knowledge, social skills, and a brash personality to transform corporate interests, via the detour of Chinese officialdom, into global profits.

Designing Women

While male professionals gain personal power and identity from converting assets across domains, there are limits to their capacity to trans-code value. Many educated Chinese men are monolingual and are extremely uncomfortable with foreign languages. Chen admits that "men have difficulty dealing with foreigners, especially when it comes to expressive communication. Chinese women are better at languages and have more complex talents in communication." He maintains that women's greater language skills, together with their subordinate gender position, make them more suitable "for lower management positions. Women are more willing. They want stable jobs, and then [to] find husbands." For their language competence and greater compliance with authority, he argues, "many [Western] companies tend to employ women." His interpretation seems excessively male chauvinist, and a reflection of his own nationalist sense of employment by, yet political independence from, foreign capitalists. Many men work with foreigners long enough to acquire new money and knowledge; their main goal is to assemble political contacts that can later be converted into personal wealth once they leave foreign employment and set up their own private businesses.

Despite male disdain, ambitious Chinese women often seek a different trajectory of personal empowerment than their male counterparts. Instead of selling themselves as gatekeepers to the political citadel, female professionals focus on cultivating cosmopolitan power that is partially situated offshore. This divergent pathway of self-empowerment is reinforced by the impact of an ever-increasing number of college graduates. Today college education is no longer reserved for the very elite. By 2004 the proportion of eighteen- to twenty-two-year-old in college had risen from 4 to 15 percent. The number of entering freshmen, about half of them female, had jumped to 4 million a year.[20]

A majority of female university graduates face deep gender-based discrimination from Chinese employers and institutions, which mostly prefer male applicants. In desperation, female job seekers advertise their physical charms by including pictures of themselves clad in miniskirts or bikinis. Others register their capacity to sing and dance as qualifications for public relations positions.[21] Furthermore, the vast majority of college-educated women do not have the kinds of networks their male counterparts use to find a job or a position themselves as political brokers. The entrenched male monopoly over Chinese institutions pushes ambitious young women to seek self-advancement mainly in the foreign sector.

Women in the lower ranks of corporate employment make themselves indispensable to foreign firms. Chen's German boss agrees that "there are more female than male white-collar workers in general. They seem more careful, future-oriented [in terms of a career within the firm], more reliable, and stable. Men are a bit don't-care-so-much [about the company]." Women capitalize on their perceived qualities of reliability and diligence as a way to rise up within the ranks of foreign firms. At the American electrical factory, for instance, a female engineer who had been employed for eight years was given a scholarship to attend a University of Washington MBA program based at Fudan University. Citibank in Shanghai has sent a number of bright female workers to enrichment programs. The personnel director expressed some frustration that the trend among aspiring young women is to use their company-sponsored training as a steppingstone to emigrate abroad, mainly to Europe and the United States.

Another avenue for seeking educational and career opportunities beyond a strictly Chinese milieu is to associate with foreign men. In Shanghai's bars and nightclubs, Chinese women carouse with European and American men, while Chinese men serve drinks. The scene could be out of colonial era Shanghai, but the qualitative difference is that the working women here are not prostitutes or simply good-time girls but highly educated white-collar workers who desire marriage to a foreign man. A transnational marriage enhances a professional woman's flexibility in both work and travel, and offers a future as part of a transcultural couple who can better bridge international markets. There are increasing numbers of high-prestige international marriages, invariably between an accomplished Chinese woman and a global businessman. Elite women can wield powerful linguistic and cultural skills in the service of cross-border businesses.

The most famous case is Wendi Deng, a mainlander married to Rupert Murdoch, the media mogul who is twice her age. "Deng has been the locomotive behind Murdoch's long push into the country, serving first as his personal interpreter at News Corp., then a mistress and an intimate adviser on China after their eventual marriage in 1999."[22] In 2007, Deng joined the board of MySpace China, a social networking web site that further advances their media frontiers. However, given the News Corp.'s past compliance with Chinese Internet censorship, Deng's new role will foster more blogging pleasures but probably not online politics.

Another example of the globally oriented female executive is Wei Christianson, the chairman of China Citigroup Global Markets Asia. China-born, Christianson was educated at Amherst College and Columbia University (where she received her J.D. degree). She is among a small but growing group of Chinese professional women valued for their translational skills and cultural flexibility. Major banks, law firms, venture capital firms, and multinational corporations are turning to Chinese-born managers, displacing an earlier reliance on overseas Chinese from Southeast Asia. Besides having a foreign education and knowledge skills, the new mainland Chinese powerbroker is valued for her capacity to open up China's social networks to foreigners. "Having the right cultural background in China and Wall Street experience: that is the most sought-after skill," said a Chinese male lawyer who worked on the successful Lenovo acquisition of IBM in 2005.[23] While many of the Chinese players in mega-deals are foreign-educated men, female executives are considered more agile because of the nuance and understanding they bring to handling both Chinese and foreign parties. Female professionals who position themselves at the nexus of global and Chinese business are appreciated for their international pizzazz and navigational skills in translating foreign investments into profitable Chinese acquisitions. Christianson, for instance, has landed big deals for Citibank such as China Unicom, Sinopec, and China Life Insurance.

At a less exalted level, other self-fashioning women carve a role for themselves as domesticators and framers of the foreign for the Chinese domestic market. Tapping into Orientalist fantasies of foreign advertising and Chinese views of women as cultural custodians, foreign businesses have turned to women to represent the foreign to the Chinese public. Global corporations in China soften their images by deploying a bevy of attractive Chinese women in the public areas of their offices, dealing with visitors and answering inquiries. By refashioning themselves as assistants, framers, and conduits of foreign interest, female professionals accentuate their perceived feminine attributes—verbal fluency, attractive personality, social ease with foreigners—into personal power. For instance, Chinese women have emerged as actors helping to create high-end markets for Western brand names. Since the 1980s, fashion magazines such as *Elle, Cosmopolitan,* and *Harper's Bazaar* have given Chinese women advice on consumer goods, lifestyles, and sex. Well-heeled urban women are already familiar with labels such as Gucci, Armani, Lanvin, and Chanel, the last two having recently staged splashy fashion shows in Shanghai. A Lanvin creative director expressed enthusiasm for the rise in sales of luxury goods. "But China is more than a market. It's not just a group of buyers. I get inspiration from its people, from its beautiful, strong women." Orientalist fantasies are lucrative for cultivating loyalty to high-end retailers among newly affluent Chinese women in China's top-tier cities.[24]

The launching of *Vogue China* signals that the passion for foreign logos has reached a scale (300 million urban consumers) ripe for further expansion of brand-name markets. The editorial director chosen by Condé Nast was Angelica Cheung. By helping them choose high-end labels, she was to be a tastemaker for potentially millions of Chinese women. Cheung is again the kind of eager young professional who has cosmopolitan knowledge and experience. Her degrees were in law and English literature, and she had been an editor of *Elle China.* Her international experience was gained in the news media in Hong Kong and in fashion circles in Paris and Milan. Having become a fashionista herself, she was eager to refashion Chinese women's lifestyle aesthetics. "The most important thing is that today in China you feel the will to be more fashionable," she said, "and the desire to live a better life is very strong. And with the new money, [Chinese consumers] have the means of doing it. But these people need guidance."[25] But tastemakers like Cheung also give advice to foreign labels about Chinese women's preferences, such as for having boutiques in mega-malls rather than as stand-alone stores, or about linking luxury labels to prestige, or "face," as a way of flaunting wealth and status; saleswomen therefore are advised to create an aura of exclusivity. By nurturing wealthy Chinese women's interest in using luxury goods as a way to build personal value, Cheung translates fashion's lust for profits in China.

It appears that elite Chinese women are more effective than their male counterparts at the international level in translating cultural images into moneymaking projects. Dancing across the fault lines of Chinese socialism and Orientalist capitalism, professional women—as multinational employees, advertising copywriters, or international executives—have become the public face of a new China. While self-propelling men excel at working the ambiguous levers of Chinese politics, women deploy their linguistic skills and understanding of an ambiguous China to help international executives capitalize on China's great investment opportunities.

• • •

In remaking selves, Shanghainese professionals capitalize as well on foreign (mis)perceptions of China, its culture, and its politics as unchanging attributes that require "Chinese" mediation. Because they both embody and activate Chinese "value" in a transnational context, these professional men and women knowingly play off images of national authenticity and cultural expertise. Their role as gatekeepers to Chinese political power casts the self-propelling activities of ambitious men as defending nationalist interests. Female professionals capitalize on Orientalist perceptions of their skills and charm thus encouraging the perception that their mediations express the "positive" or more appealing aspects of Chinese "culture." As unavoidable translators for foreigners in the Chinese environment, young professionals simultaneously bridge and reinforce the separation between foreign and Chinese worlds as arenas of distinct values.

In such a milieu, is the communist party girl a figure of political liberalism or political adventurism? What kind of social imaginary is being reconfigured by this self-propelling individualism that adroitly sidesteps self-questioning of the political condition? What notions of personhood are emerging in the encounter between global corporate culture and Chinese authoritarian socialism? There is some evidence of a Western liberal concept of individual subjectivity, the kind of independent-thinking subject who critiques social conditions of oppression. A few journalists and lawyers who champion the poor and who appear to seek a radical form of individual freedom have been mercilessly harassed and frequently imprisoned by the authorities. Meanwhile, among those CCP-approved, politically correct professionals busily managing proprietary selves, there is little conviction about the right of inalienable right. Privatization opportunities can be withdrawn at any time by the socialist state, so a key impulse in self-fashioning must be the maxim about making hay while the economic sun shines on Shanghai.

It seems appropriate to end by noting that Western journalists like Howard French, mentioned earlier in this chapter, often mistake the flashy and fashionable urban elites as harbingers of a "free-spoken civil society" in China. They tend to invest those self-fashioning individuals who nimbly interweave socialist authoritarianism and global markets with the mantle of political freedom when they are really the dancing soldiers of China's take on neoliberalism.

12. Living Buddhas, Netizens, and the Price of Religious Freedom

Dan Smyer Yü

"Dantseng Dzashi Rinpoche is a reincarnation of Guru Padmasambhava. He is bringing his teachings to Han Chinese. . . . Living Buddha Dantseng Dzashi is traveling to Shanghai, Beijing, Guangdong, and other places, accepting disciples. Those who have truthful faith in tantric teachings may join him. The contact person in Shanghai is Zhouma at this number. . . ." This Tibetan Dharma event announcement appeared on the discussion forums of four Chinese Buddhist Web sites in spring 2003. According to the instructions of Zhouma, a young woman from Gansu Province, participants were told to meet in front of two large tour buses in the parking lot of the People's Square in downtown Shanghai on a Friday morning. After the buses were loaded, she and her boyfriend collected ¥300 from everyone for the weekend-long event. After about an hour's drive, the buses arrived at a convent in a rural village on the outskirts of Shanghai. Shortly after lunch, Zhouma instructed everyone to greet Living Buddha Dantseng Dzashi at the front gate. At about 2:00 P.M. her cell phone rang. She announced that his vehicle was approaching. In the meantime, her boyfriend was asking the faithful crowd to kneel as a gesture of devotion to the Living Buddha. A black Lexus pulled up to the front gate. Two young Tibetan lamas in their late twenties stepped out of the car. Both of them looked a bit shocked to see the kneeling crowd. They grinned at each other. The younger lama whispered to Zhouma. She turned to the crowd, telling them to stand up. The greeting process continued as the young Living Buddha sat down in the Dharma Hall. The attending lama and Zhouma collected the mounting cash alms, while Zhouma's boyfriend maintained the orderly line.

Two days later a fresh comment was inserted in the discussion forums of the four Web sites where Zhouma had made her initial announcement. The comment read, "Two Tibetan youngsters fooled a crowd of ignorant Buddhists in Shanghai."

Religious Freedom and the Creative Destruction of the Global Market

This type of Web-facilitated Tibetan Buddhist event in coastal China is becoming a noticeable trend among Chinese Buddhists in spite of the fact that cross-regional religious activities are not legally permitted without official approval. In early 2006 the Chinese state released its official survey, citing the presence of 4 million Catholics, 10 million Protestants, 18 million Muslims, and over 100 million Buddhists in China.[1] These figures do not include those religious adherents who are not willing to register themselves with the Chinese state's Bureau of Religious Affairs. Among these reviving religious traditions, Tibetan Buddhism has also become a popular religious option for non-Tibetans. Its popularity is uniquely shown in its presence in the electronic infrastructure of China's global market economy. The market is the primary means for the entrance of Tibetan Buddhism into the greater social realm of China.

This religio-economic phenomenon appears to be a triumph of worldwide neoliberalism, which, as David Harvey writes, "proposes that human well-being can best be advanced by the maximization of entrepreneurial freedoms within an institutional framework characterized by private property rights, individual liberty, free markets and free trade."[2] In reality, China is not a classic case of neoliberalism as delineated by Harvey, since it permits extensive legal ambiguity in protecting private property rights and continues its suppressive measures in addressing individual liberty. What qualifies current social and economic conditions in China as a neoliberal case is the continuing process of its privatization of state resources toward privileged individuals within the elite social strata[3] and its full participation in the global economy.

Whether or not China completely fits the framework of neoliberalism is not my concern in this chapter; privatization, however, as the primary trademark of the neoliberal approach, does hold my interest. China has experienced approximately thirty years of privatization—almost exclusively the privatization of state-owned resources—signifying a transition, or rather a reversal, from China's early socialist collectivization to private ownership in the context of the global market economy. Since the late 1990s, the Chinese state has decreased its public rhetoric of privatization. The process nevertheless continues in the twenty-first century as *shichanghua*, or marketization. The social meaning of privatization as marketization is evolving beyond the mere redistribution of material resources. In the realm of religious affairs, privatization, paralleling the aforementioned transitional and redistributive process, refers to the reclamation as a private person of the collectivized, standardized self of the era of communist extremism. This private self is understood as an intangible social entity that can best be delineated by an array of religious concepts such as spirit, psyche, and the soul. Thus, the focus of my concern is the inner realm of the individual in the midst of the interplay of religious revivals and China's market economy.

Consequently, I argue that the revival of Tibetan Buddhism in a period of market reform is a process of what Harvey calls "creative destruction"—the trademark of neoliberalism in practice, if not in theory. In the case of China, my understanding of the creative aspect of this process is derived from my ethnographic observation of China's globally linked market as not only a global economic system but also a spontaneous social space in local settings where what has previously not been permitted finds room to display its social presence and make itself available for private cognitive processes without the overtly intrusive interruption of the state. In other words, this creative aspect signifies an emerging freedom of religion sanctioned not by the Chinese state but by the market, along with other fledgling public discourses in China. On the ground level, the accessibility and sustainability of religious practices for common Chinese citizens in the case of Tibetan Buddhism is heavily contingent on the electronic networks of China's market. In this sense, the creative aspect is inherently an outcome of the modern market.

When this "creativity," however, is linked with destruction, from Harvey's perspective, market-sustained religious freedom is transformed into a practice of consumption that overturns the spiritual order of things. This transformation is destructive mostly because of the exteriorization of the individual's inner yearning for authentic religious life. This type of spiritual yearning and the market's subversion of religious spirituality mirror what many contemporary Chinese intellectuals deem the *jingshen-weiji*, or "spiritual crisis," a prevalent cultural occurrence in China. Whatever is yearned for in the market bears market value. The profit-oriented teleology of the market inevitably transfigures the initial, spontaneous sense of freedom into a commercializing process. A case in point is the large cash flow that has moved Tibetan Buddhism from Tibetan regions to urban China within the networks of China's market.

Neoliberal Destabilization of the Tibetan Buddhist Tradition

Contemporary Chinese Buddhists' fascination with Tibetan Buddhism began in large part with the cyber-representation of Tibetan *tulkus* (incarnate lamas), or

Living Buddhas in Chinese, in Kham and Golok, two Tibetan regions in Sichuan and Qinghai provinces. The on-line narratives and images of Tibetan Buddhist teachers and their communities are obviously yielding great social effects. Since the late 1990s, many Chinese pilgrims to Tibetan monasteries in Kham and Golok, and those who attend Tibetan Buddhist events in their urban locales, personally own or have access to computers and Internet services. They are an integral part of the rising segment of the Chinese population known as *wangmin*, or "netizens," referring to those who formally subscribe to Internet services or who frequently Web surf or are registered with various Web sites of their choosing.

The cyberspace of Chinese Buddhist netizenship is only a part of the larger electronic infrastructure of China's market economy. China is undergoing a "digital leap forward,"[4] and in this regard the Chinese state, as an agent of global neoliberal practices, has contributed to the multidimensionality of the recent Tibetan Buddhist revival among Chinese adherents in cyberspace. Thus, Chinese Buddhist netizenship is a result of the localizing process of economic globalization, which is known for the phenomenon of compression and connectivity across geographic distances, and across differing cultures and belief systems.[5] This infrastructural condition means that virtual Tibetan Buddhism is not a single entity but a composite of many determinations. It is a tension-laden global assemblage, a term that Stephen J. Collier and Aihwa Ong define as follows: "Global implies broadly encompassing, seamless, and mobile; assemblage implies heterogeneous, contingent, unstable, partial, and situated."[6] These contingencies, instabilities, and partialities again convey a strong sense of a localized global reality in which conflicting cultural, political, and economic forces are interposed and are mutually maneuvered for their own interests. In this context, Chinese netizens' spiritual conception of Tibetan Buddhism is often susceptible to being turned into commercial capital for profit-making ventures.

Since the late 1990s, more and more Tibetan "Living Buddhas" have emerged in cyberspace. Many of their hagiographies, written by Chinese Buddhists, are like appetizers that lure hungry netizens to purchase products related to Buddhist practices. In comparison to the personal narratives of Chinese pilgrims in the earlier stages of the Tibetan Buddhist revival in Kham, these hagiographies often provoke a sense of disbelief in the reader with regard to the spiritual authenticity of the Living Buddhas represented in the virtual world. For example, Guru Gyagong, a Living Buddha from a little-known monastery in Kham, emerged online as a "Buddha of Wealth Gods" in the summer of 2002. His largest patron is a Buddhist bookstore located in the Tibetan quarter of Chengdu, which sells Buddhist publications in both print and digital versions. Its owner also boasts that the store is the largest "Web City of Buddhist Business." In the over two hundred–page hagiography of Guru Gyagong given free to the store's customers, the twenty-four previous lifetimes of this "Buddha of Wealth Gods" are meticulously narrated. To my knowledge he is the first Tibetan Living Buddha who has

Figure 5. A seventeen-year-old Khamba "Dharma King" performing an empowerment ritual in Shanghai. Courtesy of Dan Smyer Yü.

claimed to be an incarnation of three prominent Chinese historical figures, namely, Confucius, Sima Qian, and Emperor Xiaoming of the Eastern Han Dynasty. These Chinese cultural icons are attributed, respectively, to Guru Gyagong's second, fifth, and seventh incarnations. In the meantime, the sale of Guru Gyagong's Tibetan herbal medicine for liver and kidney ailments appeared to be going well on my visits to the store between 2002 and 2004.

The commercial deployment of charismatic Tibetan Living Buddhas is a prominent marker of the consumption of religion whose consequence leads to the disjointing of a religious belief from its practice. Vincent Miller says, "When consumption becomes the dominant cultural practice, belief is systematically misdirected from traditional religious practices into consumption."[7] In the case of Chinese Buddhist netizens' consumption of Tibetan Buddhist spirituality, money is the primary medium that makes such consumption possible. To be specific, money in the form of cash is the primary indicator of China's current economic prosperity on the ground level, especially in the coastal regions. In my participation in various Dharma events in Tibetan regions, I estimated that the average amount of cash that a Chinese pilgrim offered to a Living Buddha was between ¥500 and ¥1,000. In some private sessions the amount ranged from ¥20,000 in cash to pledges of a wire transfer of half a million RMB or more. It is

Figure 6. Akha Choyang Rinpoche, a charismatic Tibetan lama in Golok, blessing Tibetan and Chinese pilgrims. Courtesy of Dan Smyer Yü.

understandable that it would not be possible for Chinese pilgrims to travel with perishable items as offerings. This flood of cash, however, has caused many leading Tibetan monastic figures to worry about the fate of their monastic tradition.

While I was in Kham in 2003, I discussed issues of religious consumerism among Chinese Buddhists with Lama Gyamtso, one of the intimate disciples of the late Manser Rinpoche, a beloved tantric master based in Golok, Qinghai Province. He told me:

> This is a perverted time. Everyone believes that one's merit comes from money and power In recent years, there are many fake Living Buddhas. Money or political power can buy this title. I dare say those "Living Buddhas" and "Dharma kings" roaming in Han areas have rarely sat down for practice in their lifetime, and have no sense of enlightenment, though they skillfully reap offerings from countless Han Buddhists who blindly worship their titles.

Lama Gyamtso is not the only Tibetan teacher who is concerned about current trends in Tibetan Buddhism in China. Duoshi Rinpoche, a Geluk *tulku*, is also among the most vocal Tibetan teachers. In my conversations with him, he used the phrase "Dharma minstrels" to characterize many unqualified Tibetan tantric teachers who conduct "Dharma events" in urban regions, suggesting that they are "impostors ripping off ignorant Chinese Buddhists in the name of the Buddha." The late Khenpo Jigme Phuntsok also painstakingly tackled issues related to the activities of unqualified lamas traveling in Tibet and China. In a

Dharma talk at his academy in 2000, he pointed out: "More and more lamas have betrayed their ultimate teachers. Many of them treat their monastic liveli-hood as a conventional profession. More and more phony *tulkus* and khenpos have popped out of the earth to 'teach the Buddhadharma.' "[8]

Catallaxy and the Imagined Community of Tibetan Buddhists

In my work with on-line Chinese Buddhist forums and actual pilgrims in the Ti-betan regions of Sichuan and Qinghai provinces, I see a certain primitive trait of the market, whether global or local, and that is the potential to form sponta-neous communities among those who share similar interests. Friedrich von Hayek calls this fundamental characteristic of the market "catallaxy," or "catal-lactics," derived from the Greek terminology for economic systems. It means not only "to exchange" but also "to admit into the community" on a spontaneous basis.[9] This aspect of the ancient Greek market system seems consistent with the current neoliberal construct of a single worldwide market system. It permits the use of the networks of the global market for purposes other than profit-making ventures.

From this perspective I see the rising popularity of Tibetan Buddhism as a catallactic phenomenon of China's market economy. The development of the market has engendered various spontaneous communities such as associations of Web-based Chinese Buddhists whose religious activities are dependent on the mechanisms of the market economy. This catallactic phenomenon is an integral part of China's ongoing market reform, which aims at a full privatization that may ultimately reduce the Chinese state's responsibility for its citizens' basic so-cial safety net in terms of health insurance and retirement provisions. Sponta-neously formed communities and public discourses in China's market system suggest that there is what Richard Madsen calls a "new freedom" with "a capac-ity for personal expression" in China's current consumer revolution.[10] With re-gard to religion, the catallactic aspect of the market obviously materializes popular yearnings for reclaiming the freedom of inner expression in relation to the spiritual dimension of human life. In other words, the Chinese state's priva-tization project has inadvertently become in part a popular process of regaining and reprioritizing the self that was once collectivized in the series of political campaigns promulgated by the Chinese Communist Party. The modern market-place becomes an alternative social space where the answers to questions of ulti-mate human truth are no longer monopolized by state ideology; other options reveal themselves as more and more religious Web sites are emerging.

From Hayek's catallactic perspective, I consider China's market economy to constitute an "explosive growth of new venues and modes for socializing."[11]

These provide a platform for the enactment of religious freedom as defined not by Chinese policymakers but by religious practitioners themselves. Electronically facilitated Tibetan Buddhism relies on this platform for constituting itself as a "virtual community of faith" or a "new cybersect"[12] whose methods of communicating are the passages to a "new freedom."[13]

In this context, religious expression is becoming commonplace in the electronic network of China's market economy. In the Chinese cyberworld of Tibetan Buddhism, the virtual is not necessarily the opposite of the real; instead, it is an extension of the real from the immediate physical locations of individual Buddhist netizens. The virtual world of Tibetan Buddhism indeed functions as a public medium for the congregation of numerous individuals with a religious commonality. To a large extent, this virtual medium ultimately brings people together as pilgrims or as participants in Tibetan Buddhist events in urban settings. It has formed an imagined religious community whose members all across contemporary China are united in both cyberspace and their actual pilgrimage settings.

Chinese Tibetan Buddhists address one another as *jingang xiongdi*, or *vajra*-brothers, which is derived from *jingangcheng*, or *vajrayana* in Sanskrit, meaning the indestructible vehicle of the Buddha's teachings. Both on the pilgrimage routes and in on-line discussions, Buddhist netizens, including women, frequently use this form of address. This collective spiritual sentiment becomes a generative process as more and more newcomers come in contact with Tibetan Buddhism in cyberspace. In this process, imagination can precede action. This condition of modernity is increasingly conspicuous in twenty-first-century China, where "the imagination, especially when collective, can become the fuel for action."[14] In the midst of China's rapid economic development, however, the impulses of this imagination-based action are frequently steered toward profit-generating purposes.

Digital Hagiographic Omission and Charismatic Netizenship

The contemporary Chinese fascination with Tibetan Buddhism coincides with the popular culture of Tibetan Buddhism worldwide, which is primarily focused on incarnate lamas, including internationally renowned figures such as the Dalai Lama, Sogyal Rinpoche, the late Chögyam Trungpa Rinpoche, as well as locally celebrated ones such as Hsiabha Rinpoche, Sengji Tserang Rinpoche, Buchu Rinpoche, and Guru Jigme Phuntsok of Nianlong Village in Kham. These religious celebrities were all identified as *tulkus* when they were young boys. As Peter Moran points out, *tulkus* belong to "a special order of being."[15] They are embodiments of both Tibetan Buddhist lineages and Tibetan cultural history in the eyes of their local communities, and as such they are both cultural institutions and individuals. As institutions, they hold office and command the authority of their respective lineages, large or small. As individuals, they have both consanguineal and affinal ties, and most important of all, they have personalities which are reflected in their relationships with people around them. They do not always appear saint-like as they lead their daily lives. Unlike celibate monks, many *tulkus* live in their villages or in semi-nomadic settlements with their wives and children. *Tulkus'* institutionality and individuality are thus inextricably intertwined with their personal lives.

But when their images are digitally enhanced and transported to computer screens, when they become "Living Buddhas" among Chinese Buddhist netizens, their institutionality overshadows their individuality. They become offices uninhabited by persons. What holds the office of a Living Buddha in the netizens' digital representation is what I call "impersonalized charisma," which is based on selective hagiographic representation of the *tulku*. This is not what Max Weber calls "pure charisma," which is "self-determined and sets its own limits."[16] The involvement of the market and information technologies in the public representation of Living Buddhas often strips away the self-determination of actual Tibetan *tulkus*. The concrete personhood of the *tulku*, which is relationally embedded in his familial and communal ties, is plastered over with digitally enhanced images and hagiographical rhetoric.

Zhang, a former photojournalist based in Chengdu, is a faithful disciple of the abbot of a monastery, one of many monastic sites in Kham, currently in western Sichuan. His cyber-hagiography of the abbot, a *tulku* living with his wife and their son, is the primary theme stringing together the pages of a Web site dedicated to the monastery. The ordinariness of the abbot is eclipsed by claims of his magic powers and the extraordinariness of a saint. The hagiographic genre emphasizes the unusual foresight and the superhuman qualities of the abbot, as Zhang writes:

> When he was fifteen years old, the situation in Kham was drastically worsening. Rinpoche was locked up in prison. . . . Although his body was shut in the fortress of the prison, he was able to exit and enter it without hindrances. The magic power of his enlightenment allowed him to walk through the thick walls of the prison. . . .
>
> Once he was at Dharma Monastery, he kneaded a ball of butter into a frog at a stream nearby. He inserted a mantra written on a piece of paper into the hollow belly of the butter frog. He was going to hide it behind a rock. When he moved the rock, a deep hole appeared beneath the rock. He placed the butter frog in the hole. As soon as he let go of it, it became a real frog! The next day, some of his guests went back to the hole and saw the frog still alive. . . . This is proof of what is called "the quantified appearance of enlightenment wisdom."

Zhang's style is not unique but is rather common to many hagiographers, past and present. In Frank Reynolds and Donald Capps's book *The Biographical Process*, hagiography is defined as "sacred biography," an account "written by followers or devotees of a founder or religious savior."[17] In their reading of various sacred biographies, they find two common traits: humanization and spiritualization.[18] The humanization process identifies the "everyman" in the sacred person, in the sense of finding an overarching quality of commonly shared humanity. Thus the qualities of this "everyman" reflect the ideals of humanity—courage, forbearance, wisdom, and compassion. In the meantime, the sacred biographer "spiritualizes the subject by expunging references to his human weakness."[19] Both humanization and spiritualization involve the sacred biographer in "the inclusion or omission of materials."[20] In this respect I share the sentiment expressed by Reynolds and Capps, who state, "[Scholars] are painfully aware that the available texts provide us with very little authentic information concerning the details of [the saint's] life"[21]—except that he is the man of "everyman."[22]

It is not unique that Tibetan Living Buddhas are being transfigured into the man of everyman in contemporary China. This popular imaginative process is identical to what is happening in the West, where Tibet is actively personified as a pristine place of sacred purity. In his *Virtual Tibet*, Orville Schell remarks: "No longer is the creation of our Tibet largely the product of the written word working on our imaginations. Now it can be visited as if it were a multidimensional Web site."[23] Precisely in this multidimensional Web site in Chinese cyberspace Tibetan Living Buddhas are hagiographically crafted. They are visually molded into various fantastic images and are made easily accessible. In this sense, the cyber-mediated charisma manifests itself through acts of imagination, in which Living Buddhas are actively envisioned as charismatic totemic beings who beget a virtual totemic tribe—the Chinese netizenship of Tibetan Buddhism.

In my participation in netizens' on-line discussions and actual Dharma events, I find that charisma derives more from the crowd psychology of the Buddhist netizens than from the personal qualities of a given Tibetan incarnate lama. The digitally enhanced charisma is a transpersonal psychic state rather than a "gift of grace" that resides in only a single individual.[24] This highly impersonalized charisma, against the backdrop of China's rapid development of a market economy, pertains to a popular conception of religious spirituality that at once reflects the inner realm of the individual and begets both symbolic currencies and economic capital.

Neoliberal Erosion of the Moral Fabric

In my participation in Tibetan Buddhist Dharma events mediated by cyberspace, I noticed the obvious gullibility of Chinese Buddhists, as seen at the beginning of this chapter. Most participants do not question the authenticity of Tibetan lamas or their monastic authorization for the performance of tantric Buddhist rituals. Instead, they appear to be generous and willing to show their humility in the service of these Living Buddhas. On the cultural level, owing to the lack of familiarity on the part of the Chinese with Tibetan Buddhist culture, this type of gullibility also was seen in the Republican era, when Tibetan lamas toured southern China.[25] In the twenty-first century, a similar kind of cultural ignorance continues to exist among the Chinese. The attraction of today's Chinese spiritual seekers to Tibetan Buddhism, however, is unstoppable. It is apparently mediated by the spiritually efficacious images of Tibetan incarnate lamas in cyberspace, which do in fact evoke a strong sense of the sacred among spiritual seekers. But this does not explain why so many Chinese are desperately yearning for ritualized religious experiences. On the basis of my ethnographic, research I see this collective desperation among Chinese spiritual seekers as a primary signifier of that common phenomenon known as the "spiritual crisis."

Popular discourses on this collectively felt crisis emerged in the context of internationally recognized events in recent Chinese history, such as students' demonstrations in the late 1980s, the rampant corruption cases involving high-level officials, and intensified consumerism in the twenty-first century. A short essay titled "Do We Still Have a Spiritual Home?" by an anonymous author was widely posted in various privately operated Web sites. It alleges that the severity of China's spiritual crisis can be seen in the decline of the younger generation, who are self-centered and empty-headed, in the moral catastrophe reflected in the nationwide prostitution of young women, and in the widespread corruption in the upper strata of government.[26] The author includes his personal portrait of a family in crisis: the father sells barbecued mutton on a street corner, the mother sells pirated DVDs and CDs, and their daughter sells her body.

This is apparently a case of the effect of neoliberalism on Chinese society. As in other parts of the world, economically disadvantaged Chinese bear the primary brunt of the consequences of neoliberal creative destruction. Marketization, seen as the process of privatization, involves macro-economic structural change. In the meantime, it also gives rise to changes on a micro-economic level, such as various forms of street vending and peddling to meet one's basic needs, particularly among those who have been laid off by formerly state-owned businesses. To a large extent, this is indeed a social reality for ordinary Chinese people who provide their labor to, but do not substantially benefit from, the Chinese state's privatization and market reform. The sense of hopelessness roams at large among China's working-class population and their children. During the Chinese New Year in 2003, while I was staying in Hangzhou with a Tibetan lama from Kham, I witnessed a destitute street vendor's encounter with local law enforcement. One cold afternoon, as I was walking in the chic fashion district of the city, I saw six or seven *jing-jing*, short for "economic policemen," forcefully confiscating a dim sum cart from a woman and her handicapped son. Apparently they were "illegal" street vendors whom these economic policemen had been assigned to clear out. The woman's pleas were not heeded, as the policemen loaded the cart into their van. Suddenly, the woman and her child darted out into the street into the path of an oncoming bus, which screeched to a halt two feet from them. Then both of them dove under the front tires of the bus and refused to budge. Passengers got off the bus, and soon the crowd became large enough to create a two-hour traffic jam in the middle of the fashion district. Several people, who identified themselves as neighbors of the woman, attempted to pull her and the child from beneath the bus. Each time they were pulled out, they ran back underneath it, crying, "We don't want to live anymore!" Several carloads of traffic policemen arrived on the scene and attempted to arrest the woman. This immediately outraged the crowd, who formed a wall to block the attempt to take her into custody. Several of the woman's neighbors were explaining the cause of this commotion to a plainclothes policeman who appeared to be in charge. Not wanting to cause further outcry from the crowd, he agreed to contact these "economic policemen" and arrange for the return of the cart, while the neighbors sent the woman and the child home to their old apartment building behind the fashion district. As the crowd dwindled, an old woman told several latecomers on the scene that the woman was unemployed, while her husband was hospitalized for severe diabetes, and her ten-year-old son was nearly blind. Street vending seemed to be the only source of income for the family.

The social phenomenon of the spiritual crisis, in fact, is not limited to the economically disadvantaged. For many affluent Chinese, this crisis is not necessarily expressed in martyr-like suicides. It shows up instead in a personally felt but also commonly shared sense of "meaninglessness" among this growing elite population, as if life has lost its purpose for many of the newly rich who have reached the apex of material achievement.

At one of the Tibetan Dharma events in a rural area of Zhejiang Province, I met Mr. Liu, a successful entrepreneur in his early forties, who owns a pharmacy chain catering to the farming population of Zhejiang and Jiangsu provinces. He hires an array of store managers and licensed medical doctors for his stores. As a graduate student at a university in Beijing, he had been about to receive a master's degree in comparative literature in 1989. Because of his involvement with the leading student dissidents at Tiananmen Square, however, he was imprisoned for over two years in Beijing's Qincheng Prison for political prisoners.

In the early 1990s, he was released. With a loan from two of his high school friends who were themselves successful entrepreneurs, Liu developed his current formidable pharmaceutical business. Yet a daily sense of "meaninglessness" has haunted him. On the one hand, he still cannot get over his experience of having been abandoned by the student leaders at Tiananmen Square, who escaped and went abroad. On the other hand, he is experiencing existential fatigue with people around him, especially government officials whose administrative jurisdictions impinge on his business. In one of our conversations at his 2 million–yuan house, he lamented: "Everything has been so meaningless since I got out of prison. My 'democracy' friends were hypocrites. They ditched those of us left behind, and we had to go behind the thick walls of the prison. Now, sometimes I feel appreciative of the government for my success, but it is expensive to entertain its greedy officials. They are all over you whether or not your business is successful. Look at me. After these years of dining out with them, I am fat and have high blood pressure, and I suffer from insomnia." His material success has not brought happiness; instead, he has a raging case of cynicism toward everything. Having seen the base nature of humanity in events and people around him, he finds few ideals in life.

In cyberspace, an increasing number of Chinese intellectuals have been posting their on-line responses to this nationally felt spiritual crisis. On one Web site Yuan Zhimin, one of the writers of the TV series *River Elegies*, listed five essential factors of the spiritual crisis, namely, "the demise of the national ideology," "the absence of folk value systems," "the rupture of Chinese traditional culture," "the loss of moral conscience," and "the deserted inner world."[27] He cautioned his cyber-audience: "The spiritual crisis of mainland China has reached such a state. If it is not resolved, the Chinese will be beyond recognition and become a ferocious people."[28] This popular identification of the spiritual crisis clearly hinges on a primary index of the consequences of the iconoclastic approach of Chinese Marxism toward religions and of the creative destruction of China's rapidly growing consumerism.

On the popular level, the spiritual crisis cuts at the heart of numerous individuals' psyches and physical well-being. When the 10 percent annual economic growth of China is translated into qualitative terms, it means that people, whether poor or rich, are facing overwhelming forces of change that directly affect their psychological and material states. For example, in demographic terms, the recently suppressed Falun Gong movement attracted mostly unemployed workers and retirees without health insurance.[29] There is a clear correlation between material instability and spiritual and psychological breakdown. People are looking for alternative psychological, ideological, and spiritual solace. Both folk religions and traditional world religions, such as ancestor veneration, Buddhism, and Christianity, are experiencing a revitalization, but they are spatially confined within so-called officially registered places. To contemporary Chinese Buddhists, finding space in which to practice religion is a grave issue because most Buddhist monasteries have been integrated into the national tourism industry, and it is difficult for practitioners to congregate regularly in local monasteries that receive tourists seven days a week. These economic and sociopolitical constraints are pushing religious seekers to look for other spaces, and cyberspace is obviously a primary alternative. The emergence of Tibetan Buddhism in this virtual space opens a gateway for numerous Chinese to seek out spiritual explanations of the crisis through pragmatic and ritualized methods. In the meantime, it is subject to the forces of the market, which appears more destructive than creative.

Reversal of the Buddhist Order of Things in the Market

The rapid development of China's global market economy has engendered various "political vacuums,"[30] over which the Chinese state has attempted to take full
control, though it has not yet acquired the technology to do so. The cyberspace of
Tibetan Buddhism is one of these political interstices where regulatory forces with
authority over religion are associated more with the market than with the Chinese
state, in which the popular demand for religious practices is susceptible to being
transformed into a demand for the consumption of religious products, that is, for
religious events and ritual objects. This market-facilitated demand has been more
destructive than creative to the current revitalization of Tibetan Buddhism. In the
case of China, the neoliberal approach to the maximization of individual freedom
in the market seems to bestow a sense of empowerment on individual choice; but
the new freedom of religion in China's global market supports Madsen's observation that "the freshness of the experience of freedom depends on novelty."[31]
When the novelty of Tibetan Buddhism is transformed into a market value, it becomes transgressive to Tibetan monastic traditions.

The transgressive force of the market in the Tibetan Buddhist revival comes
into play mostly in terms of Chinese Buddhists' offerings in the form of cash.
The possession of money in China's modernization process is not just an indicator of one's wealth; it is also a measure of one's social status coupled with one's
purchasing power. This power affords Chinese Buddhists access to the novelty of
Tibetan Buddhism. In the meantime, it becomes a power of destructive dominance because of its direct connection with China's rising market economy. In
other words, instead of being a means of sustaining the emerging freedom of religion, it begins to remold Tibetan Buddhism according to the equation of supply and demand. Thus the Chinese Buddhists' alms-giving in the form of large
flows of cash is more an exhibition of purchasing power than a traditional offering to Tibetan Buddhist monasteries.

Traditionally, Buddhist almsgiving resembles Marcel Mauss's concept of the
gift economy. The difference is that this type of gift economy mostly involves the
exchange of the tangible with the intangible. In my experience, a list of gifts from
Tibetan laypeople to a *tulku* might include a scoop of yak butter for the oil lamps
in a Dharma Hall, a sack of *tsamba* (roasted highland barley), a bucket of fresh
yak milk in the morning, or a sheepskin for his winter attire. Money does appear
on the list, though it might be included in the minimum denominations of
RMB, such as coins or bills valued from ten cents to one yuan. In turn, the *tulku*
provides the laity with blessings, healing, and various initiation and empowerment rituals. In this respect, the exchange of almsgiving and ritual performance
accords with what Chris Gregory refers to as an "exchange of inalienable things
between transactors who are in a state of reciprocal dependence."[32] In a Tibetan

Buddhist community, the inalienability of both tangible and intangible things involved in this gift exchange follows from the reciprocal dependence between the *tulku* and his Tibetan lay followers.

This inalienability, however, is being rapidly breached in the modern market. In the context of religion, money raises an issue of morality pertaining to the alleged inconvertibility of what is cherished as sacred. In their discussion of money and the morality of exchange in the modern era, Jonathan Parry and Maurice Bloch, drawing on the perspective of Georg Simmel, write, "Anonymous and impersonal, money measures everything by the same yardstick and thereby—it is reasoned—reduces differences of quality to those of mere quantity."[33] This is exactly what is happening to the reviving Tibetan Buddhism in China. The inconvertibility of religious spirituality into monetary value can no longer stand high above everything else deemed material in a sophisticated modern market economy such as that of contemporary China. The value of religious spirituality is framed in the highly stereotypical moral attributes expressed in words such as "invaluable," "sacred," "indestructible," "irreducible," or "inviolable." When these spiritual attributes become enmeshed with money and mediated through the digitalized charismatic images of Living Buddhas, they do in fact generate desire on the part of those who would like to gain access to them with money. In this reality of China's market economy, the Chinese Buddhists' collective longing for something higher, loftier, more pristine and enlightening is trapped in the market economy, whose profit-oriented value system is crudely saturating and adulterating the traditionally cherished sacredness. Thus Tibetan Buddhism has become one of the many collective emotional symbols captured by the market and redeployed as a medium for cash flow.

It is no exaggeration to state that the fate of Tibetan Buddhism is in the hands of *tulkus* who have been the anchors of their communities since ancient times, as both cultural icons and religious leaders. Neither is it an overstatement to say that, more and more, contemporary *tulkus* have become almost inextricably entangled in the market economy in China as their images, hagiographies, and even personal presence are being increasingly digitalized, packaged, and marketed under the rubric "Living Buddhas" by profit-minded Chinese netizens in the name of "nonprofit" Dharma events. Without doubt, *tulkus* have become trapped in a virtual reality of Tibetan Buddhism by digitally mediated, fantastic hagiographic representations. This popular phenomenon resembles what Liah Greenfield deems the "unreflective imitation of the excited behavior of others"[34]—a crowd psychology of contemporary Chinese Buddhist netizens who seek empowerment from the supposed supernatural powers of the "Living Buddhas." Thus this electronically mediated consumption of Tibetan Buddhism is obviously fixated on the brand-names of "Living Buddhas," with their alleged specialties in performing magic. This fixation is patterned after secular consumers' fixation with brand-names such as Nike and Motorola. In this pattern of the consumption of religion, money is no longer a standard measurement of quantifiable objects in terms of conventional tangible goods and services; instead it seizes everything that comes in touch with it, including the digitally constructed biographies and images of Tibetan *tulkus* as an ancient religious institution.

The Price of Religious Freedom

In twenty-first-century China, the price of religious freedom increasingly refers to the purchasing power of the individual who yearns for such freedom from state control. It continues to be a social reality of China that religious affairs are highly regulated. Religious institutions and practitioners are subject to the authority of the Bureau of Religious Affairs, a powerful governmental organ that determines the social space and time for religious activities. The Chinese state currently permits religious activities only within officially registered religious institutions. Cross-regional religious activities like the Tibetan Dharma events in coastal Chinese cities are not legally allowed unless they are officially approved. Throughout this chapter my ethnographic narratives may have given the impression that Chinese Buddhists have increasing religious freedom; this freedom is limited, however, mostly within China's market economy, particularly its electronic infrastructure and privately arranged spaces.

This limitation is a markedly "Chinese characteristic" in comparison with the way privatization is being enacted in the market economy of former communist states of Eastern Europe. This "Chinese characteristic" has little to do with the features of traditional China; instead it can be understood as a manifestation of what Gordon White calls "market socialism."[35] The "socialist" attribute of this market economy refers to the legacy of the phenomenon of "verticality," meaning that "each individual and social group was incorporated into a hierarchically organized system of some kind as opposed to belonging to social institutions organized horizontally by their members."[36] In spite of the fact that the Chinese populace has been undergoing privatization for several decades, this socialist bureaucratic verticality continues to get in the way of resurgent horizontal social relations among individual citizens. This is clearly seen in the intimate liaison between entrepreneurs and China's socialist bureaucracy. David Wank points out that the state did not retreat during the era of market reform; instead its local bureaucratic power has been commodified and finds its clientele among entrepreneurs.[37] Harvey offers similar comments on the peculiar pattern of China's privatization as a state redistribution process: "The Chinese state has followed through a whole series of draconian steps in which assets have been conferred on a small elite to the detriment of the mass of the population."[38] Consequently, this socialist market economy obviously permits numerous incidents of high-level corruption, massive involuntary unemployment, forced relocation, and seizure of farmland for commercial development.

On the religious front, the effect of socialist verticality continues to drive religious seekers into the realm of the market for horizontal spiritual relationships as the catallactic aspect of the global market suggests a degree of spontaneous congregation of religious adherents within those networks. Thus privatization as a process of marketization in China parallels Chinese citizens' utilization of the market as an alternative space for public discourse on a variety of issues. Among them, marketized religions are becoming media for the reclamation of the private self from the previously collectivized socialist self. In the modern marketplace, however, this privatization of the self through religious orientation is a process of the exteriorization of one's inner search. The object of such inner yearning does not necessarily stay within the reach of the individual's search. More often than not, it is gripped by the commercializing forces of the market. This is where the emerging freedom of religion in the economic framework of China is subjected to the creative destruction of neoliberalism. The primary indication of this global-scale destruction, as Harvey notes, is that "the commodification of cultural forms, histories and intellectual creativity entails wholesale dispossessions."[39] In this respect, freedom of religion itself becomes a commodity with a price tag. Tibetan Buddhism in China is undoubtedly subject to the onslaught of these wholesale dispossessions as it is being accessed as an object of consumption.

13. Privatizing Control

Internet Cafés in China

Zhou Yongming

In Beijing on June 16, 2002, an Internet café called Blue Speed Limit, was set on fire. Twenty-five people perished in the disaster. It was later discovered that the café was operating without a license and the arsonists were three revenge-minded teenagers who had had a dispute with the café management. The mayor of Beijing immediately shut down all Internet cafés and launched a "rectification campaign" citywide. On June 26 the central authorities proclaimed that it would launch such a campaign nationwide in July and August, during which no new permits for setting up Internet cafés would be issued.[1] This event was widely reported by the Western media, which typically claimed that the Chinese government "has for several years staged periodic cybercafé raids . . . to shut down what is, for many Chinese, the main artery to the Internet. Control-crazy officials are struggling to monitor an information-packed online world that by its very name, the Web, is a tangle of unmanageable links to 'cultural pollution.' "[2]

I am grateful to the Committee on Scholarly Communication with China, the Woodrow Wilson Center for International Scholars, and the Graduate School of the University of Wisconsin, Madison, for their financial support for this research in 2001–2003. My thanks also go to Aihwa Ong and Li Zhang and to an anonymous reviewer for their insightful comments and suggestions on the early version of this chapter.

This report is an example of the unprecedented Western attention to the development of the Internet in China, which often focuses on the control efforts of the Chinese state. Government regulations with respect to Internet use are scrutinized, and the application of technologies for censoring and policing the information flow on the Net is protested. Government crackdowns on dissent activities in cyberspace are condemned, and details of each case are gathered and made public both on-line and through traditional media. In the earlier phase, many observers of China believed that Chinese authorities' control efforts would be in vain, claiming that the Internet, with its uniquely decentralized structure and absence of hierarchy, is uncontrollable and would change Chinese society anyway. For example, in January 1998, Radio Free Europe/Radio Liberty cited the prediction of an "expert" that "China's attempts to control the Internet were destined to fail" because most Chinese Internet users are university students who "are also [the] ones fighting most for freedom and democracy within their country" and "the ones who can cause the most damage to the communist form of government." In addition, claimed the same expert, the key to China's success in today's information age is the ability to obtain and integrate information freely at all levels. "How does one control access to information and still provide the information necessary for them to compete? The answer is simple: they can't."[3]

As is so often encountered by researchers on contemporary Chinese politics, it has turned out that this prediction was just another case of wishful thinking. The Internet is not as powerful or omnipotent as commonly thought, a force that by itself alone can change or even topple the current Chinese regime. Worse still, the Chinese decision makers have treated the Internet not as an evil monster but rather as an engine for economic and social growth, and have even adopted a proactive policy to develop the Internet. In recent years China has experienced phenomenal Internet growth without the government's losing much control. Nevertheless, Western attention still seems to focus predominantly on the control role of the state and often depicts it as a monster intent on destroying the Internet in China.[4]

I propose to de-mystify researchers' prescribed assumptions that are clearly grounded in the democratizing effect that the Internet supposedly is having on Chinese society. While most observers agree that the Internet will have its impact on Chinese politics, we have to realize that technology facilitates, it does not dictate, politics. The change is not necessarily in the direction hoped for, because the technology can be used by different parties in different ways to achieve diverse goals. The Internet can be used by the Chinese people to enlarge their space for political participation, and it can also be adopted by the Chinese state to consolidate its power.[5] Furthermore, the "democratizing" function of the Internet is itself a historical entity, not something insulating and intrinsic to change. A case in point is that not long ago, Westerners emphasized the "civilizing" or "modernizing" effects of science and technology to non-Western societies.[6] Today, in a different paradigm, the focus has shifted to the "democratizing" function of the Internet, a technology that is perceived to fit very well with, and even enhance, liberal democracy and a free market economy modeled after contemporary Western societies. Viewed from the historical perspective, however, the presupposed "democratizing" function of the Internet loses much of its persuasive power.

In a short period of time the Internet has become a serious academic topic and has received attention from many disciplines, ranging from political science and sociology to media and literary studies. Anthropology can certainly contribute to the study of the Internet through its ethnographic method, which pays special attention to human agency and the practices of everyday life while not neglecting the large-scale context in which that everyday life unfolds. As Stephen Collier and Aihwa Ong point out, to grasp the complex relationship between technology, politics, and ethics as anthropological problems, we should adopt "a mode of inquiry that remains close to practices, whether through ethnography or careful technical analysis. The result is a discerning, reflective, and critical approach that we feel is defining an important and exciting trajectory of interdisciplinary inquiry in the human sciences." And critical to this mode of inquiry is the conceptualization of these relationships as an "assemblage" that "is the product of multiple determinations" which will always be "heterogeneous, contingent, unstable, partial, and situated."[7]

In the following discussion I combine ethnographic observation on and historical analysis of the Internet café in order to discuss the politics of the Internet café in urban China and to examine how interactions among multiple parties with affiliations to the state and the market have shaped its complex, conflicting, and ever-changing development in recent years. Of different sizes, locations, and targeted customer groups, individual Internet cafés may be run in different styles, but their chief operational purpose remains the same, which is to provide Internet service to their customers and to profit from this service. Realizing this purpose, however, depends on the outcomes of daily operations. My descriptions and analyses are mainly based on my fieldwork in a Beijing Internet café called Ocean during summer 2001 and fall 2002, conducted mainly through interviews and participant observation.[8] I am fully aware that no single Internet café can claim to be representative of all. My intention here is just to present a snapshot that may help us better understand the bigger picture.

Viewing the politics of the Internet café as an assemblage comprising a contingent cluster of interacting elements also requires us to situate it in a number of broad contexts, which are themselves in continuous flux. In the discussion that follows, I try to embed my ethnographic and historical description of the Internet café in a number of theoretical formulations concerning issues of neoliberalism, privatization, governmentality, and relations between the state and the market. First, the politics of the Internet café has to be examined in the context of China's continuing turn toward neoliberalism, in which marketization and privatization have been actively promoted by the state. At first sight, using neoliberalism to describe a social order that still claims to be socialist may seem a little perplexing, yet various neoliberal practices in China have attracted scholarly attention.[9] Of special interest to this discussion is the fact that the seemingly improbable coexistence of authoritarian rule and free market economy within an ostensibly socialist system has created many neoliberal practices that are unique in the context of contemporary China. As we shall see, on the one hand, Internet cafés are primarily owned by individual entrepreneurs whose goal is profit-driven; on the other hand, the state tries to impose regulations that are contrary to key tenets of neoliberalism, which advocates "deregulation, privatization, and withdrawal of the state."[10] This brand of neoliberalism has made relationships between private entrepreneurs, the market, and the state more complicated in the arena of the operations of Internet cafés.

Second, the very fact that the Chinese state has to exert control in the context of the new market economy propels it to adopt new strategies in response. To grasp the complex and fluid picture, we have to realize that the Chinese state is not a monolithic entity, and its various elements often employ conflicting strategies and priorities concerning Internet development and control. It is clear that in facing the new challenges posed by Internet technology, the Chinese state has reacted not only defensively and passively but also proactively. In a very short period of time, the state has come up with more refined and flexible strategies to "govern" this new domain. Here Michel Foucault's concept of governmentality seems very relevant to our discussion because not only does it concern the "art of government," but also it could provide a critique of neoliberalism. As Thomas Lemke points out: "Governmentality is introduced by Foucault to study the 'autonomous' individual's capacity for self-control and how this is linked to forms of political rule and economic exploitation."[11] This concept provides a means of understanding neoliberalism as "a political rationality that seeks to govern not through command and control operations but through the calculative choice of formally free actors."[12]

Employing the concepts of neoliberalism and governmentality and situating them in contemporary China, I argue that in addition to allowing privatization in the economic domain, the state has also aimed to "privatize" certain aspects of control by devolving them to the private sectors. This new strategy is manifested in the fact that while the state continues to use coercive means to "control" and "police" cyberspace, it allots responsibilities to the private sector and individuals, resulting in a new mechanism for achieving the goal of maintaining economic privatization and political control. In the case of Chinese Internet cafés, Foucault's original emphasis on "self-control" can be expanded to include both individual users as well as owners of Internet café. The "self-control" of Internet café users is shown in the fact that they treat the café mainly as an entertainment establishment, indulging in on-line gaming and chatting while being less engaged in news reading and political discussion. To the individual cyber-entrepreneurs, their resistance to state regulations often stops when their ultimate goal of profit seeking is perceived as being in danger, for instance, in a situation such as allowing politically sensitive activities to be carried out in their cafés. By extending the right of privatization of business to this group, the state also privatizes part of its control by transferring it into the hands of cybercafé owners, in effect creating another form of "self-control."

It is at this juncture that we also have to pay attention to the role the market has played in China's neoliberal forms of governance. As we will see, in the context of economic privatization and the fast pace of development, the market has shown its dual role in either challenging or working together with the state to ensure its ultimate goal: profit making. By enlisting the market to serve its control goals, the state also initiates a process of privatization of control and lets individuals make "rational" choices of self-control within the limits set by the state. This is not to say that in the daily operations of the Internet café there are not examples of outright resistance. In fact, individual users of Internet cafés have developed diverse strategies to cope with state regulations, ranging from outright resistance to lip-service compliance. Even though my focus in this chapter is on the relationship between privatization, the market, and neoliberal governmentality, the aspect of resistance should be part of any analysis of the complex picture of Internet cafés in urban China.

Internet Cafés: A New Landscape in Chinese Urban Space

Since China commenced its open-door policy in the late 1970s, Chinese society has experienced tremendous social and economic transformations. Many Chinese cities have also experienced dramatic changes in both their physical and social landscapes. High-rise buildings, multilane freeways, and increased automobile traffic speak vividly of how "modern" many Chinese cities have become. Chinese urbanites have also been exposed to new venues of leisure on an almost daily basis, including disco halls, karaoke bars, movie theaters, beauty parlors, theme parks, shopping malls, and fast food outlets, to list only a few.[13] The Internet café has ostensibly been a new addition to the list since the end of the 1990s. In fact, Internet cafés have appeared throughout urban areas in China, and have become the newest location in the Chinese urban space to attract enthusiastic patrons seeking entertainment and/or information on-line.

To fully understand the phenomenal development of the Internet and Internet cafés in China, we should place this phenomenon in its historical context. In the early 1990s, only scientists, researchers, and university faculty located in major metropolitan areas could access the Internet. With the opening of Chinanet in

1996, Internet service was finally made available to the general public. Since 1997 China has seen an explosive increase in the number of Internet users, from a mere 620,000 in October 1997 to 162 million by the end of June 2007.[14] It seems that the explosive emergence of a large number of Internet users in China has coincided with the rise of a young urban middle class with increased consumption power. The data collected by a recent survey show that "a typical Internet user is young, male, well educated and well paid."[15] In light of the fact that 162 million Internet users constitute only 12 percent of the Chinese population, and the proportion of Internet users in the large cities is less than 50 percent, it is predictable that the number of Chinese Internet users will continue to increase at a rapid pace.[16]

Although the first Chinese Internet café appeared in Beijing in November 1996, it was not until three years later that its popularity really took off.[17] According to the statistics of the China Internet Network Information Center (CN-NIC), by the end of 1999, 11 percent of Chinese Internet users were logging on-line in Internet cafés. That figure jumped to 21 percent by the end of 2000. Since then, the figure has stabilized between 15 and 19 percent.[18] Since some log on to the Internet through multiple avenues (at home or at the office in addition to the Internet café), the actual number of people using Internet cafés exclusively may be smaller. Nonetheless, Internet café use accounts for about one-sixth of the total *wangmin* (netizens) in China.[19] This number shows that there is a big market demand for Internet cafés, and Chinese private entrepreneurs have wasted no time entering this new business domain. In a matter of a very short period of time, numerous Internet cafés appeared, most of them in urban areas. In Beijing alone there were more than 2,400 by June 2002.[20] According to one estimate, the total number of Internet cafés in China at the time was around 200,000.[21]

In addition to the growth in numbers, Internet cafés have also gone through a series of changes involving their operation. In the early days, Internet cafés were intended to provide access to a small number of customers who had both the need and the means to access the Internet in China—mainly foreign students and expatriates in metropolitan centers such as Beijing and Shanghai. In the fall of 1997 I visited an Internet café for the first time. It was located in a residential neighborhood not far from the east gate of Beijing University, and foreign students made up the majority of customers. The café had two rooms, one with half a dozen computers that were connected to the Internet through telephone lines, the other with tables and chairs where tea and coffee were served to customers. The café charged 20 yuan per hour for logging on-line, which was beyond affordability for ordinary Chinese customers. One year later the Joint Publishing House Book Store (Sanlian Shudian, the most popular bookstore among Beijing intellectuals and college students) put a dozen computers in its coffee bar on the second floor, converting it to an upscale Internet café overnight, and targeting customers from Beijing's cultural elite.

Generally speaking, the first generation of Chinese Internet cafés was closer to the meaning of the name; that is, they were not only a place to go on-line but also a place to have a drink, relax, and meet people. This kind of business operation may work well for serving a small group of relatively rich clients, but not many ordinary Chinese could afford it. In addition, consistent with the demographic distribution of Internet users in China, which indicates that about three-quarters are under thirty years old, a substantial portion of Internet café users in China were young students on a limited budget.[22] So subsequently, virtually all Internet cafés have become stripped-down versions of the early ones, emphasizing the function of providing Internet service. Even though some of the newer cafés offer soft drinks to patrons, for the most part they have turned away from the original purpose of the traditional café. Space previously reserved for coffee tables is now used for computers, and the number of computers has become a general gauge of how big and "strong" an Internet café is.

Meanwhile, the steady decrease in the cost of going on-line (down from 20 yuan per hour in the late 1990s to only 2 yuan per hour in 2004) has played an important role in transforming Internet cafés. They have gone from being a trendy elite activity to a form of mass consumption in a matter of a few years. Not only have Internet cafés increased dramatically in big cities, but also they have begun to appear in smaller cities and towns. Given the fact that a "digital divide" exists between China's coastal areas and its hinterland, with the former having the majority of both Internet users and facilities, the Internet café may increasingly serve as an avenue for providing on-line service to people in small cities in the interior of China.[23] In different areas and locations, the scale of the Internet café varies from a family-sized niche player with half a dozen computers to a super-sized Internet operation with several hundred computers. The majority of Chinese Internet cafés are believed to lie in the middle range, with several dozen computers in operation. Since there is still enormous room for growth and an increasing demand for Internet service, the Internet café is and will remain a part of the Chinese urban landscape for some time to come.

The Ocean: An Internet Café in Beijing

The Ocean is located in Beijing's college district in the northwest part of the city. The Internet café is on the second floor of a two-story commercial building; the first floor is occupied by a fast food store. Even though the building faces a busy street, the main entrance leads only to the fast food store. To get into the Ocean, one has to use the stairs at the right-hand rear side of the building. At first I was puzzled why the owner chose this location. To me, the fast food store makes too much noise, and the obscure entrance of the Ocean decreases its chances of attracting more customers. As it turned out, however, these two perceived "disadvantages" are part of the strategy of the owner. The fast food store downstairs provides convenience to those Internet "addicts" who spend several hours or even whole days on-line, while the obscure entrance is a self-protective mechanism that lowers the chance of attracting the attention of authorities who have kept close watch on the Internet cafés.

Upon walking into the narrow entrance of the Ocean, you first encounter the reception desk. A café worker greets you and asks you to sign your name. After that, the worker assigns you a computer to use. As soon as you log on to the computer using the password provided by the worker, the clock begins to count your usage time. There are about eighty computers on the floor, divided into four columns of cubicles. In general, the customers of Ocean can be divided into two categories: *changke* (regulars) and *sanke* (occasional patrons). Occasional patrons are often task-oriented, coming to Ocean to look for specific information on-line (such as information about foreign graduate school applications) and leaving when the task is completed. Regulars are those people who frequent the Ocean and spend a significant amount of time there. They are obviously favored customers, evidenced by the fact that Ocean workers often remember their names, treat them more politely, and even develop personal relationships with some of them.

The management team of the Ocean consists of the owner and about ten employees who are all college students working on a part-time basis. In 2001 the Ocean was open around the clock, and the work was divided into day and night shifts. Generally speaking, from late afternoon to midnight was the busiest time, especially on weekends, when the whole floor was often packed with customers. The work schedule for each employee is very flexible. For example, one can work a twelve-hour shift or can chip in for three- or four-hour shifts when available. The Ocean also adopted a very flexible fee schedule for its customers. During 2001–2002, the regular hourly charge was 3 yuan, but the Ocean charged half the regular price during the non-peak time, and even offered free service between 3:00 and 7:00 A.M. These tactics were aimed mainly at attracting and keeping those regulars in the café as long as possible, as the free service after midnight could lure more of them to come to the Ocean in the evening.

I conducted a survey on a busy night in October 2002 to find out who the customers were and what activities they were carrying out at the Ocean. Among the seventy-two replies I received, there were thirty-three middle and high school students and twenty college students. Only nineteen patrons categorized themselves as something other than a student. There were forty-three male customers and twenty-nine female customers, and the average age of the whole group was twenty, which was consistent with the general demographic distribution data collected by the CNNIC. As far as their activities were concerned, thirty-five said that their main activity at the café was playing on-line games, nineteen were talking in on-line chat rooms, eleven were seeking useful information on-line, and the remaining seven replied that they were checking e-mail. For those regulars, it seemed that playing on-line games and participating in chat rooms were the main reasons that kept them at the café for hour after hour. I specifically asked chat room enthusiasts whether they often visited chat rooms that focused on political and current affairs. The majority of them told me that they mainly frequented leisure-oriented chat rooms to have casual conversations with friends they met on-line, discussing topics such as sports, games, films, dating on-line, and so on. I realize that I cannot read too much into the data obtained through my survey unless it is supported by broader evidence. In 2003 Chinese researchers carried out the most comprehensive survey of Internet usage and impact in twelve Chinese cities. They found that 48 percent of all Internet users liken the Internet to an "entertainment place," and that "Internet café users read more online news about entertainment (79 percent) and sports (48 percent) than other topics."[24] A 2005 survey found the same tendency among Chinese Internet users.

Since playing on-line games and frequenting chat rooms can be very addictive, the growing popularity of Internet cafés brings an increased concern about the possible "side effects"—especially among parents worrying that their children spend too much time in the Internet café and are neglecting studying and other activities. The Chinese media have put out so many reports on how a youth addicted to the Internet can squander all of his or her time, energy, and money on games and on-line chatting, or be lured into visiting pornographic Web sites, that even some social celebrities have been prompted to propose a wholesale ban on for-profit Internet cafés in China.[25] Since 2001, authorities in various locations have adopted a number of measures in an attempt to limit the "side effects" of Internet café use among adolescents. The Administrative Rules for Internet Service–Providing Places of 2002 specifically stipulated that all Internet service locations could operate only from 8:00 A.M. to midnight, and no Internet cafés were allowed to be set up within a 200 meter radius of elementary and middle schools, as well as in residential areas. Providing service to non-adults was also prohibited.[26] Nonetheless, many Internet cafés, the Ocean included, have only paid lip service to the government regulations, since few of them want to lose the patronage of non-adults, the most profitable segment of their business.

I want to highlight several points based on the ethnographic description of the Ocean so far. First, the rapid development of Internet cafés is part of the privatization process that China is undergoing today, in which, in the area of information technologies such as the Internet, state control and privatization can go hand in hand. In the meantime, the private owners of Internet cafés have adopted a variety of "flexible" techniques, including flexible work schedules, flexible fee scales, and deliberate evasion of government regulations, to accomplish what David Harvey calls the "flexible accumulation."[27] Second, to many Chinese, Internet cafés such as Ocean serve mainly as entertainment establishments. They represent a new domain in which many Chinese youth spend their leisure time and are not perceived, contrary to Western Internet utopians, as an important place to get "free" information. Finally, the Chinese state has adopted multiple techniques in dealing with the Internet. It does not always play the role of a draconian regulator, sometimes trying instead to show itself as responding to genuine public concerns. Building on the fact that more than 87 percent of Chinese Internet users support a certain degree of government control or management of the Internet, especially on issues of pornography (88 percent) and incitement to violence (74 percent),[28] state regulation of Internet café operations with respect to non-adults has understandably not drawn much resentment from the public. As I have pointed out elsewhere, the "refined control" strategies adopted by the state could be more effective, and they show that the Chinese state is seeking improved modes of governmentality in dealing with new domains such as the Internet.[29]

A Non-monolithic State: Control-Crazy versus Development-Crazy

The Chinese government has been an active promoter of the Internet out of a conviction that this new technology could be an engine for economic and technological development. This statement may sound a little puzzling to those whose focus is on the control side. It is true that in a society where information (especially political information) has been subject to rigid control, the Chinese government has also moved quickly to regulate the Internet and has issued a number of regulations regarding it.[30] Nonetheless, the authorities are very confident that the positive aspects of the Internet outweigh the negatives. This is revealed in China's general principle regarding the Internet, which prescribes "developing it actively, strengthening its management, seeking advantages and avoiding harmfulness, making it serve our purpose."[31] The policymakers did not think the Internet was fundamentally different from newspapers or radio and TV stations: each has undergone rapid development and become more commercialized in the reform era while remaining under the firm control of the government.[32] Authorities at different levels and with different means have been promoting the Internet by using a similar approach, focusing on its technological and commercial applications while keeping an eye on its political implications.

Chinese Internet observers tend to focus their attention on the level of the central government, scrutinizing its policies for monitoring the Internet yet neglecting the fact that the Chinese state is not a monolithic entity that will carry out those policies at face value. The Internet as an area for new business growth has attracted a large amount of investment and fierce competition. Sometimes concerns about development seem to have relaxed or even outweighed concerns about control, especially in the minds of lower-level officials. The rapid spread of the Internet café is a very illuminating case. Among the Internet cafés in China, technically speaking, most were operated illegally. As pointed out by the piece quoted earlier from *Time Asia* magazine, fewer than two hundred Internet cafés were fully licensed in Beijing. Nationwide, only 46,000 out of 200,000 had permission to operate.[33] The reporter needs to look at the numbers she cited and ask herself: if officials really were "control-crazy," as she claimed, how could the existing illegal cybercafés overwhelmingly outnumber the legal ones? One plausible interpretation is that Chinese officials have not done a good job of controlling the cybercafés. Then the question becomes why not, and what factors have affected their control performance.

To answer these questions, we cannot neglect the fact that local officials often have different priorities from those set by the central authorities. It was through my interviews with the owner of Ocean, Mr. Zhou, a businessman from Taiwan in his late thirties, that I realized that the Internet café did not have all its papers and was operating illegally (such businesses are labeled "black cybercafés," *hei wang ba*, in Chinese). But the owner was not particularly worried that the Ocean was in any imminent danger of being shut down by local officials. "They only care about the figures of GDP growth and money," Mr. Zhou said contemptuously. In their view, the greater the number of Internet cafés, the better it would be for local (district-level) economic development through such benefits as adding new jobs and increasing the local tax base. So the lower-level officials generally had a more laissez-faire attitude toward allowing the setting up of new Internet cafés, even though they knew that those cafés were not fully licensed. According to the estimate by Mr. Zhou, among about a dozen Internet cafés operating within a radius of several blocks from his own, with the exception of one that put all necessary permits on display on the wall, none of them had a complete set of permits.

As Mr. Zhou explained, in order to set up an Internet café, one had to get a permit from four different government bureaus. These included the Public Security Bureau (fire and safety requirements and network security); the Cultural Bureau (Internet content control, especially pornography); the Telecommunications Bureau (network connection regulations); and the Bureau of Industrial and Commercial Administration (business operation license). To get all four permits could be a tedious process. With Internet fever raging in China and the lucrative returns the Internet cafés generated, many businessmen opted to set up and operate cybercafés without a full set of permits. Furthermore, government regulations clearly forbade foreign capital (including overseas Chinese capital) in the area of Internet café startups. Yet the local officials allowed Mr. Zhou, a Taiwanese businessman, to operate the cybercafé by registering it under the name of a local resident. In the minds of many Chinese, Internet availability is not only a convenient means of communication but also a symbol of not being "backward," both economically and technologically as well as culturally. So those local officials who allowed "black" cybercafés to operate should be more appropriately labeled "development-crazy" than "control-crazy," because their concerns about economic factors often outweighed other concerns.

Why was this practice of blatantly ignoring state regulations generally tolerated in Beijing as well as the rest of China? One has to understand the complexity of everyday life practices to make sense of many phenomena that might otherwise seem incomprehensible on paper. First, in the reform era, the Chinese state has become more than a monolithic entity (or, more accurately, the state was never monolithic but has become even more pluralistic today). There are officials who see the Internet primarily as an engine of economic development and others who see it as a threat to the existing censorship system. Local officials make their own interpretations of central policies based on local interest, and in practice, all of these make state policy seem fluid and internally contradictory. At the local level, the implementation of concrete policies and regulations is further complicated by the fact that written rules are often overstretched or even neglected in order to accommodate personal connections. And in a worst-case scenario, local officials are often bribed to allow "black" Internet cafés to exist and conduct business as corruption has become more and more rampant with China's transformation to a more market-oriented economy.

Double Role of the Market: State Regulation Challenger or Complier

The privatization process and market forces have also contributed to the astonishing growth rate of the Internet in China. At the macroscopic level, after a series of reforms in the late 1990s in the area of telecommunications, China has separated enterprise operations from direct government control and has subjected the industry to market forces. For example, in order to encourage more people to use the Internet, China Telecom offers convenient no-application Internet access called "Just Dial 163." Anyone can log on to the Internet over the telephone lines simply by dialing 163, using 163 as both the log-in name and the password. The charge appears on the telephone subscriber's monthly bill. Obviously this practice is good for business—but not as far as control is concerned. In fact, when economic development becomes the priority, "market mechanisms" often function in ways that are contrary to the government's goal of tightening control.

The market mechanism also has made the running of a cybercafé in Beijing a very complex and pressure-filled endeavor. The entrepreneurs not only have to deal with the state regulations but also have to engage in furious competition against others in a "market economy" environment. Sometimes the products of market competition can be mistaken for the effects of state control. During my fieldwork, the Ocean was once raided by the Bureau of Industrial and Commercial Administration on the grounds that it did not have the appropriate permit for conducting business. Eighty computers in the café were taken away, and the café was shut down. But to my amusement, only one week later the owner got the computers back and resumed business. I was told that Mr. Zhou was able to achieve this by first finding some connections to get in touch with top officials of the bureau. The owner then treated them to an elaborate banquet in a fancy restaurant. In addition, Mr. Zhou also presented some "gifts" to key figures, who finally consented to return his computers and let him resume business as usual.

I was not surprised by the way the Ocean owner brought his business back—a widely used practice in the Chinese sociocultural context combining bribery and *guanxi* connections.[34] What caught me off guard was that, according to Mr. Zhou, the bureau was tipped off by another Internet café owner to take action against him, out of envy, because the Ocean was prospering at the time. There were more surprises to come. Several weeks later, certain that his jealous business rival was not fully licensed either, Mr. Zhou had the rival's café raided by the Public Security Bureau on the grounds that it did not have the necessary fire safety permit. Though obviously pleased, Mr. Zhou told me that he expected his rival would be back in business shortly just as he had been, because "everybody has some connections and ultimately the money can buy you a way out, and we are kind of used to raids coming periodically. It is just a part of the business of running an Internet café."

So the raids against the Internet cafés could be launched for many reasons, and most of the cafés being raided were reopened, and new cybercafés were continually being set up. Beyond the raids resulting from fierce business competition, the periodically launched "rectification campaign" against Internet cafés in China has been aimed mainly at those "black" or "illegal" cafés that have stirred strong public resentment for providing services to adolescents. The Western reports that emphasize only the "political control" side have missed the complexity of the issue. As one puzzled observer wrote on an e-mail Listserv for people who are interested in studying the Internet in China: "Here in the Netherlands the same old 'news' appears once again in the newspapers: 17,000 Internet cafés in China are forced to close down, another 28,000 must install software that blocks certain information. If we are to believe these stories completely, it remains a mystery how it comes that over time more rather than less Internet cafés appear."[35] Only by taking into account both the promotion policy the state has adopted and the role the market mechanism has played can one respond to the observer's puzzlement. As economic development becomes the ultimate criterion of job performance, local officials have adopted more pro-growth policies, and this in part explains why the growth of Internet cafés has been so rapid, and why even though most of them are not fully licensed, they are still able to flourish in contemporary urban China. A report about the situation in Guangzhou at the end of 2003 was illustrative. After periodic "rectification campaigns," out of six hundred Internet cafés in the city, only eighty-three were fully licensed. A municipal inspecting team visited six cybercafés in one night; none of them was fully licensed, and all of them operated all night, ignoring the time limits set by the regulations.[36]

Anthropologists have noted the role played by the flow of capital in challenging the state's regulatory function. In discussing the "tension between state and capital in the cultural realm" over broadcasting Western TV programs in China, Mayfair Meihui Yang points out that "the pursuit of advertising patrons is why the station ignored a long-standing state regulation requiring stations to limit their imported TV series to two. Instead, they actually show about twenty per year."[37] This is also true in the case of Internet cafés. The desire to make a profit explains why private entrepreneurs have been enthusiasts of Internet cafés, employing the power of capital to circumvent state regulations in the name of helping accelerate economic development. What has been neglected is the fact that in the context of contemporary China, the huge market and tremendous potential for profit making could just as easily decrease capital's role in challenging the state, transforming capital itself into a regulatory force in order to safeguard its main profit-making function through a self-initiated privatization of control.

The dual role played by capital is manifested in the daily practices of the Ocean, which involve both resistance and compliance to state regulations. On the one hand, the ability of government to control the Internet is being challenged all the time. For example, though required to keep records on the personal identification of patrons of Internet cafés, the Ocean simply asked users to sign their names and did not follow the regulations requiring Internet cafés to check their authenticity by asking customers to show their personal identification cards. The workers also kept one eye closed to underage middle school students, who came mainly to play on-line games. Mr. Zhou told me that he usually did not intervene unless these youngsters refused to quit after using the Internet for an exceedingly long time (for example, more than twenty-four hours), out of fear that the angry parents might report their children's activities at the Ocean to authorities. "To take the government regulations too seriously will not do anything good to business. Nonetheless, if you do not pay any attention to regulations, you will be in trouble," the Ocean owner told me. So the "appropriate" way to deal with the regulations was to be flexible, doing the minimum to satisfy the authorities at the surface level while not driving away patrons.

On the other hand, the Ocean sometimes presents itself as a very careful follower of state regulations. Upon entering the Internet café, one can hardly fail to notice conspicuously displayed posters on the wall reminding customers not to visit forbidden Web sites (particularly reactionary and pornographic Web sites).[38] To the state Internet monitors, controlling access to Internet content has been the focal point of limiting the availability of inadmissible information. For example, the regulations on the bulletin board systems (BBS) and chat rooms require the BBS providers to remove any inadmissible content immediately, keep the relevant records, and report to the relevant authorities. In principle, the Internet café is basically an Internet service provider, not an Internet content provider. Although it is the patrons who decide what BBS or chat room to visit and how to participate, the authorities have also made the Internet café responsible for not letting its patrons log on to inadmissible Web sites. Putting numerous warning posters on its walls served as a means of self-protection, aimed at showing that the Ocean is operating in accordance with government regulations in case officials come to inspect the café—or, in an even worse scenario, to relieve itself of responsibility should some customers be caught engaging in "illegal" activities in cyberspace. In addition, the Ocean has its own system for monitoring clients' activities and usually keeps operation records for two months. In this case, the Ocean functions as an intermediary between the state and individual patrons. It assumes part of the responsibility for state control that has been privatized onto this private business operation.

Privatization of Control: Neoliberal Governing in Chinese Style

A newer development is that the state is actively promoting chain-style Internet café operations involving large amounts of capital and on a large scale. In March 2003 the Ministry of Culture proclaimed that it would issue permits for up to ten companies to operate nationwide Internet café chains, which would have relatively standardized services and management and thus be more easily subject to government regulations.[39] In early June, ten companies successfully acquired permission. Of special note is that among them were large-scale state-owned enterprises such as China Unicom as well as private companies closely linked to government organs, such as Zhongqing Wangluo Jiayuan and Zhongluo Shikong.[40] China Unicom immediately laid out its business plan of setting up seven hundred cybercafés by the end of 2003, and Zhongluo Shikong set its target at a thousand.[41] These companies' entrance into the operation of Internet cafés could represent the beginning of a closer relationship between state and capital in which the state and state-backed capital work together to achieve the twofold task of maintaining control for the former while making profit for the latter.

In the meantime, Internet café–related social news continues to attract the attention of the Chinese. In April 2004 three middle school students in Chongqing fell asleep on the railway tracks after spending too much time in a "black" Internet café. Two were killed by a train. This incident stirred another outcry in China and prompted the central authorities to send a "supervising team" to monitor the local officials carrying out the campaign to "rectify" Internet café operation in the city. Among their findings, one problem was that that there were ten different government organs with some responsibilities for the monitoring of local Internet cafés. It seems that the greater the number of organs, the less effective the monitoring. There did not seem to be a quick fix for the situation. Frustrated by the problem, more than two hundred local elders, trying to take matters into their own hands, volunteered to act as "supervisors" of the Internet cafés.[42] To address social concerns about the negative effects of Internet cafés on adolescents, China even designated March 20 as the "Day for Civilized Internet Action by Adolescents." On March 20, 2004, fifteen retired teachers and policemen were appointed as "supervisors" of Internet cafés in one Beijing community.[43]

These new developments represent the privatization of control which is part of the neoliberal mode of governing in a Chinese context. We have to keep in mind that privatization is not limited to the economic domain but also occurs in politics and through the techniques of government. Facing the twofold task of developing the economy and maintaining control of power, the Chinese state has adopted and incorporated flexible strategies for governing. As we have seen in the new Internet domain, along with the privatization of business operations, it also privatizes or subcontracts certain control responsibilities to non-state actors, such as Internet cafés, entrepreneurs, customers, and even community volunteers, through its expectation for them to exercise "self-control." In this process the market has played a dual role of both challenging and collaborating with the state. Despite the recent uproar in the West over the fact that high-tech giants such as Yahoo and Google have complied with Chinese Internet surveillance rules (by handing over on-line records and deleting politically sensitive terms from the search engine) is another good example, showing that the privatization of control can be extended to multinational companies as long as the need to penetrate China's huge market renders "self-control" a rational choice.[44]

The politics of the Internet café continue to unfold in China today. The café is a place where the complexity of Internet politics is negotiated and worked out among different players, an "assemblage" that is interrelated and ever changing. The politics of Internet cafés should be examined from the perspective of two sets of tensions embedded within the broader context of contemporary China. One set of tensions arises from the fact that the non-monolithic Chinese state is both the technology promoter and the monitor, the other from the fact that privatization and market forces both challenge and reinforce state regulations. These contradictions illustrate the complexity of a new neoliberal governmentality that is trying to find its hold in China. As long as the processes of privatization and marketization continue to flourish in a Chinese neoliberal environment, it is likely that we will see more privatization of control in many domains in China in the future.

Afterword

Thinking Outside the Leninist Corporate Box

Ralph A. Litzinger

As I was sitting down to write my reflections on this remarkable volume, a friend and colleague sent me an excerpt from Will Hutton's recently published book *The Writing on the Wall: Why We Must Embrace China as a Partner or Face It as an Enemy.*[1] Hutton was the economics editor of the *Guardian* from 1990 to 1996, and he worked for a spell as the editor of the *Observer.* He appears frequently on BBC television, and is known as an outspoken advocate for affordable housing in the United Kingdom, though in 2004 he was embroiled in a minor scandal when it was revealed that his wife's company, First Premise, was renovating rundown properties and then selling them at an enormous profit. Despite these diversions, Hutton has managed to fashion himself as a quasi-leftist public intellectual and critic of capitalism. He is perhaps best known to academics for his edited volume *Global Capitalism*, compiled with Anthony Giddens, a meandering collection of essays by authors examining from varied perspectives the logics of global capitalist restructuring in the wake of the 1999 anti-globalization protests in China.[2]

Hutton's new obsession is China. Titled "Power, Corruption, and Lies," the *Guardian* article boldly sets out to unmask the fears, anxieties, and gross misconceptions that surround the specter of China's seemingly unstoppable emergence as a global economic giant.[3] At first glance, Hutton's is a welcome intervention.

Tune in to Lou Dobbs's nightly show on CNN, or read the occasional tirades against China's trade policies, human rights record, or investment forays into various African or Latin American countries in any of a number of newspapers, magazines, or blogs, and one cannot but notice that China has emerged as a potent signifier of dread and anxiety: Is China transforming the economic logics of contemporary global capitalism? Is the once sleeping socialist giant really poised to dominate the world? What will this domination look like? Is it possible for the Western superpowers to shape China into a sustainable model for Democracy and Enlightenment? If not, what will become of the post–cold war global order? And what do we make of China in relation to India, which for many scholars and pundits has emerged "as a case study in effective Western indoctrination"?[4] Is India—where rampant metropolitan-based consumerism, rising incomes, and easy credit seem to have gone hand in hand with a supposedly flourishing democratic will among the masses—truly emerging as the Other to China? Are the big categories such as Capitalism, Globalization, Democracy, and Leninist Corporatism really the best ways to capture the complexities of the newly emergent and often highly contested experimental systems of neoliberal governance that have come to China, India, and elsewhere in the last decade or so?

Hutton begins his narrative by noting that the anxiety over China has been accompanied by a starry-eyed awe over its command of a $2 trillion economy (at the beginning of 2007). Hutton is not really interested in the politics of anxiety, and he is skeptical of anyone who characterizes China as an "unstoppable force whose economic model is unbeatable and set to swamp us." Rather the main focus of its energies is the dangerous delusion, seemingly rampant in business, government, and policy centers in the United States and Europe, that China "has abandoned communism and embraced capitalism." He sums up this grand delusion as follows:

> China's own claim—that it is building a very particular economic model around what it describes as a socialist market economy—is dismissed as hogwash, the necessary rhetoric the Communist party must use to disguise what is actually happening. China proves conclusively that liberalization, privatization, market freedoms and the embrace of globalization are the only route to prosperity. China is on its way to capitalism but will not admit it.

For Hutton, way too many of us[5] want to see China as a thriving capitalist economy with market freedoms, private firms, and individual entrepreneurs all forging ahead. We read daily reports about angry peasants and laid-off workers storming party headquarters, and an emerging NGO sector working closely with the Chinese government to address the country's economic inequalities, its environmental problems, and its social unrest. From these reports we desperately seek evidence of a robust public sphere and civil society, which we hope will ultimately challenge the autocratic rule of the Communist Party. We want to believe that the submerged forces of social justice, democratic will, and dreams of shared political representation will surface once the Communist Party, plagued by corruption and unfair extractive policies, finally implodes upon itself. The country will then awaken and remake itself in the perfect image of the West. According to Hutton, these desires are pure hogwash. He writes: "The western conception of the free exercise of property rights and business autonomy that goes with it, essential to any notion of capitalism, does *not* exist in China" (my emphasis).

Hutton's education in the Real China continues. What exists in China is a country "frozen" in a "structure" best thought of as "Leninist corporatism." Here we enter the crux of Hutton's analysis. This is not capitalism as we long for it to emerge in China. The state corporatist system is unstable, inefficient, corrupt, unfair, and unsustainable; it is nearly totalitarian in its reach and vise-like managerial grip on everyday life. Hutton builds drama into his schematic unmasking of the Real China: the Chinese Communist Party, he pontificates, "has become one of the most corrupt organizations the world has ever witnessed. The combination of absolute power and an ideology that palpably no longer describes reality is *a virus that is morally and psychologically undermining the regime*" (my emphasis). When this virus spreads and eventually devours the Leninist machine, the country will sink into chaos; quite likely this will result in new forms of repression not yet seen. This prospect is so real, so imminently on the horizon, "that the task of peacefully moving to a sustainable capitalism, and building the necessary institutions to do it, is so vital for both China and the world."

Sustainable Capitalism. Necessary Institutions. Saving China and the World from Leninist Corporatism: these are the terms of Will Hutton's Real China. Readers of *Privatizing China* are offered a strikingly different take on the economic, cultural, disciplinary, and managerial logics of reform era China. Here there is no high moral ground or sense of desperate urgency that the United States, if it plays its cards right, can transform China and get rich at the same time. No sense that the Chinese state can be summed up in the sweeping, generalized moniker Leninist Corporatism. No falling back on easy clichés that the Chinese Communist Party is being criticized from both within and beyond the party (most intellectuals working and agitating in China, and those of us who follow their work, know this already). And no shameless trafficking in the politics of hysteria which holds that China is, in all probability, on the brink of economic and political convulsion.

Hutton wants us all to believe that China has experienced great "progress" over the last twenty years or so and that this progress is in jeopardy. The contributors to this volume are skeptical of any such recourse to the faith in Progress, in part because they are grounded in ethnographic entanglements with the complexities and ambiguities of privatization, neoliberalism, and new technologies of the self that animate the politics of the mostly urban present. Progress, in any case, circulates a bit too freely in the neoliberal logics and modes of governing that this book brings into visibility. Additionally, the authors describe processes that resolutely refuse cold war imaginings of a totalitarian party-state apparatus ruthlessly repressing its populations, even while many of them argue that socialism must still be taken seriously in China today. In Hutton's analysis, an outmoded Chinese government—the Leninist Corporate machine—is portrayed as working against the interests of its own people, who are hungry for democracy and ripe for unleashing their entrepreneurial spirit. It is unclear if Hutton thinks this entrepreneurial spirit is innate to something called Chinese culture, or whether he understands it as an effect of the reform period or the ability of some people to convert prior forms of cultural and political capital into money capital.[6] In any case, society emerges as the hero in Hutton's narrative. It is uncritically assumed to be a space of public and private life, wrestling to get out from under the party-state's master grip. It is not surprising that the resurgence of neoliberal logics and rationalities around the world, coupled with the popularity of such fantasies as Thomas Friedman's that the world is now flat, has kept these cold war narrative forms alive. They profoundly influence business leaders, pundits, government officials, and think tank experts who make it their business to tell the public what an "emergent China" or a "democratic India" means to the smooth functioning of the global economy. More apropos to the critical agenda of this volume, they can see the politics of market capitalism in China only through the lens of a universal liberalism: the idea that the totally administered society must give way to the internal logics and self-regulatory practices that are believed to belong inherently to the market, civil society, and the citizenry. Rationalize the state with the rule of law; unleash the entrepreneurial powers of society; the market will do the rest. All will be well in the world again!

Privatizing China refuses the logic of Western liberalism, understood here as a mentality of rule,[7] even while it shows, contra Hutton, how powerful some of the assumptions of liberalism have become in China today. Similarly, the contributors seek to complicate simplistic views of neoliberalism as the unfettered exercise of market logics, outside of the state. The essays collected here show how the state is intimately involved in the crafting of new subjects, now called upon by the state to mobilize *individual* capacities for self-government and self-improvement. Unlike the liberal Enlightenment subject Hutton seeks to bring to China in order to save the country and the world from the monster of Leninist Corporatism, this new subject is at once private and public, at once of the state and of society, at once subjected to histories of the socialist present (socialism from afar) and to the neoliberal logic that the energies of the individual can be productively developed only through the pursuit of economic self-interest in a free market. On the one hand, then, this volume demands a shift in perspective: technologies of governing are at the heart of the practices, policies, and everyday effects of privatization. On the other, it calls for a methodological shift in the determination of just what constitutes the object of analysis. The chapters roam across, through, between, and among varied sites and places, some terrestrial, some virtual. More important, the space of inquiry is the emergence of new forms and practices that seek to care for, manage, and improve the life of populations across multiple scales and through a wide range of administrative, managerial, and everyday practices. To be sure, as some of these chapters show, life is not always improved. In the privatization of land, capital, and selves, some sectors of the population are deliberately excluded, pushed to the margins, or devalued because they have not become activist citizens, healthy subjects, sufficiently middle class, fully protected and productive workers, enterprising party members, savvy consumers of the right foodstuffs or pharmaceuticals, or people with the economic clout or geographical proximity to have access to the Internet.

Through these inclusions and exclusions, where the new powers of the self coexist and sometimes collide with state practices of rule, this book asks the reader to think through, and argue with, private villas and gated communities for China's new middle class; the changing configurations of landownership, finance, and taxation; the transnational coding and management of labor; the restless mobility and circulation of small-time media magnates; the pharmaceutical industry and the privatization of biotech knowledge; the contradictory logics of consuming and of fearing SARS; the making of new patriotic entrepreneurs and self-fashioning practices of would-be hipster party members; and, of course, the wild fantasies and creative mobilizations of self and other that are taking place in cyberspace. What emerges from all of this is a refreshingly critical perspective on just how open-ended neoliberal postsocialist China remains, where a wide range of possible political, economic, and cultural outcomes are possible.

Additionally, *Privatizing China* marks a shift away from a form of interdisciplinary academic writing that began to emerge in the 1980s. In much of this writing, the nation-state was critiqued for its totalizing discourses and was unmasked as a national space best defined by ethnic and regional diversity; peripheries haunted centers, and the borderlands and margins spoke back to the national socialism of the center. While these were once useful and productive ethnographic, historical, and literary projects (in the sense of producing new kinds of knowledge about China and its multiple sites of internal difference), they now arguably represent a kind of exhausted methodology limited to showing how heterogeneity undermines the homogenizing impulses of the nation-state. This volume, in contrast, is perhaps best thought of as a collection of ethnographic *interventions*, at once in dialogue with new modes of social theory concerned with revisiting liberal forms of governance and the details of particular practices. As interventions, they reveal how neoliberal values and modes of reasoning that seek to promote privatization, entrepreneurialism, and the crafting of new productive and consuming selves are radically indeterminate, contingent, and unsettled. Whatever privatization is in China, it is not something that can be understood as a direct and unmediated effect of the totality of economic globalization; it is not simply the instantiation of the Global, or Capitalism, or Modernity, or Democracy, or that newer fetish, the War on Terror. Similarly, as I have indicated, neoliberalism, when turned into an object of critical ethnographic inquiry, cannot be reduced to the mere expression of market logics that seek to expunge the state from the everyday care and management of populations (as happened to varying degrees in the dreamworlds of the Thatcher and Clinton administrations). Indeed, the chapters in this volume demonstrate how unequivocally neoliberalism is linked to previous and contemporary modes of socialist rule, even while those modes of rule have unleashed a new desiring subject now responsible for her own self-development.

Aihwa Ong and Li Zhang write in their introduction, "When governing depends on animating the freedom or capacities of individuals to act, politics becomes a matter of troubling the link between knowledge and ethics." The Foucault-inspired shift to an ethics of the self is one that is long overdue in the study of China, especially in a China that has seen more than two decades of spectacular economic growth and the wild profusion of all kinds of cultural crazes, from saving the earth, to McDonaldization, to five-star hotels replete with massage parlors and in-house sex workers, to the internal Orientalist love of Tibet and other ethnics among middle-class terrestrial and virtual travelers. "How one should live" is indeed the quintessential question for any rethinking of the politics of life, and the life of politics. This ethics, with its inescapable link to new forms of knowledge and new modes of rule, from afar and through the body and its desires, is one of the most important questions confronting the scholarship of China today.

In reading through this volume, I wanted to see someone push this question of ethics into the messy moral and political terrain of how one should write "neoliberal China." It seems to me that "neoliberal" China, and its associated practices in which space, land, peoples, and selves are increasingly privatized, has much to teach us about larger geopolitical developments and how these developments make sense in both a post–cold war and post-9/11 world order. At the same time, we need to think of ways to take seriously the spate of writings by journalists, former government officials, and some academics now cashing in on the new fascination with China. In part, this is why I made the choice to begin this afterword with a riff on Will Hutton's piece in the *Guardian*. I choose to juxtapose Hutton's unmasking of the Real China to the interventionist project of this book because I believe we need to think of tactics and maneuvers for talking back to the pundits who are representing China and its economic and political realities and struggles to audiences outside the academy. Perhaps Hutton's writings on China are appealing to post–cold war and War on Terror policymakers, as well the general reading public, because he has mastered the skill, as Edward Said once put it in response to Samuel Huntington's book *The Clash of Civilizations*, of cutting through the details of large masses of scholarship and experiences and boiling them down to catchy, easy-to-remember ideas and phrases[8]—the tyranny and imminent decay of the Leninist Corporate machine, for example, or the highly seductive idea that India, the new sign of Democracy-in-the-Making, is also transforming America and the world.

To rub Hutton up against these essays is to argue not that the task of this volume is to set the record straight, to prove that the old sod Hutton has got it all wrong. It is rather to show that those of us trying to write authoritative accounts of the messiness, contingencies, and uncertainties of neoliberalism in China are captured more by the details of how people are struggling with the ethics of living today in China than we are by the recycling of worn-out clichés. *Privatizing China* is instructive because we learn that there are indeed unique ways in which neoliberalism is getting assembled and reassembled in China. Hutton is instructive because we learn how pervasively the long history of Western liberalism and its associated political reason and rationalities informs how China is interpreted, depicted, and staged for Western consumption. Our ethnographic interventions have to be made from the knowledge we produce from the fieldwork we do in the cafés, malls, employment offices, schools, streets, parks, meetings, protest demonstrations, research and media centers, villages, villas, and urban neighborhoods in China. But they also have to be staged in the public domain in the West, where the myth that China needs to be saved from itself in order to ensure that global capitalism survives is gaining in both force and popularity.

Liberalism (whether Western or postsocialist) remains intractably bound to the problem of just how one is to take one's life into one's hands. But it also remains bound to a quite old form of desire, one that can see a future for China only if it buys into the rationalities of liberal globalization and the international rule of law. Hutton can imagine China only against the backdrop of what he takes to be the manifold successes of Western, liberal, industrial, and postindustrial capitalism. Others, however, are now turning to India as the new model of market democracy.[9]

In the end, Hutton's story about China and its "power, corruption, and lies" is ultimately a story about what it will take for China to become just like "us." Or perhaps what it will take for China to become more like India, the new great hope for global market democracy. What clichés such as Market Democracy, Leninist Corporatism, and State Authoritarianism miss is not just how contested these categories are in practice, but how they can't begin to capture the uncertain and open-ended futures of countries such as China and India. The refusal to fall prey to and take comfort in these clichés is what makes *Privatizing China* such a powerful intervention and such a rewarding read.

Notes

Introduction

1. David Barboza, "A Portrait of China Running Amok," *New York Times*, September 4, 2006, B1, 7.

2. Friedrich A. von Hayek, *The Road to Serfdom*, 50th anniversary ed., intro. Milton Friedman (Chicago: University of Chicago Press, 1994).

3. Ibid.

4. Nikolas Rose, *Powers of Freedom: Reframing Political Thought* (Cambridge: Cambridge University Press, 1999), 49–50.

5. Ibid., 43.

6. Aihwa Ong, *Neoliberalism as Exception: Mutations in Citizenship and Sovereignty* (Durham: Duke University Press, 2006).

7. For a note on an ethnographic approach that "stays close" to such practices, see ibid., 13.

8. This phrase is borrowed from Barbara Cruikshank, "Revolutions Within: Self-Government and Self-Esteem," in *Foucault and Political Reason*, ed. Andrew Barry, Thomas Osborne, and Nikolas Rose (Chicago: University of Chicago Press, 1996), 231–52.

9. See Lisa Hoffman, Monica DeHart, and Stephen J. Collier, "Notes on the Anthropology of Neoliberalism," *Anthropological News* 47, no. 6 (2006): 9–10.

10. Maurice Freedman, "On the Handling of Money," in *The Study of Chinese Society: Essays by Maurice Freedman*, selected and introduced by G. William Skinner (Palo Alto: Stanford University Press, 1979).

11. Susan Mann, *Local Merchants and the Chinese Bureaucracy, 1750–1950* (Stanford: Stanford University Press, 1987).

12. Martin King Whyte and William L. Parish, *Urban Life in Contemporary China* (Chicago: University of Chicago Press, 1984); Lu Xiaobo and Elizabeth J. Perry, eds., *Danwei: The Changing Chinese Workplace in Historical and Comparative Perspective* (Armonk, N.Y.: M. E. Sharpe, 1997).

13. Gordon White, *Riding the Tiger: The Politics of Economic Reform in Post-Mao China* (Stanford: Stanford University Press. 1993).

14. Karl Marx, *Capital*, vol. 1 (1867; reprint, New York: International Publishers, 1967), chap. 26.

15. Victor Mallet, "China and India: The Two Differ in Business as They Do in Politics," *Financial Times*, December 12, 2006, 11.

16. Michel Foucault, *History of Sexuality*, vol. 1, *An Introduction*, trans. Robert Hurley (New York: Vintage, 1979), 90.

17. Stephen J. Collier, "The Spatial Forms and Social Norms of 'Actually Existing Neoliberalism': Toward a Substantive Analytics," New School University, International Affairs Working Paper no. 2005–04 (2005). For another view of management technologies in socialist Europe, see Elizabeth Dunn, *Privatizing Poland* (Ithaca: Cornell University Press, 2004).

18. "Problematization," Foucault writes, "does not mean the representation of a preexistent object nor the creation through discourse of an object that did not exist. It is the ensemble of discursive and non-discursive practices that make something enter into the play of true and false and constitute it as an object of thought (whether in the form of moral reflection, scientific knowledge, political analysis, etc.)." Quoted in Paul Rabinow, *Anthropos Today* (Princeton: Princeton University Press, 2003), 18.

19. David Harvey, "Neoliberalism as Creative Destruction," http//user.chol.com/~moraz/DH-neoliberalism.doc (accessed 2002).

20. David Harvey, *A Brief History of Neoliberalism* (Oxford: Oxford University Press, 2005), 139–41.

21. Wang Hui, *China's New Order: Society, Politics, and Economy in Transition*, ed. Ted Huters (Cambridge: Harvard University Press, 2003).

22. For another critique of a single model of global capitalism, see Mayfair Yang, "Putting Global Capitalism in Its Place: Economic Hybridity, Bataille, and Ritual Expenditure," in *Current Anthropology* 41, no. 4 (2000): 477–509.

23. Michael Hardt and Antonio Negri, *Empire* (Cambridge: Harvard University Press, 2000), 23.

24. Aihwa Ong, "Introduction: Neoliberalism as Exception, Exception to Neoliberalism," in *Neoliberalism as Exception: Mutations in Citizenship and Sovereignty* (Durham: Duke University Press, 2006), 1–27.

25. Ibid., 1–30.

26. For a criticism of "Empire" from the point of environmentalism in China, see Ralph Litzinger, "Contested Sovereignties and the Critical Ecosystem Fund," *Political and Legal Anthropology Review (PoLar)* 29, no. 1 (2006): 66–87.

27. See Stephen J. Collier and Aihwa Ong, "Global Assemblages, Anthropological Problems," in *Global Assemblages: Technology, Politics, and Ethics as Anthropological Problems*, ed. Aihwa Ong and Stephen J. Collier (Malden, Mass.: Blackwell, 2005), 1–21.

28. Thomas Luhmann, *Observations on Modernity* (Stanford: Stanford University Press, 1998), 107.

29. Dorothy Solinger, "China's Urban Transients in the Transition from Socialism and the Collapse of the Communist 'Urban Public Goods Regime,' " *Comparative Politics* 27, no. 2 (January 1995): 127–46.

30. See Howard W. French, "Wealth Grows but Health Care Withers in China," *New York Times*, January 14, 2006.

31. See, for example, You-tien Hsing, *Making Capitalism in China* (Oxford: Oxford University Press, 1998).

32. See David L. Wank, *Commodifying Communism: Markets, Trust, and Politics in a South China City* (Cambridge: Cambridge University Press, 1999); and Frank N. Pieke, "Bureaucracy, Friends, and Money: The Growth of Capital Socialism in China," *Comparative Study of Society and History* 37, no. 3 (1995): 494–518.

33. Joseph Kahn, "Rights Group Urges China to End Curbs on Lawyers," *International Herald Tribune*, December 10, 2006.

34. For an influential concept of the public sphere and its limitations, see Craig Calhoun, ed., *Habermas and the Public Sphere* (Cambridge: MIT Press, 1992).

35. Craig Calhoun, *Neither Gods Nor Emperors: Students and the Struggle for Democracy in China* (Berkeley: University of California Press, 1994).

36. Deborah Davis, "Introduction: A Revolution in Consumption," in *The Consumer Revolution in Urban China*, ed. Deborah Davis (Berkeley: University of California Press, 2000), 3, 21.

37. Judith Farquhar, *Appetites: Food and Sex in Post-socialist China* (Durham: Duke University Press, 2002), 2–3. For another view of consumerism and a new cultural assertiveness, see James Watson, ed., *The Golden Arches East: McDonald's in East Asia,* 2nd ed. (Stanford: Stanford University Press, 2006).

38. Lisa Rofel, *Desiring China: Experiments with Neoliberalism, Sexuality, and Public Culture* (Durham: Duke University Press, 2007), 4–5.

39. Mayfair Yang, *Gifts, Favors, and Banquets: The Art of Guanxi in Chinese Society* (Ithaca: Cornell University Press, 1994); Yunxiang Yan, *The Flow of Gifts: Reciprocity and Social Networks in a Chinese Village* (Stanford: Stanford University Press, 1996).

40. Nikolas Rose, *Powers of Freedom: Reframing Political Thought* (Cambridge: Cambridge University Press, 1999), 98–99.

41. Ibid., 101.

42. Besides Hayek, see also Gilles Deleuze and Félix Guattari, *Anti-Oedipus: Capitalism and Schizophrenia*, reprint ed. (Minneapolis: University of Minnesota Press, 1983).

43. See Li Zhang, *Strangers in the City* (Stanford: Stanford University Press, 2001).

44. Ann Anagnost, "The Corporeal Politics of Quality (*Suzhi*)," *Public Culture* 16, no. 2 (2004): 189–208.

45. See Yan Hairong, "Neoliberal Governmentality and Neohumanism: Organizing *Suzhi*/Value Flow through Labor Recruitment Networks, "*Cultural Anthropology* 18, no. 4 (2003): 578–96.

46. See, for example, Peter Gries, *China's New Nationalism* (Berkeley: University of California Press, 2003).

47. Michel Foucault, "On the Genealogy of Ethics: An Overview of Work in Progress," in *Michel Foucault: Ethics, Subjectivity, and Truth*, vol. 1 of *Essential Works of Foucault, 1954–1984*, ed., Paul Rabinow (New York: New Press, 1997), 253–80.

48. Michel Foucault, *Technologies of the Self*, ed. Luther H. Martin, Huck Gutman, and Patrick H. Hutton (Amherst: University of Massachusetts Press, 1988), 19–20.

49. Stephen J. Collier and Andrew Lakoff, "On Regimes of Living," in *Global Assemblages: Technology, Politics and Ethics as Anthropological Problems,* ed. Aihwa Ong and Stephen J. Collier (Malden: Blackwell, 2005), 22–39.

50. This question was broached by Liu Xin in *The Otherness of Self* (Ann Arbor: University of Michigan Press, 2003).

51. Ulrich Beck, "The Reinvention of Politics: Towards a Theory of Reflexive Modernization," in *Reflexive Modernization,* ed. Ulrich Beck, Anthony Giddens, and Scott Lash (Stanford: Stanford University Press, 1994), 14–15.

Chapter 1. Private Homes, Distinct Lifestyles

1. Li Zhang, "Forced from Home: Property Rights, Civic Activism, and the Politics of Relocation in China," *Urban Anthropology* 33, nos. 2–4 (2004): 247–81; Li Zhang, "Spatiality and Urban Citizenship in Late Socialist China," *Public Culture* 14, no. 2 (Spring 2002): 311–34; C. K. Lee, "Pathways of Labor Insurgency," in *Chinese Society: Change, Conflict, and Resistance,* ed. Elizabeth Perry and Mark Selden (London: Routledge, 2000), 41–61; Dorothy Solinger, *Contesting Citizenship in Urban China: Peasant Migrants, the State, and the Logic of the Market* (Berkeley: University of California Press, 1999).

2. The social stratum I describe here is new in the sense that it is a byproduct of the recent privatization of homeownership, which was largely absent from the early 1950s to the late 1980s. Furthermore, this social group is not a structural continuation of the middle class that existed before the communist takeover.

3. My fieldwork was carried out during the summers from 2000 to 2006 with a total of approximately fifteen months of field research. Over the course of these four years, I interviewed about forty homeowners and management staff in several different communities and maintained close ties with some of my informants. I also interviewed about ten developers and local officials involved in the construction of new communities. Much time was also spent on daily observation of community life in over ten housing compounds, with a particular focus on three of them.

4. E. P. Thompson, *The Making of the English Working Class* (New York: Pantheon Books, 1964), 9.

5. I borrow this concept from Paul Willis even though it originally referred to a set of distinct, localized cultural practices and beliefs associated with working-class youth culture in a capitalist society he examined. See Paul Willis, *Learning To Labor: How Working Class Kids Get Working Class Jobs* (New York: Columbia University Press, 1977).

6. Such anxieties and instability in middle-class cultural practices have been discussed by Barbara Ehrenreich, *Fear of Falling: The Inner Life of the Middle Class* (New York: Pantheon Books, 1989); Katherine S. Newman, *Falling from Grace: Downward Mobility in the Age of Affluence* (Berkeley: University of California Press, 1999); Max Weber, *From Max Weber: Essays in Sociology,* ed. and trans. H. H. Gerth and C. Wright Mills (New York: Oxford University Press, 1981).

7. Although Weber differentiates classes from status groups in that the former is largely defined in terms of production and the latter in terms of consumption, he also emphasizes that the two modes of group formation are closely linked through property ownership, which not only determines one's class situation but also serves as the primary basis for differences in lifestyle. See the analysis by Anthony Giddens, *The Class Structure of the Advanced Societies* (London: Hutchinson & Co., 1981).

8. Thompson, *The Making of the English Working Class*.

9. For a culturally oriented understanding of class making, see Mark Liechty, *Suitably Modern: Making Middle-Class Culture in a New Consumer Society* (Princeton: Princeton University Press, 2003); and Daniel Miller, "Consumption and Commodities," *Annual Review of Anthropology* 24 (1995): 141–61.

10. Pierre Bourdieu, *Distinction* (Cambridge: Harvard University Press, 1984).He treats "habitus" as a form of structuring structure, or those elements of culture that are anchored in and shape people's daily practices. Here I do not intend to engage in the argument about whether consumption ultimately leads to emancipation or exploitation. See Deborah Davis, "Urban Consumer Culture," *China Quarterly* 47, no. 3 (2005): 461–84; and Pun Ngai, "Subsumption or Consumption?" *Cultural Anthropology* 18, no. 4 (2003): 469–92. I simply want to emphasize the active role of consumption in shaping class and the often contradictory experiences it generates.

11. This is not to deny any social and economic differences that existed among urban Chinese under Mao. Yet the very living pattern based on *danwei* simply made it difficult for people with similar economic status to live together and cultivate a shared lifestyle, a habitus, and a sense of common identification as anything other than *danwei* comrades.

12. See Jean Baudrillard, "On Consumer Society," in *Rethinking the Subject: An Anthology of Contemporary European Social Thought*, ed. James D. Faubion (Boulder: Westview Press, 1995), 193–203.

13. I thank Rebecca Karl for her critical comments on my theoretical treatment of class and status. Although we do not fully agree with each other on whether the use of *jieceng* can capture or depoliticize what is going on in Chinese society today, her engaging comments pushed me to rethink this issue more carefully.

14. By "neoliberalism" I refer to the practices and thinking associated with the privatization of property and lifestyles and with the valorization of market forces, rather than to a Foucaultian notion of neoliberalism as a form of governmentality and self-governing.

15. See Xiaobo Lu and Elizabeth J. Perry, eds., *Danwei: The Changing Chinese Workplace in Historical and Comparative Perspective* (Armonk, N.Y.: M. E. Sharpe, 1997); Martin Whyte and William L. Parish, *Urban Life in Contemporary China* (Chicago: University of Chicago Press, 1984).

16. Shanghai presents an exception, for its residents tend to maintain a strong consciousness of spatial inequality, partly owing to the city's colonial experiences. See Tianshu Pan, "Neighborhood Shanghai: Community Building in Five Mile Bridge" (Ph.D. diss., Harvard University, 2002).

17. Deborah Davis, "When a House Becomes His Home," in *Popular China: Unofficial Culture in a Globalizing Society*, ed. Perry Link, Richard Madsen, and Paul Pickowicz (Lanham, Md.: Rowman and Littlefield, 2002), 231–50; Davis Fraser, "Inventing Oasis: Luxury Housing Advertisements in Reconfiguring Domestic Space in Shanghai," in *The Consumer Revolution in Urban China*, ed. Deborah Davis (Berkeley: University of California Press, 2002), 25–53.

18. The lower-income neighborhoods include mostly privatized *danwei* housing compounds and some newly developed, state-subsidized *xiaoqu* for teachers, other low-income families, and those who were forced out of the core city districts by recent urban renewal projects or commercial developments.

19. Most new commercially developed communities in China are now regulated by property management agencies and private security guards; they thus have little contact with residents'

committees (*juweihui*) and the local police. See Benjamin Read, "Revitalizing the State's Urban 'Nerve Tips,'" *China Quarterly* 163 (2000): 806–20; and Benjamin Read, "Democratizing the Neighborhood? New Private Housing and Home-Owner Self-Organization in Urban China," *China Journal* 49 (2003): 1–29.

20. David Goodman, "The New Middle Class," in *The Paradox of China's Post-Mao Reforms,* ed. Merle Goldman and Roderick MacFarquhar (Cambridge: Harvard University Press, 1999), 241–61.

21. See Ya Ping Wang and Alan Murie, "Commercial Housing Development in Urban China," *Urban Studies* 36, no. 9 (1999): 1475–94; Ya Ping Wang and Alan Murie, *Housing Policy and Practice in China* (New York: St. Martin's Press, 1999); Xing Quan Zhang, *Privatization: A Study of Housing Policy in Urban China* (New York: Nova Science Publishers, 1998).

22. This is called *yinxing shouru* (invisible income), which often far exceeds the salary offered by one's work unit. Yet it is nearly impossible to survey such incomes for two reasons: they tend to fluctuate over time, and people are unwilling to divulge exactly how much invisible income they earn and the means by which they obtain it.

23. Li Zhang, "Forced from Home: Property Rights, Civic Activism, and the Politics of Relocation in China," *Urban Anthropology* 33, nos. 2–4 (2004): 247–81.

24. This is very similar to the situation discussed by Teresa Caldeira, *City of Walls: Crime, Segregation, and Citizenship in São Paulo* (Berkeley: University of California Press, 2000); and Setha M. Low, "The Edge and the Center: Gated Communities and the Discourse of Urban Fear," *American Anthropologist* 103, no. 1 (2001): 45–58.

25. Howard W. French, "Chinese Children Learn Class, Minus the Struggle," *New York Times,* September 22, 2006.

26. Recent anthropological studies have also demonstrated the centrality of consumption, not just production, in understanding the formation and transformation of the working-class identity and lifestyle in the era of globalization and capitalist restructuring. See Carla Freeman, *High Tech and High Heels in the Global Economy: Women, Work, and Pink-Collar Identities in the Caribbean* (Durham: Duke University Press, 2000); and Mary Beth Mills, *Thai Women in the Global Labor Force: Consuming Desires, Contested Selves* (New Brunswick, N.J.: Rutgers University Press, 1999).

27. The increased importance of consumption in post-Mao social life is clearly demonstrated by a series of studies in Davis, *The Consumer Revolution.*

28. See arguments made by Anita Chan, "The Culture of Survival: Lives of Migrant Workers through the Prism of Private Letters," in Link, Madsen, and Pickowicz, *Popular China,* 163–88; Lee, "Pathways of Labor Insurgency," 41–61; Pun Ngai, *Made in China: Women Factory Workers in a Global Workplace* (Durham: Duke University Press, 2005).

29. Benjamin Read is more optimistic about recently created homeowners' associations in China's new communities, seeing them as a possible force for democratizing the urban Chinese population. See Read, "Democratizing," 1–29. Yet my own research indicates that these associations are often short-sighted, parochial, and short-lived.

30. See Caldeira, *City of Walls*; also Low, "The Edge and the Center," 45–58; and Mike Davis, *City of Quartz: Excavating the Future in Los Angeles* (New York: Vintage Books, 1992).

31. For example, Mike Davis describes this kind of conflict and tension in the United States as a fierce "new class war" at the level of the build environment. Davis, *City of Quartz,* 228.

Chapter 2. Property Rights and Homeowner Activism
in New Neighborhoods

1. See C. B. MacPherson, *The Political Theory of Possessive Individualism: Hobbes to Locke* (London: Oxford University Press, 1964), 194–262; and Edwin G. West, "Property Rights in the History of Economic Thought: From Locke to J. S. Mill," in *Property Rights: Cooperation, Conflict, and Law*, ed. Terry L. Anderson and Fred S. McChesney (Princeton: Princeton University Press, 2003), 20–42.

2. Friedrich A. von Hayek, *The Road to Serfdom* (Chicago: University of Chicago Press, 1944), 103.

3. From a 1985 speech by John Moore quoted in Shirley Robin Letwin, *The Anatomy of Thatcherism* (New Brunswick, N.J.: Transaction, 1993), 102.

4. See, for example, Liu Junning, "Feng neng jin, yu neng jin, guowang buneng jin: zhengzhi lilun shiye de caichanquan yu renlei wenming" [The Wind and Rain May Come in, but the King May Not: Property Rights and Human Civilization in Political Philosophy], excerpted from a 1998 collection of essays, available at http://boxun.com/hero/liujn/18_1.shtml (accessed November 11, 2006).

5. Letwin, *Anatomy*, 105.

6. Kevin J. O'Brien and Lianjiang Li's *Rightful Resistance in Rural China* (Cambridge: Cambridge University Press, 2006) explores this topic in depth. See also Elizabeth J. Perry and Mark Selden, eds., *Chinese Society: Change, Conflict, and Resistance* (London: Routledge, 2000); and Peter Hays Gries and Stanley Rosen, eds., *State and Society in 21st-Century China* (New York: RoutledgeCurzon, 2004).

7. While scholarly analysis of this appears scant, it is reflected in news accounts such as the following: "Protesters Granted an Audience in Beijing: Shenyang Group Tell Officials Directly about Alleged Land Scam," *South China Morning Post*, August 29, 2003; "Three Held after Rally by Oil Well Investors," *South China Morning Post*, July 3, 2003; "Investors Besiege City Hall in Beijing," *South China Morning Post*, June 18, 2003; "Beijing Gets Cold Feet—and Freezes a Key Reform: To Placate Investors, It Cancels a Stock Issue in State Companies," *BusinessWeek*, July 15, 2002; "Demonstrators in China Test New Tolerance," *Wall Street Journal*, August 14, 1998.

8. Shai Oster, "For Chinese Consumers, a Superhero," *Christian Science Monitor*, January 25, 2000; Elisabeth Rosenthal, "Finding Fakes in China, and Fame and Fortune Too," *New York Times*, June 7, 1998.

9. The concept of corporatism as applied to the Chinese context is discussed in Bruce J. Dickson, "Cooptation and Corporatism in China: The Logic of Party Adaptation," *Political Science Quarterly* 115, no. 4 (2000–2001): 517–40; Jonathan Unger, " 'Bridges': Private Business, the Chinese Government, and the Rise of New Associations," *China Quarterly* 147 (1996): 795–819; Jonathan Unger and Anita Chan, "China, Corporatism, and the East Asian Model," *Australian Journal of Chinese Affairs* 33 (1995): 29–53; and Margaret M. Pearson, "The Janus Face of Business Associations in China: Socialist Corporatism in Foreign Enterprises," *Australian Journal of Chinese Affairs* 31 (1994): 25–46.

10. Useful starting points include Deborah S. Davis, "From Welfare Benefit to Capitalized Asset: The Re-commodification of Residential Space in Urban China," in *Housing and Social Change: East-West Perspectives*, ed. Ray Forrest and James Lee (London: Routledge, 2003); Ya Ping Wang and Alan Murie, *Housing Policy and Practice in China* (New York: St. Martin's Press, 1999); Ya Ping Wang and Alan Murie, "Commercial Housing Development in Urban China," *Urban Studies* 36, no. 9 (1999): 1475–94; and Min Zhou and John R. Logan,

"Market Transition and the Commodification of Housing in Urban China," *International Journal of Urban and Regional Research* 20, no. 3 (September 1996): 400–421.

11. This is discussed by Yongshun Cai, "Civil Resistance and Rule of Law in China: The Defense of Homeowners' Rights," in *Grassroots Political Reform in Contemporary China*, ed. Elizabeth J. Perry and Merle Goldman (Cambridge: Harvard University Press, 2007), 174–95.

12. A preliminary analysis of these new homeowners' organizations can be found in Benjamin L. Read, "Democratizing the Neighbourhood? New Private Housing and Homeowner Self-Organization in Urban China," *China Journal* 49 (January 2003): 31–59. Li Zhang's December 2003 unpublished paper "Governing at a Distance: The Politics of Privatizing Home and Community in Neoliberalizing China," discusses power relations among the state, developers, and homeowners in Kunming. Deborah S. Davis presents a case study of a Shanghai neighborhood in "Urban Chinese Homeowners as Citizen-Consumers," *The Ambivalent Consumer: Questioning Consumption in East Asia and the West*, ed. Sheldon Garon and Patricia L. Maclachlan (Ithaca, N.Y.: Cornell University Press, 2006), 281–300. Published Chinese-language analyses include Xia Jianzhong, "Zhongguo gongmin shehui de xiansheng—yi yezhu weiyuanhui wei li" [The First Signs of China's Civil Society: The Case of the Homeowner Committees], *Wen shi zhe*, no. 3 (2003): 115–21; Xia Jianzhong, "Beijing chengshi xinxing shequ zizhi zuzhi yanjiu—jianxi Beijing CY yuan yezhu weiyuanhui" [A Study of Autonomous Organizations in Urban Beijing's New Communities: Learning from the Homeowners Committee in Beijing's CY Gardens], *Beijing shehui kexue*, no. 2 (2003): 88–94; Zhang Jing, "Gonggong kongjian de shehui jichu" [Social Foundations of the Public Sphere], Working Paper 2001.004, Institute of Sociology and Anthropology, Peking University (2001); and Gui Yong, "Lüe lun chengshi jiceng minzhu fazhan de keneng ji qi shixian tujing—yi Shanghaishi wei li" [On the Development of Grassroots Democracy in Urban Areas: A Case Study of Shanghai], *Huazhong keji daxue xuebao shehui kexue ban* 15, no. 1 (February 2001): 24–27.

13. This body of work, encompassing studies of "civil society" as well as other studies of associations, is too immense to cite properly here, but some useful items include Mark E. Warren, *Democracy and Association* (Princeton: Princeton University Press, 2001); Lester M. Salamon et al., eds., *Global Civil Society: Dimensions of the Nonprofit Sector* (Baltimore: Johns Hopkins Center for Civil Society Studies, 1999); Michael Woolcock, "Social Capital and Economic Development: Toward a Theoretical Synthesis and Policy Framework," *Theory and Society* 27, no. 208 (1998): 151–208; Juan J. Linz and Alfred Stepan, *Problems of Democratic Transition and Consolidation: Southern Europe, South America, and Post-communist Europe* (Baltimore: Johns Hopkins University Press, 1996).

14. Zhonghua renmin gongheguo jianshebu ling 1994 nian 33 hao, "Chengshi xinjian zhuzhai xiaoqu guanli banfa," reprinted in Beijingshi juzhu xiaoqu guanli bangongshi, *Beijingshi wuye guanli wenjian huibian* [Compilation of Documents on Real Estate Management in the City of Beijing], vol. 1 (February 1998), 1–5.

15. The new regulations, called the *wuye guanli tiaoli*, are available on the Web site of the Ministry of Construction, http://www.cin.gov.cn/law/admin/2003062002.htm.

16. *Zhuzhai xiaoqu guanli weiyuanhui*, abbreviated as *guanweihui*, or "management committee." Over time this term gave way to another, *yezhu weiyuanhui*, abbreviated as *yeweihui*. As the Ministry of Construction adopted the latter term in its 2003 regulations, I use it here to refer to all homeowner groups.

17. Read, "Democratizing."

18. Li Zhang's unpublished paper on homeowner groups in Kunming contains a good discussion of these three factors.

19. Beixiu Huayuan is this neighborhood's real name. This sketch is based on two long interviews with the *yeweihui* leader in April 2000 and December 2003, and one newspaper article, Chen Dihao, "Yezhu chaodiao wuye gongsi" [Homeowners Fire a Property Management Company], *Nanfang zhoumo*, November 5, 1999.

20. This sketch is based on conversations with four homeowners in July 2003 and July 2004. The neighborhood is referred to with a pseudonym.

21. Lijiang Huayuan is this neighborhood's real name. Its English name is Riverside Garden. This sketch is based on interviews conducted in April 2000 and December 2003. In addition to the cited newspaper articles, it also draws on "Lijiang Huayuan weiquan ji" [Upholding Rights in Riverside Garden], a detailed unpublished account written in the spring of 2003 by Fang Sanwen, a professional journalist and Lijiang homeowner.

22. See "Wei shequ weiquan wo jiu dei you 'chou' you 'ying' " [To Uphold Rights for the Community I Have To Be Both "Stinky" and "Hard"], *Nanfang dushi bao*, February 22, 2004.

23. "Lijiang yeweihui xuanju liuchan zhi ji" [Homeowner Committee Elections Aborted in Riverside Garden], *Nanfang dushi bao*, February 21, 2004.

24. Jiashan is a pseudonym. This sketch is based on interviews with the principal organizer conducted in November 2000 and July 2003.

Chapter 3. Socialist Land Masters

1. Between 1980 and 2002 the urban population grew from 18–20 percent of the total population to 36–40 percent; in other words, about 500 million residents were added to the urban population. See George C. S. Lin, "The Growth and Structural Change of Chinese Cities: A Contextual and Geographic Analysis," *Cities* 19, no. 5 (2002): 299–316; and Yixing Zhou and Laurence J. C. Ma, "China's Urbanization Levels: Reconstructing a Baseline from the Fifth Population Census," *China Quarterly*, no. 173 (March 2003): 176–96.

2. PRC Constitution, Article 10; PRC Land Management Law (first adopted in 1986, amended in 1988, 1998, 2004), Article 2. The remainder of Article 10 stipulates that land in the countryside and in suburban areas is under collective ownership." In this chapter I choose to focus on urban instead of rural collective land.

3. My data are collected from fieldwork in Beijing, Guangzhou, and Shanghai in 2003 and 2004, and more generally from two cities in Sichuan (Chengdu and a prefecture-level city), Zhengzhou (Henan), and Changsha (Hunan) from 1997 to 2002.

4. Most of the recent work on China's changing regime of land rights has been focused on rural farmland and resource land, not urban land. See, for example, Sally Sargeson, "Full Circle? Rural Land Reforms in Globalizing China," *Critical Asian Studies* 36, no. 4 (2004): 637–56; Peter Ho, Who Owns China's Land? Policies, Property Rights, and Deliberate Institutional Ambiguity, *China Quarterly*, no. 166 (2001): 394–421; Xiaolin Guo, "Land Expropriation and Rural Conflicts in China," *China Quarterly*, no. 166 (2001): 422–39. In studies of the changing land rights regimes in eastern Europe, most works also deal with rural agricultural land. See, for example, Katherine Verdery, "The Elasticity of Land: Problems of Property Restitution in Transylvania, *Slavic Review* 53, no. 4 (1994): 1071–1109. In studies of China, works on urban land are mainly about the evolution of China's land institutions but not its urban politics. See Samuel Ho and George Lin, "Emerging Land Markets in Rural and Urban China: Policies and Practices," *China Quarterly*, no. 175 (2003): 681–707; and Fulong Wu,

"China's Changing Urban Governance in the Transition towards a More Market-Oriented Economy," *Urban Studies* 39, no. 7 (2002): 1071–93.

5. Each municipality is divided into districts. For example, as of the beginning of 2003, Beijing municipality had eighteen districts. Four of them were in the city core; Shanghai municipality had twenty-three districts, ten of them in the city core.

6. See Xiaobo Lu and Elizabeth Perry, eds., *Danwei: The Changing Chinese Workplace in Historical and Comparative Perspective* (New York: M. E. Sharpe, 1997).

7. Here I follow scholars in the social-legal studies of landed property rights, such as the contributors to Harvey Jacobs, ed., *Who Owns America? Social Conflicts over Property Rights* (Madison: University of Wisconsin Press, 1998). Research focused on the Third World is represented by de Sousa Santos, "The Law of the Oppressed: The Construction and Reproduction of Legality in Pasargada," *Law and Society Review* 12, no. 1 (1977): 5–126.

8. Here "territorial" refers to a physical and political space and to the people and resources within it. Territorial power is understood as an open, endless strategic game aimed at controlling and influencing the people and resources within the space. See David Delaney, *Territory: A Short Introduction* (Oxford: Blackwell, 2005); and Michel Foucault, "The Subject and Power," in, *Michel Foucault: Beyond Structuralism and Hermeneutics*, ed. Hubert Dreyfus and Paul Rabinow (Brighton, 1982), 221–22.

9. See John Logan and Harvey Molotch, *Urban Fortunes: The Political Economy of Growth* (Berkeley: University of California Press, 1987).

10. Interview CS0002, Changsha, June 2000.

11. See Ho and Lin, "Emerging Land Markets in Rural and Urban China."

12. In 2002 the central government demanded that 40 percent of the land appreciation tax be incorporated into the state budgetary system and be shared with the state treasury. But a municipal land management official claimed that he "did not know any city that had followed the new rule," and he felt it would be difficult for the central government to enforce that rule. Interview TJU0301 (a high-ranking official of the Tianjin Municipal Land Management and Planning Bureau), May 2003.

13. Samuel Ho and George Lin, Non-agricultural Land Use in Post-reform China, *China Quarterly*, no. 179 (2004): 758–81, esp. 765.

14. Yixing Zhou and Meng Yenchuen, *Beijingde jiaoquhua jiqi duice* [Suburbanization and Policies in Beijing] (Beijing: Science Publisher, 2000), 141.

15. *Shanghai chengshi guihua* [Shanghai's City Planning] (Shanghai: Shanghai Municipal Bureau of Urban Planning, 1998).

16. Chiling Huang, "Gaige kaifang zhong Shanghai dushi duti fazhanyu dushi kongjian zaijiegou" [Urban Land Development and Urban Space Restructuring in Shanghai during Economic Reforms] (Master's thesis, Tongji University, Shanghai, 1997). According to a 1998 survey of seventeen major cities in China, industrial land still occupied 22 percent of the total urban area. Twenty-five percent of Shanghai, 17 percent of Beijing, and 28 percent of Suzhou's urban core was still occupied by industries. See Jianhai Cao, *Zhongguo tudi gaoxiao liyung yenjiu* [Studies of Efficient Use of Urban Land in China] (Beijing: Jingji guanli, 2002), 105–7.

17. For land squandered on urban industries during the early period of socialist industrialization, see Kai-yu Fung, "Urban Sprawl in China: Some Causative Factors," in *Urban Development in Modern China*, ed. Laurence Ma and Edward Hanten (Boulder: Westview Press, 1981), 194–220.

18. For an account of the construction activities of urban *danwei*, see Duanfang Lu, "Building the Chinese Work Unit: Modernity, Scarcity, and Space, 1949–2000" (Ph.D. diss., University of California at Berkeley, 2003).

19. Article 10, clause 4 of the "Provisional Regulations on the Conveyance, Granting, and Transferring of the State Land's Use Rights in Cities and Towns," enacted by the State Council in May 1991.

20. Wenhao Zhang, "Beijing tudiye chushi" [Land Masters in Beijing], *Caijing*, no. 61 (2002): 41.

21. Interviews BJ0301 (a real estate development consultant), Beijing, June 2003; and BJ0309 (general manager of a large development company with an SOE background), Beijing, July 2003.

22. One of the largest development group companies in Beijing, Capital Land, has seven listed companies. One of them is listed on the Hong Kong Stock Exchange. The general manager of Capital Land, Liu Xiaoguang, a guru in Beijing real estate circles, is the former vice chair of Beijing's Economic Planning Committee, which had the authority to approve land development projects. Capital Land claimed to have a land reserve of 450,000 square kilometers in 2003. Interview BJ0320 (general manager of one of Capital Land's subsidiaries), July 2003. Also see Ju Xie, "Shouchuang sanwen" [Three Questions about Capital Land), *Xincaijing*, no. 41 (August 2003): 34–37.

23. In 2003 the land management system was restructured. The Ministry of Land and Resources and its provincial branches took back from local governments much of the authority to approve land lease sales and farmland conversion. It is too early to tell how effective the reinstallation of the "vertical management" system has been. Interview BJ0319 (a high-ranking official of the Ministry of Land and Resources), Beijing, August 2003.

24. See Fulong Wu, "The New Structure of Building Provision and the Transformation of the Urban Landscape in Metropolitan Guangzhou, China," *Urban Studies* 35, no. 2 (1998): 259–72.

25. See William Alonso, *Location and Land Use* (Cambridge: Harvard University Press, 1964).

26. I received more than half a dozen delegations of Chinese urban planning students while teaching at the planning school of the University of British Columbia from 1992 to 1996.

27. George Lin, "Towards a Post-socialist City? Economic Tertiarization and Urban Reformation in the Guangzhou Metropolis, China," *Eurasia Geography and Economics* 45, no. 1 (2004): 18–44.

28. Jianhai Cao, *Zhongguo tudi gaoxiao liyung yenjiu*, 108.

29. Interviews BJ0302 (an urban planning professor and consultant); and BJ0303 (a senior official on Beijing's Urban Planning Committee), both Beijing, August 2003.

30. Interview BJ0303 (a senior official of the Urban Planning Committee), Beijing, August 2003. The transaction surcharge amounted to 5 to 10 percent of total construction costs.

31. Chengshun Mo, "Hainan fangdichan paomo" [Property Bubbles in Hainan], *Caijing*, May 31, 2004.

32. Interview BJ0311 (a high-ranking official in Beijing's Center for Land Reserves), August 2003.

33. See Po Ren, "Beijing yuhui zhilu" [The Winding Path That Beijing Took], and "Chengshi tudi zhimi" [Secrets of Urban Land], *Caijing*, no. 76 (January 2003).

34. "Reinforcement of State Landed Assets Management," State Council, April 2001.

35. Interview BJ0309 (general manager of a large development company with an SOE background), August 2003.

36. Interview BJ0311 (a high-ranking official in Beijing's Center for Land Reserves), August 2003. While fees for the transfer of land use rights through individual negotiations can be paid in installments scheduled over many years, auctioned land parcels require a much larger initial investment (35 percent of the total amount) at the time of lease signing.

37. Zheng Tang, "8–31 da-xian" [The Deadline of August 31], *Caijing*, no. 110 (2004): 96–99.

38. Interviews BJ0301 (a real estate development consultant), Beijing, August 2003; and SH0401 (a planning professor and consultant), Shanghai, December 2004. It was estimated that in 2000, as many as 95 percent of land transaction cases in China still used individual negotiation rather than public tender or open auction. See Hongqiao Jiang, "Tudi shichanghua: zai liyi jiujie zhong jiannan tuijin" [Pushing Ahead Land Marketization against Vested Interests], *Economic Observer*, September 13, 2003.

39. Zongli Wong et al., eds., *Beijing fangdichan* [Beijing Real Estate] (Beijing: Hangkong-gongye Press, 1996), 147.

40. Interviews GZ0402 (a planning professor and consultant), Guangzhou, June 2004; SC0302 (a high-ranking official in the urban planning bureau of a prefecture-level city), Sichuan, January 2003; and BJ0302 (an urban planning professor and consultant), August 2003.

41. Interviews SZ9701(a high-ranking official in Shenzhen's planning and land use bureau), Shenzhen, July 1997; TJU0401 (a high-ranking Tianjin municipal official), November 2004.

42. Interviews CD9701 (a high-ranking planning official in the Institute of Urban Design and Planning), Chengdu, July 1997; and GZ0301 (a high-ranking official in a district urban planning bureau), Guangzhou, January 2003 and June 2004.

43. Interview BJ0309 (general manager of a large development company with an SOE background), August 2003.

44. Zhiling Huang, "Gaige kaifenghou Shanghai chengshi tudi kaifa yu chengshi kongjian zaijiegou," 72.

45. Shengjie Cao and Shangchun Lu, "Hepingli beijie erhao: nanyi kaizhang de chaoshi?" [No. 2 Hepingli North Street: A "Land Supermarket" That Could Not Open for Business], *Economic Observer*, September 12, 2004.

46. Mei Yuan and Xiang Zhang, "Shanghai tudi tunji zhimi" [The Puzzle of Land Hoarding in Shanghai], Caijing, no. 127 (2005): 28–34.

47. Here legitimacy is understood as the contested process of justifying claims of political authority. For a review of legitimacy issues in China's transformation, see the introduction to this volume and Vivienne Shue, "Legitimacy Crisis in China?" in *State and Society in 21st-Century China*, ed. Peter Gries and Stanley Rosen (New York: RoutledgeCurzon, 2004), 1–49.

48. Interviews BJ0401 and BJ0402 (relocated persons and protesters), Beijing, August 2004.

49. Interview BJ0304 (a sociology professor and researcher), Beijing, August 2004; Zhao Lin, *Chaiqian shinien beixiju* [Ten Years of Relocation Drama], *Southern Weekend*, September 4, 2003.

50. This movement has been generated mainly by the abolition of *danwei* housing and the new schemes for home mortgages. For a study of homeowner associations, see Benjamin Read, "Democratizing the Neighborhood? New Private Housing and Home-Owner Self-Organization in Urban China," *China Journal*, no. 49 (January 2003).

51. Interviews BJ0403 (a homeowner association activist), Beijing, July 2004; and BJ0301 (a real estate development consultant), Beijing, August 2004.

52. Interview BJ0404 (former general manager of one of China's largest development companies, now running his own development company in Beijing), Beijing, August 2004.

53. For a review of the studies on the central state, decentralization, and the local state in post-reform China, see Richard Baum and Alexei Shevchenko, "The State of the State," in *The Paradox of China's Post-Mao Reforms*, ed. Merle Goldman and Roderick Macfarquhar (Cambridge: Harvard University Press, 1999), 333–60.

Chapter 4. Tax Tensions

1. Junwei He and Wenbo Pan, "A Survey Report on the Agricultural Problems in Qipan Township of Jianli County, Hubei Province," in *Spoke the Truth to the Prime Minister*, ed. Changping Li (Beijing: Guangming Daily Press, 2002). [In Chinese.]

2. Lan Zou and Yu Zhang, "Earn Money Jiao by Jiao, Pay Money Pile by Pile: A Self-Employed Couple Talking about the Heavy Burden of Taxes and Fees," *Xinhua News Agency*, March 21, 2002. [In Chinese.] http://news.xinhuanet.com/newscenter/2002–03/21/content _325701.htm.

3. Christine P. W. Wong, "Overview of Issues in Local Public Finance in the PRC," in *Financing Local Government in the People's Republic of China*, ed. Christine P. W. Wong (New York: Oxford University Press, 1997), 27–59, quote on 33.

4. Christine P. W. Wong, "Shifting from Charges to Taxes: Extra-budgetary Funds and Intergovernmental Fiscal Relations in China," *Jinji Shehui Tizhi Bijiao* 92 (2000): 14–21. [In Chinese.]

5. See Roy Bahl, *Fiscal Policy in China: Taxation and Intergovernmental Fiscal Relations* (San Francisco: The 1990 Institute, 1999).

6. Laurence Brahm, "Exposing the Corruption Mountain," *South China Morning Post*, August 4, 2003.

7. Justin Yifu Lin, Ran Tao, Mingxing Liu, and Qi Zhang, "The Problem of Taxing Peasants in China," Working Paper (preliminary draft), China Center for Economic Research, Peking University, 2002.

8. Shuming Liu, "Unification of Urban and Rural Taxation System as Well as Adjustment Policy: A New Approach to Lessen Peasants' Burden," *Economic Research* 2 (2001): 43–39. [In Chinese.]

9. See Weiwei Jiang, "Zhang Xiaoqiang, Deputy Director of the State Development and Planning Commission of China: China's Urban-Rural Income Disparity Is Increasing," *China Youth Daily*, December 29, 2003. [In Chinese.]

10. For example, see Baoli Ding and Lijian Cheng, "An Investigative Report on the Rural Fee-Tax-Swap Project Reform in Anhui Province," *Journal of Anhui University (Philosophy and Social Sciences)* 26 (2002): 8–12. [In Chinese.]

11. A new law that was passed in March 2007 affirmed private property rights and stipulated equal protection for private and public ownership. Although commercial land use leases were not affected, land use contracts for farmers and urban residential property will automatically renew at the end of their terms.

12. Tingwei Zhang, "Urban Development and a Socialist Pro-growth Coalition in Shanghai," *Urban Affairs Review* 37 (2002): 475–99.

13. See Deci Zou, "Chinese Cities Towards the 21st Century," *City Planning Review* 22 (1998): 7–9; and Yan Zhang and Ke Fang, "Is History Repeating Itself? From Urban Renewal in the United States to Inner-City Redevelopment in China," *Journal of Planning Education and Research* 23 (2004): 286–98.

14. See Zhang, "Urban Development."

15. Ibid.

16. See Zhang and Fang, "Is History Repeating Itself?"

17. Ibid.

18. See Financial Times Information, "Control over Land Market Crucial," *Daily Business Update*, December 12, 2003.

19. Bahl, *Fiscal Policy in China*, 142.

20. See National Bureau of Statistics, *China Statistical Yearbook* (Beijing: China Statistics Press, 2003), 291.

21. Jiawang Zhou, "Beijing's Housing Price Is Too High: The House Price–to–Income Ratio Reaches 11:1," *Beijing Evening News*, December 25, 2001. [In Chinese.]

22. Yu-Hung Hong, "Myths and Realities of Public Land Leasing: Canberra and Hong Kong," *Land Lines Newsletter* [Lincoln Institute of Land Policy] 11, no. 2 (1999), http://www.lincolninst.edu/pubs/PubDetail.aspx?pubid=363.

23. See China Business InfoCenter, "Real Estate Tax Plan to Cut Housing Prices," March 16, 2004, http://www.cbiz.cn.

24. See Asia Pulse, "Will China Impose Property Tax," April 4, 2005.

25. See Andrei Shleifer and Robert W. Vishny, "Corruption," *Quarterly Journal of Economics* 108, no. 3 (1993): 599–617.

26. Ibid.

Chapter 5. "Reorganized Moralism"

1. The pioneers in this area are Stephen Frenkel, "Globalization, Athletic Footwear Commodity Chains, and Employment Relations in China," *Organization Studies*, no. 4 (2001): 531–62; Tan Shen and Liu Ka Ming, *Kuaguo gongsi di shihui zeren* [Transnational Corporate Social Responsibility in China] (Beijing: shihui kexue wenxian chubanshe, 2003); and Anita Chan and Hong-zen Wang, "Raising Labor Standards, Corporate Social Responsibility, and Missing Links: Vietnam and China Compared," paper presented at Labor Standards in China Conference, March 21–22, 2003, University of Michigan.

2. See the works of Anita Chan, in particular, *China's Workers under Assault: The Exploitation of Labor in a Globalizing Economy* (Armonk, N.Y.: M. E. Sharpe, 2001); Lee Ching Kwan, *Gender and the South China Miracle: Two Worlds of Factory Women* (Berkeley: University of California Press, 1998); and Hsing You-tien, *Making Capitalism in China: The Taiwan Connection* (Oxford: Oxford University Press, 1998).

3. Reebok International Ltd., "Toward Sustainable Code Compliance: Worker Representation in China," November 2002.

4. See Doug Guthrie, *Dragon in a Three-Piece Suit* (Princeton: Princeton University Press, 1999).

5. See Ching Kwan Lee, "From the Specter of Mao to the Spirit of the Law: Labour Insurgency in China," *Theory and Society* 31 (2002): 189–229.

6. See March J. Blecher, "Hegemony and Workers' Politics in China, *China Quarterly* 170 (2002): 283–303; Dorothy J. Solinger, "Labour Market Reform and the Plight of the Laid-Off Proletariat," *China Quarterly* 170 (2002): 304–26; Feng Chen, "Industrial Restructuring and Workers' Resistance in China," *Modern China* 29 (2003): 237–62.

7. See Jean-Paul Sajhau, "Business Ethics in the Textile, Clothing, and Footwear (TCF) Industries: Codes of Conduct," *ILO Bulletin*, no. II-9 (June 1997); Nina Ascoly, "About the Clean Clothes Campaign: A Brief Overview of the CCC's Development and Areas of Activity," paper presented at the Forum on Industrial Relations and Labour Polices in a Globalizing World," Beijing, January 9–11, 2000.

8. Some codes consist of general principles applicable to all actors in a company's business activities, including material providers, manufacturers, and retailers. Some are much more detailed and contain variations between the internal practices of the companies and the external policies of production suppliers or trade partners. Various details of codes are adopted in local labor laws and working conditions.

9. Sajhau, "Business Ethics."

10. Women Working Worldwide, "Company Codes of Conduct" (2000), http://www.poptel.org.uk/women-ww/company_coc.htm.

11. Wal-Mart, a major U.S. retailer, established a set of comprehensive company codes of conduct in 1993 which soon became the example for many U.S. clothing and footwear companies and retailers such as Sears, Nike, Reebok, J.C. Penny, Woolworth's, Liz Claiborne, The Gap, and Phillips–Van Heusen. Although European companies were much slower to take action in responding to the demand for ethical trade, a number of retailers such as C&A, Littlewoods, and the Otto mail order group developed their own company codes in the early 2000s, especially after pressure from the Clean Clothes Campaign and other campaigns such as Labour behind the Label.

12. See Tony Emerson, "A Letter to Jiang Zemin: The Quixotic Tale of Three American CEOs and Their Ill-Fated Mission to Change China from Inside," *Newsweek International*, May 29, 2000.

13. See CIC, February 2000; LARIC, July–August 2000; Global Exchange, "Executive Summary of Report on Nike and Reebok in China" (September 1997), http://www.globalexhange.org/economy/corporations/nike/NikeReebokChinaSummary.html.

14. See Frenkel, "Globalization."

15. The Clean Clothes Campaign (CCC) is a network of organizations in different countries working to improve conditions in the textile, clothing, and footwear industries. Its aim is to raise consumer awareness about how clothes are made and to put pressure on retailers to take responsibility for labor conditions throughout subcontracting chains. More information is available at the CCC Web site, http://www.cleanclothes.org/codes.

16. The identities of companies and all workers from this point on have been kept anonymous.

17. We interviewed these workers one by one in meeting rooms provided by China Miracle and also provided labor law training at China Miracle.

18. A workers' dormitory building was planned, but construction had not yet started. The company rented dormitory rooms outside for their workers, which required a fifteen-minute walk to the company premises.

19. China Miracle was certified ISO 9000 in 2000 and ISO 14000 in 2002, and aimed at certifying SA 8000 by the middle of 2003. Few companies in China really paid attention to achieving SA 8000 certification.

20. NGOs such as Oxfam International, the Clean Clothes Campaign, and the Maquila Solidarity Network are well aware of the pressure on workers to provide "correct" answers to the monitors and attempt to make recommendations regarding monitoring practices.

21. The code stated that "a contract based on local legislation has to be established between employee and employer." The code also required the contract to contain the following points: (1) workers must be paid at least the minimum legal wage; (2) overtime pay must meet the legal requirements; (3) workers must receive paid annual leave and holidays as required by law; and (4) an understandable wage statement must be provided, which includes number of days worked, wage or piece rate earned per day, hours of overtime at each specified rate, bonuses, allowances, and contractual deductions. The contracts provided by the two enterprises, however, specify only the following: the starting date; the name of the work unit; the worker's obligation to abide by factory regulations; the requirement that the worker accept any arrangement concerning a change of position without arguing against it; the obligation to ensure and respect a safe company environment; a warning of dismissal if a worker does not follow company regulations or causes loss of production; and a statement that the company pays wages, insurance, and overtime in accordance with the Labor Law.

22. According to China's Labor Law, workers should have two days off in seven.

23. The legal minimum wage in the Yangtze River region was RMB 430 in April 2002, which was raised to RMB 460 in December 2002. Management insisted that meeting the legal requirement was not a problem because most workers would receive above that amount. The workers, however, could not tell us the amount of the minimum wage, and most of them were unfamiliar with the provision.

24. The code further states that "factories may not interfere with workers who wish to lawfully and peacefully associate, organize, or bargain collectively."

25. I wish to acknowledge that most of the NGOs involved in labor code monitoring have adopted a critical stance in stating that the major limitation in code implementation is the lack of workers' participation.

Chapter 6. Neoliberalism and Hmong/Miao Transnational Media Ventures

1. Stephen J. Collier and Aihwa Ong, "Global Assemblages, Anthropological Problems," in *Global Assemblages: Technology, Politics, and Ethics as Anthropological Problems*, ed. Aihwa Ong and Stephen J. Collier (Malden, Mass.: Blackwell, 2005), 12.

2. Pierre Bourdieu and Loïc Wacquant, "New Liberal Speak: Notes on the New Planetary Vulgate," *Radical Philosophy* 105 (January–February 2001): 3.

3. Graham Burchell, "Liberal Government and the Techniques of the Self," in *Foucault and Political Reason: Liberalism, Neo-liberalism, and Rationalities of Government*, ed. Andrew Barry, Thomas Osborne, and Nikolas Rose (Chicago: University of Chicago Press, 1996), 27–29.

4. Colin Gordon, "Governmental Rationality: An Introduction," in *The Foucault Effect: Studies in Governmentality*, ed. Graham Burchell, Colin Gordon, and Peter Miller (Chicago: University of Chicago Press, 1991), 44.

5. Aihwa Ong, *Buddha Is Hiding: Refugees, Citizenship, the New America* (Berkeley: University of California Press, 2003), 89.

6. These figures are based on the 2000 U.S. Census and compiled by the Hmong National Development organization. See http://www.hndlink.org/economicstat.htm.

7. Jamie Morgan, "Words of Warning: Global Networks, Asian Local Resistance, and the Planetary Vulgate of Neoliberalism," *Positions* 11, no. 3 (2003): 543.

8. Burchell, "Liberal Government," 29; Paul Heelas and Paul Morris, *The Values of the Enterprise Culture: The Moral Debate* (London: Routledge, 1992).

9. Ong, *Buddha Is Hiding*, 267.

10. Ibid., 269.

11. Nikolas Rose, "Governing 'Advanced' Liberal Democracies," in Barry, Osborne, and Rose, *Foucault and Political Reason*, 61.

12. For an overview of the effects of Xibu Dakaifa across China, see the special issue on the subject edited by David S. G. Goodman in *China Quarterly* 178 (June 2004).

13. Jonathan Unger and Jean Xiong, "Life in the Chinese Hinterlands under the Rural Economic Reforms," *Bulletin of Concerned Asian Scholars* 22, no. 2 (1990): 4–17.

14. Hairong Yan, "Neoliberal Governmentality and Neohumanism: Organizing Suzhi/Value Flow through Labor Recruitment Networks," *Cultural Anthropology* 18, no. 4 (2003): 499.

15. Junhao Hong, *The Internationalization of Television in China: The Evolution of Ideology, Society, and Media Since the Reform* (Westport, Conn.: Praeger, 1998), 88.

16. Offices of the Guizhou Chinese Communist Party and the Guizhou Provincial Government, "Memo on Accelerating Steps for Poverty Alleviation and Development in the Mashan and Yaoshan Regions" [Guanyu Jiakuai Mashan, Yaoshan Diqu Fupin Kaifa Bufa de Tongzhi], August 5, 1994, 56–57.

17. The account in this paragraph is based on information compiled by the Miao scholar-journalist Long Jiangang of Foshan University.

18. Hong, *The Internationalization of Television*, 118.

19. Leslie Sklair, *Sociology of the Global System* (Baltimore: Johns Hopkins University Press, 1998), 201.

20. Max Horkheimer and Theodor W. Adorno, "The Culture Industry: Enlightenment as Mass Deception," in *The Dialectic of Enlightenment* (1944; reprint, New York: Continuum, 1972), 120–67.

21. Guy Debord, *The Society of the Spectacle* (1967; reprint, New York: Zone Books, 1995).

22. Yan, "Neoliberal Governmentality," 494.

23. Ibid., 495.

24. Ibid., 497. Ralph Litzinger suggests that this developmental logic was antedated by what he calls a form of "cultural governmentality," in which minority cultures were themselves valued as resources by which ethnic actors could advance themselves in line with state goals. See Ralph Litzinger, *Other Chinas: The Yao and the Politics of National Belonging* (Durham: Duke University Press, 2000), 200–201.

25. Arjun Appadurai, *Modernity at Large: Cultural Dimensions of Globalization* (Minneapolis: University of Minnesota Press, 1996).

26. Mayfair Mei-hui Yang, "Mass Media and Transnational Subjectivity in Shanghai: Notes on (Re)Cosmopolitanism in a Chinese Metropolis," in *Ungrounded Empires: The Cultural Politics of Modern Chinese Transnationalism*, ed. Aihwa Ong and Donald Nonini (New York: Routledge 1997), 287–319.

27. Louisa Schein, "Of Cargo and Satellites: Imagined Cosmopolitanism," *Postcolonial Studies* 2, no. 3 (1999): 345–75.

28. See Zhen Zhang's discussion of the phrase *yu shijie jiegui*, literally "linking up with the tracks of the world," which she glosses as "China's desire to catch the last train of global

modernity." Zhen Zhang, "Mediating Time: The Rice Bowl of Youth in Fin-de-Siècle Urban China," *Public Culture* 12, no. 1 (2000): 93.

29. Neil Smith, "Homeless/Global: Scaling Places," in *Mapping the Futures: Local Cultures, Global Change,* ed. Jon Bird, Barry Curtis, Tim Putnam, George Robertson, and Lisa Tickner (London: Routledge, 1993), 90.

30. Yan, "Neoliberal Governmentality."

31. For an extended discussion of this and other conferences as well as other dilemmas in the establishment of Hmong/Miao transnational fraternity, see Louisa Schein, "Importing Miao Brethren to Hmong America: A Not-So-Stateless Transnationalism," in *Cosmopolitics: Thinking and Feeling Beyond the Nation,* ed. Pheng Cheah and Bruce Robbins (Minneapolis: University of Minnesota Press, 1998), 163–91.

32. Nikolas Rose, *Powers of Freedom: Reframing Political Thought* (Cambridge: Cambridge University Press, 1999), 176–77.

33. Ibid., 174.

34. This section is based on Chanhia Yang's account of the partnership.

35. By late 2006, when this chapter was being revised, they had released part two, to even better sales. Yeng Tha was looking for an Asian distributor, and the couple were petitioning for a fiancée visa for Ying.

36. David Harvey, *The Condition of Postmodernity: An Enquiry into the Origins of Cultural Change* (Cambridge, Mass.: Blackwell, 1989).

37. David L. Wank, *Commodifying Communism: Business, Trust, and Politics in a Chinese City* (Cambridge: Cambridge University Press, 1999).

Chapter 7. Consuming Medicine and Biotechnology in China

1. Giorgio Agamben, *Homo Sacer: Sovereign Power and Bare Life*, trans. Daniel Heller-Roazen (Stanford: Stanford University Press, 1998), 123.

2. For my discussion of the three sectors of biotech (agricultural, pharmaceutical, and genomic) being developed in China, see the article "China's Biotech Bloom," *Genewatch* 17, no.1 (January–February 2004).

3. *European Molecular Biology Organization Reports* 4, no. 2 (2003), 111–13.

4. Shai Oster, "Tinkering with Tomorrow: China Races to Lead the World in Genetic Research, While Most of Its Citizens Are Detached from Technology" *SF Chronicle,* April 3, 2001.

5. "The Human Genome Project in China," http://hugopacific.genome.ad.jp/2contents/project.html (accessed May 15, 2002).

6. Ellen Hertz, *The Trading Crowd: An Ethnography of the Shanghai Stock Market* (Cambridge, England: Cambridge University Press, 1998).

7. Vincanne Adams, "Randomized Controlled Crimes: Postcolonial Sciences in Alternative Medicine Research," *Social Studies of Science* 32 no. 5–6 (October–December 2002), 659–90, quote at 661.

8. Nancy N. Chen, "Health, Wealth, and the Good Life," in *China Urban: Ethnographies of Contemporary China* (Durham, N.C.: Duke University Press, 2001).

9. Eric Niiler, "China's Efforts to Lure Biotechs to Bio-Island Criticized," *Nature Biotechnology* 18, no. 7 (July 2000), 708.

10. Josh Gerstein, "In China, Harvard Head Laments Study," *Boston Globe*, May 15, 2002, A12.

11. *European Molecular Biology Organization Reports* 4, no. 2 (2003), 111–13.

12. John Gittings, "Experts Call for Curbs on Human Cloning in China," *Guardian*, April 16, 2002.

13. *European Molecular Biology Organization Reports* 4, no. 2 (2003), 111–13.

14. Carol Benedict, *Bubonic Plague in Nineteenth-Century China* (Stanford: Stanford University Press, 1996).

15. Albert Camus, *The Plague*, trans. Stuart Gilbert (New York: Modern Library, 1948).

16. Warwick Anderson, "Postcolonial Technoscience: Introduction," *Social Studies of Science* 32, no. 5–6 (October–December 2002), 643–58.

Chapter 8. Should I Quit?

1. Epidemiologists began to study tobacco smoking in China on a large scale only in the late twentieth century, so long-term statistical knowledge on the subject does not exist. According to two nationwide surveys of tobacco use conducted in 1996 and 2002, rates of smoking among women in contemporary China pale in comparison to those occurring among men. In 1996, 63 percent, and in 2002, 58 percent of men over fifteen years of age who were surveyed reported that they smoked a tobacco product regularly. During the same periods, only 3.8 percent and 2.6 percent of women who were surveyed reported smoking. Chinese Association on Smoking and Health, "2002 Nian Zhongguo Renqun Xiyan Xingwei De Liuxingbingxue Diaocha [2002 Epidemiological Survey of China's Smoking Behavior]," *Newsletter of Chinese Smoking and Health* 62, no. 5 (2004): 7. In Kunming, the 1996 survey found that 77 percent of men and 4.5 percent of women were current smokers. Chinese Academy of Preventive Medicine, *1996 Nian Quanquo Xiyan Xingwei Liuxingbingxue Diaocha* [1996 Epidemiological Survey of National Smoking Behavior] (Beijing: China Science and Technology Press, 1997), 197.

2. Sven Dierig, Jens Lachmund, and Andrew Mendelsohn, eds., *Science and the City*, vol. 18, *Osiris* (Chicago: University of Chicago Press, 2003).

3. Martyn Denscombe, "Uncertain Identities and Health-Risking Behavior: The Case of Young People and Smoking in Late Modernity," *British Journal of Sociology* 52, no. 1 (2001), 155–77; Pat O'Malley, "Risk and Responsibility," in *Foucault and Political Reason: Liberalism, Neo-liberalism and Rationalities of Government*, ed. Andrew Barry, Thomas Osborne, and Nikolas Rose (Chicago: University of Chicago Press, 1996), 189–208.

4. Ulrich Beck, *Risk Society: Toward a New Modernity* (London: Sage, 1992); Anthony Giddens, *Beyond Left and Right* (Cambridge: Polity Press, 1994).

5. Michel Foucault, "Governmentality," in *The Foucault Effect: Studies in Governmentality*, ed. Graham Burchell, Colin Gordon, and Peter Miller (Chicago: University of Chicago Press, 1991), 87–104.

6. Beck, *Risk Society*; Ulrich Beck, *World Risk Society* (Cambridge: Polity Press, 1999).

7. Ulrich Beck, "The Terrorist Threat: World Risk Society Revisited," *Theory, Culture, and Society* 19, no. 4 (2002), 39–55.

8. Ulrich Beck, *Ecological Politics in an Age of Risk* (Cambridge: Polity Press, 1995); Beck, *World Risk Society*.

9. Paul Thiers, "Risk Society Comes to China: SARS, Transparency, and Public Accountability," *Asian Perspective* 27, no. 2 (2003), 241–51.

10. Also see Deborah Lupton, *Risk* (New York: Routledge, 1999); John Tulloch and Deborah Lupton, *Risk and Everyday Life* (London: Sage, 2003).

11. Yuan Tingdong, *Zhongguo Xiyan Shihua* [Historical Narrative of Smoking in China] (Beijing: International Commercial Press, 1995), 169; Jason Hughes, *Learning to Smoke: Tobacco Use in the West* (Chicago: University of Chicago Press, 2003), 36–94.

12. Ma, *Yan Jiu Cha Yu Jiankang*, 1.

13. Timothy Brook, "Smoking in Imperial China," in *Smoke: A Global History of Smoking*, ed. Sander Gilman and Zhou Xun (London: Reaktion Books, 2004), 89.

14. See Wenfei Ma, *Yan Jiu Cha Yu Jiankang* [Tobacco, Alcohol, Tea, and Health] (Beijing: Renmin Weisheng Press, 1985), 1.

15. TobaccoChina Online. "China's Tobacco Industry Registers Balanced Growth of Cigarette Production, Sales." http://www.tobaccochina.com/englishnew/content.aspx?id=28726.

16. I have spent less time, though still a considerable amount, talking to Kunming women about smoking and anti-tobacco media. Because this chapter's central focus is that of male identity formation, I will wait for another venue to describe at greater length what I have learned from my female informants.

17. David Wank, "Cigarettes and Domination in Chinese Business Networks: Institutional Change during the Market Transition," in *The Consumer Revolution in Urban China*, ed. Deborah Davis (Berkeley: University of California Press, 2000), 268–86.

18. Martin Baxendale, *Bangongshi Shengcun Zhinan/Jieyan Shengcun Zhinan* (Office: A Survival Guide/Stopping Smoking: A Survival Guide) (Beijing: Yukong Press, 2003).

19. Although decontextualized self-help manuals such as the one discussed here, when applied alone in a highly pro-tobacco environment like Kunming, seem highly problematic in terms of their likelihood of helping smokers to quit, it is more than plausible that such manuals—if designed to fit local sociocultural contexts, paired with efficacious smoking cessation drugs, and used together with counseling programs—could be useful in helping Kunming residents and other Chinese citizens to quit.

20. Michel Foucault, "Governmentality," in Burchell, Gordon, and Miller, *The Foucault Effect*, 87–104.

21. Mitchell Dean, "Foucault, Government, and the Enfolding of Authority," in Barry, Osborne, and Rose *Foucault and Political Reason*, 220; Lupton, *Risk*, 84–102.

22. Dean, "Foucault, Government, and the Enfolding of Authority," 217. The emphasis here is mine.

23. Ibid., 220.

24. Although the majority of taxi drivers are men in Yunnan's central city of Kunming, women seem to work in the profession there in greater numbers than in other large cities across China that I have visited over the years. This relatively higher rate of female drivers in Kunming has been explained to me by women drivers there as possibly owing to the large numbers of non–Han Chinese "minority" women who have been attracted to the local profession. It is also plausible that, to some degree, women are driving taxis in Kunming in greater numbers because of male cabbies' growing frustration over new constraints on driving and smoking. For further discussions of gender, space, and mobility in post-Mao China, see Matthew Kohrman, "Motorcycles for the Disabled: Mobility, Modernity, and the Transformation of Experience in Urban China," *Culture, Medicine, and Psychiatry* 23, no. 1 (1999), 133–55.

25. Office of the National Patriotic Health Campaign Committee, "Guójia Weisheng Chengshi Biaozhun" [National Clean City Criteria] (Kunming: Office of the Kunming Patriotic Health Campaign Committee, 2001), 4.

Chapter 9. Wild Consumption

1. Nikolas Rose, *Powers of Freedom: Reframing Political Thought* (Cambridge: Cambridge University Press, 1999), 87.

2. Ibid., 85.

3. Ibid., 43.

4. Aihwa Ong and Stephen Collier, "Global Assemblages, Anthropological Problems," in *Global Assemblages: Technology, Politics, and Ethics as Anthropological Problems*, ed. Aihwa Ong and Stephen J. Collier (Malden, Mass.: Blackwell, 2005), 1–21.

5. Thus, except for tracking the development of the SARS epidemic and key essays from science journals, the bulk of my fieldwork on SARS was done after the crisis was over. In this essay, then, I juxtapose personal stories with articles from science journals, popular magazines, newspapers, TV programs, and Web sites, so the form of this essay also serves as a reflection on the media of circulation, encounters, and ruptures.

6. The popularity of snake dishes at restaurants in Shanghai was related to the rise of medicinal food and female beauty products in urban China. Snakes are considered a good source of yin energy (the cool, feminine, descending, and nurturing energy). It is commonly recommended for women as a way to nourish their yin energy and thus give them smoother and more beautiful skin. Fried snake is not recommended for beauty purposes, however, because the frying process depletes yin energy.

7. The World Health Organization narrowly defines "zoonosis" as "any disease and/or infection which is naturally 'transmissible from vertebrate animals to man.'" Strikingly, the Web page where this definition is listed features a Chinese-looking boy eating out of a rice bowl. See http://www.who.int/zoonoses/en/. Many epidemics, such as the bubonic plague, are said to have had zoonotic origins. Today, mad cow disease, avian flu, and West Nile virus infection are all considered zoonotic illnesses. Upon the outbreak of SARS in Hong Kong and Guangdong, many virologists immediately pointed to the farming and eating habits of the Chinese as possible culprits.

8. See, for example, "China and SARS: Could Do Better," *Nature* 427 (January 8, 2004): 87; Jonathan Watts, "China Takes Drastic Action over SARS Threat," *Lancet* 361 (May 17, 2003): 1708–9.

9. Joseph Kahn, "Some Say China's Response to SARS Has Been Too Heavy-Handed," *New York Times*, May 23, 2003, 23.

10. For the announcement of these bans, see "Liji Tingzhi Yesheng Dongwu Shichang Jinyin Huodong" [Immediate Ban on Marketing Activities Involving Wild Animals], *People's Daily*, April 30, 2003, 2.

11. Y. Guan, B. J. Zheng, and Y. Q. He, "Isolation and Characterization of Viruses Related to the SARS Coronavirus from Animals in Southern China," *Science* 302 (2003): 226–78.

12. Chinese Forestry Administration, "Shoupi Ke Shangyexing Xunyang Fanzhi Liyong De Yesheng Dongwu Mindan Gongpu [Announcement of the First List of Wild Animals That

Are Allowed to Be Commercially Domesticated, Bred, and Utilized]," http://www.lnet .forestry.ac.cn/page/BookInfo.cbs?ResName=mrxw&no=28608&IndexWord=20030814++.

13. The statistics are from the WHO summary table of SARS cases by country, November 1, 2002–August 7, 2003, http://www.who.int/csr/sars/country/en/country2003_8_15.pdf.

14. A coronavirus is a type of virus that contains single-stranded RNA and is shaped like a crown when seen under a microscope. It is a main cause of respiratory infections among humans and animals.

15. Medical professionals in Shanghai told me that they believed that the first cases of SARS probably occurred as early as November 2002, even though the international media explosion over SARS did not occur until the end of March 2003. There have been several explanations for this delay. The North American and European scientific community and media accused the Chinese government of "cover-ups." In China, however, some suggest that the public disclosure of SARS and the subsequent intervention by the Chinese government were not just a response to "international pressure." Some medical professionals pointed out to me that the clinical symptoms and autopsy findings of SARS patients were easily confused with those indicating pneumonia; in addition, it was impossible to keep SARS a "secret" because of the fast rate at which the disease spread—causing entire hospitals to be quarantined.

16. Tong Zeng, *Zuihou Yidao Fangxian* [The Last Line of Defense] (Beijing: Chinese Social Science Press, 2003).

17. Nelson Lee, David Hui et al., "Major Outbreak of Severe Acute Respiratory Syndrome in Hong Kong, *New England Journal of Medicine* 348 (2003): 1986–94. Also see Henry Masur, Emanuel Ezekiel, and Lane Clifford, "Severe Acute Respiratory Syndrome: Providing Care in the Face of Uncertainty," *Journal of the American Medical Association* 289, no. 21 (2003): 2861–62.

18. "Wet market" is a term that describes markets in which livestock and wild animals are sold alive, especially as food items. The word "wet" emphasizes the wet and slippery floors— and, by association, the filthiness—of these markets. Interestingly, although the term had been used to describe markets in Chinatowns in the United States, its popularity in English usage soared during media coverage of the SARS outbreak.

19. For example, the April 26, 2003, issue of the *Economist* adopted for its front cover an image of Chairman Mao wearing a mask. The May 5, 2003, issue of *Time* presented on its cover a blond-haired, blue-eyed young woman wearing a mask to alert the readers to the "global threat" of SARS. Most images, however, depicted not individuals but masses of Asian bodies wearing masks. This focus on the spread of SARS through sneezing and other forms of contact thus also played on an old Orientalist image of China—and East Asia—as a densely crowded place where contamination is spread very easily.

20. Keith Bradsher and Lawrence K. Altman, "Strain of SARS Is Found in 3 Animal Species in Asia," *New York Times*, May 24, 2003, A1.

21. Ibid.

22. Guan, Zheng, and He, "Isolation and Characterization of Viruses Related to the SARS Coronavirus."

23. See, for example, Stefan Lovgren, "China Is the Perfect Breeding Ground for Viruses Like SARS, Expert Says," *National Geographic*, May 6, 2003, http://news.nationalgeographic .com/news/2003/05/0506_030506_sarschina.html (accessed June 8, 2004). Also see Elisabeth Rosenthal, "The SARS Epidemic: The Path; From China's Province, a Crafty Germ Breaks Out," *New York Times*, April 27, 2003, N1; Paul Sperry, "Did SARS Mutate from Duck, Pig Feces? China's Old-World Farming Practices Possible Culprit," *Worldnetdaily* (accessed April

25, 2003); Robert Webster, "Wet Markets: A Continuing Source of Severe Acute Respiratory Syndrome and Influenza?" *Lancet* 363 (January 17, 2004): 234–36; Jim Yardley, "The SARS Scare in China: Slaughter of the Animals," *New York Times*, January 7, 2004, A3; Geoffery York, "China's Taste for Exotic Flesh Ripens the Risk of Another SARS," *Globe and Mail*, Saturday, June 28, 2003, http://theglobeandmail.com/servlet/Article/News/TPPrint/LAC/20030628/ (accessed June 28, 2003).

24. Reuters, "Bloody Animal Trade Thrives in Post-SARS China," http://www.healthypages.net/news.asp?newsid=3788 (accessed October 26, 2003).

25. David Lynch, "Wild Animal Markets in China May Be Breeding SARS," *USA Today*, October 28, 2003, http://www.usatoday.com/news/health/2003–10–28–sars-wild-animals_x.htm.

26. See note 23.

27. As has been pointed out by Judith Farquhar in *Appetites: Food and Sex in Post-Socialist China* (Durham: Duke University Press, 2002), the large-scale marketization and consumption of food in China today has as much to do with the general "deficiency" of the Mao era as with the "excess" of a post-Mao China, in which desires for consumption are discursively cultivated and embodied. Farquhar argues that the practice of excess in postsocialist China is a response to the general state of deficiency—if not hunger itself—of the Mao era. She further points out that such excess is often localized. In contrast to the pervasive state of deficiency that characterized the Chinese state and society in general during the Mao era, the excess in consumption has so far been restricted to urban areas and the emerging middle class. It is no surprise, perhaps, that the SARS outbreak was at its worst in prosperous Guangdong Province and the capital city, Beijing—pioneers, one might say, in China's efforts in marketization and privatization.

28. For example, among the 138 SARS patients admitted to the Prince of Wales Hospital from March 11 to 25, 2003, 69 were health care workers. This was reported in Lee, Hui et al., "A Major Outbreak of Severe Acute Respiratory Syndrome in Hong Kong."

29. See Farquhar, *Appetites*; Matthew Kohrman's chapter in this book; and Mei Zhan, *Other-Worldly: Making Chinese Medicine through Encounters* (Durham: Duke University Press, forthcoming).

30. See Nancy Chen, "Health, Wealth, and the Good Life," in *China Urban*, ed. N. Chen et al. (Durham: Duke University Press, 2001), 165–82; Volker Scheid, *Chinese Medicine in Contemporary China: Plurality and Synthesis* (Durham: Duke University Press, 2002); Kim Taylor, *Chinese Medicine in Early Communist China, 1945–63* (London: RoutledgeCurzon, 2005).

31. Shaoguang Wang, "China's Health System: From Crisis to Opportunity," *Yale-China Health Journal* 3 (2004): 5–49. Wang's study came out amid intense public criticism and government scrutiny of health care reform in China. In fall 2005 the Chinese Ministry of Health declared the reform a "failure."

32. I did not subscribe to the basketball network NBA-TV.

33. Sun Wen's comments underscored the emergence of a new kind of "preventive medicine" in urban China since the late 1990s. In contrast to the "preventive medicine" of the socialist period, which focused on the prevention of infectious diseases afflicting the rural poor, this new preventive medicine promotes a cosmopolitan middle-class lifestyle that emphasizes mind-body health, self-discipline of the body, and overall well-being. See Zhan, *Other-Worldly*. The invention of the new preventive medicine in China, moreover, is mediated through trans-Pacific traffic in people, things, and ideas between China's coastal urban areas and California.

34. Live coverage of *STARS vs. SARS* on sina.com, http://sports.sina.com.cn/k/2003-05
-11/2011438896.shtml.

35. The avian flu, for example, is commonly referred to as the "Asian bird flu." "SARS," a seemingly neutral scientific term, is also suggestive of "SAR," a shorthand for "Special Administrative Region." It is perhaps more than a mere coincidence that Hong Kong not only became a SAR after returning to China in 1997, but also was suspected to be a birthplace of SARS a few years later. Moreover, these emergencies elicit immediate action and interventions that constitute gritty boundary battles between marked bodies of both human and nonhuman sorts and, as I have suggested, produce particular subjectivities shaped by contingent articulations of Orientalist and neoliberal discourses.

Chapter 10. Post-Mao Professionalism

1. The material in this chapter is based on studies conducted over the course of ten years of anthropological fieldwork in Dalian beginning in the summer of 1993 and extending through December 2003, including dissertation fieldwork from 1995 to 1996. In addition to going to job fairs regularly over the years, I interviewed human resource managers at their offices, job seekers who self-identified as "talent," several classes of graduating seniors in local universities, university employment officials, and those who managed and ran the city talent markets and human resource offices. I also conducted surveys with job seekers at major job fair events and several classes of graduating students. In addition to extended formal interviews that lasted anywhere from one to six hours, I had countless informal exchanges with people as well as social engagements with young professionals and their families across the city.

2. I use the terms "high socialism" and "traditional socialism" interchangeably in this chapter. They refer to the period known as the Maoist era (1949–1978), when China followed a centrally planned command economy system. The reform or post-Mao era began when Deng Xiaoping came to power at the end of 1978 and initiated what people call "market socialism." On this terminology, see also David Bray, *Social Space and Governance in Urban China: The Danwei System from Origins to Reform* (Stanford: Stanford University Press 2005), 204. As discussed in this chapter, important reforms in higher education and the place of educated people in national development were recognized in the 1980s, even as the "market" was only formally adopted "as a mechanism of government" in 1992, which accelerated both the pace and scope of market-based reforms. Gary Sigley, "Liberal Despotism: Population Planning, Subjectivity, and Government in Contemporary China," *Alternatives* 29 (2004): 568 and see below. For instance, a section of the 1985 decision on restructuring higher education emphasizes that China must "give full rein to the skilled people now available and to further enhance their capabilities, but also train, on a large scale, people with new types of skills who are dedicated to the socialist cause and to the nation's economic and social progress." Cited in Michael Agelasto and Bob Adamson, "Editors' Introduction," in *Higher Education in Post-Mao China*, ed. Michael Agelasto and Bob Adamson (Hong Kong: Hong Kong University Press, 1998), 3.

3. See Agelasto and Adamson, *Higher Education in Post-Mao China*; Lisa Hoffman, "The Art of Becoming an Urban Professional: The State, Gender, and Subject Formation in Late-Socialist China" (Ph.D. diss., University of California at Berkeley, 2000); and Lisa Hoffman "Guiding College Graduates to Work: Social Constructions of Labor Markets in Dalian," in

China Urban: Ethnographies of Contemporary Culture, ed. Nancy Chen, Constance Clark, Suzanne Gottschang, and Lyn Jeffrey (Durham: Duke University Press, 2001), 43–66.

4. In Feng Chao, ed., *Deng Xiaoping Sixiang Lilun Da Cidian* [Dictionary of Deng Xiaoping Theory] (Shanghai: Shanghai Dictionary Publishers), 305.

5. Sigley, "Liberal Despotism," 568.

6. See Lisa Hoffman, "Enterprising Cities and Citizens: The Re-figuring of Urban Spaces and the Making of Post-Mao Professionals," *Provincial China* 8, no. 1 (2003): 5–26.

7. Nikolas Rose, "Government, Authority, and Expertise in Advanced Liberalism," *Economy and Society* 22, no. 3 (1993): 285.

8. Michel Foucault, "The Birth of Biopolitics," in *Ethics: Subjectivity and Truth, Essential Works of Foucault, 1954–1984,* vol. 1, ed. Paul Rabinow (New York: New Press, 1997), 76; Barry Hindess, "Liberalism—What's in a Name?" in *Global Governmentality: Governing International Spaces,* ed. Wendy Larner and William Walters (London: Routledge, 2004), 26.

9. Stephen J. Collier "The Spatial Forms and Social Norms of 'Actually Existing Neoliberalism': Toward a Substantive Analysis," *International Affairs Working Paper,* New School University, New York (2005), 23.

10. In focusing on patriotism, I do not mean to imply that other forms of responsibility, such as that to the family, are unimportant. Making "responsible" decisions, in terms of both the nation and the family, overlaps with desires for success, dreams of fulfilling one's potential, and hopes for social mobility in a highly fluid social world. Techniques of rule, in other words, cross over between state, market, and familial domains. In this chapter I focus on one site where these domains intersect—the job search process. See also Vanessa Fong, "Filial Nationalism among Chinese Teenagers with Global Identities," *American Ethnologist* 31, no. 4 (2004): 631–48.

11. See Susan Brin-Hyatt, "Poverty in a 'Post-welfare' Landscape: Tenant Management Policies, Self-governance and the Democratization of Knowledge in Great Britain," in *Anthropology of Policy: Critical Perspectives on Governance and Power,* ed. Chris Shore and Susan Wright (London: Routledge, 1997): 217–38; Nikolas Rose, "Governing 'Advanced' Liberal Democracies," in *Foucault and Political Reason: Liberalism, Neo-liberalism, and Rationalities of Government,* ed. Andrew Barry, Thomas Osborne, and Nikolas Rose (Chicago: University of Chicago Press, 1996): 37–64; Nikolas Rose, "The Death of the Social? Re-figuring the Territory of Government," *Economy and Society* 25, no. 3 (1996): 327–56.

12. Lisa Hoffman, Monica DeHart, and Stephen J. Collier, "Notes on the Anthropology of Neoliberalism," *Anthropology Newsletter* 47, no. 6 (2006): 9–10.

13. Hung Yung Lee, "From Revolutionary Cadres to Bureaucratic Technocrats," in *Contemporary Chinese Politics in Historical Perspective,* ed. Brantly Womack (Cambridge: Cambridge University Press, 1991), 180–206; Hung Yung Lee, *From Revolutionary Cadres to Party Technocrats in Socialist China* (Berkeley: University of California Press, 1991); and Martin K. Whyte, "Deng Xiaoping: The Social Reformer," *China Quarterly* 135 (1993): 515–35.

14. "Freedom" in many analyses of the introduction of market competition into socialist states is understood as an "absence" of government. These arguments also suggest that the state either intervenes in people's lives or it does not, implying that one could identify a social field within which one finds neither state forms of governance nor ways of knowing that are shared with state rationalities. My analysis takes a different view of emerging "private" lives and forms of personhood. Moreover, by choosing to write about subject formation rather than about political interests and agency per se, I wish to avoid the assumption that unified and unitary subjects exist outside of power relations, regulatory norms, and discursive and nondiscursive

practices. See also Sigley, "Liberal Despotism," 560. For more on how the regulation and management of subjects happens "through freedom," see Andrew Barry, Thomas Osborne, and Nikolas Rose, "Introduction" in *Foucault and Political Reason*; Graham Burchell, "Liberal Government and Techniques of the Self," ibid., 19–36; Michel Foucault, "Governmentality," in *The Foucault Effect: Studies in Governmentality*, ed. Graham Burchell, Colin Gordon, and Peter Miller (Chicago: University of Chicago Press, 1991), 87–104; Aihwa Ong, *Buddha Is Hiding: Refugees, Citizenship, the New America* (Berkeley: University of California Press, 2003); Aihwa Ong, *Neoliberalism as Exception: Mutations in Citizenship and Sovereignty* (Durham: Duke University Press, 2006); Nikolas Rose, "Governing the Enterprising Self," in *The Values of the Enterprise Culture: The Moral Debate*, ed. Paul Heelas and Paul Morris (London: Routledge, 1992), 141–64; Rose, "Government, Authority, and Expertise"; Rose, "Governing 'Advanced' Liberal Democracies"; and Nikolas Rose, *Powers of Freedom: Reframing Political Thought* (Cambridge: Cambridge University Press, 1999).

15. Rose, "Governing 'Advanced' Liberal Democracies," 57; Rose, "Government, Authority, and Expertise," 285; and Rose, "Governing 'Advanced' Liberal Democracies," 54.

16. Bray, *Social Space and Governance in Urban China*, 179. These discourses ignore issues of unemployment and financial and social insecurity also generated by these new forms of governing.

17. For more on how the implementation of neoliberal techniques of governing in China does not contradict the state's continued importance in the decisions professionals make—autonomously—see Lisa Hoffman, "Autonomous Choices and Patriotic Professionalism: On Governmentality in Late-Socialist China," *Economy and Society* 35, no. 4 (2006): 550–70.

18. Wendy Larner, "Neoliberalism?" *Environment and Planning D: Society and Space* 21 (2003): 510.

19. Sigley, "Liberal Despotism," 563. See also Ong, *Neoliberalism as Exception*, on graduated sovereignty.

20. Foucault, "Birth of Biopolitics," 74.

21. Collier, "Spatial Forms and Social Norms of 'Actually Existing Neoliberalism,'" 11. Aihwa Ong puts this well when she argues that it "seems appropriate to study neoliberalism not as a 'culture' or a 'structure' but as mobile calculative techniques of governing" (*Neoliberalism as Exception*, 13). See also Larner, "Neoliberalism?"

22. Stephen J. Collier and Aihwa Ong, "Global Assemblages, Anthropological Problems," in *Global Assemblages: Technology, Politics, and Ethics as Anthropological Problems,* ed. Aihwa Ong and Stephen J. Collier (Malden, Mass.: Blackwell, 2005), 3–21. See also Ong, *Neoliberalism as Exception*.

23. See also Hoffman, "Enterprising Cities and Citizens"; Amy Hanser, "Youth Job Searches in Urban China: The Use of Social Connections in a Changing Labor Market," in *Social Connections in China: Institutions, Culture, and the Changing Nature of Guanxi*, ed. Thomas Gold, Doug Guthrie, and David Wank (Cambridge: Cambridge University Press, 2002), 137–61; and Amy Hanser, "The Chinese Enterprising Self: Young, Educated Urbanites and the Search for Work," in *Popular China: Unofficial Culture in a Globalizing Society*, ed. Perry Link, Richard Madsen, and Paul Pickowicz (Lanham, Md.: Rowman and Littlefield, 2002), 189–206.

24. Rose, "Governing 'Advanced' Liberal Democracies," 42.

25. Ibid.

26. Yanjie Bian, *Work and Inequality in Urban China* (Albany, N.Y.: State University of New York Press, 1994), 51.

27. Ibid., 96.

28. Kai-ming Cheng, "Reforms in the Administration and Financing of Higher Education," in Agelasto and Adamson, *Higher Education in Post-Mao China*, 23.

29. Deborah Davis, "Urban Job Mobility," in *Chinese Society on the Eve of Tiananmen: The Impact of Reforms*, ed. Deborah Davis and Ezra Vogel (Cambridge: Harvard University Press, 1990), 89; Deborah Davis, "Social Class Transformation in Urban China: Training, Hiring, and Promoting Urban Professionals and Managers after 1949," *Modern China* 26, no. 3 (2000): 251–75.

30. Davis, "Urban Job Mobility."

31. Cited in Bray, *Social Space and Governance in Urban China*, 60.

32. Foucault, "Birth of Biopolitics," 75.

33. See entries for Rose, 1996, for example, in note 11.

34. Zhongren Liu, ed., *Daxuesheng xuanye zhinan* [College Graduate Guide for Choosing a Profession] (Beijing: China Materials Publisher, 1999), 4–6; see also Wei-Yuan Zhang, *Young People and Careers: School Careers Guidance in Shanghai* (Hong Kong: Comparative Education Research Center, University of Hong Kong, 1998).

35. Fuxiang Wen, "Enhancing Students' Overall Quality and Promoting Society's All-around Development," in *East-West Dialogue in Knowledge and Higher Education*, ed. Ruth Hayhoe and Julia Pan (Armonk, N.Y.: M. E. Sharpe, 1996), 276.

36. Alexa Olesen, "Chinese President Issues List of Virtues," *International Business Times*, March 15, 2006, http://in.ibtimes.com/articles/20060315/ju-huntao-virtues.htm.

37. See also Peter Hay Gries, *China's New Nationalism: Pride, Politics, and Diplomacy* (Berkeley: University of California Press, 2004).

38. Fong "Filial Nationalism"; Zhongdan Pan, Lee Chin-chuan, Joseph Man Chan, and Clement K. Y. So, "To Cheer for the Family-Nation: The Construction of Chinese Nationalism during the Hong Kong Handover," in *Cultural Studies in China*, ed. Dongfeng Tao and Yuanpu Jin (Singapore: Marshall Cavendish Academic Press, 2005), 40–67.

39. Gries (*China's New Nationalism*, 116–134) argues that the party is in fact losing control of popular nationalism, as evidenced in protests over the bombing of the Chinese embassy in Belgrade in 1999 and the fervor in 1996 and 1997 over the publication of Song Qiang, Zhang Zangzang, Zhang Xiaobo, Tang Zhengyu, Qiao Bian, and Gu Qingsheng, *Zhongguo keyi shuobu* [China Can Say No] (Beijing: Zhonghua gongshang lianhe chubanshe, 1996), and Song Qiang, Zhang Zangzang, Qiao Bian, Tang Zhengyu, and Gu Qingsheng, *Zhongguo haishe neng shuobu* [China Can Still Say No] (Beijing: Zhongguo wenlian chubanshe, 1996).

40. Hanna Beech, "Changing the Game in China," *Time*, June 27, 2005, 40–44.

41. Laurie Duthie "White-Collar China: Global Capitalism and the Formation of a New Social Identity in Urban China," presented at China Colloquium, Jackson School of International Studies, University of Washington, Seattle, 2006.

42. Hoffman, "Art of Becoming an Urban Professional."

43. I thank the anonymous reviewer of this volume for pushing me on this point.

Chapter 11. Self-fashioning Shanghainese

1. My description of the blog and quotations are drawn from Howard W. French, "A Party Girl Leads China's Online Revolution," *New York Times*, November 24, 2005, A1.

2. Aihwa Ong, "Neoliberalism as Exception, Exception to Neoliberalism," in *Neoliberalism as Exception: Mutations in Citizenship and Sovereignty* (Durham: Duke University Press, 2006), 1–30.

3. G. W. F. Hegel, *Philosophy of Right*, trans. T. M. Knox (London: Oxford University Press, 1967), 42–43.

4. Michel Foucault, *Technologies of the Self*, ed. Luther H. Martin, Huck Gutman, and Patrick H. Hutton (Amherst: University of Massachusetts Press, 1988), 18.

5. Michel Foucault, "On the Genealogy of Ethics: An Overview of Work in Progress," in *Michel Foucault: Ethics, Subjectivity, and Truth*, vol. 1 of *Essential Works of Foucault, 1954–1984*, ser. ed. Paul Rabinow (New York: New Press, 1997), 253–80.

6. Nikolas Rose, *Powers of Freedom: Reframing Political Thought* (Cambridge: Cambridge University Press), 1999.

7. Mayfair Yang, *Gifts, Favors, and Banquets: The Art of Social Relationships in China* (Ithaca: Cornell University Press, 1994).

8. Aihwa Ong, "Re-engineering the 'Chinese Soul' in Shanghai?" in *Neoliberalism as Exception*, 219–39.

9. As indicated in the text, I use "translation" here to refer to individual knowledge practices in dynamic everyday situations, very differently from Lydia H. Liu, who has examined linguistic translation across comparative scholarship in *Translingual Practice: Literature, National Culture, and Translated Modernity—China, 1900–1937* (Durham: Duke University Press, 1997), and the use of words as gifts, missiles, and mirrors in international relations in her edited volume *Tokens of Exchange: The Problem of Translation in Global Circulations (Post-contemporary Interventions)* (Durham: Duke University Press, 2000).

10. Ulrich Beck, "The Reinvention of Politics: Towards a Theory of Reflexive Modernity," in *Reflexive Modernization: Politics, Tradition and Aesthetics in the Modern Social Order*, ed. Ulrich Beck, Anthony Giddens, and Scott Lash (Stanford: Stanford University Press, 1995), 14–15.

11. Rose, *Powers of Freedom*, 188.

12. Marilyn Strathern, "Introduction: New Accountabilities," in *Audit Cultures: Anthropological Studies in Accountability, Ethics, and the Academy*, ed. Marilyn Strathern (London: Routledge, 2000), 1–18.

13. Nigel Thrift, "The Globalization of the System of Business Knowledge," in *Globalization and the Asia-Pacific: Contested Territories*, ed. K. Olds et al. (London: Routledge, 1999), 59.

14. For a discussion of "assemblage" as a field of analysis, see Stephen J. Collier and Aihwa Ong, "Global Assemblages, Anthropological Problems," in *Global Assemblages: Technology, Politics, and Ethics as Anthropological Problems*, ed. Aihwa Ong and Stephen J. Collier (Malden, Mass.: Blackwell, 2005), 3–21.

15. Arjun Appadurai, "Introduction: Commodities and the Politics of Value," in *The Social Life of Things: Commodities in Cultural Perspective* (Cambridge: Cambridge University Press, 1983), 25.

16. Barbara Czarniawska and Guje Sevon, "Translation Is a Vehicle, Imitation Its Motor, and Fashion Sits at the Wheel," in *Global Ideas: How Ideas, Objects, and Practices Travel in the Global Economy* (Copenhagen: Copenhagen Business School Press, 2005), 7–14.

17. Ibid., 11.

18. Hai Ren, "Consuming Ethnic Culture and the Formation of the Chinese Business Class," paper presented at the Association of Asian Studies, Chicago, March 31–April 3, 2005.

19. For more on American management woes, see Aihwa Ong, "Re-engineering the 'Chinese Soul.'"

20. Jim Yardley, "It's Out of College and Onto Jobless Rolls in China," *New York Times*, May 29, 2004.

21. Xing Zhigang, "Job Hunt an Uphill Battle for Female Graduates," *China Daily*, April 4, 2004, 47.

22. Shu-Ching Jean Chen, "Mrs. Murdoch Takes the Wheel at MySpace China," *Forbes*, June 28, 2007, http://www.forbes.com/2007/06/28/myspace-china-deng-markets-equity-cx _jc_0628markets2_print.html.

23. David Barboza, "The New Power Brokers: Born in China, Now Closing Deals for U.S. Firms," *New York Times*, July 7 and 19, 2005, C1.

24. Jen Lin-Liu, "Catering to China's Fashionistas," *Wall Street Journal*, September 2005.

25. Sarah R. Larendaudie, "A Tastemaker in China," *International Herald Tribune*, October 8, 2005.

Chapter 12. Living Buddhas, Netizens, and the Price of Religious Freedom

1. Central United Front Department (中央统战部), "The Current State of Religion in ChinaD" (中国的宗教现状), http://www.zytzb.org.cn/zytzbwz/religion/index.htm.

2. David Harvey, "Neoliberalism as Creative Destruction," http://user.chol.com/ ~moraz/DH-neoliberalism.doc, 1.

3. Ibid., 14.

4. Christopher R. Hughes and Gudrun Wacker, "Introduction: China's Digital Leap Forward," in *China and the Internet: Politics of the Digital Leap Forward*, ed. Christopher R. Hughes and Gudrun Wacker (London: RoutledgeCurzon, 2003), 1–7.

5. John Tomlinson, *Globalization and Culture* (Chicago: University of Chicago Press, 1999).

6. Stephen J. Collier and Aihwa Ong, "Global Assemblages, Anthropological Problems," in *Global Assemblages: Technology, Politics, and Ethics as Anthropological Problems*, ed. Aihwa Ong and Stephen J. Collier (Malden, Mass.: Blackwell Publishing, 2005), 1–21.

7. Vincent J. Miller, *Consuming Religion: Christian Faith and Practice in a Consumer Culture* (New York: Continuum, 2004), 225.

8. Jigme Phuntsok, "The Essence of Wisdom and Compassion" [智悲心滴], in *Methods for Tantric Practice* [密宗实修法], ed. Khenpo Soudaji (Hong Kong: Hong Kong China PressD, 2003 [香港中华出版社]).

9. F. A. Hayek, *Studies in Philosophy, Politics, and Economics* (Chicago: University of Chicago Press, 1967), 164.

10. Richard Madsen, "Epilogue: The Second Liberation," in *The Consumer Revolution in Urban China*, ed. Deborah Davis (Berkeley: University of California Press, 2000), 314.

11. Davis, *The Consumer Revolution in Urban China*, 14.

12. Patricia M. Thornton, "The New Cybersects: Resistance and Repression in the Reform Era," in *Chinese Society: Change, Conflict, and Resistance*, ed. Elizabeth J. Perry and Mark Selden (London: RoutledgeCurzon, 2003).

13. Madsen, "Epilogue," 313–21.

14. Arjun Appadurai, *Modernity at Large: Cultural Dimensions of Globalization* (Minneapolis: University of Minnesota Press, 1996), 7.

15. Peter Moran, *Buddhism Observed: Travelers, Exiles, and Tibetan Dharma in Kathmandu* (London: RoutledgeCurzon, 2004), 14.

16. Max Weber, *Economy and Society: An Outline of Interpretive Sociology*, vol. 2 (Berkeley: University of California Press, 1978), 1112.

17. Frank E. Reynolds and Donald Capps, *The Biographical Process: Studies in the History of Psychology of Religion* (Paris: Mouton, 1976), 3.

18. Ibid.

19. Ibid.

20. Ibid.

21. Ibid.

22. Erich Neumann, *The Place of Creation* (Princeton: Princeton University Press. 1989), 115.

23. Orville Schell, *Virtual Tibet: Searching for Shangri-La from the Himalayas to Hollywood* (New York: Metropolitan Books, 2000), 208.

24. Weber, *Economy and Society*, 1121.

25. Gray Tuttle, *Tibetan Buddhists in the Making of Modern China* (New York: Columbia University Press, 2005), 74.

26. See http://education.legend-net.com/xinwen/fb/jshjy.html and http://21exit.com/51/ShowAricle.asp?AricleID=260.

27. Yuan Zhiming and Su Wenfeng, "The Flow of the Spirit," http://www.http://oc.org/gb_txt/oc2420a.htm.

28. Ibid.

29. Hu Ping, "Was the Self-Immolator a Falun Gong Member?" http://bjzc.org/bjs/bc/95/37.

30. Li Zhang, *Strangers in the City: Reconfigurations of Space, Power, and Social Networks within China's Floating Population* (Stanford: Stanford University Press, 2001), 2.

31. Madsen, "Epilogue," 313.

32. C. A. Gregory, *Gifts and Commodities* (London: Academic Press, 1982), 12.

33. Jonathan Parry and Maurice Bloch, *Money and the Morality of Exchange* (Cambridge: Cambridge University Press, 1989), 6.

34. Liah Greenfield, "Reflections on Two Charismas," *British Journal of Sociology* 36 (1985): 117–32, quote at 127.

35. Gordon White, *Riding the Tiger: The Politics of Economic Reform in Post-Mao China* (Stanford: Stanford University Press, 1993), 233.

36. Ibid., 200.

37. David Wank, *Commodifying Communism: Business, Trust, and Politics in a Chinese City* (Cambridge: Cambridge University Press, 1999), 9–10.

38. David Harvey, "Neoliberalism as Creative Destruction," *Annals of the American Academy of Political and Social Science* 610, no. 1 (2007), 21—44.

39. Ibid.

Chapter 13. Privatizing Control

1. For details about the fire and its repercussions, see relevant reports at http://www.chinanews.com.cn/zhuanti/wangba/index.html (accessed October 12, 2002).

2. Hannah Beech, "China Unplugged," *Time Asia* magazine, July 15, 2002, http://www
.time.com/time/asia/magazine/article/0,13673,501020715–300685,00.html (accessed August
8, 2002).

3. Julie Moffett, "China: Government Makes Vain Attempts to Control Internet," http://
www.rferl.org/nca/features/1998/01/F.RU.980106133925.asp (accessed July 19, 2003).

4. News headlines are often phrased in eye-catching ways, ranging from "China Enacts
Sweeping Rules on Internet Firms" (Reuters) to the more misleading "Amnesty International: China Orders Death Penalty for Internet Use" (NewsMax.com). See http://www.cnn
.com/2000/ASIANOW/east/10/02/china.internet.reut/index.html (accessed May 5,
2003); http://www.newsmax.com/showinside.shtml?a=2002/11/30/120649 (accessed May
5, 2003).

5. For details, see Shanthi Kalathil and Taylor Boas, "Internet and State Control in Authoritarian Regimes: China, Cuba, and the Counterrevolution" (Washington, D.C.: Carnegie
Endowment Working Paper no. 21, 2001); Nina Hachigian, "The Internet and Power in
One-Party East Asian States," *Washington Quarterly* 25, no. 3 (2001): 41–58; "China's Cyber-
strategy," *Foreign Affairs* 80, no. 2 (2002): 118–33. For a case study of how the Internet has
been used by the Chinese to promote antidemocratic and nationalist discourse, see Zhou
Yongming, "Informed Nationalism: Military Websites in Chinese Cyberspace," *Journal of
Contemporary China* 14, no. 44 (2005): 543–62.

6. Michael Adas, *Machines as the Measure of Men: Science, Technology, and Ideologies of
Western Dominance* (Ithaca: Cornell University Press, 1989).

7. Stephen J. Collier and Aihwa Ong, "Global Assemblages, Anthropological Problems,"
in *Global Assemblages: Technology, Politics, and Ethics as Anthropological Problems*, ed. Aihwa Ong
and Stephen Collier (Malden, Mass.: Blackwell Publishing, 2005), 4 and 12.

8. Its real name has been altered to protect the owner's identity.

9. For example, Yan Hairong, "Neoliberal Governmentality and Neohumanism: Organizing Suzhi/Value Flow through Labor Recruitment Networks," *Cultural Anthropology* 18,
no. 4 (2003): 493–523; Li Zhang, "Privatizing Urban Housing and Governmentality in
Reform-Era China," unpublished manuscript (2004). Also see David Harvey, *A Brief History
of Neoliberalism* (Oxford: Oxford University Press, 2005), esp. chap. 5 on China; And Wang
Hui, *China's New Order: Society, Politics, and Economy in Transition* (Cambridge, Mass.: Harvard University Press, 2003).

10. Harvey, *A Brief History of Neoliberalism*, 3.

11. Thomas Lemke, "Foucault, Governmentality, and Critique," *Rethinking Marxism* 14,
no. 3 (2002): 52. Also see Graham Burchell, Colin Gordon, and Peter Miller, eds., *The Foucault
Effect: Studies in Governmentality* (Chicago: University of Chicago Press, 1991).

12. Nikolas Rose, "Governing 'Advanced' Liberal Democracies," in *Foucault and Political
Reason: Liberalism, Neo-liberalism, and Rationalities of Government*, ed. Andrew Barry, Thomas
Osborne, and Nikolas Rose (Chicago: University of Chicago Press, 1996), 37–64. The quota-
tion is from Collier and Ong, "Global Assemblages," 13.

13. McDonald's in China is used not only as a place to eat but also as a place to spend
leisure time and to consume "modernity." See Yan Yunxiang, "McDonald's in Beijing," in
Golden Arches East: McDonald's in East Asia, ed. James Watson (Stanford: Stanford University
Press, 1998), 9–22.

14. China Internet Network Information Center (CNNIC), Semiannual Survey Report
on the Development of China's Internet (1997–2006), http://www.cnnic.org.cn/index/0E/
00/11/index.htm (accessed September 5, 2007).

15. Guo Liang, "Surveying Internet Usage and Impact in Five Chinese Cities: The CASS Internet Survey Report, 2005," http://www.markle.org/downloadable_assets/china_final_11_2005.pdf (accessed December 16, 2005).

16. Ibid.

17. Chen Yan, *Internet gaibian zhongguo* [The Internet Changes China] (Beijing: Beijing daxue chubanshe, 1999), 343.

18. For details, see CNNIC, http://www.cnnic.net.cn/develst/report.shtml (accessed March 13, 2004).

19. *Wangmin* is the Chinese translation of "netizens," a term first coined by Michael Hauben in 1992. Hauben believed in the democratizing function of the Internet and championed the participation of netizens to build a global community on the Net. For details, see Michael Hauben and Ronda Hauben, *Netizens: On the History and Impact of Usenet and the Internet* (Los Alamitos, Calif.: Wiley-IEEE Computer Society Press, 1997). The Chinese translation *wangmin* maintains the original connotation of being citizens of the Internet, which is of political significance, as suggested by Aihwa Ong.

20. Xinhua News Agency, June 16, 2002, "Beijing Jinji Bushu Fanghuo Anquan, Zhengdun Suoyou Wangba" [Beijing Makes Urgent Arrangements Concerning Fire Safety and Rectifying All Internet Cafés], http://www.people.com.cn/GB/shehui/47/20020616/753947.html (accessed October 9, 2002).

21. Beech, "China Unplugged."

22. According to a CNNIC Survey of July 2003, 19.5 percent of Internet users in China had no income, and 30.1 percent of all Chinese Internet users were students. See http://www.cnnic.net.cn/html/Dir/2003/11/05/1204.htm (accessed February 2, 2004).

23. In October 1997 Internet users in Beijing, Shanghai, and Guangdong Province accounted for 52 percent of all Internet users in China. Even though the figure had dropped to 22 percent at the end of 2003, it was still significant because the population of these three urbanized costal areas accounts for 9.5 percent of the total Chinese population. See CNNIC, http://www.cnnic.org.cn/index/0E/00/11/index.htm (accessed July 5, 2004).

24. Guo Liang, "Surveying Internet Usage and Impact in Twelve Chinese Cities," http://www.markle.org/downloadable_assets/chinainternet_usage.pdf (accessed July 18, 2004). Internet users under age seventeen were not included in the survey.

25. During the fourth session of the Ninth Chinese People's Political Consultative Conference National Committee in March 2001, with the support of a couple of National Committee members, Zhang Haidi, who had been a role model in China for overcoming a handicap, suggested a ban on all "commercial" Internet cafés in order to protect the youth from being "poisoned" by pornographic Web sites. Her suggestion subsequently stirred an outcry among Internet users in China and never materialized. See Wu Yan, "Fengsha Wangba" [Shutting Down Internet Cafés], http://www.people.com.cn/GB/shehui/47/20010322/423586.html (accessed October 11, 2003).

26. The Administrative Rules for Internet Service–Providing Places [Hulianwang shangwang fuwu yingye changsuo guanli tiaoli]. The version of 2002 can be found at http://news.xinhuanet.com/zhengfu/2002–10/11/content_593298.htm (accessed March 4, 2005).

27. David Harvey, *The Condition of Postmodernity* (Oxford: Blackwell, 1989).

28. Guo, "Surveying Internet Usage and Impact in Twelve Chinese Cities."

29. For details, see Zhou Yongming, "Living on the Cyber Border: Minjian Political Writers in Chinese Cyberspace," *Current Anthropology* 5 (2005): 779–803; and "Negotiating Power Online: The Party State, Intellectuals, and the Internet," chap. 7 of *Historicizing Online*

Politics: Telegraphy, the Internet, and Political Participation in China (Stanford: Stanford University Press, 2006), 155–80.

30. A list of recent regulations can be found on the CNNIC Web site at http://www.cnnic .net.cn/index/0F/index.htm. On a macroscopic level, generally speaking, regulation of the Internet lagged behind the rapid development of the technology. Regulations are often vaguely written, are sometimes conflicting, are interpreted in different ways by different Internet players, and are not always implemented, just as is the case with regulations and laws in other areas in China.

31. Zhou Baoxin, "Chinese Internet: Current Conditions and Future Development," *Technologies of Broadcasting, Television, and Networking* 8 (2001): 18.

32. This does not mean that the authorities do not realize the difference between the Internet and other forms of media. The point is that as long as the current effective media control system is intact, they have enough confidence that the Internet can also be brought under control, just as they dealt with previous challenges presented by the appearance of television, the fax machine, and more recently satellite television. The case of Rupert Murdoch's satellite television network in China may bear the closest resemblance to that of the Internet. For details, see Michael Curtin, "Murdoch's Dilemma, or 'What's the Price of TV in China?'" *Media, Culture, and Society* 27, no. 2 (2005): 155–75.

33. Beech, "China Unplugged."

34. The importance of *guanxi* in Chinese society has been thoroughly studied by anthropologists. See Yan Yunxiang, *The Flow of Gifts* (Stanford: Stanford University Press, 1996); Mayfair Meihui Yang, *Gifts, Favors, and Banquets* (Ithaca: Cornell University Press, 1994); and Andrew B. Kipnis, *Producing Guanxi* (Durham: Duke University Press, 1997).

35. The message was posted on chineseinternetresearch@yahoogroups.com on November 12, 2001.

36. "Guangzhou 800 Jia Wangba Jin 83 Jia Zhengzhao Qi" [Only 83 Internet Cafés Are Fully Licensed among 800 Cafés in Guangzhou], http://news.sina.com.cn/c/2003–11–13/12431112767s.shtml (accessed January 27, 2004).

37. Mayfair Meihui Yang, "Mass Media and Transnational Subjectivity in Shanghai: Notes on (Re) Cosmopolitanism in a Chinese Metropolis," in *The Anthropology of Globalization: A Reader*, ed. Jonathan Xavier Inda and Renato Rosaldo (Malden, Mass.: Blackwell, 2002), 334.

38. According to the Telecommunication Regulations issued in September 2000, "reactionary" Web sites include those which are against the basic principles established by the Constitution; which endanger national security, reveal state secrets, undermine state sovereignty, and injure national unity; which harm national dignity and interest; which provoke hatred and discrimination among nationalities and injure national solidarity; which undermine state religious policy and advocate cult and feudal superstitions; and which disseminate rumors, disrupt social order, and injure social stability. For details, see http://www.cnnic.net.cn/html/Dir/2000/09/25/0651.htm (accessed November 21, 2003).

39. "Wenhuabu Guanyu Jiaqiang Hulianwang Shangwang Fuwu Yingye Changsuo Liansuo Jingyin Guanli De Tongzhi" [A Notice to Strengthen the Management of Internet Service Chain Stores by the Ministry of Culture], http://www.chinaweblaw.com/news/show.aspx?id=6866&cid=9 (accessed December 25, 2004).

40. The former is linked to the Central Committee of Chinese Communist Youth League, and the latter is linked to the Ministry of Culture.

41. "Liansuo Wangba Shi Nailao Haishi Jile" [Is Internet Café Chain Good or Bad?], http://www.chinabyte.com/ColumnArea/217034812114862080/20030611/1706942.shtml (accessed July 19, 2004).

42. "Zhongyang Duchazhu Gang Fu Chongqing" [A Supervisory Team of Central Government Is Swiftly Dispatched to Chongqing], http://news.sina.com.cn/c/2004–04–09/20402266971s.shtml (accessed May 20, 2004).

43. "Jintian Yancha Wangba" [Strict Internet Café Inspection Will Be Carried Out Today], http://tech.sina.com.cn/i/w/2004–03–20/2147336754.shtml (accessed May 18, 2004).

44. "Yahoo Says It Gave China Internet Data, Journalist Jailed by Tracing E-mail," http://www.washingtonpost.com/wp-dyn/content/article/2005/09/10/AR2005091001222.html (accessed December 18, 2005); "Hi-Tech Firms Censured over China," http://news.bbc.co.uk/2/hi/technology/4541524.stm (accessed December 20, 2005).

Afterword

1. See William Hutton, *The Writing on the Wall: Why We Must Embrace China as a Partner or Face It as an Enemy* (New York: Free Press, 2007). All citations are to this source. Special thanks to Hairong Yan for sending the excerpt my way.

2. William Hutton and Anthony Giddens, eds., *Global Capitalism* (New York: New Press, 2001).

3. See the on-line issue of the *Guardian,* http://books.guardian.co.uk/extracts/story/0,,1984961,00.html (accessed January 8, 2007).

4. In a review in *The Nation,* from which this quote is taken, Siddhartha Deb takes issue with the celebratory analyses of journalists such as Thomas Friedman and recent books by Edward Luce (2007) and Mira Kamdar (2007) which uncritically champion India as the world's fastest-growing instantiation of "democratic capitalism." See Siddhartha Deb, "The Spoils of India Democracy," *The Nation,* March 26, 2007, 36–42; Mira Kamdar, *Planet India: How the Fastest-Growing Democracy Is Transforming America and the World* (New York: Scribner, 2007); Edward Luce, *In Spite of the Gods: The Strange Rise of Modern India* (New York: Doubleday, 2007).

5. Hutton never clarifies who this collective "us" really is, though one can assume, at the very least, that he is referring to the educated readers who subscribe to the *Guardian.* Discursively and rhetorically, Hutton's collective "we" assumes anyone who has a stake in really wanting to know what is happening in China and what the economic and political effects of a Chinese superpower presence on the world will be.

6. Ann Anagnost, preface to *Narratives of the Chinese Economic Reforms: Individual Pathways from Plan to Market,* ed. Dorothy Solinger (Lewiston, N.Y.: Edwin Mellen Press, 2005).

7. Nikolas Rose, "Governing 'Advanced' Liberal Democracies," in *Foucault and Political Reason: Liberalism, Neo-liberalism, and Rationalities of Government,* ed. Andrew Barry, Thomas Osborne, and Nikolas Rose (Chicago: University of Chicago Press, 1996), 37–64.

8. Edward Said, cited in Catherine Besteman and Hugh Gusterson, *Why America's Top Pundits Are Wrong: Anthropologists Talk Back* (Berkeley: University of California Press, 2005), 3.

9. See Fareed Zakaria, "India Rising," *Newsweek,* March 6, 2006, 32–42.

Contributors

Nancy N. Chen is Associate Professor of Anthropology at the University of California at Santa Cruz. She is the author of *Breathing Spaces: Qigong, Psychiatry, and Healing in China* (2003) and co-editor of *China Urban: Ethnographies of Contemporary Culture* (2001) and *Bodies in the Making: Transgressions and Transformation* (2006).

Lisa M. Hoffman is Assistant Professor of Urban Studies at the University of Washington, Tacoma, and conducts research in China on urban professionalism and in the United States on homelessness and citizenship. Her interests include issues of self-formation, new forms of governing, neoliberalism, and urban transformation. She is currently completing a book about young professionals in Dalian.

You-tien Hsing is Associate Professor of Geography at the University of California, Berkeley. She is the author of *Making Capitalism in China: The Taiwan Connection*. She is now completing her second book, *The Great Urban Transformation: The Politics of Land Development in China*.

Matthew Kohrman is Assistant Professor in Stanford University's Department of Cultural and Social Anthropology. In 2005 he capped a decade of research, publishing *Bodies of Difference: Experiences of Disability and Institutional Advocacy in Modern China*. His current research projects examine under-studied relationships between the transnational promotion and proscription of tobacco and the making of state, gender, and subjectivity in contemporary China.

Bei Li is a Ph.D. student of economics at the University of California, Davis. She has a bachelor's degree in engineering from Hunan University in China and obtained her M.A. in economics from the University of California, Davis, in 2003. She is at present working on her doctoral dissertation on U.S. property tax limitation policies.

Ralph A. Litzinger is an Associate Professor in the Department of Cultural Anthropology at Duke University and the Director of the Asian/Pacific Studies Institute. He is the author of *Other Chinas: The Yao and the Politics of National Belonging* and numerous essays in anthropology, cultural studies, and East Asia studies journals. He is completing a book on global environmentalism and advocacy politics in northeastern Yunnan and Eastern Tibet.

Pun Ngai is an Associate Professor in the Division of Social Science, Hong Kong University of Science and Technology. She is the author of *Made in China: Women Factory Workers in a Global Workplace* (2005) and, with Agnes Ku, *Remaking Citizenship in Hong Kong: Community, Nation, and the Global City* (2004).

Aihwa Ong is Professor of Socio-Cultural Anthropology at the University of California, Berkeley. Her books on different aspects of the global include *Flexible Citizenship* (1999), *Buddha Is Hiding* (2003), *Global Assemblages* (2005), and *Neoliberalism as Exception* (2006). She has spoken at global conferences including the World Economic Forum, and her writings have been translated into German, Italian, and Chinese.

Benjamin L. Read is Assistant Professor of Politics, University of California, Santa Cruz. His research concerns grassroots-level associations in China and Taiwan. In addition to studying homeowner groups, he is writing a book on state-fostered neighborhood organizations.

Louisa Schein is Associate Professor in the departments of Anthropology and Women's and Gender Studies at Rutgers University. She is the author of *Minority Rules: The Miao and the Feminine in China's Cultural Politics* (2000) and has published articles in leading journals. She is currently completing a book, *Rewind to Home: Hmong Media and Gendered Diaspora*, on media, transnationalism, and sexuality/gender in the Hmong/Miao diaspora and co-editing a volume on media, erotics, and transnational Asia.

Steven M. Sheffrin is Professor of Economics and Dean of the Division of Social Sciences at the University of California, Davis. He received his Ph.D. from the Massachusetts Institute of Technology and his B.A. from Wesleyan University. His research interests include public finance, taxation, and macroeconomics.

Dan Smyer Yü is Director of the Language and Ethnic Studies Program at the Council on International Educational Exchange. His research topics range from globalization and the revival of world religions to the emerging civil discourses on modern science and religious worldviews and the interplay between religion and ethnic identity in contemporary China.

Mei Zhan is Assistant Professor of Anthropology at the University of California, Irvine. Her book *Other-Worldly: Making Chinese Medicine through Encounters* is forthcoming with Duke University Press. Her articles have appeared in *American Anthropologist* and *Cultural Anthropology*.

Li Zhang is Associate Professor of Anthropology and the former Director of the East Asian Studies Program at the University of California, Davis. She is the author of *Strangers in the City* (2001) and is completing a new book that explores the emerging configurations of property, class, and lifestyle in a booming Chinese metropolis.

Zhou Yongming is Associate Professor of Anthropology at the University of Wisconsin, Madison. He is the author of *Anti-drug Crusades in Twentieth-Century China: Nationalism, History, and State-Building* (1999) and *Historicizing Online Politics: Telegraphy, the Internet, and Political Participation in China* (2006).

Index